IN CONTRA

MW01073163

In Contradiction

A Study of the Transconsistent

Expanded Edition

by

GRAHAM PRIEST

CLARENDON PRESS · OXFORD

*This book has been printed digitally and produced in a standard specification
in order to ensure its continuing availability*

OXFORD
UNIVERSITY PRESS

Great Clarendon Street, Oxford OX2 6DP

Oxford University Press is a department of the University of Oxford.
It furthers the University's objective of excellence in research, scholarship,
and education by publishing worldwide in

Oxford New York

Auckland Cape Town Dar es Salaam Hong Kong Karachi
Kuala Lumpur Madrid Melbourne Mexico City Nairobi
New Delhi Shanghai Taipei Toronto
With offices in
Argentina Austria Brazil Chile Czech Republic France Greece
Guatemala Hungary Italy Japan South Korea Poland Portugal
Singapore Switzerland Thailand Turkey Ukraine Vietnam

Oxford is a registered trade mark of Oxford University Press
in the UK and in certain other countries

Published in the United States
by Oxford University Press Inc., New York

First edition published 1987 by Martinus Nijhoff Publishers
This expanded edition first published 2006

Reprinted 2010

ISBN 978-0-19-926330-1

To the end of exploitation and oppression
in all its forms and wherever it may be.

Table of Contents

Acknowledgements of First Edition   xii
Preface of First Edition   xiii
Preface of Second Edition   xvii

INTRODUCTION

0 Dialetheism   3

PART I: THE LOGICAL PARADOXES

1 Semantic Paradoxes   9

   1.1 Logical Paradoxes   9
   1.2 Semantical Paradoxes: The Tarski Conditions   10
   1.3 Truth Value Gaps   12
   1.4 In Defence of the T-scheme   17
   1.5 The Demise of a Hierarchy   18
   1.6 ...or Two   20
   1.7 Extended Semantic Paradoxes and Semantic Ascent   23
   1.8 Appendix: Berry's Paradox   25

2 Set Theoretic Paradoxes   28

   2.1 Set Theoretic Paradoxes   28
   2.2 The Cumulative Hierarchy: Its Lack of Rationale   30
   2.3 ...and its Inadequacy in Category Theory   32
   2.4 ...and Logic   36
   2.5 Semantics and Set Theory   37

3 Gödel's Theorem   39

   3.1 Gödel's Theorem   39
   3.2 Naive Proof   40
   3.3 ...and Dialetheism   44
   3.4 Inconsistency *v.* Incompleteness   46
   3.5 Appendix: Proof of Gödel's Theorem   48

Table of Contents

PART II: DIALETHEIC LOGICAL THEORY

4 Truth and Falsity   53

   4.1 Preliminary Issues   53
   4.2 The T-scheme   55
   4.3 ... and Meaning   56
   4.4 But Truth is More than This   59
   4.5 The Teleological Account of Truth   61
   4.6 Assertion   62
   4.7 Truth or Falsity: Truth Value Gaps   64
   4.8 Truth and Falsity: Dialetheism   67
   4.9 Untruth   69

5 Dialetheic Semantics for Extensional Connectives   73

   5.1 Formal Languages: Abstraction   73
   5.2 Extensional Sentential Connectives   74
   5.3 Quantifiers and Identity   76
   5.4 The Truth Predicate   78
   5.5 Appendix: Proofs of Theorems   80

6 Entailment   82

   6.1 Preliminary Issues   82
   6.2 Curry Paradoxes   83
   6.3 Entailment   84
   6.4 The Omniscience of G   86
   6.5 Non-Contraposible Implications   88
   6.6 Relevant Logic   89
   6.7 Quantification and Identity   92

7 Pragmatics   94

   7.1 Pragmatics   94
   7.2 Assertion: Content   94
   7.3 Belief: Acceptance and Rejection   96
   7.4 Rational Belief   99
   7.5 Rational Change of Belief   103
   7.6 Appendix: Probability Theory   107

8 The Disjunctive Syllogism and Quasi-Validity   110

   8.1 The Disjunctive Syllogism   110
   8.2 What it is Not   111

8.3 ... and What it is		113
8.4 The Improbability of Inconsistency		115
8.5 The Classical Recapture		117
8.6 Appendix: *Consequence		119

PART III: APPLICATIONS

9 Semantic Closure and the Philosophy of Language		**125**
9.1 Applications of Dialetheism		125
9.2 A Semantically Closed Theory		125
9.3 Comments on the Construction		130
9.4 Truth and Meaning		132
9.5 Appendix: Proofs of Theorems		136
10 Set Theory and the Philosophy of Mathematics		**141**
10.1 Naive Set Theory		141
10.2 Substitutional Semantics		143
10.3 Analyticity and Paradoxicality		146
10.4 Mathematical Realism		148
10.5 ... and Anti-Realism		152
10.6 Cardinality and Syntax		154
11 The Metaphysics of Change I: The Instant of Change		**159**
11.1 Contradictions in the World		159
11.2 The Instant of Change		160
11.3 Dialectical Tense Logic		162
11.4 The Leibniz Continuity Condition		165
11.5 The LCC and Contradiction		169
12 The Metaphysics of Change II: Motion		**172**
12.1 Change and Motion		172
12.2 The Orthodox Account of Motion		172
12.3 The Hegelean Account of Motion		175
12.4 ... and its Consequences		179
13 Norms and the Philosophy of Law		**182**
13.1 Inconsistent Obligations		182
13.2 Legal Dialetheias		184
13.3 Deontic Semantics		188

13.4 Some Semantic Invalidities   195
13.5 Other Norms, Rules and Games   197
13.6 The Resolution of Dialetheias   200
13.7 Language Games   203

CONCLUSION

14 The Transconsistent   207

PART IV: MATERIAL NEW TO THE
SECOND EDITION

15 The Metaphysics of Change III: Time   213
    15.1 The Spread Hypothesis and the Hegelean
         Definition of Change   213
    15.2 The Flow of Time   215
    15.3 The Direction and Duration of Time   216
    15.4 Some Variations and Extensions   217

16 Minimally Inconsistent *LP*   221
    16.1 The Classical Recapture   221
    16.2 Limiting the Models   222
    16.3 Semantics for *LP*   223
    16.4 Semantics for *LPm*   224
    16.5 Properties of *LPm*   224
    16.6 Reassurance: the Propositional Case   226
    16.7 Reassurance: the First Order Case   226
    16.8 Appendix Proofs of Lemmas   228

17 Inconsistent Arithmetic   231
    17.1 Some History   231
    17.2 Collapsed Models of Arithmetic   232
    17.3 Consistent *v.* Inconsistent Arithmetics   234
    17.4 Gödel's Theorems   236
    17.5 The Naive Notion of Proof   237
    17.6 Shapiro's Criticisms   239
    17.7 The Inconsistency of Peano Arithmetic   240
    17.8 The Incredulous Stare   241
    17.9 Appendix: The Structure of Inconsistent Models of Arithmetic   244

18 Paraconsistent Set Theory 247

18.1 Paraconsistent Set Theory: Background 247
18.2 The Material Strategy 249
18.3 The Relevant Strategy 251
18.4 The Model-Theoretic Strategy 256
18.5 Metatheory of Paraconsistent Logic 258
18.6 Technical Appendix 260

19 Autocommentary on the First Edition 262

19.1 Twenty Years On 262
19.2 Chapter 0 263
19.3 Chapter 1 263
19.4 Chapter 2 265
19.5 Chapter 3 266
19.6 Chapter 4 266
19.7 Chapter 5 269
19.8 Chapter 6 269
19.9 Chapter 7 273
19.10 Chapter 8 275
19.11 Chapter 9 276
19.12 Chapter 10 277
19.13 Chapter 11 281
19.14 Chapter 12 281
19.15 Chapter 13 282
19.16 Chapter 14 283

20 Comments on Some Critics 284

20.1 The Empire Strikes Back 284
20.2 Dialetheic Logic 284
20.3 The Extended Liar Paradox 287
20.4 Expressability 290
20.5 Motion 295
20.6 Contradictions in the World 299

Bibliography 303
Index 317

Acknowledgements of First Edition

I would like to thank the Department of Philosophy of the University of Pittsburgh, where this book was drafted, for its hospitality. I would also like to thank the Department of Philosophy of the Research School of Social Sciences, Australian National University, for two Visiting Fellowships during which a significant amount of the initial work was done. A special thanks goes to Lee Carter, who prepared the index. Some of the book has appeared in print before. Part of chapter 7 appeared as 'Contradiction, Belief and Rationality' in the *Proceedings of the Aristotelian Society* 86 (1986). Chapter 12 is a very slightly modified version of 'Inconsistencies in Motion', *American Philosophical Quarterly* 22 (1985). Part of chapter 3 appeared essentially as sections 5–7 of 'Logic of Paradox Revisited', *Journal of Philosophical Logic* 13 (1984). Chapters 2 and 11 contain material that first appeared in 'Semantic Closure' and 'To be and not to be: Dialectical Tense Logic', *Studia Logica* 43 (1984) and 41 (1982), respectively. I am grateful to the Editors of the *American Philosophical Quarterly* and *Studia Logica*, the Aristotelian Society and D. Reidel Publishing Company for their permission to reproduce. I am also greatly indebted to Jeff Rohl for the use of the facilities of the Department of Computer Science of the University of Western Australia, which were used to prepare the manuscript. Lastly, but most importantly, my thanks go to my wife, Annie, for her support and encouragement over the years.

Preface of First Edition

This book is a greatly expanded and extended version of my essay 'Logic of Paradox' (1979a).[1] However, its gestation period commenced well before that paper was written. In 1974 I wrote a doctoral thesis on the philosophy of mathematics.[2] The thesis left hanging what I thought was a relatively minor problem. It was clear that, for a completely satisfactory solution to the problems concerned, an account of semantic closure was required; the problem was what this account was. The right approach, I had become convinced some years earlier,[3] was to allow contradictions to arise, and to jettison the classical principle *ex contradictione quodlibet*. I planned to sort out the problem of how this was to be done, add this to the content of the thesis, and publish the result as a book. This is the book.

The problem and its offspring came to dominate my philosophical thinking after 1974. By 1976 I had worked out a number of the technical details of semantic closure, and had also reached the conclusion that the only suitable philosophical underpinning for the enterprise is dialetheism. These investigations were recorded in 'Logic of Paradox', whose manuscript I took with me when I came to Australia. The investigations of dialetheism that followed were published in a number of different papers (most of which are referred to in the book) and, as I followed through its implications, came to range over a number of areas in logic, epistemology, and metaphysics. In 1982 I had a year's study leave, and I decided to spend the time pulling together the threads of the previous eight years' work and making it a coherent whole. The book was drafted then. The original material on the philosophy of mathematics, reworked, had by then dwindled in significance and now occupies only a chapter, which is, perhaps still, the least satisfactory.

There are very few ideas in the book, at least in its first two parts, whose germs are not to be found in 'Logic of Paradox', but there are many things on which I have changed my mind over the years. As a result, the positions adopted in this book on various matters often differ in small but significant ways from the positions adopted in previous publications. I have not tried to note the changes in the book. They will be obvious enough to anyone to whom this is important, should there be any such person.

---

[1] References cited in this fashion can be found in the bibliography at the end of the book.
[2] 'Type Theory in which Variables Range Over Predicates', University of London.
[3] See my 'Bedside Reader's Guide to the Conventionalist Philosophy of Mathematics' in *Proceedings of the Bertrand Russell Memorial Logic Conference, Denmark 1971*, ed. J. Bell *et al.*, Leeds 1973.

While on the question of what is not in the book, let me note that there are a number of issues raised which deserve more discussion than they get, but which I have not pursued here. These include the arguments for constructivism, the philosophical underpinning of possible world semantics, and relevance. The book is not neutral on these issues; but I decided on a policy of fighting one battle at a time, especially this one. And, as I indicate in the text, though these issues might bear on the precise formulation and consequences of dialetheism, they do not bear on dialetheism itself. Finally, on the subject of omissions from the book, there are some technical questions raised that are not settled. My excuse is that I do not know the answers.

The subject is unavoidably technical in places. The import of the book is primarily philosophical, however, and can survive numerous technical emendations. Hence I have tried to make the material as accessible as possible to non-logicians. To this end I have suppressed as much technical material as possible, or relegated it to appendices (and the occasional footnote), which can happily be omitted by readers without damaging their understanding of the book. The amount of logic required of a reader can also be minimised by selective reading. The first part of the book is self-contained and may be omitted almost entirely by someone uninterested in logical paradoxes. All that readers need take into Part Two of the book is the thought that these provide a strong motivation for dialetheism. The second part of the book is its heart, and cannot be omitted. The chapters in Part Three depend on Part Two, but are more or less independent of each other (except for chapter 12, which presupposes chapter 11). This part can therefore be read selectively. Unfortunately, logical notation cannot be read selectively. I have tried to keep it as simple and perspicuous as possible. This has caused me to elide use and mention systematically in certain contexts (though not where this is important). I take it that rigour should never become *rigor mortis*. (The joke is an old one, but well worth repeating.) Notation that is not completely standard is explained where it is introduced.

It is impossible for me to cite all of the people who have in some way contributed to the content of the book. A list of those who have patiently listened to ideas, and given criticisms and suggestions, would include virtually all my friends and colleagues over the years. However, I am very grateful to Stewart Candlish for taking a number of bugs out of one draft. The logicians who comprise the Australasian Association of Logic also deserve a special mention. Had it not been for the fertile Australian soil, my sapling dialetheism would probably have withered. There is also one of this number to whom I am particularly indebted: Richard Routley (now Sylvan). Though he will disagree profoundly with much of the book, it is with him, more than anyone else, that I have struck a chord of mutual philosophical sympathy over the past ten years. His resolution has also been a lesson to me: whenever my spirits have flagged in defending the outrageous, they have been revived by his stalwart defence of the even more outrageous.

Dialetheism *is* outrageous, at least to the spirit of contemporary philosophy. For this reason, many may be tempted to dismiss the idea out of hand. I ask only that they remember how many scientific theories that came to be accepted started their history wearing this mark, and give the idea a fair hearing. I am confident that if this be done the merits of the position will speak for themselves.

G.P.
Perth,
1987

Preface of Second Edition

As the preface to the first edition of this book says, *In Contradiction* was drafted in 1982. The final draft was written in 1983. The content is now, therefore, a little over twenty years old. The book did not appear until 1987, however. The reason for this is that it was rejected by ten major publishers before one accepted it.[1] It was therefore with great relief that I heard that Martinus Nijhoff (now part of Kluwer Academic Publishers) was prepared to publish it, and I remain deeply grateful to them for having enough faith in myself and the book to do so.[2]

Most of the rejections from the other publishers I approached were simply polite refusals. But a couple of publishers did send readers' comments, and I am sure that they are typical of the advice the publishers received. Not all the readers' recommendations were negative. Thus, one reader (for a publisher that turned the book down) said:

Some of the basic ideas—true contradictions... and the rejection of *ex contradictione quodlibet* for example—have been on the philosophical scene for a number of years, but this ms. is the most ambitious and broadly conceived (and most persuasive) presentation I know of... The content is effectively organized. The argument is easy to follow. Despite occasional infelicities... the writing is crisp and clear, and the overall tone is appealingly enthusiastic, energetic, and self-confident. I enjoyed reading the ms...
I recommend publication despite some reservations, and although I am not a convert to dialetheism, because I enjoyed reading the ms. and felt that I learned much from it. It deals with a central topic in logical theory in an imaginative, attractive and intellectually courageous fashion. The author has obviously lived with the issues raised for many years, and has produced a ms. that is filled with interesting and provocative arguments.

But most of the reports recommended against publication, and for essentially the same reasons. Here is what one (in the context, not unsympathetic) reader said:

The book is highly competent, and, indeed, highly original. It is also true that the topic it deals with is one in which there is increasing interest. But, the fundamental point is that the main idea will strike most philosophers as totally wrong-headed in the most radical way possible. For the main idea is that there are *contradictions*—statements of the form: '*A* and it is not the case that *A*'—that are *true*. Unless one can swallow that main idea, the development in the book can have only formal or mathematical interest; and that will,

---

[1] For the record, the publication of the related Priest, Routley, and Norman (1989) also took a long time, but for quite different reasons. The completed typescript of this was sent to the publishers early in 1982. For various reasons, they took seven years to produce the book.

[2] Nijhoff required a camera-ready copy of the manuscript. I produced it on one of the first 512K Macs. Given the primitive nature of word processing in those days, and the fact that I had never had anything to do with the production of a book before, the result was a little rough. It did, however, allow me to get away with unorthodox things, such as calling the first chapter 'Chapter 0'.

I think, ensure rather small sales. The situation might be different if the book were a "jazzy" and irresponsible one. Then it might attract a certain kind of frivolous reader. But this is a cool, responsible, and fairly technical book; and it calls for some considerable knowledge of logic and the philosophy of mathematics. Consequently, its likely readership comprises those serious members of the profession who have the requisite knowledge *and* fancy true contradictions, plus those—relatively few—who will find the formal development interesting in its own right.

Of course, the book does not ask the reader to accept ("swallow") the main idea, dialetheism, on the basis of faith. The whole thing is a sustained argument for the conclusion. But arguments against an entrenched orthodoxy have a hard time making any impact. As the same reader says a little later in the report:

A crucial chapter in this part is chapter 7, where Priest addresses the question of rational belief in contradictions. It goes without saying that most readers are bound to be unpersuaded by what he says about this, but that will be because—like me—they cannot accept the main idea.

In other words, people will disregard the arguments because they have already rejected the conclusion. What this says about rationality in operation, I leave the reader to ponder.

Perhaps the most typical reaction by readers was expressed in its most extreme form by one of them as follows:

The author grants that his thesis is outrageous.[3] I came to this manuscript with the belief that the thesis was not just outrageous, but silly, and after having read it I still think so. But while I cannot take the thesis seriously (I don't know how to take it seriously since I don't know how to understand it so that it might be true), I was prepared to try to enter into the author's game to see if the development and defense of the thesis might produce some fruitful and interesting results, either technical or philosophical. I don't, however, think that the book meets this standard.

I still find it hard to see how any half-way competent attack on an orthodoxy that is some two and a half thousand years old, and scarcely defended during that period, can fail to have some 'fruitful and interesting' results. Even if it the attack is wrong, discovering why this is so cannot but help deepen our understanding of the orthodoxy. The suggestion that there was nothing of significance to be learned from the book was therefore a singularly depressing one. In fact, a major irony of this report was that, after having said this, and having called the view silly, the reader then went on at great length—for another five pages—engaging with the arguments of the book. (As the publisher said, 'It is unusual for a reader to spell out in such detail the problems he finds with an author's argument.') This was effectively, it seemed to me, a covert admission that the view overtly expressed could not be sustained.

---

[3] What *In Contradiction* actually says (p. xv) is 'Dialetheism *is* outrageous—at least to the spirit of contemporary philosophy.'

At one point in the lengthy struggle to find a publisher for the book, the late David Lewis interceded with one publisher on my behalf. He sent me a copy of his letter to the publisher, from which I quote:

As to the market: The reader thinks that the likely readership is limited to those who have the expertise and fancy true contradictions, plus a few who find the formal development interesting in its own right. I think this is quite wrong. And not just because there are many who do not now fancy true contradictions but might readily be persuaded to. I think that there are many reasons for an implacable opponent of true contradictions— such as myself—to take great interest in what Priest and his allies are doing.[4]

If the book is a commercial success, as I think it might be, here is the form I think its success might take. The *immediate, readymade* market does indeed consist of the sympathizers, and is indeed small. After that, the book makes its own market. Some outraged defender of classical virtue (I have in mind here the very man for the part, but let me not name him) hears of this new heresy and decides to squash it once and for all—and it is apparent to all that his attempt is question-begging and worthless. Others set out to do the job properly: of course we all know that Priest is wrong, but you have to refute him *this* way. No, that won't work, it has to be *this* way . . . Then the difference splitters: you have to grant Priest this much but then you can hold the line *here* . . . In short: a snowballing, complicated debate among opponents about how the paraconsistent position might best be resisted—and of course the paraconsistent manifesto is required reading for participants in the debate. The increasingly obvious disarray of the opponents helps Priest to gather converts who themselves pitch in. . . .

I premise this scenario on two beliefs. (1) Many people will think that it is an easy thing to refute Priest's position, decisively and in accordance with customary rules of debate. It is *not* an easy thing. I myself think that it is an impossible thing: so much is called into question that debate will bog down into question-begging and deadlock. (On this point, Priest disagrees with me: he thinks that shared principles of methodology might provide enough common ground.) I think this calls in question the very idea that philosophy always can and should proceed by debate—itself a heretical view, likely to be vigorously opposed.[5] (2) Many philosophers hold an unprincipled and unstable position: they have been persuaded by Quine and Putnam that logic is in principle open to revision, they are prepared to contemplate revisions of logic that seem to them to require only small and esoteric changes, yet they still think it absurd to countenance true contradictions. Give these folks a good shaking, and I suppose we'll see a lot of conversions—some souls saved for staunch classicism, some lost to Priest, and doubtless some novel positions as well.

With hindsight, one can see the prescience of Lewis's view. Though the debate is, I think, still a young one, events have proceeded much as Lewis envisaged. There were a few reviews of the book; these were generally critical but kind (da Costa and French 1988, Cargile 1989, Makinson 1990, Smith 1991). After

---

[4] Lewis remained a staunch opponent of dialetheism till the end of his life. The fact that he was prepared to go to bat for it is a small illustration of the magnanimous sort of person that he was. It did occasion him to wonder why one should support philosophers whose views one thinks to be entirely wrong, though. The results of his reflections can be found in Lewis (2000).

[5] Lewis maintained this view till the end. See Lewis (2004).

a while the unsympathetic weighed in—Denyer (1989), Smiley (1993), Everett (1993, 1994, 1996); and the compromisers—T.Parsons (1990), Beall and Ripley (2004); and the sympathetic—Mortensen (1995, 1997), Beall and Armour Garb (Beall 1999, Armour-Garb and Beall 2001, Armour-Garb 2004), Garfield (Garfield and Priest 2003); and those who wanted to turn the screws on Quine—Arnold and Shapiro (forthcoming). An important role in helping to persuade philosophers that there were important issues to be thought about here was played by a few notable people who were orthodox but open-minded. (A major one of these is Sainsbury. In his book on paradoxes (1987) he devoted a whole chapter to dialetheism; this was expanded to a longer one in the second edition.) The debate is now attracting numerous logicians and philosophers, as is witnessed by the collection of papers in Priest, Beall and Armour-Garb (2005). In the process of all this, *In Contradiction* has become something like the canonical manifesto of dialetheism.

The first edition of the book has now been effectively out of print for a number of years. It therefore gave me great pleasure when an opportunity arose to produce a second edition. The opportunity arose largely thanks to the efforts of Peter Momtchiloff at Oxford University Press, to whom I am particularly grateful. In the introduction to the second edition of *Beyond the Limits of Thought* (also with Oxford University Press), I wrote:[6]

As I read through the first edition in preparing the second, I was surprised (and a little alarmed!) to see that there was virtually nothing in it that I wished to change . . . This has allowed the reproduction of the first edition pretty much intact.

In producing the second edition of *In Contradiction*, I have adopted the same policy: the original text has been reproduced as it was in the first edition, with the exception of a few minor corrections, largely of typographical errors;[7] all the new material in the edition (other than this preface) is in the new part of the book, Part Four. The policy was not adopted for the same reason, however; indeed, the reason is the diametrical opposite—if I were to write the book again now, it would have to be a quite different book (showing that something can be different from itself!). I have not changed my mind on most of the issues of substance in the book; but under the stimulation of discussion with friends and foes alike, my views on the matters in the book have evolved considerably. Part Four of the new edition documents this.

Part Four contains six new chapters. Chapters 15, 'Metaphysics of Change III: Time', and 16, 'Minimally Inconsistent *LP*', are essays that were written soon after the publication of the first edition, but continue its trajectory. I would certainly have included this material in the first edition had it been available at

---

[6] Priest (1995), p. xvii.
[7] The text contains various temporal references which indicate when it was written: towards the end of the twentieth century. I decided not to change these. The reader should therefore bear in mind that the first and second editions straddle the turn of century.

the appropriate time. Chapter 15 would have appeared after Chapters 11 and 12; Chapter 16 would effectively have replaced section 8.6. Chapters 17, 'Inconsistent Arithmetic', and 18, 'Paraconsistent Set Theory', are much more recent essays which survey developments in their respective areas (and were originally written for that purpose). These four chapters are based, respectively, on Priest (1991*a*, 1992, 2003, and forthcoming *a*), though I have edited the material (for example making the notation uniform) to fit more cleanly into the new context, and also added to or revised material in the process.[8] I am grateful to the editors and publishers of these volumes for permission to reuse the material.

The last two chapters of Part Four, Chapters 19 and 20, are both new. The first of these is an autocommentary on the first edition; in this I explain, chapter by chapter, what modifications and extensions I would now make to the material of the first edition. In the second I comment on a number of the more significant issues that have been brought up by commentators on the first edition, not dealt with elsewhere. These chapters refer to the other chapters new to the second edition, but also to *Beyond the Limits of Thought, Introduction to Non-Classical Logic*, and especially *Doubt Truth to be a Liar*.[9] The last of these, in particular, articulates many of the core notions concerning dialetheism, such as truth and rationality, in a much more extended way than is possible in this volume. Indeed, this edition of *In Contradiction* and *Doubt Truth to be a Liar* have been produced in tandem, and can be thought of as companion volumes.

This edition has been produced largely on a year's sabbatical leave from the University of Melbourne. I am grateful to the University for maintaining the conditions under which research can flourish. Much of the work was done during months spent at the Universities of Kyoto and Berkeley. I am grateful to them both for their hospitality during this period, and particularly to Yasuo Deguchi and Alan Code for making the visits both possible and happy. Finally, this edition bears the marks of many with whom I have discussed relevant matters since the appearance of the first edition—in print, in private correspondence, in seminars and conferences, in bars and restaurants, in walks, buses, and planes, and in all the other places where philosophy gets done. It is impossible to mention all such people, and it would be invidious to single out a few. But to all, I would say a warm thank you.

G.P.
Melbourne
16 January 2005

---

[8] There are also some minor notational changes between the first and second edition material. I note these where appropriate.   [9] Priest (1995, 2001, and 2006).

INTRODUCTION

According to Kant, ... thought has a natural tendency to issue in contradictions or antinomies, whenever it seeks to apprehend the infinite. But
Kant ... never penetrated to the discovery of what the antinomies really
and positively mean. The true and positive meaning of the antinomies is
this: that every actual thing involves a coexistence of opposed elements. ...
The old metaphysic, ... when it studied the object of which it sought
metaphysical knowledge, went to work by applying the categories abstractly
and to the exclusion of their opposites. Kant, on the other hand, tried to
prove that the statements issuing through this method could be met by
other statements of contrary import with equal warrant and necessity.

Hegel, *Lesser Logic*, section 48

0

Dialetheism

The central concerns of this book are certain notions drawn from logic. They include truth, negation, proof, sethood and sundry others. None of these is a category in the sense of traditional logic. Yet they share with traditional categories certain key features. In particular, both these notions and the traditional categories of logic are general notions which are fundamental to thought, language, and their relationships to the world. They must therefore be understood if we are to understand these important areas of philosophical concern. It is this which gives the following investigations more than purely local and esoteric significance.

In his discussion of the categories in the *Critique of Pure Reason*,[1] Kant argued that our categories have a natural range of application. Specifically, the categories can be applied to (and only to) intuitions. In non-Kantian jargon, we can put it thus: the natural range of application of our notions, such as time, is the set of things we can experience, such as the mail man arriving. If we try to apply these concepts outwith this range, then, according to Kant, trouble occurs. Specifically, contradictions arise. For example, if we apply our temporal notions to the whole universe, a totality which cannot be experienced (as such), we shall, by reasoning in a totally legitimate way, be able to prove that the universe is both temporally bounded and temporally infinite.[2] This shows, according to Kant, that the application of our concepts beyond the bounds of experience is illegitimate, and must be avoided if coherence is to be maintained. Such is the thrust of the Transcendental Dialectic. At the hands of Hegel, the Transcendental Dialectic underwent an important transformation. In his *Logic*,[3] Hegel agreed with Kant that the antinomies, the arguments that end in contradiction, proceed by perfectly legitimate reasoning. However, he found no basis for ruling the applications of concepts within them to be illegitimate. Indeed, Hegel's idealism meant that the distinction between objects that are experienced and mere "objects of thought" has no particular ontological significance. Thus, according to Hegel, perfectly correct reasoning, using legitimate applications of certain concepts, leads to contradiction: the concepts are contradictory. And since a sound argument

---

[1] In the *Transcendental Dialectic*, bk II, ch. 2.

[2] For a fuller discussion of this and the following remarks on Kant and Hegel, see Priest and Routley (1983), ch. 2, sects. 4, 5.

[3] See sect. 48 of *Logic*, pt I of the *Encyclopaedia of the Philosophical Sciences*.

must have a true conclusion, there must be contradictions which are true. Moreover, according to Hegel, Kant's antinomies are just the tip of an iceberg. In fact, he held that all our concepts are contradictory. This fact was of crucial importance; for it produced a train of conceptual development (the dialectic of the categories) and hence, via Hegel's idealism, of the world. We need not go into all these aspects of Hegel here. The only point that I wish to isolate and highlight is Hegel's contention that our concepts are contradictory, that there are true contradictions. The notion of true contradiction is at the heart of this book. Awkward as neologisms are, it will therefore be convenient to have a word for it. I will use 'dialetheia'.[4] So to avoid any confusion, let me say, right at the start, that a dialetheia is any true statement of the form: α and it is not the case that α.

Few people, if any, would now accept the Hegelean contention that there are dialetheias. The arguments which produce the Kantian antinomies all seem to contain fallacies, and the arguments for contradiction in Hegel's *Logic* strike the modern reader either as sophistical or else as totally incomprehensible. Most would reject the idea that our concepts are inconsistent, or at least would suppose that, if they are, then they are incoherent and need to be changed. In neither case would they accept that there are dialetheias. It is the main claim of this book that Hegel was right: our concepts, or some of them anyway, are inconsistent, and produce dialetheias.

Let me put the point in more familiar terms; for the twentieth century has preferred talk of language to talk of concepts and categories. Language contains certain constructions which are of very general (topic-neutral) application. In English some of these can be expressed by the phrases '... is true', 'it is not the case that...', '...is a member of...', etc., though presumably all natural languages will contain phrases which function in the same way. The senses of these constructions are determined by certain conditions which lay down the criteria for the correct applications of the phrases concerned. Thus, for example, the following might partially determine the senses of 'not', 'true' and 'member':

'not-α' is true $\leftrightarrow$ 'α' is false

'α' is true $\leftrightarrow$ α

x is a member of $\{y \,|\, α(y)\} \leftrightarrow α(x)$

and so on.[5] The principles are *a priori* and, one might argue, analytic, specifying as they do (at least in part) the defining conditions of the notions concerned. At any rate, they are true. Now the point is that such principles, possibly on their

---

[4] The word 'dialetheia' owes its coinage to Richard Routley and myself. Although it is not a *bona fide* Greek word, its Greek roots are meant to be indicative of the Janus-headed nature (Wittgenstein 1956, pt IV, sect. 59) of a true contradiction: if α ∧ ¬α is a true contradiction, α "faces" both truth and falsity.

[5] In ch. 6 I shall discuss various implication connectives, and in sect. 6.3 and thereafter I shall use $\rightarrow$ for a specific one of them: the entailment connective. Until then I use the sign as a generic sign of implication, and where particular assumptions are made about its properties these are made explicit.

own, possibly with the connivance of other contingent truths donated by the world, entail statements of the form: α and not-α, which must therefore be true, entailment preserving truth. Thus our conceptual net, or the set of meaning connections of our language, produces dialetheias.

There are a couple of preliminary skirmishing points that might as well be dealt with straightaway. The first is the contention that the principles cited above are not those governing the senses of the constructions concerned. This is a genuine issue which I will pursue at various points in the book. It might be suggested that no further investigations are necessary, since the contradictions produced show *ipso facto* that the principles are not correct. Not so. The inconsistency of our linguistic principles is the very thesis I am affirming. Hence, in discussions of what these principles are, consistency cannot be invoked as a regulative principle without begging the question against me. But, even putting this aside, there is no legitimate presupposition of consistency here. Rather, the natural presupposition is that of inconsistency. For language and the principles that govern it have developed piecemeal and under no central direction. As logicians know, inconsistency is the natural outcome of spontaneity. Consistency has to be fought for. Therefore, *prima facie*, it would indeed be surprising if our concepts were internally and mutually consistent. There are deeper arguments for the claim that our language must be consistent. However, I will deal with these in due course.

A second objection is that, even if our concepts are inconsistent, all this shows is that they are incoherent. Nothing should therefore hang on them, as on the babblings of a raving person. If there is a philosophical job to be done, it is in revising our concepts to produce consistent ones. An appeal to the authority of Hegel might be thought possible here. After all, didn't he say that the inconsistencies in concepts were to be transcended to produce more universal concepts? There is nothing to be gained by an appeal to Hegel; for, though he did indeed maintain that inconsistencies were to be transcended, this did not produce consistency, but further inconsistencies. Everything (including the Aim of it All, the Absolute) is inconsistent. It follows that Hegel would certainly not have accepted that inconsistency implies incoherence.

But more important than what Hegel thought is the question of whether inconsistency actually does imply incoherence. There is an obvious question here about what, exactly, 'incoherence' should be taken to mean. The answer is not at all clear, but incoherence should at least be taken to entail unusability. Again, there may be some deep arguments here. I will look at them in due course. One superficial argument that might be used (unfortunately, one that too commonly prevents discussion of deeper issues) is that, if a contradiction were true, everything would be true. Hence language would be unusable. Whatever we are to make of this last inference, the crux of the argument is the appeal to the received logical principle $\{\alpha \wedge \neg\alpha\} \vdash \beta$, *ex contradictione quodlibet.* The objection is superficial because it is clear that, since not every β is true, any dialetheia will produce a counter-example to this principle. An appeal to this principle, or to classical logic in general, can only, therefore, beg the question. What account we are to give of validity, and the status of the received logical theory, I will discuss in due course; but it is clear that, if I succeed in making good the claim that our language is inconsistent (which I hope to achieve by the end of the book), it will follow naturally that inconsistency does not entail incoherence. For the usability of an inconsistent language follows naturally from the fact that one is used.

To return to the main point and conclude: the aim of this book is to argue for the existence of dialetheias, and to discuss their logic, epistemology, and some issues in their metaphysics. Logically, the starting place for this is, perhaps, a discussion of truth itself; but heuristically, the best way to start the discussion is with the production of some dialetheias. Hence I will postpone more systematic discussion to Part Two of the book. I have already said that I cannot accept the Kantian examples of dialetheias. Neither can I accept any other of the examples which Hegel cites or produces (with the possible exception of one of Zeno's paradoxes, to which we will come). By the end of the book I will, in fact, have produced many examples of dialetheias. One kind of example, however, is of singular importance: the logical paradoxes. (Undoubtedly Hegel would have made great use of these had he known about them.) Motivationally, these have been important for all that follows. But more importantly, the logical paradoxes are the site of a fault-line in the whole tectonic of "classical" logic. Though painfully aware of it, logicians this century have had as little success with it as their geological counterparts have had with the San Andreas fault. By applying a little pressure along the crack, I hope to blow the whole configuration asunder.

PART I

THE LOGICAL PARADOXES

...sitting round a table. Smoke filled the room. The dispute had been going on for some hours. The point at issue was whether or not it was possible, legitimately, to make reference to a collection of things which might themselves refer to this reference. Aleph maintained that this would clearly lead to an infinite regress which would deprive the reference of any clear sense. Beth held that though the reference would make sense, the regress would prevent what was said from being either determinately true or determinately false. Gimmel disagreed with both of them. To make his point he gave an illustration, and this was the illustration he gave: There were three philosophers. They were...

Trad., arr. Priest

1

Semantic Paradoxes

1.1 LOGICAL PARADOXES

By the logical paradoxes, I mean the paradoxes of self reference, some of which, such as the liar, are very old, but most of which were discovered around the turn of this century. The paradoxes are all arguments starting with apparently analytic principles concerning truth, membership, etc., and proceeding via apparently valid reasoning to a conclusion of the form 'α and not-α'. *Prima facie*, therefore, they show the existence of dialetheias. Those who would deny dialetheism have to show what is wrong with the arguments—of every single argument, that is. For every single argument they must locate a premise that is untrue, or a step that is invalid. Of course, choosing a point at which to break each argument is not difficult: we can just choose one at random. The problem is to justify the choice. It is my contention that no choice has been satisfactorily justified and, moreover, that no choice can be.

It is not at issue that we can devise formal theories which are consistent, or even provably consistent. What is at issue is the consistency of the familiar concepts which give rise to the paradoxes, or, what comes to the same thing, the consistency of the semantics of fragments of natural language. For example, we may set up a theory in a formal language containing the words 'is true', and this may be consistent. However, the crucial question remains: how adequate a formalisation is this of the phenomenon we are trying to model: natural reasoning? It is disturbing to see how many logicians think that the problem has been solved once some formal construction, which is (putatively) consistent, has been given.

To discuss these issues, it will be convenient to divide the paradoxes into two families: the semantic and the set theoretic. The former comprises the paradoxes of truth, denotation, predication, and so on (the liar, Grelling's, Berry's, Richard's, Köenig's, etc.). The latter comprises the paradoxes of membership, cardinality, etc. (Russell's, Cantor's, Burali-Forti's, Mirimanoff's etc.). The received wisdom on the subject, dating back to Peano,[1] is that the two families are quite distinct, the former belonging not to mathematics but to "linguistics". Since the advent of mathematical semantics, and of Tarski's

---

[1] Peano (1906) p. 157.

definition of 'truth' in a set theoretic metalanguage, etc., this distinction has become virtually impossible to draw satisfactorily. There is also an obvious formal isomorphism between the abstraction scheme of set theory and the Tarski satisfaction scheme:

$$x \in \{y \mid \alpha\} \leftrightarrow \alpha(y/x)$$
$$x \text{ satisfies } \underline{\alpha} \leftrightarrow \alpha(y/x)$$

where $\underline{\alpha}$ is a formula with one free variable, y, $\alpha(y/x)$ is α with all free occurrences of 'y' replaced by 'x' (with the usual precautions concerning clash of variables taken), and underlining is used for quotation. With a little ingenuity, we can extend the isomorphism to the case where α contains free variables other than y.[2] Moreover, under the isomorphism, some of the semantic paradoxes transform into some of the set theoretic ones and vice versa. For example, Grelling's paradox and Russell's transform into each other. It is not surprising, therefore, that we have witnessed a number of papers resurrecting Russell's original view[3] that there is really only one family here.[4]

Despite all this, there are reasons for keeping the two families apart. One is that there are some set theoretic paradoxes which have no natural semantic counterpart (e.g. Burali-Forti's), and vice versa (e.g. the definability paradoxes). More importantly in the present polemic context, the set theoretic paradoxes have a solution that is widely agreed upon (at least by mathematical logicians), while the semantic paradoxes have none. Hence I will treat them separately. I will return to the connection between the two families in section 2.5. With these preliminary words said, let us turn to the semantic paradoxes.

1.2 THE SEMANTIC PARADOXES

My aim here is to defend the view that the semantic paradoxes are *bona fide* sound arguments. In virtue of the multitude of incompatible proffered reasons why they are not, much of the discussion must consist of criticism of other people's views. This is not a particularly constructive exercise, but it is a necessary one: the dialetheist position will seem less attractive while some consistent positions are seen as plausible. To make the discussion as integrated as possible, I will proceed as follows. I will state a set of conditions sufficient for contradiction and then defend against all comers the view that natural language satisfies these conditions (or if not these, then others which have the same effect). The upshot of the discussion will be that the putative solutions to the paradoxes betray a pattern which not only gives strong inductive evidence that the paradoxes cannot be solved, but also indicates why not.

---

[2] See e.g. C. Parsons (1974).   [3] Russell and Whitehead (1910), vol. I, Introduction, ch. 2.
[4] See e.g. Thompson (1962).

Tarski (1936) located the root of the semantic paradoxes in semantic closure, and more specifically in a set of closure conditions. Tarski's point may be shown as follows. For simplicity, let us restrict our attention to formulas of one free variable. I will say that a formal theory satisfies the *Tarski conditions* if it is such that:

(1) For every formula, α, there is a term of the language, $\underline{\alpha}$, its name.
(2) There is a formula of two free variables, Sat($x\,y$), such that every instance of the scheme

$$\text{Sat}(t\ \underline{\alpha}) \leftrightarrow \alpha(v/t) \qquad\qquad (*)$$

is a theorem, where t is any term, α is any formula of one free variable, v, and $\alpha(v/t)$ is α with all free occurrences of 'v' replaced by 't' (with the usual precautions concerning the binding of variables free in t).
(3) The rule of inference $\{\alpha \leftrightarrow \neg\alpha\} \vdash \alpha \land \neg\alpha$ is valid in the logic underlying the theory.

Now to show that any theory which satisfies the Tarski closure conditions is inconsistent, we need only take for α the formula $\neg\text{Sat}(v\,v)$ and for t the term $\underline{\neg\text{Sat}(v\,v)}$. (*) then gives us

$$\text{Sat}(\underline{\neg\text{Sat}(v\,v)}\ \underline{\neg\text{Sat}(v\,v)}) \leftrightarrow \neg\text{Sat}(\underline{\neg\text{Sat}(v\,v)}\ \underline{\neg\text{Sat}(v\,v)})$$

Applying the rule of inference in clause 3 now gives us the contradiction. This paradox is just the heterological paradox, since $\neg\text{Sat}(v\,v)$ says that v is not truly predicable of itself.

In his 1936, Tarski uses the truth predicate, T, rather than the satisfaction predicate, to make the same point. For this reason, he needs an extra "empirical" premise to obtain the contradiction, namely the existence of a formula, α, of the form $\neg T\underline{\alpha}$. This is strictly necessary, since it can be shown that without it a theory with its own truth predicate may be consistent.[5] None the less, given the satisfaction scheme, we can define truth, denotation, etc., in the usual way and, possibly with a bit of extra machinery, prove the other semantic paradoxes. But this is unnecessary for the purpose at hand, since the point is shown: these closure conditions give rise to contradiction.

So much for formal theories. Let us turn now to natural language. Tarski claimed, and I shall agree with him, that a natural language, such as English, satisfies these closure conditions. However, we must take some care here, for the

---

[5] See Priest (1984). Moreover, it suggests that paradoxes may be solved by simply denying the contingent premise. In effect, the argument can be construed as a *reductio* of this premise (see Prior 1961). This move cannot effect a general solution to the paradoxes since, as we see, a contingent premise is not always to be found. However, the strategy has produced some astounding claims: that it may be impossible for one to be thinking that snow is white, even when it appears to oneself that one is; that it may be impossible even to utter words that normally mean this, when it appears to oneself that one does (see Prior 1961). These are indicative of the desperation that prolonged failure to solve the paradoxes has induced in people.

above closure conditions cannot be applied as they stand to a natural language. The problem is, of course, that the definition is couched in terms of 'formula', 'term', 'theorem', etc.—jargon applying only to formal languages. Still, it is easy enough to rephrase the conditions while retaining their spirit. A natural language satisfies the *Tarski conditions* iff:

(1) For every phrase α, there is a noun phrase $\underline{\alpha}$, its name.
(2) There is a phrase Sat, requiring two noun phrases to be inserted to make a sentence, such that every sentence of the form

Sat($t\ \underline{\alpha}$) iff $\alpha(t)$

is true, where α is any phrase requiring a noun phrase, t, to be inserted to make a sentence, and parentheses mark insertion.[6]
(3) The following rule of inference is truth preserving:

α iff it is not the case that α.

Hence, α and it is not the case that α.

This definition, though rather cumbersome, is obviously the analogue of the previous definition. The only real point of interest is that we have changed 'is a theorem' to 'is true'. We can now proceed, exactly as before, to establish that any natural language that satisfies the Tarski conditions contains true sentences of the form 'α and it is not the case that α'.[7]

A natural language which satisfies the Tarski conditions therefore contains true contradictions. Of course, it might be doubted that natural languages do satisfy these conditions. To this I now turn.

1.3 TRUTH VALUE GAPS

To deny that English satisfies the Tarski conditions, one has to deny that one of the above three conditions holds for English. The prospects for denying clause 1 seem bleak indeed. Every phrase in English has an English name. Given a phrase, to form its name we simply enclose it in quotation marks. Before quotation marks became a regular feature of the vernacular, the same function was performed (and still is, especially in spoken language) by allowing the phrase to denote itself. In medieval jargon, the phrase, when used thus, had *material supposition*. There is, therefore, little scope for denying clause 1. The major arguments must therefore concern clauses 2 and 3. I will take these in reverse order.

---

[6] Those who do not like sentences being called true may replace 'is true' with 'expresses a true proposition', 'can always be used to make a true statement'—or whatever their favourite theory is— and continue to do so until further notice.

[7] Strictly speaking, we do need an extra assumption in this case, namely, the existence of a noun phrase 'itself' such that Sat(t itself) has the same truth conditions as Sat($t\ t$). We now take α to be 'It is not the case that Sat(itself)', and t to be $\underline{\alpha}$.

There is one (and perhaps only one), plausible reason for rejecting the *reductio* principle of 3, and this is the existence of truth value gaps, sentences that are neither true nor false. Not that an intuitionist will think that these cause the principle to fail: the principle is valid intuitionistically. But suppose we are thinking in more classical terms and that we have a sentence, α, such that both α and $\neg\alpha$ fail to be true. Then $\alpha \wedge \neg\alpha$ will fail to be true (assuming a normal conjunction, as I will do throughout). But, given a conditional that is not simply a gap-in/gap-out conditional (where the valuelessness of a part spreads to that of the whole), $\alpha \rightarrow \neg\alpha$ and its converse may hold, and their conjunction may be true. In this case the inference fails. In fact, under very weak conditions the *reductio* scheme is equivalent to the law of excluded middle,[8] whose failure can very naturally be taken to express the existence of truth value gaps. Hence if we may take paradoxical sentences to be neither true nor false, this particular argument to dialetheism may be blocked.[9] I shall argue in section 4.7 that there are no truth value gaps. However, for the present let us suppose, at least for the sake of argument, that there are. I will argue that dialetheism is not to be avoided in this way.

But first a preliminary point of clarification. The thesis that sentences may be truth valueless comes in two varieties. According to the first, while sentences are the *kind* of thing that are true or false (perhaps relativised to a context), some sentences are neither. A more complex version holds that it is what is expressed by (perhaps the use of) a sentence that is true or false, and that some (uses of) sentences fail to express anything. This idea itself comes in two varieties, according to whether it is statements or propositions which are said to be expressed. I do not now wish to discuss the issue of whether it is sentenes, statements, or propositions that are the primary bearers of truth (on which, see Haack and Haack 1970). I intend my discussion to apply to all versions and sub-versions of the thesis. To this end, I will now write 'true', 'false', and their cognates with initial capitals. Those who think sentences are true/false can read 'True/False sentence' in the obvious way. Those who think that it is statements or propositions that are true/false can read it as 'sentence (the use of) which makes a true/false statement/proposition', depending on their preferred theory. The thesis that there are truth valueless sentences can now be expressed as: there are some (indicative) sentences that are neither True nor False. Let us call such sentences 'Valueless'.

So much for preliminaries. The first main point is this: even granted that Valueless sentences vitiate the *reductio* scheme, this does not, *per se*, solve the paradoxes. It is also necessary to show that the paradoxical sentences are valueless; for, unless we are given an independent reason for supposing this, the "solution"

---

[8] Specifically, the equivalence holds given only the principles of first degree entailment.

[9] A truth value gap approach to the paradoxes has been suggested by many people: to name but a few, Fitch (1952), Bar-Hillel (1957), Martin (1967), van Fraassen (1968), Kripke (1975), Goddard and Goldstein (1980).

is worthless. As I have already noted, it is not in doubt that we can avoid the paradoxes if we can make any move we like. For just this reason, a putative solution that is not backed up by an independent rationale is just an intellectual fraud. Neither is the fact that if the sentenses were not Valueless a contradiction would arise, a sufficient rationale in the present context. As I have stressed already in chapter 0, this would just beg the question.

Now some rationales have been offered, but none of them is very satisfactory. For example, some (e.g. Martin 1967) have suggested that paradoxical sentences are category mistakes, and therefore Valueless. This appears most implausible. For example, in 'This sentence is False', the subject appears to be the right *kind* of thing for the predicate to be about. The essential *ad hoc*-ness of this move is witnessed by the fact that, in Martin's "decision procedure" for category correctness, a special clause is required to eliminate paradoxical sentences, which would otherwise seem to pass the test. The clause is the familiar one for filtering out "loopy" sentences. In fact, the ineliminability of a demonstrative or similar referring phrase from a paradoxical sentence due to a loop is frequently cited as a reason for its Valuelessness. For example, Ryle (1950) suggests that this ineliminability shows that no statement is made by the utterance of a paradoxical sentence. This essential ineliminability is closely related to Kripke's notion of groundedness.[10] Only grounded sentences receive a truth value when these are assigned in a certain well founded fashion. A basic problem with these rationales is that, while eliminability, groundedness, or whatever, may be a sufficient condition for having a Value, it is not at all obvious why it should be supposed to be necessary too. Take, for example, Ryle's position. Suppose that my father asserts the mendacity of all one-legged men in town; suppose also that there is only one one-legged man in town who, unbeknown to us, has asserted the veracity of my father. If Ryle is right, then either my father or this one-legged man failed to make a statement. Without loss of generality, let us suppose it to be my father. Yet, by all the standard tests for making a statement, he did. I understood what he said; I can draw inferences from it; I can act on the information contained in it, and so on.[11] Alternatively, take Kripke's position. Let α be any sentence that obtains no truth value at a fixed point. Then, obviously, 'α is not true' should be true at the fixed point (at least if truth at the fixed point models the behaviour of truth in English!), though in the construction it receives no truth value.[12] Hence it seems that none of the motivations will do what is required.

Any doubts that we might have that, even if there are Valueless sentences, paradoxical sentences are not among them are magnified when we consider the pair

This sentence is True   (1)

This sentence is False   (2)

---

[10] For the connection, see Yablo (1982).   [11] The point is wittily made by Popper (1954).
[12] For some further telling criticisms along the same lines, see Gupta (1982).

There is something odd about both these sentences, but, *prima facie* at least, it is not the same in both cases. In the case of (1) the semantic rules governing the use of the demonstrative 'this sentence' and those governing the predicate 'is True' appear not to be sufficient to determine the Truth value of the sentence. In other words, the semantic rules involved underdetermine its Truth value. Such a sentence is an obvious candidate for a Truth value gap. By contrast, in the case of (2) the semantic conditions of the words involved seem to overdetermine its Truth value. (2) would therefore seem a much more plausible candidate for a Truth value "glut" than a truth value gap, which is exactly, of course, what it is.

The second main point against Value gap solutions to the semantic paradoxes concerns extended paradoxes. Let us suppose that there are Valueless sentences, and that the claim that paradoxical sentences are Valueless can be substantiated. This allows us, in effect, to maintain that, although a paradoxical sentence such as 'This sentence is False' is True iff it is False, since it is neither, the derivation of a contradiction is blocked. There is, however, a standard argument to show that this ploy will not work.[13] Some sentences are neither True nor False. Obviously we are capable of expressing this idea in English: we have just done so. (Moreover anyone who maintains that paradoxical sentences are Valueless must accept this on pain of obvious self refutation.) In particular, for any sentence α that is neither True nor False, 'α is not True' must be True. (Again, anyone who maintains a Value gap solution to the paradoxes must accept this, or face a devastating *ad hominem* argument.) This does not necessarily mean that 'α is True' is False, since it is possible to maintain that 'α is True' is Valueless, and that negation transforms a Valueless sentence into a True one. It is beyond question, though, that

if α is not True, 'α is not True' is True. (3)

Now consider the "extended" (or "strengthened") liar paradox:

(4) is not True. (4)

This sentence is either True, False or Valueless. If it is True, then (by the T-scheme, which is not here at issue) it is not True. Similarly, if it is not True (i.e. False or Valueless), then it is True. Hence, whatever it is, we have a contradiction. One might object to the inference from (4)'s being Valueless to its being True. If, for example, we suppose that (4) makes no statement, then it should not follow that it makes a true one (see Goddard and Goldstein 1980). Yet we have agreed (and the Valuegappist is committed) to (3), an instance of which is

if (4) is not True, then '(4) is not True' is True

i.e. if (4) is not True, then (4) is true. Hence there is no way out here.

It may be objected that the above argument still uses the law of excluded middle in the form of the assumption: (4) is True or it is not True (False or Valueless). However, this is just an *instance* of the law of excluded middle, and

---

[13] For references and an excellent discussion, see Burge (1979).

one, moreover, that is unimpeachable for classical logic augmented with truth value gaps. (For the intuitionist the situation might be different, but we have already dealt with him.) Indeed, given that the Valuegappist is committed to the view that (4) is Valueless, and hence that it is not True, he can hardly deny that it is either True or not True.

Of course, attempts have been made to avoid the extended liar paradox. The most popular move is simply to rule that notions necessary for the formulation of the paradox (and in particular the notion of Valuelessness) are not expressible in the language in question. (And hence the Valuegappist's own discussion must be considered as occurring in a different language.[14]) But if this is right, it is an admission that the language for which the semantics has been given is not English, since these notions obviously are expressible in English. Thus the problem, which was to show how the English concepts are consistent, has not been solved. We meet here a situation which will recur several times, namely that purported solutions of the liar paradox allow for the formulation of other paradoxes which can be avoided only by denying that the language in question has a certain expressive power. I will discuss the significance of this in section 1.7. For now I just want to flag the phenomenon so that its constant return, like that of a bad penny, will be noted.[15]

Anyway, to return to the issue at hand, even if all the preceding discussion were incorrect, the denial of the law of excluded middle would still not avoid dialetheism. This is for the very simple reason that there are proofs of contradictions which do not use it. Take Berry's paradox, for example: English has a finite vocabulary. Hence there is a finite number of noun phrases with less than 100 letters. Consequently there can be only a finite number of natural numbers which are denoted by a noun phrase of this kind. Since there is an infinite number of natural numbers, there must be numbers which are not so denoted. Hence there must be a least. Consider the least number not denoted by a noun phrase with fewer than 100 letters. By definition, this cannot be denoted by a noun phrase with fewer than 100 letters, but we have just so denoted it. Contradiction. This argument appeals nowhere to the law of excluded middle. Both horns of the dilemma are given a direct proof. *Reductio*, or its equivalent, the law of the excluded middle, is not appealed to at all. It might be thought that I have smuggled the law into the proof somewhere, and with an informal proof this is always a legitimate worry. It is possible, however, to give a formal proof of Berry's paradox which uses no propositional logical machinery other than that of first degree entailment. This can be found in the appendix to this chapter, section 1.8, and removes that worry.

---

[14] This line is taken by, e.g. van Fraassen (1970), Fitch (1964), Kripke (1975).

[15] Gupta and Martin (1984) show that, provided we suppose that all truth functions are of the gap-in/gap-out variety, a theory can contain its own 'Valueless' predicate. However, this does not avoid the problem: what the theory cannot now express is that a sentence is not True. It will not do to say that the sentence is False or Valueless, since if the sentence is Valueless this claim is itself Valueless.

1.4 IN DEFENCE OF THE T-SCHEME

We have seen that denying the law of excluded middle is not sufficient to avoid the dialetheist conclusion provided by the paradoxes. The only other possibility for avoiding the conclusion is a denial of clause two of the Tarski conditions, i.e. a denial of the fact that English has a predicate satisfying the satisfaction scheme. It is time to consider this possibility. In fact, I will discuss not satisfaction and the satisfaction scheme, but truth and the T-scheme:

$$T\underline{\alpha} \leftrightarrow \alpha$$

where α is any closed (and non-indexical) sentence. There is no harm in this since both biconditionals should clearly be treated in the same way, and this approach has the merit not only of keeping the discussion simpler, but of tying it more closely to discussions of more orthodox views.

Pretty obviously, English has a truth predicate, viz. 'is true'. There is also a very strong presupposition that it satisfies the T-scheme.[16] For it is exactly that which characterises it as a *truth* predicate (at least extensionally) and not some *ersatz*. It is this point which Tarski underlined by calling the T-scheme a condition of adequacy on any definition of truth. Hence, the onus of proof is on those who claim that instances of the T-scheme fail. What reasons can be given for the failure of instances of the T-scheme? There are, as far as I know, only three basic reasons that have been offered in any detail as to why instances may fail. I will treat each of these in turn.

The first reason that has been offered is, again, the existence of Truth value gaps. In the light of the discussion in the previous section, this can be dealt with quite quickly. First, the points about the non-existence of Truth value gaps and the *ad hoc*-ness of appealing to them in this context carry over. Second, and in any case, Valueless sentences do not vitiate the T-scheme. To see this, consider why they might be thought to do so. Take any Valueless sentence, α, and consider the sentence $T\underline{\alpha}$. Since α is not True, this sentence is, presumably, False. Hence the biconditional, $T\underline{\alpha} \leftrightarrow \alpha$, whatever it is, is not True. This reasoning is not particularly cogent. First, it does not follow that $T\underline{\alpha}$ is false. It may, in fact, be Valueless. This depends on what truth conditions for the Truth predicate are correct, given the existence of Truth value gaps. Since α is *ex hypothesi* not True, and this is supposed to be English we are dealing with, $\neg T\underline{\alpha}$ must be True, but it does not follow that $T\underline{\alpha}$ is False. For the negation may be of the "external" kind which turns a Valueless sentence into a True one. This, therefore, does not settle the matter. More importantly however, whether $T\underline{\alpha}$ is False or Valueless, nothing follows about the Truth value of the biconditional until we have decided what semantics are appropriate for conditionals. For example, if we apply the

---

[16] In fact, there is more than a strong presupposition. The correctness of the T-scheme follows from a number of considerations. I will return to these in sects. 4.2 and 4.3.

simplistic condition gap-in/gap-out, then, whichever way a Truth value is assigned to $T\underline{\alpha}$, the biconditional comes out Valueless; if we take a biconditional to be True provided both of its sides have the same value, and give $T\underline{\alpha}$ the same value as α, the T-scheme will come out True. Or again, if we take the conditional to be a relevant one, then the information about Truth values just is not sufficient to settle the question.

Which account of the conditional is the correct one is, of course, contentious. Neither do I wish to try to settle the issue here. So let us not assume any particular formal account of the conditional, but try to settle the issue without this. It is possible to do this since the following observation seems to show that, however we end up distributing Truth value gaps across Truth predicates, conditionals, etc., the T-scheme ought not to be disturbed: the inference from α to $T\underline{\alpha}$ is at least Truth preserving, and not just materially, but necessarily so. For, whatever values are given to the components of α, if α is True, so is $T\underline{\alpha}$.[17] Moreover, the converse inference is also necessarily Truth preserving. In virtue of this, we can always deduce the one from the other. Furthermore, both inferences are clearly *relevant*. Each premise is used essentially to infer the appropriate conclusion. Therefore, on anyone's informal conditions for a true biconditional, the T-scheme passes.

The third reason why invoking Truth value gaps will not disturb the dialetheist conclusion is that, even if they did vitiate the general T-scheme, they leave enough instances to produce dialetheias anyway. To see this, merely consider the extended liar paradox again. Take the extended liar sentence to be the sentence 'This sentence is not True'. Call this α. Then, as we saw in the previous section, the Valuegappist is committed to the claim that α is not True, i.e. α. In other words, this particular sentence *has* a Truth value. Hence the instance of the T-scheme for it holds. The extended paradoxes therefore break through the Valuegappist defences on both fronts of his attack against dialetheism.

1.5 THE DEMISE OF A HIERARCHY

The second well worked out reason for supposing that instances of the T-scheme may be false is provided by the thought that the truth predicate of English may not be univocal. English, it is suggested, is not one language, but a hierarchy of semantically open languages. Each language in the hierarchy has a truth predicate (which we may write as T_i where i is the index of the language) which can be applied legitimately to the sentences of the language below, and only to those of the language below. If we suppose, as we may, that the names of all the sentences

---

[17] It is argued in Wallace (1972) that the T-scheme is not necessarily true, on the ground that the words in a sentence may have different meanings in different "possible worlds". This argument is well answered in Gupta (1978) and Peacocke (1978), who point out, in effect, that all is well, provided we suppose the language to be specified rigidly.

in the hierarchy occur at all levels, this view implies that the T-scheme at level $i + 1$ is true if the sentence involved, α, is in the language of level i, but otherwise may be false. This construction is, of course, due to Tarski (though the idea of a hierarchy of truth predicates goes back to Russell). In fairness to him, it must be emphasised that he did not think that a natural language such as English is of this form. However, many logicians have supposed, *faute de mieux*, that it is.

There are many things wrong with this view. First, English certainly does not seem to be of this form. Its "surface" structure is certainly not of this form: what reasons are there for supposing that its "deep" structure is? There is, as far as I am aware, no linguistic or grammatical evidence at all that the English predicate 'is true' does typically ambiguous duty for an infinite hierarchy of predicates at the deep level. And, just as with Truth value gaps, this is sufficient to make the suggestion unsatisfactory as a solution to the paradoxes. Moreover, it is not difficult to show that English cannot be of this form. Consider, for example, the sentence 'All the sentences on page 19 of the second edition of *In Contradiction* are true.' This sentence is a perfectly good English sentence. Its sense is clear, and, assuming that there is at least one plain false sentence on the page, it has a perfectly determinate truth value—false. Yet this sentence cannot be a sentence of the hierarchy, because it attributes truth to itself. The hierarchy is not, therefore, English. This illustrates a general criticism of the mooted solution to the semantic paradoxes made by Kripke (1975), namely that whether or not a sentence is paradoxical depends not just on factors intrinsic to the syntax and semantics of the sentence, but on contingent factors such as the references of certain noun phrases and what those referents have been up to. Any semantico-syntactic constraint which succeeds in ruling out paradoxes will therefore also rule out perfectly ordinary, non-paradoxical assertions too. In other words, all languages (or hierarchies thereof) which satisfy these constraints will be expressively weaker than English.

This fact can be illustrated by considering another objection to this attempt to solve the semantic paradoxes. This is the extended liar paradox again. Let us call the ordinal of the (lowest) language of which a sentence is a member the sentence's *rank*. (This may be an infinite ordinal if the hierarchy is a transfinite one.) Intuitively, the true sentences in the hierarchy are just those which are true at their rank. Therefore the extended liar now takes the form 'This sentence is not true at its rank', which we might write as

$$\neg T_{rk(\alpha)}\underline{\alpha} \qquad (\alpha)$$

If this is a sentence of the hierarchy, then it has a rank i. By the T-scheme for rank i,

$$T_i\underline{\alpha} \leftrightarrow \neg T_{rk(\alpha)}\underline{\alpha}$$

Putting i for $rk(\alpha)$ gives us the contradiction. As usual, the only way out of this problem for the hierarchist is to deny that the extended liar sentence, and, crucially, the quantification into the indices of truth predicates which makes the notion of rank definable, is expressible in any language in the hierarchy. But again, as usual, this just shows that the hierarchy is not English, since the notion of rank is expressible in English: I have just expressed it. Again, we see that the problem of the paradoxes is "solved" only by moving to a language *weaker than* English. A final irony is that, even to explain what the hierarchy is, we must assert (among many other things) the existence, for each index i, of a truth predicate T_i, which is just what cannot be done on the hierarchy view. Hence any theory to the effect that the hierarchy is English is self refuting (or inconsistent).[18]

To show the expressive weakness of the hierarchy, it is not necessary to employ contorted sentences. Many quite banal claims cannot be expressed in the hierarchy. Consider the presumably true claim that any sentence is false iff its negation is true. However we fill in the index of the truth predicate, this is actually *false* on the hierarchy view: for any truth predicate, there are sentences of higher rank such that neither they nor their negations satisfy this truth predicate. In reply to this, a hierarchist can say only that when we assert that each sentence is true iff its negation is not, what we mean is that, for any rank, i, all sentences of language i are true at rank i iff their negations are false there. However, this cannot be said in the hierarchy since it uses the notion of rank. An attempt to get round this is the notorious doctrine of typical ambiguity. This is the idea that we can, by asserting a single sentence of English, make an infinite number of statements, one for each language of the hierarchy. Thus, we can assert the sentence $T_i\neg\alpha \leftrightarrow \neg T_i\alpha$ schematically, as it were, in i. This suggestion is disingenuous. For what such a typically ambiguous assertion means, what we are supposed to understand by it, is just what is expressed by a single sentence which quantifies universally over i. If this cannot be said in the language, it is not a solution to the problem, but just a tacit admission that the language is expressively incomplete.

For all these reasons, it is clear that the theory of the Tarski hierarchy cannot be used to show that the semantic concepts of English are consistent.[19]

1.6 ...OR TWO

The third sort of reason that has been given for supposing that instances of the T-scheme fail concerns another hierarchical construction. This time English is supposed to be a single language with a single truth predicate, but interpretations

[18] The point about the self refuting nature of such hierarchical theories is well established by Fitch (1964) in the context of type theory.

[19] There is a modification of the hierarchy conception due to Burge (1979), according to which the truth predicate of English should be conceived not as typically ambiguous but as indexical. In effect, this is little more than a nominal change, and my objections can be correspondingly reworded. One cannot now, of course, talk about quantifying into the indices of truth predicates, but one can obtain the same effect by quantifying over the range of possible values of the indexical. For further criticisms of this approach, see Gupta (1982).

of it form a hierarchy.[20] The members of the hierarchy differ only in the extension they assign to the truth predicate. Given an arbitrary extension at level 0, the extension at ordinal level i, E_i, can be defined in a variety of ways. For present purposes, these make no real difference, and the simplest suggestion is to let E_i be the set of sentences, α, such that for some ordinal, $j < i$, and for all ordinals, k, such that $j \leq k < i$, α holds in the interpretation of level k. At a certain height in the hierarchy a certain stability emerges. Some sentences enter the extension of the truth predicate never to depart. Call these *stably true*. If the negation of a sentence is stably true, call it *stably false*. The *stable sentences* (which include all sentences not containing the truth predicate and all sentences logically true) are just those which are stably true or stably false. An interpretation is stabilised if all stable sentences have assumed their ultimate truth value. In some sense, the unstabilised interpretations are unimportant: it is the stabilised interpretations (or at least the class of them) which manifest the important properties of sentences. Now, given a sentence α, the T-scheme for α is guaranteed to hold at a stabilised interpretation only if α is stable; and paradoxical sentences, such as the liar, are, of course, unstable.

So. For unstable sentences the T-scheme may fail at stabilised interpretations. But what exactly is this supposed to show? A major problem here is that it is not at all clear how this formal construction is supposed to relate to English and its semantics. English, we must suppose, has not just one interpretation, but a whole hierarchy. But what does this *mean*, and what are we to make of the "jump" construction which takes us from one interpretation to another? Unfortunately, little has yet been said about this, though it is a *sine qua non* if this construction is to be given serious philosophical consideration as a solution to the paradoxes.

It would seem, however, that, whatever story is ultimately told, this proposal will fare little better than the two suggestions we have already considered. There are several reasons why. Here is one. The hierarchy of interpretations must, in some sense, spell out the meaning of the language in question. Meaning is something that is grasped by users of the language. Hence, if this hierarchical construction gives a correct account of the meanings of sentences, it follows that we must be able to attribute to language users an implicit grasp of the notions involved. These include the notions of a transfinite ordinal, of definition by transfinite induction and so on. The implausibility of this need hardly be laboured. (We could raise a similar objection against the Tarski hierarchy if it is suggested that it be extrapolated into the transfinite.)

For a second objection, let us start by considering an aspect of truth which is not captured by formal constructions, but which is essential to an understanding of the notion. It is part of the notion of truth that the true is that which is aimed

---

[20] This kind of construction is given by Gupta (1982), and Herzberger (1982). The construction by Kripke (1975) is obviously related, but, because it uses truth value gaps, has already been dealt with. Closely related also is the construction of Woodruff (1984). Since this construction incorporates truth value "gluts", I do not need to argue against it.

at in certain cognitive processes, such as asserting, theorising and so on.[21] Now the extension of the truth predicate in the construction under consideration varies from interpretation to interpretation, so which sentences are we to take as being in the target set? It could, I suppose, be suggested that the process of ascending the ordinals should be considered a temporal one, and thus that the target set changes over time; but this seems implausible. Apart from the arbitrariness of fixing the temporal unit, the difficulty of interpreting limiting processes, and so on, it would seem most implausible that the liar sentence should be assertible on Mondays, Wednesdays, and Fridays and deniable on Tuesdays, and Thursdays, and Saturdays, or some such. I take it that this is not what the instigators of this model intend. Perhaps then the target set is the union of all the extensions of the truth predicate (at least in stabilised interpretations). But this is certainly inconsistent. Hence dialetheism is not to be avoided in this way. More likely, it is the intersection of all these sets, the set of all stable truths, that is to be taken as the target. This is the most plausible assumption. However, once we get this far, the proposal ceases to be as novel as it appears. For, in effect, this proposal now reduces to the truth value gap proposal; the construction divides sentences into the true (i.e. the really, stably true), the false (i.e. the really, stably false) and the neither (i.e. the unstable sentences). So however novel the route was, the destination is one with which we are quite familiar and already know to be unsatisfactory.

In particular, the extended liar paradox is again forthcoming. This time it now takes the form: 'This sentence is not stably true', or

α is not stably true (α)

either α is stably true or it is not. (Classical logic holds in all interpretations in the hierarchy.) If it is stably true, it is true in all stabilised interpretations. Hence by the T-scheme for α, which holds in all stabilised interpretations, 'α is not stably true' is stably true. Hence we may assert something which says of itself that it cannot be asserted. Contradiction. Thus we have shown, and can therefore assert, that α is not stably true. Hence again we must assert something which says of itself that it is unassertible. Contradiction.[22]

Of the few ways to avoid this problem that have been suggested,[23] only one has any novelty. This is the suggestion that the predicate 'is stably true' has itself an extension which varies over the hierarchy. Exactly how this is meant to work is not at all clear. The obvious suggestion is to set the extension of this predicate at level i as the set of formulas which *appear* at that level to have become stably true; but this would just make the truth predicate and the stable truth predicate coextensional. The notion of stable truth would therefore become vacuous. Even supposing that we can find a suitable way of defining the extensions of the

[21] For more on this, see sect. 4.5.
[22] This informal argument, which shows that this position ends up in a tangle, can be made quite precise in terms of an indefinability result which shows that the position is self refuting. See Priest (1987).   [23] By Gupta (1982).

predicate, how this is supposed to solve the extended liar paradox is quite opaque; for the only novelty that this approach to stable truth adds is the possibility that assertions which involve the notion of stable truth may themselves be unstable. But this is irrelevant to the extended liar paradox, which does not assume that they are. In fact, it takes into account quite explicitly the possibility that the sentence is not.

Thus, the only real solution open to this version of the hierarchist is the familiar one of denying that the notion of stable truth is expressible in the language at all. It is not necessary to go over the inadequacy of this response again.

We have seen that this, the last standard way of justifying the failure of instances of the T-scheme, will not work. The claim that English satisfies the Tarski conditions, or at least, if it doesn't, that it satisfies other equally inconsistent conditions, therefore stands.

1.7 EXTENDED SEMANTIC PARADOXES AND SEMANTIC ASCENT

It is now time to return to the point noted in section 1.3, the recurrence of the extended-paradoxes/inexpressibility couple. For each of the "solutions" we have considered, it transpires that the solution generates concepts which allow a different version of the paradox to be given. Thus, nothing has been gained. Ultimately the only consistency-generating move is to deny that those concepts in which the solution is expressed (which is English) are expressible in the language for which the solution is being given, which is just an admission that the problem of showing English to be consistent has not been solved.

Nor is this phenomenon purely accidental; this situation is ultimately inevitable with any purported solution. To see this, let us start by considering the significance of extended paradoxes. The paradox phenomenon starts with a set of *bona fide*, truths, which are assertible. (Normally these will be just the plain truths, but each solution may allow us to describe them in slightly different terms—true at their rank, stably true, etc.) Those that are left over we will call "the Rest". The essence of the liar paradox is a particular twisted construction which forces a sentence, if it is in the *bona fide* truths, to be in the Rest (too); conversely, if it is in the Rest, it is in the *bona fide* truths. The pristine liar 'This sentence is false' is only a manifestation of this problem arrived at by taking the Rest to be the false. In this case, we can get out of the problem by insisting that the false is only a proper part of the Rest. This creates a gap in which the liar can conveniently lie. But this solves the problem only at the cost of showing that it was inadequately posed; for, if the false is only a proper part of the Rest, then the pristine liar is not the correct formulation of the problem. What extended paradoxes, such as 'This sentence is false or neither true nor false', do is remind us of this fact. If we ever try to get out of the problem by formulating the paradox in terms of a category that does not coincide with the Rest, we can pose the original problem by describing the Rest in some other way. Thus, the extended paradoxes are not really novel paradoxes, but merely manifestations of one and the same problem, suitable to different contexts. In virtue of this, the only move which will produce consistency is that which bans the expressibility of certain key concepts (truth, Value gaps, stable truth etc.) from the language. This requires the paradox-solver to insist that she herself is talking in a language different from the one for which the semantics are being offered (the "metalanguage").

The claim that consistency ultimately drives one to a self defeating meta-language can be supported by other reasons too. The paradox-solving problem is to produce a consistent theory that can express its own semantic notions. But this is a classical chimera: if a theory is to give an account of its own semantics, it must give an interpretation of some kind for the language of the theory. Then, to show that it is a semantics for the theory, it must be able to give a soundness proof for the theory with respect to the interpretation. But (classically) soundness implies consistency, and, provided that the language is sufficiently strong, we know that an internal consistency proof is impossible by Gödel's second incompleteness theorem. What the Gödel incompleteness theorem thus shows is that, classically, consistency can be maintained only by giving the semantics of a theory in a different theory. Thus, any consistent theory must be incapable of giving its own semantics either by the requisite notions failing to be expressible in the language of the theory, or by the requisite principles about them failing to be provable in the theory. The theory must therefore be either expressively incomplete or proof-theoretically incomplete. In particular, when proof methods are informal, so that no prior constraints are imposed on them, we must suppose expressive incompleteness, and thus we must (if we are to be consistent) consider ourselves to be talking in a "metalanguage".[24] This is why this move comes up again (with Tarski), and again (with Truth value gaps), and again (with stability).

We have now seen not only why no satisfactory consistent solution to the semantic paradoxes has been given, but why none can be given. English is, in a sense, over-rich in its expressive power, and consistency can be purchased only by docking that expressive power in some way or other.

The most recent part of the programme to solve the semantic paradoxes started in all seriousness around the turn of this century. The central assumption, or "hard core", of the programme, is the assumption that no contradiction is true, and hence that the reasoning that results in the contradiction is fallacious. The aim of the programme is to locate the fallacies and to articulate a theory which explains the data: the highly plausible yet invalid reasoning. The basic strategies, or "positive heuristics", for achieving this end have been charted in previous sections. The

---

[24] On more specific grounds, Herzberger (1970) argues that consistency requires expressive incompleteness, or, rather, argues just for incompleteness, consistency being taken as read. It is an irony of Herzberger's paper that he manages to express in English the very thing he takes to be proved to be inexpressible in English, viz. 'is a grounded predicate of English'.

programme is, however, a degenerating one.[25] No agreed solution has been found. On the contrary, variants of the basic strategies have multiplied spectacularly. Show that one distinction does not work, and a dozen appear in its place; show that a putative solution runs into trouble with a well supported philosophical theory, and a dozen patched-up versions appear to replace it. Much time is spent in trying to solve problems created by the purported solutions themselves; but in the last analysis, no progress is made in resolving the fundamental problem: it is merely shifted to a new location. This is, as we have seen, the significance of the extended paradoxes. And, though each purported solution may criticise the others, each is, in its turn, forced into the same inadequate move: the appeal to the notion of a metalanguage. This, in its turn, may trigger a new, but ultimately equally futile, "solution". It is about time the whole programme was put out of its misery.

1.8 APPENDIX: BERRY'S PARADOX

The following is a formal proof of Berry's paradox showing that the law of excluded middle is not used in the proof. A proof is given in Priest (1983). Here I will give a slightly modified version which does not assume that all terms denote.[26] The proof is carried out in the language of first order arithmetic with a finite number of variables, augmented by a least number operator,[27] μ, an implication operator, $\rightarrow$, a two place predicate, D, and a one-place function symbol, lg. I will use # to denote a Gödel coding, and underlining to indicate the numeral corresponding to a number. The axioms are:

0. All true arithmetical equations
1. $\exists x\alpha \rightarrow (\alpha(x/\mu x\alpha) \wedge \exists y\, y = \mu x\alpha)$
2. $(\alpha \wedge t_1 = t_2) \rightarrow \alpha(t_1/t_2)$
3. $\underline{n} \neq \underline{m}$ if n and m are distinct.
4. $D\,\#t\,x \leftrightarrow t = x$ for all closed terms, t.
5. $\lg\underline{\#t} = \underline{n}$ where n is the number of symbols in t.
6. $(\lg y < \underline{n} \wedge \lg y \neq \underline{0}) \leftrightarrow \bigvee_{t \in T_n} y = \underline{\#t}$,   where T_n is the set of terms with length less than n.

In 1 and 2 the usual precautions are taken concerning free variables. Note that, in virtue of the fact that not all terms denote, universal instantiation need not be universally valid, but it is certainly valid in the form

$$(\forall x\beta \wedge \exists y\, y = t) \rightarrow \beta(x/t)$$

---

[25] The terminology is taken from Lakatos; see e.g. Lakatos (1970). For these notions applied to non-empirical programs, see Lakatos (1968).

[26] And hence sidesteps the objections of Brady (1984).

[27] μ-terms may, of course, fail to denote in the natural way. The following axioms are compatible with numerous ways of handling this failure, e.g. truth value gaps, fixed but arbitrary reference, Meinongianism, etc. My preferred approach, at least in this context, would be that of Priest (1979).

with the usual precautions concerning free variables taken; similarly for existential generalisation. We might note also that we assume that, for every number n, there is an axiom of the form $\exists x\; x = \underline{n}$ so that we can always instantiate with numerals. The proof now goes as follows. Let α be the formula

$$\forall y \neg (\lg y \neq \underline{0} \wedge Dyx \wedge \lg y < \underline{10}.\underline{10})$$

where $x < y$ is defined, in the usual way as: $\exists z\; x + z + 1 = y$. If we can show that

$$\exists x \alpha \tag{7}$$

we can derive a contradiction as follows. By 1 and 7,

$$\forall y \neg (\lg y \neq \underline{0} \wedge Dy\; \mu x \alpha \wedge \lg y < \underline{10}.\underline{10})$$

and hence

$$\neg (\lg \#\mu x \alpha \neq \underline{0} \wedge D\; \#\mu x \alpha\; \mu x \alpha \wedge \lg \#\mu x \alpha < \underline{10}.\underline{10}) \tag{8}$$

But by 4 and 1,

$$D\; \#\mu x \alpha\; \mu x \alpha$$

Moreover, '$\mu x \alpha$' has 52 symbols. Hence by 5,

$$\lg \#\mu x \alpha = \underline{52}$$

Thus,

$$\lg \#\mu x \alpha \neq \underline{0} \wedge \lg \#\mu x \alpha < \underline{10}.\underline{10}$$

by 3, 0, and 2; and hence

$$\lg \#\mu x \alpha \neq \underline{0} \wedge D\; \#\mu x \alpha\; \mu x \alpha \wedge \lg \#\mu x \alpha < \underline{10}.\underline{10}$$

contradicting 8.

To show 7, we proceed as follows. By 6, and the substitutivity of equivalents,

$$\neg \exists x \alpha \rightarrow \forall x \exists y (Dy\; x \wedge \bigvee_{t \in T_{100}} y = \underline{\#t})$$

$$\rightarrow \forall x \bigvee_{t \in T_{100}} D\underline{\#t}\; x$$

by 2 and distributivity. By 4,

$$\rightarrow \forall x \bigvee_{t \in T_{100}} x = t$$

$$\rightarrow \bigvee_{t \in T_{100}} \underline{k} = t$$

for any $\underline{k}$. Call this formula $\beta(\underline{k})$. Let c be the cardinality of T_{100}, and let δ be the conjunction of $\beta(\underline{k})$ for $0 \leq k \leq c$. Then $\neg \exists x \alpha$ implies δ. Hence by general distributivity $\neg \exists x \alpha$ implies a disjunction of conjunctions. Each disjunct is of the form

$$\underline{0} = t_0 \wedge \underline{1} = t_1 \wedge \ldots \wedge \underline{k} = t_c$$

Now, since there are only c distinct ts, two of the ts in this enumeration must be identical. Hence, for some distinct n_i and m_i the conjunction implies a formula of the form $\underline{n}_i = \underline{m}_i$. Thus,

$$\neg \exists x \alpha \;\rightarrow\; \bigvee_{k \in K} \underline{n}_k = \underline{m}_k \quad \text{for a certain index set } K.$$

But for each k, $\neg \underline{n}_k = \underline{m}_k$, by 3. Hence, by de Morgan laws, contraposition, and double negation, $\exists x \alpha$, as required.

2

Set Theoretic Paradoxes

2.1 SET THEORETIC PARADOXES

Let us turn from the semantic to the set theoretic paradoxes. The situation here is somewhat clearer than in the semantic case. This is for two reasons. First, it is reasonably clear what the naive account of set is, and secondly, there is a general consensus as to what is wrong with it. Let us take the first point in this section and move to the second in the next.

Semantics was never a mathematical theory in the sense that geometry, group theory, and set theory are: the theory has never been developed for the sake of its interesting theorems, etc. This means that in disputes about what naive semantics is there is no well developed mathematical practice to which an independent appeal can be made to help settle the matter. Moreover, although semantics is now a formalised theory (since Tarski), the formalisation came after the semantic paradoxes were well known, and with an eye to avoiding them. Thus, the formalisation is far too self-conscious to be of much help here either.

The situation with set theory is very different. First, there was a short, though definite, practice of set theory before mathematicians became worried by paradox. Secondly, the early formalisations, and in particular Frege's, were not deformed by conscious attempt to avoid paradox. Hence we can be reasonably happy that Frege's formalisation does capture our naive notion. At any rate, I am not aware of any substantial criticism—other than that it is inconsistent—to the effect that it does not. We can take Frege's theory to be encapsulated in the two principles:

$$\exists y \forall x (x \in y \leftrightarrow \beta) \qquad (Abs)$$

$$\forall x (x \in z \leftrightarrow x \in y) \rightarrow z = y \quad (Ext)$$

where β is any formula which does not contain y free. Of course, this is somewhat anachronistic. Frege's actual formalisation was a second order one, and $\in$ was defined. However, (Abs) and (Ext) certainly held according to Frege, and it is easy enough to interpret Frege's axioms in the above theory (since second order quantification is equivalent to quantification over arbitrary sets). Hence we may, without injustice, take the above formalisation of the notion of set to be Frege's. The central feature of this account for present purposes is that *every* condition is taken to define a set. Hence, according to the naive theory, a set just is the extension of an arbitrary condition, and that's that.

In this context, it is also informative to note Cantor's definition of set:[1]

By an "aggregate" (*Menge*), we are to understand any collection into a whole M of definite and separate objects m of our intuition or of our thought.

Though this does not actually say that every property determines a set, it is difficult to see what else 'any collection' might be taken sensibly to mean. Some time later Cantor was to distinguish between consistent and inconsistent multiplicities, but this was in response to the paradoxes.[2]

As hardly needs to be said, the naive conception of set is inconsistent. The simplest contradiction is Russell's paradox, which is derived thus:

$$\exists y \forall x (x \in y \leftrightarrow x \notin x)$$
$$\exists y (y \in y \leftrightarrow y \notin y)$$
$$\exists y (y \in y \wedge y \notin y)$$

The last step is an application of *reductio*, or the law of excluded middle. Unlike semanticists, most set theorists have not been keen to suggest that contradiction should be avoided by denying this. Reasoning by the law of excluded middle is a well entrenched part of orthodox set theoretic practice. And if one is tempted by this line, one can dismiss it quickly. Essentially the same replies can be made to it as to the corresponding suggestion with the semantic paradoxes (see section 1.3.) For example, with an "external" negation we can produce extended variants of the paradoxes. Likewise, set theoretic paradoxes can be produced which do not use the law of excluded middle or *reductio*. In Burali-Forti's paradox, a direct argument is given that the set of all (von Neumann) ordinals is not an ordinal, and a different argument that it is. An example with fewer technical presuppositions is Mirimanoff's paradox concerning the collection of all well-founded sets. Define a *regress* from z to be a function from the natural numbers, f, such that $f(0) = z$, and for all n, $f(n) = \phi$ or $f(n+1) \in f(n)$. Call a regress *bounded* if, for some n, $f(n) = \phi$. Let W be the set of all well-founded sets, that is, the set of all sets z such that every regress from z is bounded. Let f be any regress from W. If $f(0) = \phi$ then the regress is bounded. So suppose that $f(1) \in W$. Let the function g be such that $g(n) = f(n+1)$. g is a regress from $g(0) = f(1) \in W$. Hence g is bounded, whence, again, f is bounded. Thus all regresses from W are bounded, so $W \in W$. But now define the function h such that, for all n, $h(n) = W$. Then h is an unbounded regress from W. Hence $W \notin W$.

[1] Cantor (1895).
[2] Against the myopic view that Cantor *et al* did not initially suppose all conditions to determine sets, see Quine (1973), pp. 102–3. As an aside, it is interesting to note that Cantor, unlike Kant, takes it that sets (which are just extensionalised categories), may be applied legitimately not only to objects of intuition but also to objects of thought. Hegel would, of course, have approved (see ch. 0). In virtue of this, Cantor might well have expected inconsistencies to appear in the theory.

We see that our naive notion of set (even without the help of the law of excluded middle) is inconsistent.

2.2 THE CUMULATIVE HIERARCHY: ITS LACK OF RATIONALE

So far so good. Our naive notion of set as enshrined in (*Abs*) and (*Ext*) is inconsistent. Most mathematical logicians would be inclined to go along with this, if interpreted in the sense that (*Abs*) and (*Ext*) are the untutored beliefs we all have about sets. But most would claim that (*Abs*) at least, like most untutored beliefs, is false. Against this, I wish to claim that (*Abs*) and (*Ext*) are true, and in fact that they analytically *characterise* the notion of set.

The fact that (*Abs*) and (*Ext*) enshrine our naive notion, in the sense agreed upon, puts the onus on those who think that they are not true to specify which postulates do characterise the notion of set and to explain what is wrong with, in particular, (*Abs*). Thirty years ago there would perhaps have been little consensus on the answers to these questions. There is now, however, a consensus among set theorists. The received answer concerns the cumulative hierarchy. This is, essentially, the structure one gets if one starts with a collection of objects (possibly empty), takes its power set, *its* power set, and so on, collecting up as we go (though this is unnecessary if the original set is the empty set). The construction is continued into the transfinite, the sequence of steps being indexed by the ordinals. At limit ordinals we simply collect up what has gone before. The ordinal stage at which a set appears in this construction is called its *rank*.

The received solution to the set theoretic paradoxes is that only the instances of (*Abs*) that hold in the cumulative hierarchy are true, that is, that the only sets that exist are those in the cumulative hierarchy. Other instances of (*Abs*) are without warrant. It should be noted that the claim that there are no sets other than those in the cumulative hierarchy is the central one. The agnostic position which allows that there may be sets outside the hierarchy[3] is quite compatible with the dialetheist position. It is not at issue that the hierarchy is an important and interesting set theoretic structure. What is at issue is whether there are other sets, i.e. whether there are instances of (*Abs*) which are true but which fail in the hierarchy. As solutions to the paradoxes go, there is really no extant alternative to the claim that the cumulative hierarchy exhausts the universe of sets. It is a remarkable fact that virtually every consistent set theory that has been proposed this century can be shown to hold in an initial segment of the hierarchy, i.e. in the collection of all those sets which appear before some fixed ordinal level in the construction. (Provided we assume that the construction has gone far enough—technically that there are large enough ordinals.[4]) The only set theory that does not hold in some

---

[3] To be found in, e.g. Drake (1974), p. 1.
[4] See e.g. Fraenkel, Bar-Hillel, and Levy (1973), pp. 321 ff.

segment (has no natural model) is Quine's system *NF* (and its class extension *ML*). It is a mark of the measure of the hegemony that the cumulative hierarchy has achieved that Quine's system is now widely regarded as little more than a curiosity. At any rate, the cumulative hierarchy is now standardly given by set theorists as *the* notion of set.[5] Hence I will concentrate squarely on this.

The claim that the only instances of (*Abs*) that are true are those which hold in the cumulative hierarchy is unsatisfactory for many reasons. First, it is not even clear that the notion of the cumulative hierarchy makes sense without a prior and different notion of set. For it is clear that the construction is parasitic upon a prior notion of ordinal. Until we have specified "how long" the construction is to go on, that is, how far the ordinals extend, the cumulative hierarchy is ill defined. But this is an issue that can be settled only set theoretically. Indeed, an original motivation for set theory was precisely to map the ordinals and their infinities. Given a (the naive) notion of set, this can be used to specify a theory of ordinals, and hence define the cumulative hierarchy, but there seems no other adequate way of characterising the ordinals. Hence the cumulative hierarchy seems to presuppose a different notion of set. Could the notion of ordinal be provided by a set theory such as ZF? Not without damaging circularity, since this is one of the very set theories whose rationale pegs it to the cumulative hierarchy.

Secondly, if the only instances of (*Abs*) that are true were those that held in the cumulative hierarchy, our naive supposition that all conditions do define sets would appear inexplicable. From this perspective, it does not even seem plausible. Thus, the naive theory, which does explain why we believe this (it is, after all, true) exceeds the theory based on the cumulative hierarchy in explanatory power.

Thirdly, the claim that the only sets are those in the hierarchy has no satisfactory independent justification. As I stressed in the last chapter, in connection with solutions proposed for the semantic paradoxes, this is sufficient to show a solution to be quite unsatisfactory.[6] The normal attempt to justify the claim goes something like this:[7]

Fundamental to set theory is the concept of being able to regard any collection of objects as a single entity. But before we can form a collection of objects, those objects must first be "available" to us . . . Before we can build sets of objects, we must have the sets of objects out of which to build these sets. The crucial word here is, of course, 'build'. Naturally we are not thinking of *actually building* sets in any sense, but our set theory should reflect this idea.

The argument employs a temporal metaphor of sets coming into existence only after their members. However, the temporal metaphor is quite out of place. Sets

---

[5] See e.g. Shoenfield (1967) pp. 238–9; Devlin (1980) pp. 42–6.

[6] In the terms of Lakatos (1976), it is merely the version of "exception barring" called 'strategic withdrawal to a safe domain'.

[7] Devlin *op. cit.* p. 43, italics original. Similarly Shoenfield *op. cit.*, p. 238 says '[Russell's paradox] does not really contradict the intuitive [*sic*] notion of a set. According to this notion, a set *A* is formed by gathering together certain objects to form a single object, which is the set *A*. Thus before the set *A* is formed, we must have available all of the objects which are to be members of *A*. It follows that the set *A* is not one of the possible members of *A*; so the Russell paradox disappears.'

are not constructed in time, and the metaphor of building sets from the bottom up, say, from the empty set, is no better than the reverse metaphor of building sets from the top down, say, from the universal set, as one might build a chain suspended from a rafter (which obviously allows for non-wellfoundedness). If we try to state the central claim in non-metaphorical terms, it comes to something like this: a set is conceptually posterior to its members. It is difficult to make any clear sense of this claim, but even if one could, it would not follow that all sets are well founded; for there is no reason why this dependency should not stretch "back" indefinitely. For exactly the same reason, the cosmological argument for the existence of God, which this argument closely resembles, is fallacious.

There is only one attempt that I am aware of to show that the regress can not go on indefinitely.[8] According to this, the conceptual dependence is one of determinacy: the determinacy of any set presupposes that of each of its members. And hence, the argument continues, any argument for the determinacy of a set must proceed via arguments for that of each of its members. Thus, to establish the determinacy of a non-wellfounded set would require a non-wellfounded argument; but 'it is obvious that no argument whose premises proceed in a circle or a regress to infinity can be valid.'[9] Unfortunately, this argument does not work. First, it is not true that regressive arguments are invalid, or even unsound. The argument α, because α, because α, because . . . is a paradigm of validity. Secondly, the claim that any conclusion that *x* is determinate must have a premise that *y* is determinate for each member *y* of *x* does not follow at all. We may, for example, have a single "super-premise" (for example the abstraction scheme itself) from which the determinacy of *x* and each of its members (and each of their members, etc.) follows in one step. *Maybe* a "direct" proof would have the structure Mayberry suggests, but there are plenty of perfectly valid indirect proofs. (Mayberry says that the fact that sets are purely extensional entities implies that any argument for the determinateness of a set *must* go from the determinateness of its members. This claim seems to me to be a complete *non-sequitur*.) Thirdly, the whole argument is fallacious since it moves from the conclusion that we cannot *show* the determinateness of a set to the claim that such a set is not determinate. It therefore confuses epistemological and ontological questions, and can only be made to work by some illicit reduction of truth to verification. For all these reasons, the argument will not work, and there is no good reason for supposing that all sets are well founded. In fact, not all sets are in the hierarchy, as we will now see.

2.3 . . . AND ITS INADEQUACY IN CATEGORY THEORY

The fourth, and major, objection against the orthodox solution to the set theoretic paradoxes is just that there are instances of the abstraction scheme that are

---

[8] Mayberry (1977). [9] Mayberry (1977), p. 31.

true but do not hold in the cumulative hierarchy, i.e. that there are sets and set theoretic operations that cannot be accommodated in the hierarchy. In particular, the universal set *V*, the absolute complement of any set in the hierarchy, and more generally any collection that has members of arbitrarily high rank, though *perfectly good set theoretic constructions*, are not to be found there.

There is a myopic view to the effect that these set theoretic objects and constructions are not *bona fide*, since they are not required for standard mathematical practice. The view is myopic, since it can appear a plausible claim only if one focuses on the practice of the years 1920–1960, and then forgets that much of this was tailored to the hierarchy anyway.

To see this, consider first the practice of set theory before 1900. The constructions in question were an integral part of this practice. For example, Dedekind used the set of all sets to prove the infinitude of the domain of sets.[10] And Cantor used the "overlarge" set of all ordinals to prove that every cardinal is an Aleph.[11] Constructions used by the founding fathers of set theory are not to be taken lightly. After 1900 set theory was rewritten in such a way as to try to avoid the use of these constructions. Much of this was done by Zermelo, who not only proposed a (presumably) consistent set theory, but also excised the appeal to large sets from Cantor's proof that every cardinal is an Aleph. In any rewrite of history, there are parts that do not fit and have to be consigned to the rubbish bin. So it was here. In particular, Dedekind's proof of the existence of infinite sets had to be junked.[12]

It seemed for a time that the excision of large sets from mathematics could be accomplished. Certain things had to be taken as axiomatic which were before proven (the benefits of theft . . .), but ordinary mathematics did not seem to need "inconsistent multiplicities". This is now no longer the case however, as we can see by looking at more recent mathematical practice. For in category theory, in particular, we have a global theory which has run into trouble in just the place where Zermelo pared down the universe of sets.

The inadequacy of the cumulative hierarchy for category theory is well acknowledged.[13] (Though it is usually expressed as the inadequacy of *set theory*. This is because set theory has become identified with the cumulative hierarchy. It should be noted that the "problematic" constructions required by category theory are quite unproblematic in axiomatic naive set theory.) There are two major problems. First, category theorists want to deal with categories such as the category of all groups, all sets, and even the category of all categories. These are just the "overlarge" totalities that do not exist in the cumulative hierarchy. Secondly, and even worse, not only do category theorists want to talk about these

---

[10] Dedekind (1888), theorem 66.   [11] See Cantor (1899).

[12] However, Dedekind's proof is in fact perfectly good, and can be given in axiomatic naive set theory (see sect. 10.1). The function which maps every set to its singleton is a map from *V* into a proper subset of itself. *V* is therefore Dedekind-infinite.

[13] See e.g. Feferman (1977), Bell (1981), Fraenkel, Bar-Hillel, and Levy (1973), pp. 143–4.

objects, they want to operate on them. In particular, given "large" categories C, D, they want to from the functor category, C^D, of all functors from D to C. Such constructions are not possible in the hierarchy.

Of course, suggestions have been made as to how to get around these problems, but none is adequate. One suggestion is that large categories, such as the collection of all groups, should be regarded as proper classes, that is, subcollections of the hierarchy which do not themselves occur in the hierarchy, and which cannot be members of any other collection. But this will not work. First, proper classes, if we are to take them seriously (and not just as *façons de parler*), are a masquerade. The cumulative hierarchy was proposed as an analysis of the notion of set. It is supposed to contain all sets. If we are forced to admit that there are sets outside the hierarchy, this just shows that the analysis is wrong. And calling them by a different *name* is just a trivial evasion. Moreover, the insistence that proper classes cannot be members of other collections can have no satisfactory rationale. If they are determinate collections with determinate members, there is no reason why we should not consider them to be members of other collections, for example their singletons.

The second reason why an appeal to proper classes will not solve the problems of category theory is that, though this may allow us to conceptualise large categories, since they can not be members of other collections, it does not allow us to operate on them, form functor categories, etc. The only way out is to admit that proper classes can be members of other collections. However, this does not solve the problem, but merely underlines the weakness of the notion of proper class; for, by the very construction of the cumulative hierarchy, the proper classes, collections of proper classes, etc., are just sets of higher rank than those we started with. In other words, the fact that this construction is possible shows that we are still going up the cumulative hierarchy, so the original universe was not, contrary to supposition, the total universe of sets. (And conversely, if the original totality were the universe of sets, this evasive move would not be possible.)

In virtue of this, those who have a penchant for the notion of proper class would be better off to bite the bullet and admit that we did not have the entire universe of sets in the first place. This brings us to the second proposed solution. We suppose the existence of an inaccessible cardinal, ϑ. The sets of rank less than ϑ have certain pleasant closure properties, so that we may interpret category theory in the "sub-universe" of sets of rank less than ϑ. The "large" categories and their combinations are now simply members of the hierarchy with rank greater than ϑ. Hence standard set theoretic manipulation is possible. Again, this stratagem hardly solves the problem. While it may produce a model for category theory, it is hardly the intended model. In particular, category theory does not apply to sets of rank greater than ϑ. This defeats the aim of category theory, which is to chart structural isomorphisms between all algebraic structures of a certain kind. A sophistication of this idea due to Gröthendieck postulates, not just one, but arbitrarily many inaccessibles, so that every set is in a mini-universe in which category theory may be interpreted. We must now regard every sentence of the language of category theory as "typically ambiguous" (in fact, infinitely ambiguous inaccessibly many times), to be interpreted in every mini-universe. This hierarchy is a sophisticated form of type theory, and it fails for exactly the same reason that type theories always fail: namely, that we want to, and do, make statements that cross types.[14] For example,[15] suppose that $R(x\,y)$ is a relationship holding between groups x and y, and suppose we prove category-theoretically that $\exists x \forall y R(x\,y)$. The theorem might be a representation theorem for example. This shows that there is a group which bears the relationship R to *every* group (of all ranks). If we interpret the theorem typically ambiguously, however, all it says is that, for any mini-universe, there is a group in that universe which bears the relation R to all groups in that universe. The uniqueness of said group to all groups is lost—nay, cannot even be expressed.

In fact, the original problem has not been solved at all, but merely hidden. For the problem was how to form and operate on e.g. the set of *all* groups, and we still cannot do this. And what is the price paid for this solution that will not work? The price is that it commits category theorists to the claim that there are inaccessibly many inaccessible cardinals. However dubious this claim is (and this is something we might argue about), it is not one to which category theory *per se* should be committed. Category theory is widely regarded as the theory of mathematical structure *par excellence*. As such, it should apply to mathematical structure whatever it is: it should not have to depend upon "contingent" assumptions.

Thus, there is no way around the fact that the cumulative hierarchy, the universe of sets decimated in the name of consistency, cannot provide adequate set theoretic constructions for category theory. As one perceptive commentator puts it:[16]

[T]he operations on large categories which appear so natural to category-theorists are not justified by current set theoretic foundations and so appear to demand an extension or reformulation of the set theoretic framework to accommodate them. In this connection, however, it should be noted that the failure of set theory to justify the unlimited application of category-theoretic operations is a consequence of its success in eschewing the overcomprehensive collections which were originally deemed responsible for the paradoxes... In fact, set theory's failure to embrace the notion of arbitrary *category* (or structure) is really just another way of expressing its failure to capture completely the notion of arbitrary property...

or, better, 'the notion of *set determined by an arbitrary property*'. In other words, there is more in the heaven and earth of set theory than is dreamt of in the philosophy of the cumulative hierarchy: there are all the other sets that are specified by an arbitrary condition, as the naive theory has it.

---

[14] We met this phenomenon dealing with typical ambiguity in connection with the Tarski hierarchy (see sect. 1.5).   [15] Fraenkel, Bar-Hillel, and Levy (1973), pp. 143–4.
[16] Bell (1981), p. 356. Italics original.

2.4...AND LOGIC

The cumulative hierarchy is, as we have seen, an inadequate and seriously incomplete account of sets. This conclusion, though coming into prominence in recent years, has been on the horizon since the 1930s. For the semantics of first order logic poses *exactly* the same problem as category theory; its solution is, therefore, just as intractable classically. Take a first order language and consider the definition of logical validity for that language:

$\Sigma \models \alpha$ iff *in every interpretation* in which all the members of Σ are true, α is true

An interpretation is a set theoretic entity whose domain is an arbitrary set. Hence there are interpretations of arbitrarily high rank. Thus, the definition of validity has quantifiers that range over the universe of sets, which is not, according to the cumulative hierarchy, a set. But now consider the language in which this definition is given. Normally this is just a fragment of mathematical English. What is its semantics? Obviously it *has* semantics, since we make perfectly meaningful and true assertions in it. No coherent answer can be given, at least if we adhere to the cumulative hierarchy. For an interpretation is a pair, $\langle D, I \rangle$, where D here is the domain of quantification. But D is not a set, so this is just nonsense.

The same responses that we have already met in the previous section might be suggested. They are just as inadequate here. The notion of proper class would not help, even if it could be given a suitable rationale. For even if we assume that D is a proper class, the definition is still nonsense since, in an interpretation, D is a member of another set. And if we assume that proper classes can be members of hyper-properclasses, this just launches us off up the cumulative hierarchy again, as we saw in connection with category theory. The suggestion that we restrict the quantifiers to a suitable set—say, the set of sets of rank less than the first inaccessible—will not help either. For it is important that, in the definition of logical consequence, 'every' means *every*: the whole point of logical consequence is that a valid inference may be applied to any domain of reasoning. If an inference were truth-preserving only in finite domains, or only in domains of rank less than the first inaccessible cardinal, it would not be universally valid.[17] It might be thought that the downward Löwenheim–Skolem theorem could get us out of the jam; for it shows that in the definition of validity we need quantify only over *countable* structures and, though there are countable structures of arbitrarily high rank, these will all be isomorphic to countable structures of some small and bounded rank. However, this does not solve the problem but just underlines it.

---

[17] In other words, there would be situations that do not fall within the soundness proof for the relation of logical consequence, and where we have no right, therefore, to use the logic to reason. Or, to put it another way, given that we do use logic in this context, and apparently successfully, how this is so becomes a complete mystery.

For we cannot even state, let alone prove, the Löwenheim–Skolem theorem without quantifying over all structures. Hence any suggestion that the theorem shows the problem to be solved is self-refuting. Finally, as with category theory, an appeal to a suitable hierarchy and the notion of typical ambiguity will not help. For even to state the very idea of typical ambiguity, that the definition of logical consequence should be interpreted ambiguously (in every mini-universe in the Gröthendieck hierarchy, say), requires us to quantify over the universe of sets. Again, the suggestion is therefore self-refuting. There is no escape.[18]

The problem can be seen as a special case of a more general one. The specification of the semantics of a first order language is normally thought of as being couched in a set theoretic metalanguage. Hence the language the specification of whose semantics poses problems is set theory itself. The interpretation of a set theoretic language is a pair, $\langle D, I \rangle$, where D is the domain of all sets. Assuming the cumulative hierarchy to be the correct account of set, the semantics of set theory thus becomes impossible to specify in a coherent fashion.

2.5 SEMANTICS AND SET THEORY

As we have seen, both category theory and logic show the inadequacy of the cumulative hierarchy as an account of sets. Both theories are global in nature and put demands on set theory that no well founded structure can satisfy. Specifically, both require the application of set theoretic operations, and in particular the powerset operation, to a totality greater than which cannot be conceived. Yet if the original domain is well founded, the sets produced must be new. Hence the trouble. The only way out of the problem is to operate with a totality of sets which is not well founded. For then applications of the set theoretic principles produce nothing new, but merely turn us back into the totality from which we started. (It is just this which gives them their power to produce contradictions, of course. For we need only add a twist on the return journey and . . .)

The problem of global theories *v.* wellfoundedness is crucial and should have been visible as soon as it became clear what was involved in the giving of semantics. It is to the credit of category theorists that they have explicitly formulated the problem and tried to tackle it, and to the discredit of logicians that they have not.[19] By and large they have not noticed the problem, or, if they have,

---

[18] Well, there is always the heroic solution: throwing the ladder away: '[A]nyone who understands me eventually recognises [my propositions] as nonsense when he has used them—as steps—to climb up beyond them. (He must, so to speak, throw away the ladder he has climbed up)' (*Tractatus*, 6.54). Unfortunately, this is not a serious possibility: if the propositions are understood, they are not nonsense, and conversely, if they are nonsense they cannot be understood.

[19] A notable exception is Mayberry (1977), whose analysis of the situation is acute. Unfortunately, his solution is less inspiring. He insists that, in a "logically perfect language", all quantifiers be bounded (i.e. of the form $\exists x \in y$, $\forall x \in y$). The semantic conditions of no single formula, therefore, require us to refer to the domain of all sets. Unfortunately, it is necessary to quantify over

have responded to it with a "two set theory" policy, having one formal set theory for which to give semantics, and another informal set theory in which to give them. In fact, this is just our old friend, the language/metalanguage distinction set theoretically writ. For, despite the rather different starting point, we have returned to the point at which we concluded the last chapter: the metalinguistic ascent. As we saw in section 1.7, the constructions inherent in our semantic concepts force us, given any semantically open theory, to ascend to a stronger metalanguage in order to express certain facts about it. We have now seen that, given any well founded totality, constructions inherent in our set theoretic concepts, and in particular the powerset operation, force us into a similar ascent, this time, in effect, up the cumulative hierarchy. But these two ascents, despite different appearances, are closely related. For, since Tarski, we know what set theoretic machinery we need to define appropriate semantic notions for a theory T: second order T, that is, the theory whose intended interpretation is the powerset of that of T.[20] Hence, in a sense, there is only one construction which pushes us ever on to bigger and better things (if we wish to remain consistent), which may manifest either a set theoretic or a semantic aspect.[21] This, incidentally, explains an apparently strange fact in the history of set theory. Modern set theories tied to the cumulative hierarchy, such as ZF, were designed with an eye to avoiding the set theoretic paradoxes. This was before it was shown how to define semantic concepts in set theoretic terms. Once it was known how to do this, it was found that, for subtle reasons and apparently "accidentally", these set theories could not define their own truth predicates and could not, therefore, be shown to be inconsistent via the semantic paradoxes (or prove their own consistency). The explanation for this is now apparent: the two paradox-generating tendencies, the inner tensions that produce dialetheias, are, at root, one.

all sets if we wish to specify the semantics of the whole language, frame its account of logical consequence, etc.; so the main problem is not solved. The only possible response here is the heroic one of insisting that these notions are either ineffable, or literally unintelligible. However, both these claims make Mayberry's papers self-refuting, since in his informal exposition Mayberry himself frequently quantifies over the domain of all sets. (In Mayberry (1980), p. 352, he even points out a place where he does this.)

[20] There are some fine distinctions to be drawn here concerning the degree of impredicativity that is required, but essentially the claim is right enough. Details can be found in Wang (1962), ch. 18 or, more schematically, in Fraenkel, Bar-Hillel, and Levy (1973), pp. 321 ff.

[21] This is noted in C. Parsons (1974). Parsons also notes the unstable nature of any semantically open theory/well founded structure. His suggested solution to the problem is an appeal to typical ambiguity, which he regards as 'uncomfortable' (p. 11) and which we have already seen to be inadequate. I will return to the connection between the set theoretic and the semantic paradoxes in sect. 10.3.

3

Gödel's Theorem

3.1 GÖDEL'S THEOREM

In the last two chapters I have argued that dialetheism is correct by producing examples of dialetheias. These were the semantical and set theoretical paradoxes. In this chapter I wish to produce a third argument for dialetheism which draws on Gödel's first incompleteness theorem.[1] This is a non-constructive argument, which does not produce dialetheias explicitly, but shows that that there must be some. Although the argument starts at some distance from the ground we have already traversed, we will, as might be expected, end up in the same terrain: the logical paradoxes and the trade-off between consistency and completeness.

Gödel's first incompleteness theorem is a theorem whose profundity is agreed upon, though on what this profundity comprises there has been little agreement. The theorem comes in many shapes and sizes. I want it in a particular form, so it will pay to be precise about this. Let us start with a statement of the theorem.

Gödel's Theorem
Let T be a theory which can represent all recursive functions and whose proof relation is recursive. Then there is a formula φ such that (i) if T is consistent, φ is not provable in T, and (ii) if the axioms and rules of T are intuitively correct, we can establish by an intuitively correct argument that φ is true.[2]

To say that the theory's proof relation is recursive is to say that we can effectively recognise a proof in T when given one. To say that the theory can represent all recursive functions is just to say that it has an ability to express certain truths of arithmetic. By coding syntactic entities, such as sentences and proofs, as numbers, this gives it the power to express certain facts about the syntax of the language in question. The sentence in question, φ, is effectively of the form $\neg \exists x \Pi(x, \underline{n})$, where $\Pi(x, y)$ is a formula with two free variables, whose

---

[1] The argument first appeared in Priest (1979a, 1984a), the second of which was, in part, a reply to Chihara (1984).

[2] Strictly speaking, one needs to make certain assumptions about the underlying logic of T too. Though this is normally assumed to be classical logic, classical logic is far stronger than necessary. As will be seen from the proof, little more is needed than *modus ponens*, existential generalisation, and the substitutivity of identicals.

informal sense is that x is (the code of) a proof of formula (with code) y, n is the code of φ, and $\underline{n}$ is its numeral.

A proof of Gödel's theorem in this form can be found in the appendix to this chapter, section 3.5. Perhaps the most crucial aspect of the proof is that it involves an informal soundness proof for T which uses the informally correct principles of T themselves. The rest of this chapter is intelligible to someone who has not followed through the details of the proof.

3.2 NAIVE PROOF

So much for the formulation of Gödel's theorem. The argument for dialetheism is obtained by applying the theorem to the naive notion of proof in such a way as to show it to be inconsistent. Hence I need to explain what I take the naive notion of proof to be, and argue that Gödel's theorem is applicable to it.

Proof, as understood by mathematicians (not logicians), is that process of deductive argumentation by which we establish certain mathematical claims to be true. In other words, suppose we have a mathematical assertion, say a claim of number theory, whose truth or falsity we wish to establish. We look for a proof or a refutation, that is, a proof of its negation. (Though it may be that various non-deductive arguments can also be used to support a mathematical claim, these are not, strictly speaking, proof.) But a proof from what? Presumably from other things already known to be true. We may of course ask how we know these claims to be true, and it may be because we have proofs of them. However, on pain of infinite regress, we cannot go on like this indefinitely. Sooner or later, we must come to arguments whose premises are known to be true without our having to look for a proof; where the question of proof does not, as it were, arise. Let us call these *basic statements*. It does not matter what the basic statements are or how we know them to be true. All that matters is that there are such things.[3] Basic statements in arithmetic are, presumably, claims such as that every number has a successor, or the basic facts about addition. (We can look for formal proofs of such things in a foundational system such as *Principia*. But these are not proofs in the sense with which we are concerned: means of coming to know that the thing proved is true.) I will call the informal deductive arguments from basic statements *naive proofs*. I do not want to rule out the possibility that standards of

[3] There may, from time, to time, be disputes over whether a mathematical assertion is a basic statement, and, more, generally, over canons of proof. Still, perhaps the amazing thing about mathematics (in virtue of its non-empirical nature) is the unanimity of the mathematical community at any one time about what constitutes a legitimate proof. (Witness the fact that with very few exceptions intuitionism has made hardly any inroads into mathematics departments of universities.) There may be periods when consensus breaks down. These tend to occur when powerful new mathematical theories emerge. However, they are relatively short-lived, and the mathematical community regroups around new standards. The situation is well described by Kuhn (1962). One might even say that this consensus is necessary for there to be a notion of mathematical proof at all. As Wittgenstein stressed, without consensus the whole "language game" of proof would break down.

naive proof may change over time. Hence, to be definite, the standards of proof in question are those in force now.

So much for the naive notion of proof. I want now to argue that it satisfies the conditions of Gödel's theorem. It should be said at once that naive proof, or at least the naive theory it generates, is not a formal theory in the sense of the theorem; but it is accepted by mathematicians that informal mathematics could be formalised if there were ever a point to doing so, and the belief seems quite legitimate. The language of naive proof, a fragment of English, could have its syntax tidied up so that it was a formal language, and the set of naive theorems expressed in this language would be deductively closed. Hence we may, without injustice, talk about the naive theory as if it were a formal theory. When regarded in this way, there seems no doubt that the theory can represent all recursive functions. For our naive canons of proof contain those of ordinary arithmetic, in which all recursive functions are specifiable in the usual way.

Somewhat more contentious is the claim that the proof relation of the theory is recursive. It is, however, part of the very notion of proof that a proof should be effectively recognisable as such. For the very point of a proof is that it gives us a way of settling whether something is true or not. It is, therefore, a proof only when it is recognized as such. The point is a common enough one. As Church[4] puts it,

[C]onsider the situation which arises if the notion of proof is non-effective. There is then no certain means by which, when a sequence of formulas has been put forward as a proof, the auditor may determine whether it is in fact a proof. Therefore he may fairly demand a proof, in any given case, that the sequence of formulas put forward is a proof; and until the supplementary proof is provided, he may refuse to be convinced that the alleged theorem is proved. This supplementary proof ought to be regarded, it seems, as part of the whole proof of the theorem . . .

If the proof relation is effectively recognisable, then by Church's thesis it is recursive.

This appeal to essence may be bolstered by the following considerations. The naive notion of proof is a social one. In particular, it is one which is taught and, correspondingly, learnt. Yet the collection of proofs is (potentially) infinite. Hence the notion cannot be taught by giving a simple finite list. If proof is not a recursive notion, then the process whereby it is learnt becomes unintelligible. Consider the following analogy. People are able to produce (potentially) infinitely many numerals. Moreover, everyone can agree that what is produced is a numeral. This is perfectly understandable in virtue of the fact that numerals can be produced by applications of effective rules to a finite vocabulary. (They are a recursive class.) If this were not the case, then that agreement is achieved would be a mysterious and even mystical process. So it is with proof.

We see that there are excellent reasons for supposing that the naive notion of proof is recursive. What reasons are there against it? Several grounds might be

---

[4] Church (1956), p. 53.

adduced, most of suspect cogency. Intuitionists have sometimes been unwilling
to tie themselves down to formal systems. None the less, they do not deny the
effective recognisability of proof. As Dummett puts it,[5]

[I]ntuitionists incline to write as though, while we cannot delimit in advance the realm of
all possible intuitionistically valid proofs, still we can be certain for particular proofs given,
and particular principles of proof enunciated, that they are intuitionistically correct.

Nor can they deny this. For, as Dummett has argued, the only cogent argument
for intuitionism turns on the meaning and use of mathematical language and, in
particular, on the fact that in mathematics truth is not, in general, effectively
recognisable while proof is.[6] Hence there are no specifically intuitionist grounds
for doubting this point.

Another reason sometimes adduced against the recursiveness of proof is
Gödel's theorem itself as used, for example, by anti-mechanists.[7] But, as might be
expected, in the present context this just begs the question. The situation is this:
both the anti-mechanist and I agree that the recursiveness and the consistency of
proof are incompatible. But to infer the non-recursivencess of proof from this
invokes consistency, and hence begs the question. To the extent that arguments
for consistency are produced, they usually invoke *ex contradictione quodlibet*, and
so beg the question again.[8] We may even, in fact, turn the anti-mechanist's
argument on its head. If we assume a materialist theory of mind (which is, I
think, correct, though I do not intend to argue for it here), then, plausibly,
mechanism follows. For the neural circuitry of the brain can presumably be
reproduced (in theory) by vastly more clumsy electro-mechanical devices. But
then (at least according to the anti-mechanist) naive proof must be recursive, and
naive theorems recursively enumerable.[9] Notice also that there are—as far as I
know—no arguments against the recursiveness of proof from a non-materialist
theory of mind.

There is one final argument against the recursiveness of proof, perhaps the
major one, that needs to be considered. It is sometimes suggested that proof may
not be recursive since we may, from time to time, add to our axioms or rules of
proof new ones in a non-rule-governed way, or at least in a way not governed
by the current rules of proof. (Thus, e.g., Gödel (1947) suggests that we may add

---

[5] Dummett (1959), p. 184 of reprint.   [6] Dummett (1975).
[7] See e.g. Lucas (1961).
[8] Lucas (1961), p. 53 of reprint. It is important to appreciate the strength of this rejoinder. I am
in the process of giving an argument against consistency. One cannot, therefore, dogmatically
invoke consistency or the law of non-contradiction to show that the argument fails. Any satisfactory
objection must give independent arguments for consistency, and these would attempt a global
refutation of dialetheism, not just a local refutation of a step in this particular argument for
dialetheism. I will confront what better arguments for consistency there are in ch. 7.
[9] Strictly speaking, this argument shows only the recursive enumerability of the set of theorems
establishable by one person. However, the naive notion of proof is a social, and not a purely
subjective, one. The connection between these two things would therefore need to be spelt out if we
were to pursue the argument.

new axioms when they are known to imply many things already known to be true and nothing known to be false.) This cannot *per se* be used as an argument against the thesis of the recursiveness of proof being defended here, since the canons of proof in question were specified synchronically. However, it is sometimes suggested that the mere formulation and proof of the Gödel sentence for a theory launches us into a revision of the very proof procedures in force. Hence the pertinent notion of naive proof here is the diachronic one, and, while each synchronic slice of this may be recursive, the whole is not.[10] Any plausibility that this line has will depend on how the idea that novel proof procedures are generated is substantiated. So how exactly is this supposed to be achieved?

A simple suggestion is that the proof relation is changed by the addition of, say, the Gödel sentence as an extra axiom. This suggestion does not, however, do justice to the facts.[11] For it is clear that in the new proof procedures the Gödel sentence is not axiomatic, but is provable (the proof being essentially that given in section 3.5). Moreover, there is a clear sense in which, whatever the changes are that are made to allow this proof, they are not arbitrary, but are a natural projection of the prior proof procedures. The only plausible account of this I know is that according to which the specification of the proof relation necessary in formulating the Gödel sentence introduces new concepts or vocabulary, which can then be slotted into proof procedures that are, in some sense, schematic, to increase their strength. This has been suggested by Dummett:[12]

[O]nce a system has been formulated, we can, by reference to it, define new properties not expressible in it, such as the property of being a true statement in the system; hence, by applying induction to such new properties, we can arrive at conclusions not provable in it.

The idea is clear enough, but it will not work. The crucial question is why the property specifiable in terms of the systematisation should be logically novel, i.e. not already in the range of the schematic (or second order) variables of principles such as that of induction. Dummett gives no arguments why this is so, and, in fact, it is not. For the proof relation of the old system is (as is being conceded) recursive, and hence is specifiable in the arithmetic vocabulary to hand. (Though the combination of symbols involved in the specification may be temporally novel.) Moreover, the predicate 'true statement of the system' is equivalent to 'true and a formula of the system'. The second conjunct is, as with the proof relation, arithmetic, and the first conjunct can be novel only once, and not indefinitely as required. If it be claimed that at every state a *novel* truth predicate is added, and hence that this progression takes us up the Tarski hierarchy, the reply is that this account of truth is indefensible, as we saw in section 1.5.

---

[10] A formal model of this process might be something like the construction of Feferman (1962), where we have a hierarchy of theories each of which is recursively enumerable and each of which can prove the Gödel sentence for lower members of the hierarchy.

[11] Though this is how, in effect, the Feferman construction proceeds.

[12] Dummett (1963), p. 195 of reprint.

Even if the indefinite revisability of vocabulary could be substantiated, this line of argument would still not work; for, even granted that it is the diachronic proof relation that is relevant in this context, there are good reasons for supposing this to be recursive too. As we have noted, the manoeuvre which is used in transcending the old system is not a random or arbitrary one, but a quite determinate rule-governed one. Thus, on this conception we have not only rules of proof for generating theorems, but also rules for generating rules of proof for generating theorems. But theorems in the diachronic sense are still generated by effective rules, and so are recursively enumerable. By Craig's theorem, the system has a decidable set of axioms, and therefore a recursive proof relation. Indeed, given that this whole process is just as teachable and learnable as the synchronic one, similar considerations will push us to the conclusion that diachronic proof is recursive.[13]

Thus, it is more than reasonable to suppose that the naive theory satisfies the conditions of Gödel's theorem.

3.3 ...AND DIALETHEISM

So much for Gödel's theorem itself and the naive notion of proof. Let us now put the preceding discussion to the service of dialetheism. By the facts established in the previous sections, the consistency of our naive proof procedures entails a contradiction. For let T be (the formalisation of) our naive proof procedures. Then, since T satisfies the conditions of Gödel's theorem, if T is consistent there is a sentence φ which is not provable in T, but which we can establish as true by a naive proof, and hence *is* provable in T. The only way out of the problem, other than to accept the contradiction, and thus dialetheism anyway, is to accept the inconsistency of naive proof.[14] So we are forced to admit that our naive proof procedures are inconsistent. But our naive proof procedures just are those methods of deductive argument by which things are established as true. It follows that some contradictions are true; that is, dialetheism is correct.

Against this, one might object as follows. Granted that our naive proof procedures are inconsistent, they may not, despite our beliefs, be sound. After all, accepted proof procedures do change: we come to reject some previously accepted standards of proof. In reply to this, several points are relevant. First, the general objection that *something* may be wrong with the accepted standards of argument carries little weight. After all, it can be raised against any argument, and hence, if it were sufficient to destroy an argument, general scepticism would

---

[13] One should note that the cumulative proof relations of both the Tarski and the Feferman hierachies become non-recursive only when they go well into the transfinite. Because of this, the claim that they model any human cognitive process must be highly doubtful.

[14] Alternatively, the *reductio* can be avoided by rephrasing the argument thus: if φ is provable, T is inconsistent; but φ is provable; hence ...

result. If my argument falls only to general scepticism, I am quite content. If the point is to have any more weight than this, it must not just cast merely confused doubt on our naive proof procedures but must produce legitimate grounds for doubt concerning some particular principle used.

A second and somewhat deeper reply is that the intelligibility of this objection hinges on the assumption that we can make sense of the idea that the proof procedures that define a practice may themselves be incorrect. This assumption is not at all easy to sustain. It must be said straightaway that our views or theories about what those procedures are may indeed be incorrect. Here there can be a logical gap between theory and its object, which makes falsity possible. However, with the case of the practices themselves, it is not at all clear that there can be such a logical gap.[15] For the standards themselves create the object. The point has been made by many writers, but one naturally thinks first of Wittgenstein,[16] who emphasised that the rules of procedure in a practice may define what correctness is. The point is not the foolish one that any set of rules must be sound. It is that, once a set of rules is embedded in a practice so that it defines that practice, and to an extent the meaning of the very language used in that practice, the possibility of making global mistakes lacks any clear content.[17]

But what of the historical evidence? Do we not now know that some past mathematical practices were fallacious? Unfortunately, our knowledge of the history of mathematics suffers from serious historiographical faults. Most history of mathematics this century has been written in a positivist vein, which commits the anachronism of supposing that past standards of proof are simply crude versions of current standards. This has been well stressed by Lakatos (1976). A superficial reading of Lakatos himself would, however, support the view that old standards of proof may be fallacious. After all, he shows that old theorems may be refuted. But a careful reading shows that this happens only because of a certain amount of "concept stretching". In other words, a theorem that is "refuted" has had its meaning changed to make a counter-example possible. The old theorem—or, more precisely, the sentence with its old meaning—has not therefore been shown to be false.[18] Hence there is no comfort for the objection here.

[15] I will return to the distinction between our proof procedures and our theories about them in ch. 14.　　　　　　　　　　　　　　　　　　　[16] Particularly Wittgenstein (1953, 1956).

[17] This conclusion may be avoidable if we can locate something in virtue of which we can make sense of the notion of a global mistake. If we could substantiate mathematical realism or "platonism", this might do. But, as Wittgenstein himself saw, mathematical realism is untenable. I will not discuss this now but will return to the issue in sect. 10.4.

[18] 'For the polyhedra they [the first people to prove the Descartes–Euler conjecture] had in mind the conjecture *was* true as it stood and the proof was flawless. Then came the refutationists. In their critical zeal they stretched the concept of polyhedron, to cover objects that were alien to the intended interpretation. The conjecture was true in the *intended interpretation*, it was only false in an *unintended interpretation* smuggled in by the refutationists. Their "refutation" revealed no *error* in the original conjecture, no *mistake* in the original proof: it revealed the falsehood of a *new* conjecture which nobody had stated or thought of before' (Lakatos 1976, pp. 84–5; italics original).

The third, and perhaps most decisive, reply is that it makes very little difference to the argument if our present proof procedures *are* unsound. Suppose our naive proof procedures, T, are unsound. Suppose we reformulate them into a theory T' that is sound. Now either T' is consistent or it is inconsistent. If it is consistent, then we can apply the argument concerning Gödel's theorem to it to give a (classically) untenable contradiction. Hence it must be inconsistent, and, since it is sound, dialetheism follows. This argument presupposes that T' satisfies the conditions for the applicability and proof of Gödel's theorem. But these are very weak, and it is difficult to see how they might fail to apply. As before, we can argue that T' must have a recursive proof relation, and, unless one wishes to maintain that recursive arithmetic is unsound (a desperate move) T' will be able to represent all recursive functions too. It might be suggested that, once our informal proof procedures have been modified, there is no longer any guarantee that we can produce the informal proof of the undecidable sentence, and in particular the informal soundness proof of T'; but the principles required to prove the soundness of T' are very little more than T' itself, amounting to just second order T'. We would therefore have to suppose that the theory T' is both consistent and sound, but that if we replace the schematic letters in some axiom scheme of T' by second order variables then unsoundness results. This is obviously another desperation move. (As I pointed out in the first reply, it is not good enough to cast merely confused suspicion; specific grounds for doubting specific principles must be produced.) Attempts to get around the problem by consistentising will not work.

3.4 INCONSISTENCY *V.* INCOMPLETENESS

As many have observed, there is a connection between Gödel's theorem and the logical paradoxes. There is in fact a very tight connection, and it will pay us to pin this down.

Given the major conclusion of the previous section, that our naive proof procedures are inconsistent, it does not follow that the Gödel sentence for the naive theory is unprovable in the theory. Indeed, it is provable. What is the proof? Essentially, as it always was. The proof of φ given in the appendix, including the soundness proof for T, is now considered as being given within T itself. And as the proof also shows, the negation of φ is also provable in T. We see, therefore, what some of the inconsistencies in the theory are. In fact, in this context the Gödel sentence becomes a recognisably paradoxical sentence. In informal terms, the paradox is this. Consider the sentence 'This sentence is not provably true.' Suppose the sentence is false. Then it is provably true, and hence true. By *reductio* it is true. Moreover, we have just proved this. Hence it is provably true. And since it is true, it is not provably true. Contradiction. This paradox is not the only one forthcoming in the theory. For, as the theory can prove its own soundness, it must be capable of giving its own semantics. In particular, the T-scheme for the language of the theory is provable in the theory. Hence, as we saw in chapter 1, the semantic paradoxes will all be provable in the theory. Gödel's "paradox" is just a special case of this.

Our naive theory is semantically closed and inconsistent. By contrast, any consistent theory cannot be semantically closed. Hence, semantic reasoning about the theory (which, as we noted in section 2.5, always allows us to transcend any consistent theory) cannot be represented in the theory. But it is essentially semantic reasoning that allows us to prove the Gödel sentence. Thus is the disjuncture between what can be informally established and what can be proved in a consistent system formed. Gödel's theorem therefore bears witness to the general fact noted in section 1.7, that there is a necessary trade-off between consistency and completeness: consistency forces on a theory a certain incompleteness, either expressive or proof theoretic. And it is the failure of a consistent theory to be able to express its own truth predicate which prevents it from being able to prove its Gödel sentence. Conversely, any (expressively) complete proof theory is inconsistent.[19]

In view of this, we might say that our naive proof procedures are not just contingently inconsistent, but *essentially* so. This can be seen as vindicating the Kant/Hegel thesis that Reason is inherently, by its very nature, inconsistent. Indeed, it is easy to paint the logical paradoxes in the appropriate colours. As we saw in Chapter 0, according to Kant, the categories of thought provide a framework for categorising the objects of experience. Thought itself produces objects—objects of thought—but the categories cannot be legitimately applied to them. According to Hegel, it is not possible to stop the categories applying to the objects of thought, and the attendant contradictions have to be accepted. The logical paradoxes can be seen to make the Hegelean point. Sets, which are just extensionalised categories, may originally have functioned in our conceptualisation and manipulation of concrete objects; but, sets having been "invented", it transpired that these objects of thought are subject to the very conceptualisation they produce. Similarly, we may suppose that, in response to the need to describe and explain the workings of language, semantic language was produced. But having been produced, it was found that this very language applies to itself. Thus, the very acts of conceptualisation produce the closures which give paradox. Even though our conceptualisation/linguistic structure is, in a sense, a human product, it does not follow that we have complete control over what we produce. (This, after all, is the moral of *Frankenstein*, and, in a much more horrific way, of *Capital*.) In particular, a consequence of conceptualisation which must conceive, *inter alia*, of itself is contradiction. We

---

[19] There is, however, no guarantee that inconsistent, naive proof theory is complete in another sense, namely that every true sentence is provable. Thus, there may still be sentences that are undecidable with respect to this theory. Whether or not this is so I do not know. At any rate (and by definition), anything that can be *shown* to be true is provable in this theory.

might think of the cumulative hierarchy or the Tarski hierarchy as latterday Kantian attempts to retain a certain control over conceptual production. But as we have seen, such constraints are ultimately of no avail: dialetheism is inherent in thought.

3.5 APPENDIX: PROOF OF GÖDEL'S THEOREM

In this section I will give a proof of Gödel's theorem as stated in section 3.1. But first, two preliminary comments. A more normal statement of Gödel's theorem would have it that, if T is (ω-)consistent, φ is neither provable nor refutable. This stronger claim is unnecessary for present purposes, though it is true. And given this, there must be true sentences that are not provable in T, since either φ or its negation is true. For present purposes, however, we need to *show* that one of the unprovable sentences is true. The second comment is just that the proof makes no use of the orthodox assumption that soundness implies consistency.

A proof of Gödel's theorem goes as follows. Given a theory T that satisfies the conditions of the theorem, we code each formula and proof of T as a number, in an effective and well known way. If α is any formula, we will let #α be the code of α, and, given any number n, $\underline{n}$ will be its numeral. Thus #$\underline{\alpha}$ is the numeral of the code of α. If $\alpha(v)$ is any formula with one free variable, v, the *diagonalisation* of α is the formula $\alpha(\underline{k})$ where k is the code of $\alpha(v)$. (The diagonalisation of a formula not of this form can be defined as the formula itself.) Diagonalisation is clearly an effective procedure. Hence, by Church's thesis (the appeal to which could be avoided if we were more specific about the coding), diagonalisation is a recursive function of formula codes. This is representable in T since all recursive functions are. There is therefore a term of the language, $\delta(x)$, of one free variable, such that:

If m is the (code of) the diagonalisation of the formula (with code) n,
$$T \vdash \delta(\underline{n}) = \underline{m}^{20}$$

We can now prove the following.

Diagonal Lemma
If $\alpha(v)$ is any formula with one free variable v, then there is a sentence β such that

$$T \vdash \beta \leftrightarrow \alpha\,(\underline{\#\beta})$$

---

[20] Alternatively, we could suppose the existence of a formula with two free variables, $\Delta\,(x, y)$, such that $T \vdash \forall\, x \,\exists\,!\, y\, \Delta\,(x, y) \wedge \Delta\,(\underline{n}, \underline{m})$. But the functional version streamlines the proof.

Proof

Consider the formula $\alpha(\delta(v))$. Suppose this has code n. Then its diagonalisation is $\alpha(\delta(\underline{n}))$. Let this have code k. We know that $T \vdash \delta(\underline{n}) = \underline{k}$. Hence, by the properties of identity, $T \vdash \alpha(\delta(\underline{n})) \leftrightarrow \alpha(\underline{k})$. Thus, $\alpha(\delta(\underline{n}))$ is the required formula.

We can now prove the main theorem. Given a pair of numbers $\langle m, n \rangle$, by the conditions of the theorem we can effectively tell whether m is the code of a proof of a formula with code n. Hence by Church's thesis (which could, again, be avoided if we were to make details of the coding explicit) the characteristic function of this relation is recursive. By representability, we can find a term of the language with two free variables $\pi(x, y)$, such that

If m is the code of a proof of the formula with code n, then

$$T \vdash \pi(\underline{m}, \underline{n}) = \underline{1} \tag{1}$$

and if not,

$$T \vdash \pi(\underline{m}, n) \neq \underline{1} \tag{2}$$

Now write $\Pi(x, y)$ for $\pi(x, y) = \underline{1}$ and consider the formula $\neg \exists x \, \Pi(x, y)$. By the diagonal lemma, we can find a formula φ such that

$$T \vdash \varphi \leftrightarrow \neg \exists x \, \Pi(x, \#\varphi) \tag{3}$$

Suppose that $T \vdash \varphi$. Then $T \vdash \neg \exists x \, \Pi(x, \#\varphi)$, by (3). But also, some m is the code of a proof of φ. Hence $T \vdash \Pi(\underline{m}, \overline{\#\varphi})$ by (1), and thus $T \vdash \exists x \, \Pi(x, \#\varphi)$. Thus T is inconsistent. Contrapositively, if T is consistent, then it is not the case that $T \vdash \varphi$. This proves the first part of the theorem.

To prove the second part of the theorem, we first prove the conditional: if T is sound, φ is true. This is proved as follows. If φ is provable, then by soundness, φ is true. If φ is not provable, then no number is a code of its proof. Thus, for every m, $T \vdash \neg \Pi(\underline{m}, \overline{\#\varphi})$ by (2). By soundness, every formula of this form is true. Hence $\forall x \, \neg \Pi(x, \overline{\#\varphi})$ is true, whence φ follows by (3) and the soundness of T. In either case, φ is therefore true.

To complete the proof, we need an argument for the soundness of T. Since we are assuming the intuitive correctness of the axioms and rules of T, this is possible by a simple induction over the length of proofs in T, of a kind familiar to logicians. For example this sort of proof is used to show that Peano Arithmetic holds in the standard model of arithmetic. The proof can be written in second order T. To carry out the proof in detail, we may need to assume the correctness not just of any axiom scheme of T but of its second order form. However, this seems unproblematical, since whatever intuition supports the one would seem to support the other.

In more detail, the proof goes essentially as follows.[21] If α is any axiom of T, we can infer from α that $\#\alpha$ is true. Now suppose that α is inferred from $\alpha_1, \ldots, \alpha_n$ by

---

[21] Full details of this sort of proof can be found in, e.g. Wang (1962), ch. 18.

rule R, and that we have established that $\#\alpha_1, \ldots, \#\alpha_n$ are true. Then we infer that $\#\alpha$ is true by, essentially, rule R, which is intuitively correct. (For example, if R is *modus ponens* and α_2 is $\alpha_1 \rightarrow \alpha$, then from '$\#\alpha_2$ is true' we can infer '$\#\alpha_1$ is true $\rightarrow \#\alpha$ is true', and hence derive the conclusion by an application of *modus ponens*.) By induction, all theorems of T are true.

This completes the proof of the second part of the theorem.

PART II

DIALETHEIC LOGICAL THEORY

Indeed, even at this stage, I predict a time when there will be mathematical investigations of calculi containing contradictions, and people will actually be proud of having emancipated themselves from consistency.

Wittgenstein (1964), p. 322

4

Truth and Falsity

4.1 PRELIMINARY ISSUES

In the previous chapters I have argued a case for dialetheism based on the logical paradoxes. Once dialetheism is accepted, some obvious problems are posed. Orthodox logical theory, both formal and informal, takes no account of dialetheias. What, then, should a more adequate logical theory be like, and how does this relate to the received theory? It is the purpose of this part of the book to address these questions. In particular, I will discuss various important logical and epistemological notions, such as implication and rational acceptability. These will include some novel notions generated by dialetheism itself, such as quasi-validity. In the course of this discussion, I shall provide a formal logical theory that is more adequate than the orthodox one. In this chapter I will start with, arguably, the most important logical notion: truth.

Dialetheism, the view that some contradictions are true, does not commit one *per se* to any particular account of truth. A dialetheist who holds a correspondence account of truth will hold that there are inconsistent facts (whatever, in the end, this is taken to mean). One who holds a verificationist/pragmatist account of truth will hold that some contradictions are warranted by the evidence, and so on. None the less, there are many issues that need to be sorted out before a formal logical theory can be properly formulated, and some of these, such as falsity and truth value gaps, need us to get a clear position on truth first. Hence we start here.

It is customary to begin the philosophical analysis of some notion with a discussion of the standard views on the matter. In the present case this would require a discussion of the correspondence theory of truth, the coherence theory, and so on. But this would take us a long way off track and, in any case, would have a mainly negative outcome, the objections to all these views being well known. Hence I will not follow this approach, but will move straightaway to what is, I think, the correct account. Before I do this, it will pay dividends to get a few preliminary issues straight. We will be concerned with truth, or more precisely with the attribution of truth. The problem is what it is to say of something that it is true. A first point that probably does not need to be made, but might just, is that this is a different question from that of how one knows something to be true (or when it is reasonable to believe that something is true). I shall say a little more about this question in section 7.4, but for the moment it is sufficient to note that these are distinct questions. No chemist would make the mistake of confusing the question of what gold is (an element with a certain atomic number) with the question of how you know you have it (a positive response to certain physico-chemical tests). Presumably it is the fact that truth is less concrete than gold which has caused some philosophers to make a similar mistake. Of course, it may be that, having sorted out the nature of truth, a position on the knowledge of truth follows (or, at least, is strongly suggested); but this may not be the case, and in any case, if a connection does exist it needs to be established, not assumed.

The second, and more substantial, preliminary point concerns what sort of thing it is of which truth is predicated. In English, truth is predicated of many different sorts of things: friends, coins, beliefs, sentences, etc. I shall be concerned with only one of these: sentences. Thus, I will take 'is true' to be a predicate of grammatically well formed indicative sentences (and, as throughout the book, I will take these to be sentences without indexicals). About the more general question of truth, 'What do *all* attributions of truth have in common?', I shall have nothing to say. Few logicians would berate me for ignoring the attribution of truth to friends and coins, but many might do so for considering its attribution to sentences rather than statements, beliefs, or some other kind of cognitive entity. A few words therefore need to be said by way of justification.

First, since Tarski, it has become standard to predicate truth of sentences, and this kind of approach has proved very fruitful. In fact, as far as formal logical theory goes, there is really no alternative. On all the formal semantics I know, truth conditions are specified by a recursion over grammatical structure. But statements, for example, have no intrinsic grammatical structure. (If the notion of statement is to be genuinely different from that of sentence, then different sentences can express the same statement.) Hence this procedure is not available for them. Similar remarks apply to beliefs, propositions, and so on.

Secondly, I do not want to enter the hoary old issue of what sorts of entities are the primary bearers of truth—whatever that means. Fortunately, this can be avoided in any case. All I require is that there is *some* sense in which we can attribute truth to sentences, and this is granted even by those who take, e.g., statements to be the primary bearers of truth; for they concede that we may speak of a sentence as true (in a derived sense) if it expresses a true statement. As long as there is some sense in which we can legitimately predicate truth of sentences, this is what I wish to discuss.

Thirdly, under some reasonable enough assumptions, we can define the attribution of truth to other sorts of cognitive entity in terms of the truth of sentences. For example, 'the belief/statement x is true' may be defined as 'for some sentence y, y expresses the belief/statement x and y is true'. This presupposes that there are no ineffable beliefs/statements (i.e. beliefs/statements not expressible in any language). But such an assumption is very reasonable, and even if it is not true this shows only that truth for these notions is *sui generis*, a position we can face with equanimity.

4.2 THE T-SCHEME

Having discussed these preliminary issues, let us return to the main one: given a language, L, what does it mean to say of a sentence of L that it is true?[1] As Tarski observed,[2] if L had only a finite number of sentences, we might try to characterise truth, at least extensionally, as follows: Let $\alpha_1, \ldots, \alpha_n$ be the sentences of L, and let α' be the translation of α into English (or α itself if L is English). Then

$$Tx \leftrightarrow (x = \underline{\alpha}_1 \wedge \alpha_1{}') \vee \ldots \vee (x = \underline{\alpha}_n \wedge \alpha_n{}')$$

But any sensible language, certainly any natural language, contains an infinity of sentences. Hence this approach is not possible. A slightly different approach will, however, work. The axiom scheme

$$T\underline{\alpha} \leftrightarrow \alpha',$$

the general T-scheme, will do the job. For let P be any predicate satisfying the scheme $P\underline{\alpha} \leftrightarrow \alpha'$; then by transitivity, $P\underline{\alpha} \leftrightarrow T\underline{\alpha}$. Thus, T and P have the same extension (at least as far as sentences of L go, and if they differ elsewhere, we need only consider their respective conjunctions with 'x is a sentence of L').

Evidently, this argument assumes that truth does satisfy the truth scheme. I have already argued that it does in section 1.4, but in virtue of the central importance of the principle it is worth giving some more arguments for it. One argument concerns the "disquotational" features of truth.[3] We frequently wish to endorse the words of another. If we know what the person said, there is nothing simpler. We merely say what they said, possibly using the same sentence. However, we sometimes wish to do this even when we do not know what was said. Maybe they have not even said it yet! We must therefore proceed differently, and we resort to the truth predicate. For example, to endorse the words of a Pope, we might say 'The first *ex cathedra* pronouncement of the Pope in the year 2000 is (will be) true.' Notice that this is not only standard practice, but is, in effect, the only way language gives us of endorsing what is said.[4] Yet a little thought shows that this practice presupposes the truth of the T-scheme. For suppose the Pope utters α. We would like to assert α' (the Pope will, of course, speak in Latin), but we cannot. Instead, we form a noun phrase which refers to α, i.e. $\underline{\alpha}$, and assert $T\underline{\alpha}$. Clearly, this construction will fail if $T\underline{\alpha}$ does not imply α' or vice versa. In other words, the T-scheme holds. Moreover, since we intend to endorse

---

[1] In what follows, I will continue to use lower case Greek letters schematically for sentences of L, underlining to form names, and T for the truth predicate for L.

[2] Tarski (1936), p. 188 of reprint.   [3] See Quine (1970), pp. 10–13.

[4] We can say 'I endorse x', but this means no more than 'I say x to be true'.

what the Pope says, *whatever he says*, the universal validity of the T-scheme must be a presupposition of this linguistic construction.

In a similar way, we sometimes wish to endorse not only each of a finite collection of sentences, but each of an infinite collection. Suppose, for example, that we wish to endorse all the sentences in the set Y, $\{$'$\underline{n}$ is a number' $\mid n$ is an integer$\}$. We do this by asserting that every member of Y is true:

$$\forall x \in Y \; Tx \tag{1}$$

Again, notice that the validity of the T-scheme is presupposed. For in asserting (1) we are certainly committed to, e.g., the claim that '37 is a number' is true. But unless the T-scheme holds, we are not committed to 37 being a number. Moreover, since we may use this way of endorsing an infinite set of sentences whatever it is (in fact it is the only way we have), the universal validity of the T-scheme is presupposed.

A particular instance of this situation concerns the T-scheme itself. This has an infinite number of instances, and the only way we can endorse them all is to say that *every instance of the T-scheme is true*. For any instance of the T-scheme, β, this commits us to $T\underline{\beta}$, but without the T-scheme itself it does not follow that we are endorsing β. We can use this fact to construct an *ad hominem* argument against those who would deny the T-scheme's universal validity. For such a person must assert that *some instances of the T-scheme fail*; i.e., for some instance of the T-scheme β, $\neg T\underline{\beta}$. But if the person is right and the T-scheme does fail in general, this linguistic act may misfire badly, since this assertion is, by the person's own admission, *quite compatible with β'*.

This *ad hominem* argument aside, we have seen that certain of our linguistic constructions presuppose the validity of the T-scheme in an essential way. Indeed, it would seem that in practice the point of having a truth predicate is just to give us the means of expressing these things, which would otherwise be inexpressible. (Recall the point noted in section 3.4 that any semantically open language is expressively incomplete.) We could say that the point of the T-scheme is to ensure that there is an operator inverse to quotation. This is not quite right, for in fact, the truth predicate turns all mention into use, and quotation is only one form of mentioning. Perhaps, then, we could call truth the *unmentioning functor*. Call it what you will; unmentioning is an important role of the truth predicate and, since it presupposes the validity of the T-scheme, one which provides an argument for it.

4.3 ...AND MEANING

I want now to give a second argument for the T-scheme. This one also lays the ground for the next section on the inadequacy of the T-scheme to characterise truth. At the heart of a theory of meaning for a language is a theory of truth. This claim is not contentious. It arises from Frege's observation that to give the meaning of a sentence is to give its truth conditions. What *is* contentious is how exactly this claim is to be understood. Davidson and Davidsonians interpret the claim in a very strict form. A theory of meaning for a language just is a Tarski-type theory of truth of a certain kind.[5] The pristine T-scheme, $T\underline{\alpha} \leftrightarrow \alpha'$, states the meaning of α. For semanticists of a possible world variety, such as Montague, Lewis, and Routley,[6] we need to give not simply truth conditions, but truth-in-a-possible-world conditions. Thus, meaning-giving truth conditions are of the form: α is true in world w iff α', where α' will now contain w as a parameter. (We might write this as $T_w\underline{\alpha} \leftrightarrow \alpha'(w)$.) The T-scheme proper now reappears as a special case, viz., when w is the "actual world", G. For those of a verificationist stripe, such as Dummett,[7] we do not have to generalise the T-scheme to possible worlds. Rather, we have to understand truth in a constructive sense. None the less, the T-scheme still holds, and states the conditions under which a sentence is true (= warrantedly assertible), these conditions giving its meaning.

As we see, any theory of meaning presupposes a theory of truth.[8] Moreover, the meaning of a sentence is given by the T-scheme for that sentence (or at least its generalisation to possible worlds). This observation provides the second argument for the T-scheme. The T-scheme must hold for any meaningful sentence since this is (part of) the specification of its meaning.[9]

Before we leave the T-scheme, let me make two further comments about truth-theories in Tarski's sense. First, the T-scheme, $T\underline{\alpha} \leftrightarrow \alpha'$, tells us what it is for any particular sentence, α, to be true, that is, its truth conditions. A theory of truth for a language (or a part of a language) spells out in a systematic way the truth conditions for all the sentences of that language. There is no reason why this should be done in the same way for all kinds of sentences. If the truth theory is to be the basis of a theory of meaning, then the specification should be recursive, since it must explain how the meaning of a whole is dependent on the meanings of its parts. This still leaves plenty of scope for differences, however. For example, it may be that the truth conditions of sentences about the empirical world should be given realistically. That is, truth conditions should be specified via the notion of satisfaction by a domain of extra-linguistic entities. By contrast, those for mathematical discourse might best be given in terms of substitutional quantification, whence the detour through satisfaction is unnecessary. (For more on this, see chapter 10.) And maybe there are other ways appropriate to evaluative discourse. For any domain of discourse, the correct way of giving the truth conditions will always be a matter for separate investigation.

[5] Davidson (1967). As usual, I am supposing the language in question not to contain indexicals.
[6] Montague (1974), especially ch. 6; Lewis (1972); Routley *et al.* (1982).
[7] See Dummett (1978), especially ch. 14. N.B. also p. xxii.
[8] Grice's theory of meaning does not involve the notion of truth, and so might be thought to show this claim to be false. However, Grice's theory is inadequate precisely because it is unable to show how meanings of wholes are dependent on meanings of parts, something which truth-conditional theories excel at.　　　　　　　　[9] I will take this point up again in sect. 9.4.

The second comment is this: it is not necessary that the theory of truth conditions be convertible into an explicit definition of truth in the manner of Tarski. If the truth (or satisfaction) conditions of atomic formulas are specified without reference to truth (or satisfaction), then the recursive clauses can be turned into a second order explicit definition in the usual way. When this happens, it is a bonus, but one can give perfectly acceptable truth conditions without this, as the following example shows.[10]

Consider a simple language L, whose atomic sentences are made up from two monadic predicates T and S, and a stock of individual constants $\{a_i \mid i \in J\}$. Other formulas are built up from these with just negation and conjunction. The truth conditions of the sentences of this language are given as follows. Let D, the domain of the interpretation, contain the set of sentences of the language. Let d be the denotation function of the language; i.e., for all $i \in J$, $d(a_i) \in D$. Then:

> Sa_i is true iff $d(a_i)$ is a sentence of L
> Ta_i is true iff $d(a_i)$ is true
> $\alpha \wedge \beta$ is true iff α is true and β is true
> $\neg\alpha$ is true iff α is not true

These clauses give the recursive truth conditions of the language; but the conditions cannot be converted into an explicit second order definition, because the truth conditions of T itself concern truth. Despite this, these clauses give each sentence determinate truth conditions, and even allow us to show the truth of many sentences. For example, suppose that $d(a_1) = Sa_0$, and $d(a_2) = Sa_1$. Then Sa_1 is true since $d(a_1)$ is a sentence of L, and hence Ta_2 is true too.

Of course, there may be cases where the truth conditions go round in loops. For example, suppose that $d(a_0) = Ta_0$; then

> Ta_0 is true   iff $d(a_0)$ is true
>   iff Ta_0 is true

Or if $d(a_1) = \neg Ta_1$, then

> Ta_1 is true   iff $d(a_1)$ is true
>   iff $\neg Ta_1$ is true
>   iff Ta_1 is not true

In the second case, the truth conditions imply that a_1 is both true and not true. In the first case the conditions neither imply that a_0 is true nor do they imply that it is not true. These are familiar paradox-type situations and I will say more about them in sections 4.7 and 4.8. For the moment we need only note that, though the truth conditions are recursive, it does not follow that they have to be "well founded".

----

[10] We will have more sophisticated examples in chs. 9 and 10.

4.4 BUT TRUTH IS MORE THAN THIS

We have seen that the T-scheme characterises truth, at least extensionally. We must now ask whether it produces an adequate characterisation *simpliciter:* If some predicate satisfies the T-scheme, is it, *ipso facto*, truth?

In general, an extensional characterisation of a notion is not enough. This follows simply from the fact that there are different notions which have the same extension, such as 'featherless biped' and 'animal who habitually practises genocide'. But it might be hoped that the T-scheme gives us slightly more than an extensional characterisation, for the following reason. I have formulated the T-scheme using the symbol ' ↔ ', but I have not yet said what I take this to be. Normally the T-scheme is taken to be a material biconditional, and it is certainly at least this. But there are good reasons for thinking that it is stronger than this. First, to anticipate a little, we shall see in the next chapter that the material (bi)conditional is not detachable: we cannot infer β from α and $\alpha \supset \beta$. Yet the inferences from a sentence to its truth and vice versa certainly seem detachable. Given that nuclear weapons are folly, we can infer that 'Nuclear weapons are folly' is true. Moreover, as I shall suggest in chapter 6, we can distinguish between a material conditional and a genuine conditional. The latter of these is an intensional notion for which detachment is certainly possible. Once we do make this distinction, it is fairly clear that the connection between a sentence and its truth is one of genuine, and not material, conditionality. *If* capitalism exploits employees, *then* 'Capitalism exploits employees' is indeed true, and vice versa. Thus we should take ↔ to be a genuine conditional connective. Which intensional connective it is, we need not worry about now. (I will return to the question in section 4.9.) All that is necessary for the present is to note that the connective in the T-scheme is stronger than a material conditional, and thus (to return to the main point) we might hope that the T-scheme provides more than a merely extensional characterisation.

Clearly, the T-scheme is not an explicit definition: it does not allow us to eliminate 'is true' uniformly from all contexts. Still, explicit definitions are not the only ways of characterising notions. Indeed, they are not even always possible. And, given any sentence, the T-scheme tells us what it is for *that* sentence to be true. So one might reasonably wonder whether the T-scheme provides an implicit definition of truth in the way that the axioms of group theory provide an implicit characterisation of the notion of group. There is nothing to being a group over and above satisfying the axioms of group theory. Is there anything to truth over and above satisfying the T-scheme?

The answer is 'yes'. The T-scheme does not provide an implicit character-isation of truth. This may be seen in a number of ways; however, the basic objection is that the T-scheme does not show what the *point* of calling something true is, though this is an integral part of the characterisation of truth. Put baldly like this, the objection will be somewhat opaque, so let me try to lead up to it.

As we saw in the last section, truth is at the heart of meaning. To give the meaning of a sentence is to give its truth conditions, and the sentence which does this is, as I argued in the last section, the T-scheme:[11]

$$T\underline{\alpha} \leftrightarrow \alpha' \tag{1}$$

But now the T-scheme cannot be considered as simultaneously specifying *both* the sense of α and what it is for α to be true, which is what it would do if the T-scheme were all there is to truth. (1) must be read either as: **α is true iff . . .** , or as: α **is true** iff . . . It cannot be read in both ways at once. If this is not clear, just suppose that I have no prior grasp either of truth or of the senses of sentences of *L*. If I know only that *T* is a predicate such that, and the senses of sentences of *L* are such that, (1) is true, I can infer nothing about either. For example, (1) would be satisfied if every sentence of *L* had, as a matter of fact, the sense of its negation and *T* were the falsity predicate.

We might illustrate the point by considering a simple propositional language with extensional connectives $\wedge$, $\vee$, and $\neg$. We now formulate a truth theory for the language by taking as axioms

$$T\underline{p} \leftrightarrow p'$$

for each propositional parameter, p, of *L*, and adding the following recursive schemes for the connectives:

$T\underline{\alpha \wedge \beta} \leftrightarrow T\underline{\alpha}$ and $T\underline{\beta}$

$T\underline{\alpha \vee \beta} \leftrightarrow T\underline{\alpha}$ or $T\underline{\beta}$

$T\underline{\neg\alpha} \ \leftrightarrow$ It is not the case that $T\underline{\alpha}$

For every sentence, α, of the language *L*, we can now prove the T-scheme for α in the usual way. However, the above theory neither fixes the senses of the sentences of *L*, nor determines that *T* is a truth predicate for *L*. For the correctness of the above theory is quite compatible with *T* being the falsity predicate for *L*, every atomic sentence having the sense of its normal negation, ' $\wedge$ ' meaning *or*, and ' $\vee$ ' meaning *and*. Thus, we see that the T-scheme or, even stronger, a Tarski-type truth theory for a language, which specifies recursive truth conditions for the connectives, cannot force *T* to be a truth predicate. Truth and meaning are mutually dependent variables. Fix one, and we can obtain information about the other. But fix neither, and no information about either is forthcoming. This point is essentially Dummett's. As he puts it,[12]

---

[11] For those of a possible worlds bent, it is not the truth scheme *simpliciter* that states the meaning, but the truth-in-a-possible-world scheme: $T_w\underline{\alpha} \leftrightarrow \alpha'(w)$. The argument that follows can obviously be made to apply equally to this.   [12] Dummett (1978), p. xxi.

[A]cceptance of the redundancy theory [of truth] preclude[s] the possibility of using the notion of truth in a general account of what it is to grasp the meaning of a sentence . . . [T]he truth definition, which lays down the conditions under which an arbitrary sentence of the object language is true, cannot simultaneously provide us with a grasp of the meaning of each sentence, unless, indeed, we already know in advance what the point of the predicate, so defined, is supposed to be. But, if we do know in advance the point of introducing the predicate 'true', then we know something about the concept of truth expressed by that predicate which is not embodied in that, or any other, truth-definition, stipulating the application of the predicate to the sentences of some language: and hence the redundancy theory must be false.

The T-scheme on its own does not give an adequate implicit characterisation of truth.[13]

4.5 THE TELEOLOGICAL ACCOUNT OF TRUTH

What, then, needs to be added to it to provide such a characterisation? The answer is, I think, essentially as follows.[14] The inadequacy of the T-scheme to characterise truth stems from the fact that it can capture only a certain set of logical relations between sentences. Yet the sentences of a language are part of a practice, and truth relates to how sentences are used in that practice, something that cannot be reduced to a set of logical relations between sentences. In particular, the primary use of indicative sentences in a natural language is to make assertions. Asserting, like other human activities, has a *telos* or point, and the *telos* of asserting is truth. That is, the aim of asserting, as such, is saying something true. As Dummett puts it in his own inimitable fashion,[15]

[T]he class of true sentences is the class the utterance of a member of which a speaker of the language is aiming at when he employs what is recognizably the assertoric use.

Dummett compares asserting with playing a game, and speaking the truth with winning. The analogy is an excellent one. Playing a game has a *telos*: winning (or more precisely, obtaining a winning position). There is no one thing which counts as winning in every game. We could specify extensionally what it is to have a winning position in bridge, chess, and so on, but someone who knew only this would not know what winning is. What they would need to know is that winning is what people play the game to achieve. Similarly, the T-scheme may characterise what it is for each particular sentence to be true. But unless a person knows that the truth is what people who assert aim to speak, she will not know what truth is. Of course, in saying this, I do not wish to imply that when

---

[13] If the right-hand side of the T-scheme is a translation of α proper, that is, if the translation is not "homophonic", there is an even quicker argument against the adequacy of the T-scheme to characterise truth. For the notion of translation presupposes that of meaning, and hence that of truth.   [14] The idea is due to Dummett. See Dummett (1959*a*).

[15] Dummett (1973), p. 320.

any person asserts, their personal aim is to speak the truth: they may well be intending to deceive. Equally, for perverse reasons of my own, I may play a game to lose; the points of these activities *as such* are speaking truly and winning, respectively. But it does mean that these practices work on the basis that, by and large, people do engage in those activities for those ends. For if everyone started playing chess "to lose", losing would become winning. All that would change would be that what we used to call a winning position we would now call a losing one, and vice versa. Similary, if everyone went around trying to utter falsehoods, then "speaking falsely" would become speaking truly and vice versa. People would be berated/accused of deception for speaking "truly" and so on. In effect, the senses of sentences would change to those which had previously been expressed by prefixing a negation. We saw in the last section how truth and sense are mutually dependant variables. This underlies this fact.

The connection between truth and assertion comes out very clearly when we consider how an abstract theory of truth of the appropriate kind is tested to see whether it is the core of a theory of meaning for a particular language in use.[16] This is done, essentially, as follows. Suppose we have a putative theory of truth for the language. The meaning-giving T-sentence for an indicative sentence, α, is of the form $T\underline{\alpha} \leftrightarrow \alpha'$. We take a number of sentences, α, and see whether speakers of the language are prepared to assert α when they may reasonably be taken to believe that α' (or at least may reasonably be taken to intend the hearer to believe (that they believe that) α'). And the better the fit in this direction, the better the theory. Thus, it is the use to which the truth predicate is put, and in particular its connection with the things that speakers wish to or are prepared to assert, that completes its characterisation.

In virtue of the fact that this account of truth takes truth (or rather the speaking of truth) to be a certain kind of *telos*, we might call it the teleological account of truth.

4.6 ASSERTION

Having explained the teleological account of truth, let me, in this section, consider a couple of objections to it. The first is that, as a definition, it is circular. For truth is defined in terms of assertion. But what is asserting, as opposed to, say, commanding or questioning? An obvious answer is that asserting is the uttering of something true or false, and if this is right the definition clearly is circular. But assertings are not merely utterings: if they were, parrots and those who talk in their sleep would assert, which they do not. To assert, one must have

---

[16] The process has been discussed most by Davidsonians, but similar empirical tests would have to be performed on a Montague grammar.

certain intentions. Spelling this out in detail requires some care. Fortunately, we can take a leaf out of Grice's book[17] and take asserting to be a certain kind of meaning(N.N.) something. More specifically, we can say that x asserts p if she utters something for an audience A, with the intention that

(1) a certain response, r, be produced in A;
(2) A recognises that intention;
(3) the response be produced in part by A's recognition of this intention.

Specifying the response, r, is a sensitive business. But normally the response will be that A believes that p, or at least, believes that x believes that p. And more recondite cases may require a further depth of nesting of beliefs.

Now many objections have been raised against Grice's notion. To the extent that they are against basing an account of meaning on it (as opposed to basing it on the notion of truth conditions), we can agree with them. There are, however, various examples which might be taken to show that someone can assert without satisfying the Grice conditions. Those familiar with the Grice literature will be pleased to know that I do not intend to consider these here. Let me concede that some fine tuning of the account in virtue of these examples may be in order.[18] It remains true that the above account will do as a first approximation, and suffices to show that assertion may be characterised in non-circular terms.

A second objection to the teleological account of truth is that it is possible for something other than truth to be the point of asserting. We have seen that it is quite compatible with the teleological account that people may individually assert things without aiming to speak the truth. It is the point of asserting as such that is at issue. But if we could find a whole practice where the aim as such was not to speak the truth, this would be a counter-example. One such practice which might spring to mind immediately is acting, story telling, and the like. This can be dealt with quickly. For in this case we can simply deny that assertions are being made. Actors just do not have the intentions of inducing the right kind of beliefs in their audience. A tougher example is the following hypothetical one. We may suppose that the inhabitants of a certain island are notorious fawners: they never speak but to tell the hearer what they think he would like to hear. ('You have a nice ear-ring'; 'You are about to get a wage rise.') Hence on this island the aim of asserting is not to speak the truth but to please the listener. Unlike the actor case, these people certainly assert. Despite initial appearances, this hypothethical counter-example is logically impossible. For fawning is, in fact, parasitic upon the practice of telling the truth. The fawner tries to get the hearer to believe something (or at least, believe that they believe it) which is favourable to the hearer. But unless speakers normally said what they took to be true, mere assertion could not have this effect. If, for example, you say X, I have no reason to believe X (or believe that you believe it) if you are not aiming to say

---

[17] Grice (1957, 1968).   [18] As, e.g. in Davies (1981), ch. 1.

what you believe to be true. Since there is, *ex hypothesi*, no practice of telling the truth on this island, there can be no fawning either. The example is incoherent. Hence, instead of undercutting the primacy of truth to assertion, it underlines it.

These two objections do not, therefore, show the teleological account to be incorrect.

4.7 TRUTH OR FALSITY: TRUTH VALUE GAPS

So much for truth. Let us now make a dialectical switch and consider falsity. We will say that a sentence, α, is false, $F\underline{\alpha}$, just if its negation is true. We might write this thus:

$$F\underline{\alpha} \leftrightarrow T\underline{\neg\alpha}$$

This defines falsity in terms of truth and negation. A legitimate question, therefore, is what negation is. If we are searching for a definition, I confess I have none to offer. Negation is that sentential function which turns a true sentence into a false one, and vice versa. This is true enough, though as a definition entirely circular. Alternatively, we could use these clauses to define negation, but then our definition of falsity would become circular. It would seem that falsity and negation can be defined in terms of each other, but neither can be defined without the other. (Nor would it help, obviously, if we were to define a false sentence as one which is *not* true.) The situation is a common enough one in philosophy: we are faced with a circle of interdefinable terms, and in this case one of very small radius. Nor is this anything to do with dialetheism: the situation is exactly the same for classical logic. Orthodox truth-tables define negation in terms of truth and falsity. But falsity can be defined only in terms of, or by using, negation.

The indefinability of negation does not, however, mean that we can say nothing intelligible about it. In particular, there is much that can be said about the conditions under which a negated sentence is true. For a start, a sufficient condition for the truth of a negated sentence, $\neg\alpha$, is the failure of the truth of α. In other words, if a sentence is not true, it is false:

$$\neg T\underline{\alpha} \rightarrow F\underline{\alpha}$$

This fact about falsity follows from the analysis of truth we have just had. To speak truly is to succeed in a certain activity. And in the context of asserting, anything less than success is failure. There is no question of falling into some limbo between the two. To use the game analogy again, a draw is possible in a two-player game, for neither player may achieve his end. In a one-player game either the player achieves his end or he does not: there is no third possibility. Asserting is a one-player game. The point, again, is Dummett's. As he puts it,[19]

---

[19] Dummett (1959*a*), p. 8 of reprint. Italics original.

A statement, so long as it is not ambiguous or vague, divides all states of affairs into just *two* classes. For a given state of affairs, either the statement is used in such a way that a man who asserted it but envisaged that state of affairs as a possibility would be held to have spoken misleadingly, or the assertion of the statement would not be taken as expressing the speaker's exclusion of that possibility. If a state of affairs of the first kind obtains, the statement is false; if all actual states of affairs are of the second kind, it is true.

Now many people have, of course, given reasons for supposing there to be truth value gaps, that is, a limbo between truth and falsity. We should therefore see why their reasons are incorrect. Among the arguments for the existence of truth value gaps, we may first distinguish a couple of special ones. One of these concerns the logical paradoxes. I have already dealt with this in section 1.3. Another is Aristotle's argument in *De Interpretatione*, chapter 9, concerning future contingents. The lack of cogency of this argument is well established[20] and I need not discuss it further. The other arguments for the existence of truth value gaps appear to be a motley crew concerning non-denoting terms and other kinds of "presupposition failure"; category mistakes and other "nonsense"; sentences undecidable by the appropriate mathematical or empirical techniques; and so on. (I make no claim that this list exhausts the possibilities.) Despite this, it seems to me that this apparent variety is produced by but a single rationale, which might be described as follows. The correspondence theory of truth may not be correct, but it captures an important insight concerning truth: for something to be true, there must be something in the world which makes it so. This need not be a state of affairs as traditionally conceived of by correspondence theorists. It might, in the case of a mathematical truth for example, be our possession (in principle) of a proof. In the case of a statement of legal right, it might be certain activities of a legislature. But there must be something, some Fact, such that if (counterfactually) it did not hold, the sentence would not be true. The rationale can now be stated simply thus: for certain sentences, α, there is no Fact which makes α true, neither is there a Fact which makes $\neg\alpha$ true. For example, in the case of reference failure, there is no state of affairs which is either the King of France's being bald, or his not being bald. For the case of undecidable empirical sentences, there is no possible experiment which would verify either that a particle has a certain momentum, or that it does not have it. And so on.

In each case, one might take issue with the *particular* grounds offered for this conclusion. This would involve us in questions such as Meinongianism, realism in quantum mechanics and in mathematics. These are deep questions, and I will not discuss them here. For, whatever the particular case, there is a *general* reason why this argument fails. In a nutshell, if there is no Fact that makes α true, there is a Fact that makes $\neg\alpha$ true, viz. the Fact that there is no Fact that makes α true. Less cryptically, the point is this. Suppose that α is a sentence, and suppose that there is nothing in the world in virtue of which α is true—no fact, no proof, no

---

[20] See Haack (1974), ch. 4.

experimental test. Then this is the Fact in virtue of which $\neg\alpha$ is true. We may not know that this Fact obtains, but this is irrelevant. And we might be able to distinguish between different kinds of Fact which make $\neg\alpha$ true. For example,[21] in the case of denotation failure, we might distinguish between the case where 'John's brother is a butcher' is false because John has no brother, and that where it is false because he has a brother who is a French-polisher. But this is not a significant difference as far as truth and falsity *simpliciter* go.

There is one important reply here: the intuitionist one. It may be argued that the point that we cannot, in general, recognise when α fails *is* important. For Facts of this kind cannot play the required semantic role. This is, I think, incorrect. However, to discuss this issue here would take us too far away from the central theme of the book, and so I will not do so. In view of my rejection of the intuitionist claim and my consequent endorsement of the law of excluded middle and related principles, the position I am advocating might be called "classical dialetheism". It would be equally possible to have an "intuitionist dialetheism", which took a constructive stance on negation (so that a proof of the impossibility of a proof of α was required for the truth of $\neg\alpha$) and the other logical constants. (We noted in section 1.3 that the proofs of many logical paradoxes do not require the law of excluded middle or other intuitionistically invalid principles.) The paradoxical features of intuitionist implication, such as $\neg\alpha \supset (\alpha \supset \beta)$, could not be incorporated. But these have always been dubious features of intuitionism anyway.[22]

To return to classical dialetheism: as we have seen, if α is any atomic sentence of a kind whose members have been proposed as truth valueless, $\neg\alpha$ is true. Thus, 'Julius Caesar is not a prime number', 'The man next door does not have a television set' (when there is no man next door), and so on are simply true. This may strike some as strange, since it would be unusual to assert such sentences. Unusual perhaps, but not impossible. For example, if a door-to-door salesman enquires whether the man next door has a television, it would be quite appropriate to say: 'No he doesn't. In fact there is no man next door: the house has been empty for some time.' Similarly, it would be quite on the cards to say (perhaps by way of explaining that a category mistake has been made): 'Julius Caesar isn't a prime number, and for that matter he's not a composite number either. He isn't a number at all.'

As a final application of the position, let us return to the example given in section 4.3 of the sentence Ta_0; in effect, 'This sentence is true'. We saw there that the truth conditions of this sentence imply neither the truth of this sentence nor its falsity. There is therefore no question of an *a priori* proof (or refutation) of it. By its nature, this is the only kind of Fact which could make it true. No experiment is going to decide the issue. Hence, by the previous discussion, this sentence is simply false and its negation is true.[23]

---

[21] This case is examined in more detail in Priest (1979).

[22] See e.g. Haack (1974), pp. 101–2.

[23] In fact, the supposition that the sentence is neither true nor false leads to problems of its own. See Mortensen and Priest (1981).

4.8 TRUTH AND FALSITY: DIALETHEISM

So far I have argued that the mere failure of truth of a sentence is sufficient ground for the truth of its negation; that is, that truth and falsity are mutually exhaustive. The next question is whether they are mutually exclusive. This is obviously the question of whether dialetheism is true, which I have already answered positively in the first part of the book: some sentences are both true and false. The arguments for dialetheism used in Part One are of a very specific kind and concern, essentially, just the logical paradoxes. These, however, are not the only kinds of considerations which drive us towards dialetheism, though perhaps they are the most striking. There are, in fact, several areas where very natural considerations push us towards the conclusion that something may be both true and false. One of these concerns change and other dialectical situations. Another concerns legal norms, moral norms, and other rule-like situations. I will consider these in Part Three of the book (in chapters 11–13).[24] And since detailed arguments for dialetheism are to be found elsewhere in the book, I will not rehearse them here, but will content myself with a somewhat picturesque summary of the general situation.

Suppose we have a language, a language in use, such as English. Sentences of the language have specific uses. Each sentence has a set of situations where it is applicable. (How fuzzy this set is need not concern us here.) Now the uses of various sentences are, of course, interconnected. But, natural language being what it is, we should not necessarily expect the pieces of language to fit together neatly, like some multi-dimensional jigsaw puzzle. There may well be mis-matches. In particular, the conditions of application of a sentence may well overlap those of the application of its negation, especially if the world arranges itself in an unkind fashion. At such spots in the weft and warp of language, we have dialetheias.

With dialetheism assumed, let us return to the issue, raised in the last section, of the conditions under which a negated sentence is true. There, I argued that the mere failure of the truth of α is sufficient ground for the truth of $\neg\alpha$. Now consider the situation in which both α and $\neg\alpha$ are true. Here the Fact in virtue of which $\neg\alpha$ is true cannot be the mere "negative" one that α is not true. There must be a "positive" Fact. What sort of thing this may be we have already seen. The existence of an *a priori* and sound argument whose conclusion is $\neg\alpha$ (as with some of the logical paradoxes) may be this Fact. This may arise because of the paradoxical sort of truth conditions which we noted in section 4.3.

The Fact in virtue of which $\neg\alpha$ is true, may not, however, be purely *a priori*, but may be a combination of the empirical and the *a priori*. For example, some logical paradoxes have an empirical premise. As another example, consider the

---

[24] Other sorts of situation from which arguments for dialetheism can be extracted concern vagueness, infinitesimals, and non-existent objects. These will not be considered in any detail in this book. Some details can be found in Priest and Routley (1983), ch. 5.

following sort of situation. Suppose, *in abstracto*, that we have some domain of discourse and a set of predicates, F, G, . . . to discuss the objects in the domain. Each of the predicates has a set of conditions of application, or criteria, such that if they are satisfied the predicate is truly applicable. But the predicates may also be internally related to each other in the way that, for example, colour predicates, or the major predicates of a taxonomy, or truth and falsity, are. In each case there is an *a priori* determination that F, G, . . . are mutually exhaustive, and, particularly, mutually exclusive. That is, $Fx \rightarrow \neg Gx$, and so on. Now if the world is cantankerous enough to present us with a situation where the criteria for both F and G are fulfilled by some object, a, then Fa and Ga, and hence, by the internal relation of F and G, $\neg Ga$, will be true.

For example, consider the terms 'right wing' and 'left wing' as applied to political groups. These form a taxonomy of political parties. Maybe we need to add 'centre' to the taxonomy to complete it. But at any rate, if a party is right-wing it is not left-wing, and vice versa. The criteria for belonging to these categories are not, however, cut and dried. Certainly there is no single test the passing of which is sufficient to make a group left-wing. Rather, there is a whole set of conditions associated with being left-wing, such that satisfaction of sufficiently many of them (or maybe just a couple of them, if they are sufficiently important in the context) makes a party left-wing. These include endorsing social and economic equality; a dislike of private enterprise; a desire to change the system; a belief in the value and autonomy of the individual; and so on. A similar set of conditions is associated with being right-wing: social conservatism; a belief in free enterprise; acceptance of traditional moral standards, etc. Now suppose that a political group arises which has an unusual combination of principles. It may well be that the party is both left and right, and hence not left. Actual examples are bound to be contentious; but national socialists and right-wing anarchists would seem to be plausible examples; and if they are not, the reader is free to select a few of the criteria above, more or less at random, and envisage a political party with those features. This can be done since the conditions are pretty independent—and even where they are not, a brief glance at many extant political parties will show that a political group may well have inconsistent aims!

The fact that I have chosen an example where the criteria for the application of a term are, in one sense, vague may suggest that this is essentially a phenomenon of vagueness. It is not. Consider the family of predicates 'has a temperature between 10n and $10(n + 1)$ degrees absolute', where n is a natural number. No one would claim that these are vague. And, clearly, they form a taxonomy of temperatures. However, we have many criteria for determining temperature: the behaviour of correctly functioning mercury and alcohol thermometers, of electro-chemical thermometers, the frequency of black-body radiation emitted, and so on. Frequently the ranges of application of these criteria do not coincide. (For example, different means have to be used to measure the temperature of liquid nitrogen and that of a distant star.) But sometimes they do. For example, we can use both a mercury thermometer and an electro-chemical thermometer to measure the temperature of sea-water. Moreover, it seems to be an empirical fact that, when we do, the results of these two coincide (to within experimental error). But it is obviously quite possible that at some time and place, and because of factors of which we are, as yet, totally unaware, the results of such tests will diverge. In such a case, we might have, for example, an object which is between 200 and 210 degrees absolute (because of one criterion), and between 210 and 220 degrees absolute—and hence not between 200 and 210 degrees (because of another). This is, of course, a hypothetical example. It is possible to cite specific historical examples of where this situation seems to have arisen, but since it is the possibility of this situation rather than its actuality which concerns us here, we need not go into them.[25]

The above discussion shows how there may be negated sentences that are true in virtue of "positive" Facts. I certainly do not want to claim that these exhaust the sorts of positive ground for the truth of a negated sentence, but they will suffice to make the point. The claim that there may be positive grounds for the truth of a negated sentence is not peculiar to dialetheism. It is shared by intuitionism. As I noted in the last section, according to the intuitionist, the ground for something's being true must be something we can (in principle) effectively recognise. The mere failure of certain other grounds, since it may not be effectively recognisable, is insufficient. In particular, the ground for the truth of $\neg\alpha$ is a proof that there is no proof of α (or a proof of $\alpha \supset f$). To this extent, both dialetheism and intuitionism have classical logic, which insists that the grounds for the truth of a negated sentence be purely negative, as a common antithesis. "Intuitionist dialetheism" may well, therefore, bear further investigation.[26]

As a final observation, note that the fact that there may be positive grounds for the truth of a negated sentence means that the truth and falsity of a sentence are partially independent. Thus, the falsity conditions of a sentence cannot simply be read off from its truth conditions, and a formal semantics will have to specify both truth conditions and falsity conditions separately. We will see how this is to be done in the next chapter.

4.9 UNTRUTH

Falsity is one of the notions antithetical to truth. There is another, which I will call *untruth*. A sentence, α, is untrue if it is not true, $\neg T\underline{\alpha}$. What is the relationship between falsity and untruth?

[25] See sect. 13.6 for an example. A further discussion of multi-criterial terms, with some replies to objections, can be found in Priest and Routley (1983), ch. 5.
[26] The propensity of verificationism to produce dialetheism as well as intuitionism is noted in Papineau (1979), pp. 91–2.

Consider the principles

$$\neg T\underline{\alpha} \rightarrow T\neg\underline{\alpha} \quad (1)$$

$$T\neg\underline{\alpha} \rightarrow \neg T\underline{\alpha} \quad (2)$$

Let us call these the *exhaustion* and *exclusion* principles, respectively, since in one sense they express the exhaustiveness and exclusiveness of truth and falsity.

Classical logic endorses both (1) and (2), and thus takes falsity and untruth to be equivalent. A logic which allows for truth value gaps will normally endorse (2) but not (1).[27] Conversely, it would appear, classical dialetheism is committed to (1) but not (2). I have already endorsed (1) in section 4.7, and (2) would appear to fail since there are some false sentences that *are* true. However, matters are not that simple. If for some α_0 we have both $T\underline{\alpha}_0$ and $T\neg\underline{\alpha}_0$, then (2) gives us that $T\underline{\alpha}_0 \wedge \neg T\underline{\alpha}_0$. Thus an "internal" contradiction generates an "external" one. If "external" contradictions were quite unacceptable, then so too would (2) be. But for all that has been said so far, the external contradiction may well be acceptable. Hence this argument is less than conclusive.

It has been felt by some[28] that, even if our object-theory is inconsistent, our metatheory should be consistent, i.e. that semantic notions such as truth, satisfaction, etc., should behave consistently; and if this were right "external" contradictions would be unacceptable. It should go without saying by now that I reject this view categorically. The whole distinction between object theory and metatheory should be abolished, at least in the sense that it is normally understood. (That is, that the metatheory must be a different, and in fact stronger, theory than the object theory.) The whole thrust of chapter 1 was that this distinction is a spurious one based on incorrect attempts to impose consistency. A natural language (or a formal language that models that aspect of its behaviour) can give its own semantics. Naturally, we can still consider that part of a theory which concerns its own semantic notions (and we might call this the metatheory, though in virtue of the misleading overtones, it would be better to avoid this name altogether), but this will now be a *subtheory* of the main theory. Once we rid ourselves of the misleading notion of a metalanguage, the claim that our own semantic discourse should be consistent has no plausibility. Indeed, semantics is a paradigm example of an inconsistent area.

Thus, it is quite possible for a dialetheist to accept both (1) and (2). Moreover, there are considerations which suggest that (2) should be accepted. Perhaps the strongest of these is as follows. The T-scheme gives us

$$T\neg\underline{\alpha} \leftrightarrow \neg\alpha$$

and the contraposed T-scheme gives

$$\neg T\underline{\alpha} \leftrightarrow \neg\alpha$$

---

[27] Though an intuitionist may endorse both if she uses an untensed notion of truth (see Dummett (1977), p. 19).   [28] e.g. Rescher and Brandom (1980), sect. 26.

These, with transitivity, give both (1) and (2).

This argument is, itself, less than conclusive. In section 4.4 I suggested that the connective of the T-scheme is an intensional and detachable one, but I left open the question of which such connective it is. In particular, the question of whether or not it is contraposible, has not been broached. In section 6.3 I will argue that entailment is contraposible but there are certainly non-contraposible intensional conditionals (as writers such as Stalnaker (1968) have noted) and I will look at some of these in section 6.5. The crucial question here is whether the connective of the T-scheme is an entailment or a non-contraposible implication. Nothing I have said so far seems to bear on the issue,[29] but there are some considerations which at least suggest that it is non-contraposible. I will defer a discussion of these till section 5.4. For the present, we need note only that this argument for the exclusion principle carries little weight. And I know of no other argument that does.

We have seen that the exclusion principle spreads contradictions, and in virtue of the failure of the above argument it would seem to do so beyond necessity. To look ahead once again, in section 8.4 I will argue that contradictions should not be multiplied beyond necessity. On the basis of this, I tentatively reject the exclusion principle.

Falsity and untruth are therefore distinct, and if this is so the next question is what significant differences there are between them. The answer is 'surprisingly little'. In particular, truth and untruth are exhaustive and nonexclusive, just as truth and falsity are.

Truth and untruth are exhaustive since $T\underline{\alpha} \vee \neg T\underline{\alpha}$ is an instance of the law of excluded middle, which holds in virtue of the "negative" conditions for the truth of a negated sentence (see section 4.7). Indeed, since it is only an instance, we might well argue that it would hold even if the general law were to fail.[30] An orthodox truth value gap theorist would certainly agree that all sentences are either true or not true, even though some sentences are neither true nor false.

Truth and untruth are not exclusive since there are sentences which are both. Consider the "extended" liar paradox:

α is untrue   (α)

The T-scheme for this gives

α is true ↔ α is untrue

Hence, by the exhaustiveness of truth and untruth, α is both true and untrue.

---

[29] The fact that I have so far written the connective as ↔, which I will later use as the (bi) entailment connective, is irrelevant. See ch. 0, fn 5.

[30] We might argue for this as follows. Suppose that we augment the semantic values to be described in the next chapter by the empty set, thus allowing naturally for the possibility of sentences that are neither true nor false. Then, for any sentence α and any evaluation v (and so for the actual evaluation), $v(\alpha) = \{1\}$ or $\{0\}$ or $\{1, 0\}$ or ϕ. But $1 \in \{1\}$, $1 \in \{1, 0\}$, $1 \notin \{0\}$ and $1 \notin \phi$. Hence $1 \in v(\alpha)$ or $1 \notin v(\alpha)$: all sentences are true or not true.

There is one difference between untruth and falsity that is worth noting. I have just argued that

$$\exists x (Tx \wedge \neg Tx) \tag{3}$$

But, from the law of excluded middle, $\forall x\, (Tx \vee \neg Tx)$, it follows, by de Morgan laws and simple quantifier principles, that

$$\neg \exists x (Tx \wedge \neg Tx) \tag{4}$$

In this sense, truth and untruth are both exclusive and not exclusive. For falsity, on the other hand, though it is easy enough to argue for $\exists x(Tx \wedge Fx)$ (the analogue of (3)) on the basis of the liar paradox, it seems impossible to argue for $\neg \exists x(Tx \wedge Fx)$ (the analogue of (4)), at least without the exclusion principle. Truth and untruth are, therefore, "more inconsistent" than truth and falsity.

Let me make the situation with respect to truth and untruth here quite clear. I am affirming both (3) and (4). This is, of course, a contradiction. (Till now I have asserted contradictions only by implication. The T-scheme is necessary to extract a naked contradiction from the claim that a certain contradiction is true.) If I were attempting to produce a consistent theory of the inconsistent, this would be fatal. However, the aim of the enterprise is not to eliminate contradictions but to accommodate them.[31]

I will address the general question of the rationality of accepting contradictions in chapter 7. For the present, and concerning the rationality of accepting this contradiction, I will just say this: in virtue of the fact that the contradictory claims are semantical, and that a self referential construction (the liar paradox) was necessary to prove one of them, (3), this is exactly where I have urged that contradictions should be *expected* to turn up. In a sense, therefore my position is quite self-consistent, though this is hardly a happy way of expressing the matter! So let us just say that it is self-coherent.

---

[31] The matter is discussed a little further in Priest (1984), sect. 3.

5

Dialetheic Semantics for Extensional Connectives

5.1 FORMAL LANGUAGES: ABSTRACTION

The discussion of truth, falsity, and associated notions in the preceding chapter provides enough philosophical underpinning for the specification of a formal semantics adequate for purely extensional connectives. Some connectives are not purely extensional. One important non-extensional connective is implication; consideration of this will be deferred to next chapter.

A number of formal semantics for paraconsistent logics have been suggested. They are not all of equal merit, especially for dialetheism. I do not intend to survey and evaluate them here. (This is done in Priest and Routley 1983, ch. 3.) The following formal semantics is, I take it, correct, and follows naturally from the discussion of the preceding chapter. However, since in the first part of the book I stressed that what was at issue in dialetheism was the consistency of natural language, and I will (in orthodox logical fashion) give semantics for a formal language, it behoves me to say what I take the relationship of the latter to the former to be.

A standard scientific procedure when analysing situations or phenomena is abstraction. The factors which are deemed to be of central importance are selected, and the interrelationships between them laid out. Other factors which are of no, or of only secondary, importance are ignored. It is not supposed that all aspects of the concrete, real-life situation are captured by the abstraction, but the abstraction captures the essential features of the situation, at least to a first (or better) approximation. Thus, Newton's analysis of planetary motion concerned the central mechanism at work here: gravity. Factors such as the colours of the planets were ignored. Even factors which were admitted to be relevant, such as the gravitational influence of each planet on the others, were ignored as of minor importance for the basic analysis. When, in science, abstraction is used, the abstracted structure is frequently called a 'model' of the concrete situation. The term is not singularly appropriate, but it seems to be standard.

Now a good way of conceiving formal languages and their semantics is as a model for, or abstraction of, certain aspects of natural language: specifically, those aspects which are central to (deductive) inference. Naturally, in abstracting in this way, certain aspects of the use of language are ignored altogether and others, perhaps, simplified. But one hopes that the abstraction captures the relevant dominant tendency. It is no criticism of a model to point out that it *is* (just) a model, that there are aspects of the situation that are ignored, though this kind of criticism was far too common at certain times and places where it was fashionable to denigrate formal languages. Much more to the point is a criticism according to which the abstraction is wrong, that is, according to which the dominant aspects of the situation have not been selected, or have been selected but the fundamental relationships between them have been mis-specified. It is very difficult to make criticisms of this kind stick. Precisely because it is an abstraction, it is possible to suppose, at least initially, that the abstraction is correct but has gone too far, ignoring important factors which have a determining influence greater than the cut-off threshold. The debate between those who claim that material implication is not a correct understanding of the truth conditions of the English conditional, and those who claim that it is, but suggest that other factors (such as conversational implicature) are required to explain certain aspects of its use, is exactly of this kind. At any rate, an abstraction, once accepted, is rarely, if ever, displaced by mere criticism: an alternative and superior account is required.

There is a second way in which formal languages and their semantics may be understood, which adds to the picture of abstraction just painted. Suppose we accept the transformational grammarian's distinction between surface and deep structure. The deep structure is where the "semantical action" is. Surface structures are produced from deep structures by a sequence of meaning-preserving transformations. A formal language and its semantics may then be thought of as the deep structure of natural language, or at least a part of it. This has been suggested by a number of logicians[1] and seems to be the working philosophy of many others. It also offers the prospect of tying logic in with linguistics and the psychology of language use. If the reader wishes to view the formal semantics given in this book in this light, I shall not complain.

5.2 EXTENSIONAL SENTENTIAL CONNECTIVES

I am now in a position to formulate the semantics of extensional connectives.[2] To this end, we will consider a simple propositional language, whose class of propositional parameters is P, and whose set of formulas, F, is the closure of P under conjunction, $\wedge$, disjunction, $\vee$, and negation, $\neg$. $\alpha \supset \beta$ may be thought of as defined as $\neg\alpha \vee \beta$.

[1] For example, Harman (1972); Hacking (1975), ch. 8.
[2] The following material comes from Priest (1979*a*), as reformulated in the appendix of Priest (1980) in the manner of Dunn (1976).

The orthodox conception of a semantic evaluation is a function which maps the formulas, F, to two "truth values", distinct objects conventionally represented by 0 and 1. The functionality of the evaluation captures the idea that truth and falsity are exclusive, and the fact that the evaluation is total captures the idea that truth and falsity are exhaustive. According to the discussion of sections 4.7 and 4.8, we may retain the exhaustiveness of truth and falsity, but we must allow for the possibility that they are not exclusive. It follows that the only change to the orthodox conception we need to make here is to drop the functional requirement on an evaluation. Thus we can conceive of an evaluation as a subset of $F \times \{1, 0\}$, where every member of F occurs as the first member of at least one pair in the evaluation. Actually, it is technically simpler to think of an evaluation, equivalently, as a function which maps a formula to the set of truth values to which the formula is related, so this is how we will proceed. Let $\pi = \{\{0\}, \{1\}, \{0, 1\}\}$. Let v be an evaluation of the propositional parameters, that is, a map from P to π. We can extend this to an evaluation (which, by an abuse of notation, we will also call v) of all formulas by the following conditions:

(1a) $1 \in v(\neg\alpha)$ iff $0 \in v(\alpha)$

(1b) $0 \in v(\neg\alpha)$ iff $1 \in v(\alpha)$

(2a) $1 \in v(\alpha \wedge \beta)$ iff $1 \in v(\alpha)$ and $1 \in v(\beta)$

(2b) $0 \in v(\alpha \wedge \beta)$ iff $0 \in v(\alpha)$ or $0 \in v(\beta)$

(3a) $1 \in v(\alpha \vee \beta)$ iff $1 \in v(\alpha)$ or $1 \in v(\beta)$

(3b) $0 \in v(\alpha \vee \beta)$ iff $0 \in v(\alpha)$ and $0 \in v(\beta)$

It is easy enough to check that v, so defined, is a map from F to π.[3]

We can read '$1 \in v(\alpha)$' as 'α is true under v' and '$0 \in v(\alpha)$' as 'α is false under v'; and, using this to decode the slightly unfamiliar notation, we can see that these conditions are just the familiar ones of classical semantics. The only difference is that in the classical case, because truth and falsity are exclusive, the second condition of each pair is redundant. Once truth and falsity are agreed to have a certain amount of independence, however, this is no longer the case.

Notions of logical truth and semantic consequence can be defined in a standard way. If $F \supseteq \Sigma$ and $\alpha \in F$,

$\Sigma \models \alpha$ iff it is true of any evaluation, v, that if $1 \in v(\beta)$ for all $\beta \in \Sigma$ then $1 \in v(\alpha)$;

$\models \alpha$ iff it is true of any evaution, v, that $1 \in v(\alpha)$.

---

[3] It is clear how this semantic conception can be modified to allow for truth value gaps. We simply allow the empty set, ϕ, to be a member of π (as in Dunn 1976). As I have argued, this is not correct philosophically.

The following facts are then easy enough to establish. For those who wish them, proofs can be found in the appendix to this chapter, section 5.5, as can the proofs of all subsequently enumerated facts.

Fact 1

$\models \alpha$ iff α is a two-valued logical truth.

Fact 2

If $\Sigma \models \alpha$, then α is a classical two-valued semantical consequence of Σ.

Fact 3

The converse of fact 2 does not hold. In particular, neither of the following is true in general: $\{\alpha \wedge \neg\alpha\} \models \beta$; $\{\alpha, \neg\alpha \vee \beta\} \models \beta$.

It is also straightforward to produce a natural deduction system with respect to which these semantics are sound and complete. The details of this need not concern us here.[4]

If one thinks that these semantics appear to have a very familiar ring to them, it is because they are very familiar. But for one change—dropping the assumption that truth value is unique—they are exactly classical. Even the sets of logical truths are the same. In particular, *nota bene*, both contain the law of non-contradiction, $\neg(\alpha \wedge \neg\alpha)$. Anyway, as we see, in a very obvious sense, the semantics subsume those of classical logic. For classical logic is just the special case where no parameter (and hence no formula) takes the dialetheic value $\{0, 1\}$. All that is wrong with classical semantics for the extensional connectives (and classical logic recognises no others) is that it "forgets" this particular case.

5.3 QUANTIFIERS AND IDENTITY

The addition of quantifiers and other first order logical machinery produces even fewer novelties.[5] We may therefore spell out the semantics with very little comment. We now suppose ourselves to be dealing with a first order language with a set of variables, Var, individual constants, Con, n-place function symbols, Func_n, and n-place predicate symbols, Pred_n, the last two for all n. The set of terms, Term, and formulas, Form, are defined as usual. An interpretation for this

---

[4] They can be found, in effect, in Priest (1982).

[5] At least if this is done in the orthodox way, though the following point is worth noting. The loss of inferential force by material implication means that a restricted universal quantifier (All *A*s are *B*s) can no longer be taken to be a quantifier plus a truth function. An intensional connective can be used instead, but this destroys some expected connections between restricted universal and restricted existential quantification. It may therefore be the case that a new approach to restricted quantification (and perhaps, therefore, quantification in general) will have to be developed.

language is a pair, $M = \langle D, d \rangle$, where D is the non-empty domain of the interpretation, and d is the denotation function such that:

(1) for all $c \in \text{Con}$, $\quad d(c) \in D$;

(2) for all $f \in \text{Func}_n$, $\quad d(f) : D^n \to D$;

(3) for all $P \in \text{Pred}_n$, $\quad d(P) = \langle E, F \rangle$, where $E \cup F = D^n$.

We will write E and F as $d^+(P)$ and $d^-(P)$, and call them the *extension* and *anti-extension* of P, respectively. Intuitively, they are the sets of things which satisfy P and its negation. As for truth values, they are exhaustive but not, in general, exclusive.

Given an interpretation, M, and a function $s: \text{Var} \to D$, which specifies the denotation of each variable, we can define the denotation, $\text{den}(t)$, of every term, t, as usual, thus:

(1) If $t \in \text{Var}$, $\quad \text{den}(t) = s(t)$

(2) If $t \in \text{Con}$, $\quad \text{den}(t) = d(t)$

(3) If $f \in \text{Func}_n$ and $t_1, \ldots, t_n \in \text{Term}$,

$\text{den}(ft_1 \ldots t_n) = d(f)(\text{den}(t_1) \ldots \text{den}(t_n))$

An evaluation is now a function $v: \text{Form} \times D^{\text{Var}} \to \pi$, such that, if $t_1 \ldots t_n \in \text{Term}$, and $P \in \text{Pred}_n$,

(0a) $1 \in v(Pt_1 \ldots t_n, s)$ iff $\langle \text{den}(t_1) \ldots \text{den}(t_n) \rangle > \in d^+(P)$

(0b) $0 \in v(Pt_1 \ldots t_n, s)$ iff $\langle \text{den}(t_1) \ldots \text{den}(t_n) \rangle > \in d^-(P)$

(1a) $1 \in v(\neg\alpha, s)$ iff $0 \in v(\alpha, s)$

(1b) $0 \in v(\neg\alpha, s)$ iff $1 \in v(\alpha, s)$

(2a) $1 \in v(\alpha \wedge \beta, s)$ iff $1 \in v(\alpha, s)$ and $1 \in v(\beta, s)$

(2b) $0 \in v(\alpha \wedge \beta, s)$ iff $0 \in v(\alpha, s)$ or $0 \in v(\beta, s)$

(3a) $1 \in v(\alpha \vee \beta, s)$ iff $1 \in v(\alpha, s)$ or $1 \in v(\beta, s)$

(3b) $0 \in v(\alpha \vee \beta, s)$ iff $0 \in v(\alpha, s)$ and $0 \in v(\beta, s)$

(4a) $1 \in v(\forall x\beta, s)$ iff for all $b \in D, 1 \in v(\beta, s(x/b))$

(4b) $0 \in v(\forall x\beta, s)$ iff for some $b \in D, 0 \in v(\beta, s(x/b))$

(5a) $1 \in v(\exists x\beta, s)$ iff for some $b \in D, 1 \in v(\beta, s(x/b))$

(5b) $0 \in v(\exists x\beta, s)$ iff for all $b \in D, 0 \in v(\beta, s(x/b))$

where, in 4 and 5, $x \in \text{Var}$, and $s(x/a)$ is the same as s except that its value at x is a. Again, it is easy to check that v, so defined, is a map from $\text{Form} \times D^{\text{Var}}$ to π.

Notions of logical truth and logical consequence can, again, be defined in a standard way. If Form $\supseteq \Sigma$ and $\alpha \in$ Form,

$\Sigma \models \alpha$ iff   it is true of all interpretations, $<D, d>$, and all $s :$ Var $\to D$, that if for all $\beta \in \Sigma$ $1 \in v(\beta, s)$ then $1 \in v(\alpha, s)$.

$\models \alpha$ iff   it is true of all interpretations, $<D, d>$, and all $s :$ Var $\to D$, that $1 \in v(\alpha, s)$.

The following are now easy to establish.

Fact 4
$\models \alpha$ iff α is a logical truth of first order logic.

Fact 5
If $\Sigma \models \alpha$, α is a classical first order logical consequence of Σ; but the converse is, in general, false.

As with the propositional case, it is straightforward to specify a proof theory with respect to which these semantics are sound and complete, though this need not concern us here. It is worth observing[6] that all the rules of Gentzen's *LK*, with the exception of cut, are sound with respect to these semantics (where the sequent $\alpha_1 \ldots \alpha_n \to \beta_1 \ldots, \beta_m$ is interpreted as the formula $(\alpha_1 \wedge \ldots \wedge \alpha_n) \supset (\beta_1 \vee \ldots \vee \beta_m)$). By the Cut Theorem and Fact 4, they are also complete.

The final part of first order machinery, identity, can be simply accommodated. We merely take ' $=$ ' to be a particular two-place predicate such that

$$d^+(=) = \{<x, x>|x \in D\}.$$

$d^-(=)$ is arbitrary, except that $d^+(=) \cup d^-(=) = D^2$. (There may be philosophical arguments for placing other constraints on $d^-(=)$, but they need not concern us here.) We can now state the final Fact.

Fact 6
As for facts 4 and 5, but with 'first order logic' replaced by 'first order logic with identity'.

We see that dialetheism can handle the conceptual apparatus of first order logic with no major surprises.

5.4 THE TRUTH PREDICATE

Suppose we take the domain of an interpretation to include the formulas of the language. Then among the predicates of the language we may single out one of

---

[6] I owe this observation to Uwe Petersen.

the one-place predicates, T, as a truth predicate for the language. What semantic conditions should this satisfy? First, it should satisfy the T-scheme, $T\underline{\alpha} \leftrightarrow \alpha$, where $\underline{\alpha}$ is now a constant of the language such that den($\underline{\alpha}$) is α itself. Actually, the T-scheme cannot be formulated in this language since it has no implication operator. However, in this context it will do no harm to think of $\beta \to \alpha$ as meaning $\{\beta\} \models \alpha$; and $\beta \leftrightarrow \alpha$ as $\{\beta\} \models \alpha$ and $\{\alpha\} \models \beta$. The validity of the T-scheme is essentially the condition

$$1 \in v(\alpha) \text{ iff } \alpha \in d^+(T) \tag{1}$$

where α is any closed sentence.

For closed α, the exhaustion principle, $\neg T\underline{\alpha} \to T\neg\underline{\alpha}$, should also be validated. This is essentially the condition:[7]

$$\text{if } \alpha \in d^-(T) \text{ then } 0 \in v(\alpha) \tag{2}$$

Should we require the converse condition?

$$\text{if } 0 \in v(\alpha) \text{ then } \alpha \in d^-(T) \tag{3}$$

This is essentially the exclusion principle, and the answer would seem to be 'no'. If $v(\alpha) = \{0\}$ then $1 \notin v(\alpha)$. Hence $\alpha \notin d^+(T)$ by (1), and so $\alpha \in d^-(T)$. Suppose, on the other hand, that $v(\alpha) = \{1, 0\}$. There would certainly seem to be some sentences, α, such that $v(\alpha) = v(T\underline{\alpha}) = \{1, 0\}$. For example, if α_0, is the liar sentence, $\neg T\underline{\alpha}_0$, then

$$T\underline{\alpha}_0 \leftrightarrow \neg T\underline{\alpha}_0$$

and hence $v(T\underline{\alpha}_0) = \{1, 0\}$. But $\alpha_0 \leftrightarrow T\underline{\alpha}_0 \leftrightarrow \neg T\underline{\alpha}_0$. Hence $v(\alpha_0) = \{1, 0\}$ by (1) and (2). The liar sentence seems to be a very special case, however, just because it is equivalent to (the denial of) its own truth. There seems to be no reason why, *in general*, if α is a dialetheia, $T\underline{\alpha}$ is too. If α is a dialetheia, $T\underline{\alpha}$ is certainly true, but it might be simply true, and not also false. The truth predicate is therefore a *partial consistenciser*.

Thus, we should require only (1) and (2) of the truth predicate. Note also that if the T-scheme were fully contraposible then (3) would hold. For in that case

$$
\begin{aligned}
0 \in v(\alpha) \quad &\text{iff } 1 \in v(\neg\alpha) \\
&\text{iff } 1 \in v(\neg T\underline{\alpha}) \quad \text{by contraposibility} \\
&\text{iff } 0 \in v(T\underline{\alpha}) \\
&\text{iff } \alpha \in d^-(T).
\end{aligned}
$$

---

[7] If $1 \in v(\neg T\underline{\alpha})$ then $0 \in v(T\underline{\alpha})$
then $\alpha \in d^-(T)$
then $0 \in v(\alpha)$ by (2)
then $1 \in v(\neg\alpha)$
then $\neg\alpha \in d^+(T)$ by (1)
then $1 \in v(T\underline{\neg\alpha})$

These are the considerations I referred to in section 4.9 against the contra-posibility of the T-scheme.

Of course, we cannot simply define d in an interpretation to satisfy (1) and (2): this would be viciously circular. But it is quite possible to show that there are interpretations that satisfy these conditions. A trivial one is obtained by setting

$$d^+(P) = d^-(P) = D^n$$

for all n-place predicates, P, and all n. Then for all α, $v(\alpha) = \{1, 0\}$. Non-trivial interpretations can also be constructed (as in Dowden 1984 and Woodruff 1984). These interpretations all satisfy (3) too. As far as I am aware, establishing that there are interpretations which satisfy (1) and (2) but not (3) is an open problem.

We may single out, as well as a truth predicate, a one-place predicate which is the falsity predicate. This will satisfy the dual conditions, and in particular, will satisfy the F-scheme:

$$F(\underline{\alpha}) \leftrightarrow \neg\alpha$$

With these two predicates in the language, we can produce a theory which gives the truth conditions of the language itself. I will show how this is done in chapter 9.

5.5 APPENDIX: PROOFS OF THEOREMS

The following are outlines of the proofs of the Facts cited in sections 5.2 and 5.3.

Fact 1
If α is true under all evaluations, it is true under all classical evaluations (i.e. valuations, v, such that for all α, $v(\alpha) = \{1\}$ or $v(\alpha) = \{0\}$). Hence α is a two valued logical truth. Conversely, suppose that it is not the case that $\models \alpha$. Let v be such that $1 \notin v(\alpha)$. Let v' be the same as v except that, for all propositional parameters, p, if $v(p) = \{0, 1\}$, $v'(p) = \{1\}$. It is easily shown by induction that, for all $\beta \in F$, $v(\beta) \supseteq v'(\beta)$. Hence $1 \notin v'(\alpha)$. And since v' is a classical evaluation, α is not a two valued logical truth.

Fact 2
If $\Sigma \models \alpha$, then all evaluations are truth preserving and, *a fortiori*, all classical evaluations are truth preserving. Hence α is a two valued consequence of Σ.

Fact 3
For p, $q \in P$, let $v(p) = \{0,1\}$ and $v(q) = \{0\}$. Then it is straightforward to show that $v(p) = v(p \wedge \neg p) = v(\neg p \vee q) = \{1,0\}$. This evaluation is therefore a counter-example to the two inferences.

Fact 4

The proof is an obvious modification of the proof of Fact 1. Consistencising an interpretation in this way preserves classical truth values.

Fact 5

The proof is an obvious modification of those for Facts 2 and 3.

Fact 6

The proof is an obvious extension of those for Facts 4 and 5.

6

Entailment

6.1 PRELIMINARY ISSUES

In the last chapter I specified the semantics of the common extensional connectives. In this chapter I will discuss the most important intensional notion: implication. Primarily, what is required is a philosophically adequate formal semantics for 'if' in at least one of its many senses. This is, of course, a well known and thorny problem. It is not directly connected with dialetheism as such. As we have seen, the semantical problems of dialetheism are already raised and solved at the extensional level. In virtue of this, it is perhaps desirable to leave the issue out of a book on dialetheism. Unfortunately, this is not possible on the approach I have followed, if only because the two main inconsistent theories I have discussed so far, set theory and semantics, have central principles formulated in terms of implication and associated notions (notably, the T-scheme and the Abstraction scheme). Thus, for the sake of circumscribing the legitimacy of reasoning with these principles, it is necessary to face the problem of the conditional. The subject is a sensitive one, where the web of linguistic intuition, entrenched accounts, and various shibboleths form a set of nearly impossible constraints. Hence, any solution is bound to have some difficulties. I certainly do not want to claim that the account that follows is entirely unproblematic. Still, it will, I trust, provide at least auxiliary machinery for the rest of the book.

Before turning to the account, there are a couple of preliminary issues to be dealt with. The primary notion here is that of the connective of entailment, that is, the connective such that, given sentences α and β, 'α entails β' is true just if β follows from α. (Exactly what this means is, of course, the main problem.) It can be argued that in English the word 'entails' is not used this way: it is not a connective but a relation. Thus, if α and β are sentences, 'α' entails 'β' is a relation between these two sentences. We need not discuss the matter in any depth here. Those who do not like using the word 'entails' as a connective can read instead 'if . . . then logically . . . ' or 'if . . . then it follows logically that . . . ' or some similar locution, with the conditional suitably qualified adverbially. (A defence of the use of 'entails' as a connective can be found in the appendix to Anderson and Belnap 1975.)

Few would now suggest that "material implication" is the entailment connective; but many would hold that it is the ordinary conditional ('if' when this is used in its implicational sense[1]) and that its necessitation is the entailment connective. This view does not stand up to inspection. There are damning counter-examples to the claim that material implication is the conditional.[2] We need not go in to these; we need only note that dialetheism disposes, once and for all, of "material implication". The reason is simple. Any conditional worth its salt, $\rightarrow$, should satisfy the *modus ponens* principle: $\{\alpha, \alpha \rightarrow \beta\} \models \beta$. This is, indeed, analytically part of what implication is. Yet this principle fails for material implication as we saw (section 5.2, Fact 3). $\{\alpha, \neg\alpha \vee \beta\} \models \beta$ is not, in general, true. Hence material implication is not the conditional. For exactly the same reason, its necessitation is not the entailment connective either. Let α be some paradoxical sentence, which is not only a dialetheia, but necessarily so (such as the liar sentence). Then, for any β, $\neg\alpha \vee \beta$ is not only true, but necessarily so. This helps not a whit in inferring β from α.

6.2 CURRY PARADOXES

Before turning to an analysis of entailment, there is one more preliminary point which needs to be made: entailment must not fall foul of Curry paradoxes. Curry's paradox, as he proposed it, concerns the principle of inference called 'absorption':

$$\{\alpha \rightarrow (\alpha \rightarrow \beta)\} \vdash \alpha \rightarrow \beta$$

I will give the strongest form of it I know, which concerns the principle called 'assertion':[3]

$$(\alpha \wedge (\alpha \rightarrow \beta)) \rightarrow \beta$$

Given an arbitrary sentence, β, by diagonalisation, self reference or a similar device, we can find a sentence, δ, of the form $T\underline{\delta} \rightarrow \beta$ ('If this sentence is true, β'.) The T-scheme for this sentence gives $T\underline{\delta} \leftrightarrow (T\underline{\delta} \rightarrow \beta)$. Let us write this as[4]

$$\alpha \leftrightarrow (\alpha \rightarrow \beta) \tag{1}$$

Now suppose that assertion holds. Then, by substitutivity of equivalents, $(\alpha \wedge \alpha) \rightarrow \beta$; whence, by properties of conjunction,

$$\alpha \rightarrow \beta \tag{2}$$

(Alternatively, (2) may be inferred from (1) by absorption.) Hence by (1) and *modus ponens*, α; and by (2) and *modus ponens*, β. But β was arbitrary. Thus,

---

[1] On the variety of senses of 'if' see Routley *et al.* (1982), sect. 1.5.

[2] See e.g. Routley *et al.* (1982), sect. 1.2.

[3] Curry's original paper is (1942). The assertion form is due to Meyer *et al.* (1979). In the context of first degree entailments, assertion gives the rule form of absorption.

[4] Alternatively, the abstraction principle of set theory gives us $\exists y \forall x (x \in y \leftrightarrow (x \in x \rightarrow \beta))$; whence, by instantiation, we obtain a formula of the form $\alpha \leftrightarrow (\alpha \rightarrow \beta)$.

semantics (or set theory) based on a logic which contains the assertion principle is trival: everything is provable. It is therefore suitable for no purpose, dialetheic or otherwise.

It must be admitted that the assertion principle *looks* acceptable enough, but appearances may be deceptive. I will return to the subject of the validity of the principle in section 6.4. For the time being, all we need to note is that a criterion of adequacy for the solution to the problem of formulating an account of implication is that it must not validate assertion (or absorption).[5] This rules out most extant accounts of entailment: ordinary strict implication (if it were not already ruled out by *ex contradictione quodlibet*), Anderson and Belnap's *E* and *R*, and so on.

6.3 ENTAILMENT

As I observed, in effect, in section 6.1, a necessary condition for entailment is truth preservation from antecedent to consequent. Truth preservation may not, on its own, be sufficient, however. For not only do we use the fact that something is entailed by true sentences to prove it, but we use the fact that something entails false ones to refute it. Thus, we require an entailment to preserve falsity from consequent to antecedent too. Of course, classically, truth preservation forwards and falsity preservation backwards go together. However, once truth and falsity are seen to be partially independent, this is no longer the case. We therefore need to specify that both truth and falsity be preserved in appropriate directions. Moreover, this preservation should occur not just contingently, but *a priori*. Thus, we may tell independently of an examination of contingent facts that truth and falsity are preserved. This is why deduction is so useful. Hence the necessary preservation of truth and falsity in the appropriate directions is a necessary condition for entailment.

The next question is whether it is also sufficient. One may argue that it is as follows: the central uses of deductive argument are (i) to establish new truths from old (as in mathematics) and (ii) to establish old falsehoods from new (as in experimental refutation). And if these are the *point* of deduction, then truth and falsity preservation are all we need be concerned with in the truth conditions for an entailment to hold (at a possible world). There are some counter-arguments, but let us leave the issue there for the time being. I will return to it in section 6.6.

This gives a preliminary answer to the question of when an entailment is true. Naturally, we must also say under what conditions it is false. If the antecedent is true and the consequent is false, then this is clearly sufficient. But again, the mere possibility of this will suffice, since facts about entailment are *a priori*. Hence we

---

[5] In fact, this is just a special case of the more general constraint on the specification of a logical theory: that set theory, semantics, and other important inconsistent theories based on this logic be non-trivial.

may say that an entailment is false if it is possible for the antecedent to be true and the consequent false.

There now arises the question of how necessity and possibility are to be analysed. Fortunately there is a well worked out semantic theory of necessity: possible world semantics. Though it is not without its problems, we need have no quarrel with it here. In particular, we do not need to discuss the sensitive issue of how, philosophically speaking, the semantics are to be understood. Fortunately, the metaphysical issues here are, by and large, not particularly relevant to dialetheism. What we do need to take issue with is the orthodox conception of what "possible worlds" there are. Whatever else possible worlds are, they are at least extensions of standard extensional evaluations, and we saw in the last chapter that dialetheism countenances a wider class of evaluations than does classical logic. This, therefore, needs to be taken into account. Having done this, however, we may specify a modal semantics in the usual way.

Consider a propositional language that is the same as that of section 5.2, except that it is augmented by an entailment operator, $\rightarrow$. (Henceforth I shall use this symbol exclusively for the entailment operator.) A semantic interpretation for the language is a quadruple $M = \langle W, R, G, v \rangle$, where W is an index set (of possible worlds); R is a binary relation on W; G is a particular member of w, the "real world" or assignment which is in accord with the actual; and v is an evaluation of the propositional parameters, i.e. a map from $W \times P$ (the set of propositional parameters) into π, $(\{\{1\}, \{0\}, \{1, 0\}\})$. We will write $v(w, \alpha) = x$ as $v_w(\alpha) = x$. Given such a v, it can be extended to an evaluation of all formulas (which we will also write as v) by the following conditions. The conditions for the extensional connectives are just those of section 5.2 (now appropriately relativised to w). For $\rightarrow$, they are the obvious (in virtue of the preceding discussion):

$1 \in v_w(\alpha \rightarrow \beta)$ iff for all w' such that $w'Rw$,
  if $1 \in v_{w'}(\alpha)$ then $1 \in v_{w'}(\beta)$, and if $0 \in v_{w'}(\beta)$ then $0 \in v_{w'}(\alpha)$.

$0 \in v_w(\alpha \rightarrow \beta)$ iff for some w' such that $w'Rw$, $1 \in v_{w'}(\alpha)$ and $0 \in v_{w'}(\beta)$.

It is easy enough to see that, so defined, v_w maps all formulas into π. Definitions of semantic consequence and logical truth can now be given in a standard way:

$\Sigma \models \alpha$ iff for all interpretations, M, it is true of the evaluation, v, that
  if $1 \in v_G(\beta)$ for all $\beta \in \Sigma$ then $1 \in v_G(\alpha)$.

$\models \alpha$ iff for all interpretations, M, it is true of the evaluation, v, that
  $1 \in v_G(\alpha)$.

It is clear that these semantics incorporate and extend the truth-functional semantics of the previous chapter. All of Facts 1–3 of section 5.2 therefore carry over. In particular, all truth-functional tautologies are logical truths. The specifically implicational principles delivered by the semantics are illustrated by the following Fact.

Fact 1
The following hold (where $\leftrightarrow$ is defined in the usual way, and standard conventions concerning the relative scopes of connectives are employed):

1. $\models \alpha \rightarrow \alpha$
2. $\models \alpha \leftrightarrow \neg\neg\alpha$
3. $\models \alpha \wedge \beta \rightarrow \alpha$
4. $\models \alpha \rightarrow \alpha \vee \beta$
5. $\models \alpha \wedge (\beta \vee \gamma) \leftrightarrow (\alpha \wedge \beta) \vee (\alpha \wedge \gamma)$
6. $\models (\alpha \rightarrow \beta) \wedge (\beta \rightarrow \gamma) \rightarrow (\alpha \rightarrow \gamma)$
7. $\models (\alpha \rightarrow \beta) \wedge (\alpha \rightarrow \gamma) \rightarrow (\alpha \rightarrow \beta \wedge \gamma)$
8. $\models (\alpha \rightarrow \gamma) \wedge (\beta \rightarrow \gamma) \rightarrow (\alpha \vee \beta \rightarrow \gamma)$
9. $\models (\alpha \rightarrow \beta) \rightarrow (\neg\beta \rightarrow \neg\alpha)$
10. $\{\alpha, \beta\} \models \alpha \wedge \beta$

The validation of these principles is sufficiently straightforward (though somewhat more tedious than usual, because of having to check both truth and falsity preservation) to be left as an exercise. So much for what is valid.

6.4 THE OMNISCIENCE OF G

In section 6.2 I noted that a criterion of adequacy on any account of entailment is that the assertion principle fails. It is therefore a welcome observation that this principle fails in the above semantics. This follows from the following counter-model. Let M be $\langle W, R, G, v\rangle$, where $W = \{G, w\}$, GRG, wRG, and GRw, $v_G(p) = v_G(q) = v_w(p) = \{1\}$ and $v_w(q) = \{0\}$. It is easy enough to check that $v_G(p \wedge (p \rightarrow q) \rightarrow q) = \{0\}$. A similar counter-model to absorption can be given. I leave this as an exercise.

The crucial feature which destroys the validity of assertion (and absorption) is the failure of reflexivity of R. If R is reflexive, then, as may easily be checked, assertion always holds. However, the failure of reflexivity in general does cause one unwanted consequence; for it is clear that $\{\alpha, \alpha \rightarrow \beta\} \models \beta$ fails in general; and, as I have stressed, *modus ponens* is a *sine qua non* of any implication connective. The situation may be remedied merely by requiring that GRG. It is then easily checked that *modus ponens* holds, while, as the above counter-model shows, assertion still fails. We shall henceforth demand that G is reflexive. In fact, we shall demand something slightly stronger: namely that, for all $w \in W$, wRG. Let us call this condition *the omniscience of G*. This will do the trick, as well as validating some other useful principles, as we shall see.

What, however, is the philosophical rationale for the omniscience of G? This is an interesting question and one which cannot be entirely divorced from that of the philosophical interpretation of possible-world semantics. Still, let me, at least, indicate an answer. In a nutshell, the reason why we should expect G to be omniscient is that possibility is possibility *for us*. It is *we* who inhabit G, who say what possibility is; or better, it is our notion of possibility that is being analysed. The totality of possible worlds just is, therefore, the totality of possible worlds accessible from G. Let me try to spell this out more carefully. The set of things true in a world is a description of how the world might be (or, in the case of G, is). This description will include the conditions under which people (if there are any) live: their languages, cognitive processes, and so on. The set of possibilities relative to such a specification may be thought of as the set of situations conceivable, in some sense, by people living under those conditions. Now, how do we know that all the "possible worlds" in an interpretation are conceivable by people living under those conditions of G? Simply because we are those people (by definition), and we do conceive them. It is we who are theorising, specifying what interpretations are, and we who can spell out any particular v_w. If we were to live under a different set of conditions, however, there would be no guarantee that we would be able to think all of this. Indeed, had we not evolved, we might have been highly maladapted to our environment, and might not even, therefore, have been able to conceive properly of the conditions under which we actually lived. G is omniscient, but there is no reason, therefore, why any other world should be omniscient or even reflexive.

Returning to purely technical questions, the omniscience of G delivers a second fact.

Fact 2
The following hold:

1. $\{\alpha, \alpha \rightarrow \beta\} \models \beta$
2. $\{\alpha \wedge \neg\beta\} \models \neg(\alpha \rightarrow \beta)$
3. $\{\alpha \rightarrow \beta\} \models (\gamma \rightarrow \alpha) \rightarrow (\gamma \rightarrow \beta)$
4. $\{\alpha \rightarrow \beta\} \models (\beta \rightarrow \gamma) \rightarrow (\alpha \rightarrow \gamma)$
5. $\{\alpha \leftrightarrow \beta\} \models \delta \leftrightarrow \delta(\alpha/\beta)$
6. $\{\alpha \rightarrow \neg\alpha\} \models \neg\alpha$

where $\delta(\alpha/\beta)$ is δ with any subformula, α, replaced by β. Again, the verifications of these facts are sufficiently routine to be left as exercises.

6.5 NON-CONTRAPOSIBLE IMPLICATIONS

We have examined the entailment connective 'if ... then logically ... '. Though this is the central implicational connective, it is not the only one. Entailment, as we have seen, contraposes. But there are certainly non-contraposible conditionals, as I noted in section 4.9; and as I also argued there the main connective of the T-scheme is one such. In this section I will discuss two non-contraposible implication connectives. The first of these is the simpler, and I will use it in subsequent chapters where a non-contraposible conditional is required. I will write it as $\Rightarrow$. How to give its truth conditions is entirely implicit in the previous semantical discussion. We simply take the truth conditions for $\rightarrow$ and drop the requirement that falsity be preserved backwards. Thus:

$$1 \in v_w(\alpha \Rightarrow \beta) \text{ iff for all } w'Rw, \text{ if } 1 \in v_{w'}(\alpha) \text{ then } 1 \in v_{w'}(\beta)$$

The falsity conditions for $\Rightarrow$ are the same as those for $\rightarrow$. Once we have $\Rightarrow$ in the language, $\rightarrow$ may be taken as defined thus:

$$(\alpha \rightarrow \beta) \text{ is } (\alpha \Rightarrow \beta) \wedge (\neg\beta \Rightarrow \neg\alpha)$$

The *definiens* and the *definiendum* have both the same truth and the same falsity conditions.

As a little thought makes clear, $\Rightarrow$ behaves exactly the same as $\rightarrow$, except possibly where negation is concerned essentially. In particular, though contraposition may fail, all of the other claims of Fact 1 (section 6.3) hold when $\rightarrow$ is replaced by $\Rightarrow$. Moreover, all the claims of Fact 2 (section 6.4) hold when $\rightarrow$ is replaced by $\Rightarrow$, with the exception that Fact 5 may fail if δ contains negation. How exactly one should read $\Rightarrow$ in English, I am not sure. Nothing pithy springs to the lips.

The second non-contraposible implication does, however, have a natural reading. This is the simple English conditional 'if', used in its implicational sense, but where the implication is not one of entailment. This is the sense of 'if' in, for example, 'If you tear your Achilles tendon you will not be able to play football next week.' We have already seen that the simple conditional cannot be a material implication; and, indeed, many authors have noted that the English conditional is not contraposible. Moreover, several writers have shown how the truth conditions of a simple conditional can be given in possible world semantics augmented by a similarity relation on worlds.[6] Suppose we write the conditional as '$>$'. Then the basic idea is that we take $\alpha > \beta$ to be true at world w iff β holds in the world most similar to w in which α holds. The basic idea can be modified in a number of ways depending on what properties one takes the similarity

---

[6] See e.g. Stalnaker (1968); Lewis (1973).

relation to have. (The above conditions are appropriate to a well-ordering, for example.) We need not discuss here which variation is the correct one. It is sufficient for my purposes to note that, whichever modification is correct, the construction with that modification can be applied equally to the possible world semantics of the previous section, to give a dialetheic theory of the conditional. How this is to be done is, in principle, quite clear. There are many important details, but they need not now concern us. I will therefore make only one more comment. In all the orthodox conditional semantics, any necessarily false statement implies everything. The counter-intuitiveness of this is quite clear. For example, it is certainly true that, if an angle of 17 degrees could be constructed with ruler and compasses, then an angle of 34 degrees could be so constructed; but, it does not appear to be the case that, if an angle of 17 degrees could be constructed with ruler and compasses, Hitler was a communist. As might be expected, this counter-intuitiveness no longer obtains for a dialetheic theory of conditionals. For any sentence is true at some possible world, albeit an impossible one. For example, consider the world, w, accessible to itself only, where every propositional parameter has the value $\{0, 1\}$. This world is the trivial one in which everything is true. Moreover, given any sentence, α, there is a non-trivial world in which it is true. For take any propositional parameter, p, not occurring in α, and consider the world, w', which is exactly the same as w except that $v_{w'}(p) = \{0\}$. Then α still holds in this world, though p fails. Thus, on the dialetheic construction only some conditionals with necessarily false antecedents will come out true, as should be the case.

6.6 RELEVANT LOGIC

The semantics for entailment specified in the previous sections, let us call them Δ, are very simple and natural. They can, of course, be criticised. From one side they can be criticised for being too weak. The admission of "impossible worlds" and the general failure of the reflexivity of R eliminate some things that would be delivered by an orthodox identification of entailment as a strict implication. Defences against these criticisms are explicit in the preceding chapters and sections: these features are required by dialetheism. From the other side, Δ can be criticised as being too strong, and as verifying incorrect principles of entailment. Such criticism would come from the direction of relevant logic, and reraises the question, set in abeyance in section 6.3, of whether the necessary preservation of truth and falsity in the appropriate directions is sufficient for an entailment to hold. This now requires further discussion.

First, let us note that Δ is irrelevant, or, to put it in less question-begging terms, has logical truths of the form $\alpha \rightarrow \beta$, where α and β have no common propositional parameter. For example, since $\beta \vee \neg\beta$ is always true and $\alpha \wedge \neg\alpha$ is

always false, the semantics does appear to verify the principle $\alpha \land \neg\alpha \to \beta \lor \neg\beta$.[7]
More generally, suppose we define a modal operator, L, thus:

$L\alpha$ is $\neg\alpha \to \alpha$

Then it follows that

$1 \in v_w(L\alpha)$ iff for all $w'Rw, 1 \in v_{w'}(\alpha)$

$0 \in v_w(L\alpha)$ iff for some $w'Rw, 0 \in v_{w'}(\alpha)$

L is therefore a necessity operator. Furthermore, if we define $M\alpha$ as $\neg L\neg\alpha$, M is a possibility operator with the dual truth conditions:

$1 \in v_w(M\alpha)$ iff for some $w'Rw, 1 \in v_{w'}(\alpha)$

$0 \in v_w(M\alpha)$ iff for all $w'Rw, 0 \in v_{w'}(\alpha)$

At any rate, it can now be checked that the semantics verify

$\{L\neg\alpha, L\beta\} \models \alpha \to \beta$

A relevant logician would insist that this indicates that Δ is not the correct account of entailment.

Let us examine reasons why. First, there is the point that this is highly counter-intuitive, which must be conceded. However, on its own the point carries little weight. Intuition may provide an important part of the data against which a logical theory is measured. But a theory which is strong and satisfactory in other respects can itself show the data to be wrong. We may also go some way towards explaining why the entailment is counter-intuitive, as follows. The normal conditions of utterance of an entailment are precisely those where the status of the consequent (or the antecedent, if a *modus tollens* argument is involved) is not known, or is in dispute. Hence it would be unusual to utter the conditional if the grounds were precisely the statuses of the antecedent and consequent.[8]

The major argument, it seems to me, against taking entailment to be a strict implication is that, characteristically, strict implication allows the suppression of necessarily true antecedents and of necessarily false consequents. That is, the following are valid:

$$\{L\alpha, \alpha \land \beta \to \gamma\} \models \beta \to \gamma \tag{1}$$

$$\{L\neg\gamma, \alpha \to \beta \lor \gamma\} \models \alpha \to \beta \tag{2}$$

Arguably, there are a number of things wrong with suppression.[9] One of the most crucial is that it produces the result that everything entails a necessary truth

---

[7] Though one might justifiably doubt this. The argument for semantic validity is essentially of the form $\forall x\delta$; hence $\forall x$ (if γ then δ). This is certainly not valid if 'if' is the entailment connective.

[8] This explains the reaction of Anderson and Belnap's journal editor (1975, p. 17), who naturally expected some other ground for the assertion of an entailment.

[9] See Routley and Routley (1972) and Routley *et al.* (1982), sect. 2.10. Indeed, the Routleys argue cogently that the failure of relevance, in the technical sense, is but a symptom of suppression, which is the fundamental malaise.

and is entailed by a necessary falsehood. Thus, suppose that α is a necessary truth. Since $\alpha \wedge \beta \rightarrow \alpha$, $\beta \rightarrow \alpha$ by (1). Similarly, suppose that β is a necessary falsehood. Since $\beta \rightarrow \alpha \vee \beta$, $\beta \rightarrow \alpha$ by (2). What is wrong with this result is seen most clearly when one takes bi-entailment, in a natural way, to be necessary and sufficient for the identity of logical (or propositional) contents. It then follows that all necessary truths have the same content, as do all necessary falsehoods. But this is absurd. A necessary theorem of mathematics, such as that the number of primes is infinite, has a very different content from the trivial analytic claim that all men are men. It is therefore important to note that (1) and (2) fail in Δ. This follows from the fact that there are necessary truths that do not entail one another and necessary falsehoods that do not entail one another.[10]

Another argument that has been produced against taking entailment to be a form of strict implication[11] is that this may give rise to so-called "Ackermann fallacies". An Ackermann fallacy is a theorem of the form $p \rightarrow (\alpha \rightarrow \beta)$, where p is a propositional parameter. That there is something wrong specifically with "Ackermann fallacies" has not, to my mind, been conclusively argued. We need not, however, pursue this issue here, since there are no such theorems in Δ.[12]

A final argument that might be thought to tell against the proposed account of entailment is that of the medieval writer "Pseudo Scotus".[13] Scotus produced an ingenious argument with a necessarily true conclusion but which is provably invalid. This is not a counter-example to the proposed account of entailment, since in Δ a necessarily true conclusion is not sufficient for an entailment. One might try to direct the argument, instead, against the definition of semantic consequence. But here, too, it would fail. This is because it relies explicitly on the principle of what we might call 'necessity transmission', namely, if $\{\alpha\} \models \beta$ then $\{L\alpha\} \models L\beta$, and this fails for Δ.[14]

We see that the above arguments do not make mandatory the claim that entailment is (technically) relevant. Possibly there are others, though I am not aware of any that are stronger. If, none the less, the case for relevance can be sustained, it follows that my account of entailment is wrong and needs to be

---

[10] To show this, take an interpretation that has only one world, G, and such that $v_G(p) = \{1\}$ and $v_G(q) = \{1, 0\}$. Then $p \vee \neg p \leftrightarrow q \vee \neg q$ fails in this interpretation. Dually, the two necessary falsehoods $(p \wedge \neg p)$ and $(q \wedge \neg q)$ are not equivalent at G. Note that, since $p \vee \neg p$ and $q \vee \neg q$ are both logical truths as well as necessary truths, the above shows that logical truths cannot be suppressed either.

[11] See Anderson and Belnap (1975), sect. 5.2.1, and Routley *et al.* (1982), sect. 1.4.

[12] The proof of this is as follows. Take any formula of the form $p \rightarrow (\alpha \rightarrow \beta)$. Consider an interpretation where the only world other than G is w. Other than the omniscience of G, the only accessibility relation to hold is wRw. Let $v_G(p) = \{1\}$, and for every propositional parameter, q, $v_w(q) = \{1, 0\}$. Then for all γ, $v_w(\gamma) = \{1, 0\}$. Hence $0 \in V_G(\alpha \rightarrow \beta)$ and $1 \notin V_G(p \rightarrow (\alpha \rightarrow \beta))$.

[13] It certainly tells against the identification of entailment as orthodox strict implication, and much else besides. See Priest and Routley (1984).

[14] For example, $\{MM\alpha\} \models M\alpha$, since R is transitive at G, but $\{LMM\alpha\} \models LM\alpha$ fails in general, since R is not necessarily transitive at other worlds.

modified. It is quite possible to do this. One way that this can be done is by moving from a binary R to a ternary R.[15] Another way is to base an account of entailment on a de Morgan algebra of propositional contents.[16] Both of these approaches can be used to produce a notion of entailment which is, essentially, Δ minus the irrelevancies.[17] While these constructions are undoubtedly technically sound, it is not always clear that they are philosophically defensible. In particular, apart from the problem of making sense of the basic semantical apparatus, to get beyond a very minimal logic a number of *ad hoc* modelling conditions have to be imposed, which seem difficult to motivate. Compared with these constructions, the simplicity and philosophical perspicuity of Δ give much to recommend it.

6.7 QUANTIFICATION AND IDENTITY

Having sorted out the propositional part of the logical theory, the quantificational part is, again, relatively straightforward. The modal propositional semantics discussed so far may be extended in any of the standard ways to modal first order semantics. Since the differences between the variants of quantified modal logic, though important, are not directly relevant here, I will just spell out briefly the details of the simplest case: constant domain semantics. Take a language that is exactly the same as the extensional language of section 5.3, except that it is augmented by an entailment operator, $\rightarrow$. A semantic interpretation for this language is now a 5-tuple $\langle W, R, G, D, d \rangle$, where W, R, and G are as before, D is the non-empty domain of quantification, and d is the denotation function, exactly the same as in section 5.3 except that its values for predicates are now world-relativised. Given any function, s, which assigns a (world-invariant) member of D to each variable, we can define the denotation of each term, t, $\text{den}(t)$, as in section 5.3. An evaluation, v, is now a world-relativised function which maps a formula and s into π. The map v satisfies the obvious recursive conditions. The conditions for the extensional connectives and quantifiers are as in section 5.3, except that v and the extensions of predicates are both world-relativised. And the conditions for $\rightarrow$ are the obvious generalisations of those in section 6.3:

$$1 \in v_w(\alpha \rightarrow \beta, s) \text{ iff for all } w'Rw, \text{ if } 1 \in v_{w'}(\alpha, s) \text{ then } 1 \in v_{w'}(\beta, s)$$
$$\text{and if } 0 \in v_{w'}(\beta, s) \text{ then } 0 \in v_{w'}(\alpha, s).$$

$$0 \in v_w(\alpha \rightarrow \beta, s) \text{ iff for some } w'Rw, 1 \in v_{w'}(\alpha, s) \text{ and } 0 \in v_{w'}(\beta, s).$$

The definitions of semantic consequence and logical validity are the obvious ones. Again, it is clear that these semantics incorporate and extend those of

---

[15] The details can be found in Routley (1984).   [16] As in Priest (1980).
[17] Routley's *DK* (Routley *et al.* 1982, sect. 4.1).

section 5.3. Facts 4 and 5 of that section therefore carry over. The quantifier-*cum*-entailment principles delivered are standard enough to require no comment. Hence, for the record,

1. If $\Sigma \models \beta$ then $\Sigma \models \forall x \beta$, provided x is free in no member of Σ.
2. $\models \forall x \beta \rightarrow \beta(x/t)$, provide no variable free in t is bound in $\beta(x/t)$.
3. $\models \neg \forall x \beta \leftrightarrow \exists x \neg \beta$
4. $\models \forall x(\beta \rightarrow \gamma) \rightarrow (\forall x \beta \rightarrow \forall x \gamma)$
5. $\models \forall x(\beta \wedge \gamma) \rightarrow \forall x \beta$
6. $\models \exists x \beta \rightarrow \exists x(\beta \vee \gamma)$

And so on. The verifications of these points are also orthodox enough to require no further comment.

Identity, too, gets a standard treatment. '$=$' is a two-place predicate whose interpretation is the world-invariant set specified in section 5.3. Expected identity principles are forthcoming. (I will, here as throughout the book, write '$=xy$' in the more normal form '$x=y$'.)

7. $\models \forall x \; x = x$
8. $\{x = y\} \models \beta \leftrightarrow \beta(x/y)$, provided y is free in $\beta(x/y)$.
9. $\models (x = y \wedge \beta) \rightarrow \beta(x/y)$, provided y is free in $\beta(x/y)$.

Full first order logic with an entailment operator therefore contains no additional surprises. The formal apparatus can be further extended to allow for descriptions, predicate modifiers, tense operators, and the rest of the usual bag of logical tricks. Some of these will be considered when the appropriate philosophical occasions arise in Part Three of the book. The others will have to be left to the reader's imagination. At any rate, this chapter and the last provide enough formal logical apparatus for the general purposes of the book.

7

Pragmatics

7.1 PRAGMATICS

In the last three chapters I have discussed the formal and informal semantics of dialetheism. There is more to logic than semantics. In particular there is, what might be called for want of a better word, pragmatics. This word might be understood in many ways, but I use it to mean the theory of the application of logic, and in particular its relation to the notions of assertion, belief, and rationality. In general, the theory of pragmatics is in a much more under-developed state than that of semantics: we have a good idea of what a semantics theory should be like, but the shape of a coherent and general approach to pragmatics is much less clear. I shall not try to work one out in this chapter. Rather, the aim of this chapter is to show that dialetheism poses no particular problems for pragmatics; that is, a dialetheic pragmatics faces no problems other than those faced by a non-dialetheic one. It is very necessary to argue this. For most of the substantial objections to dialetheism fall in the realm of pragmatics. Hence I will structure this chapter by formulating and answering a number of objections to dialetheism drawn from this realm. I will consider, in turn, the areas of assertion, belief, rational belief, and rational change of belief.

7.2 ASSERTION: CONTENT

Dialetheism claims that certain contradictions are true. Moreover, in chapter 4 I claimed that truth was the *telos* of assertion. It follows that contradictions may be assertible. Moreover, I have already endorsed some explicit contradictions (for example in section 4.9). Hence, again, I am committed to the possibility of asserting contradictions. But contradictions are not assertible.

All save the last sentence are undoubtedly correct, and many have felt that the last sentence is correct too. Clearly, I must reject it. The question is, therefore, what reasons there are for supposing it to be true? This kind of claim goes back, essentially, to Aristotle. In *Metaphysics* Γ4 Aristotle argues that, though the law of non-contradiction cannot be formally proved, it cannot be denied coherently since any assertion presupposes it. I do not want to discuss the arguments of

Metaphysics Γ4 directly. This is for two reasons. First, they were already thoroughly destroyed by Łukasiewicz in 1910.[1] Secondly, and anyway, this is not the right way to put an objection to the version of dialetheism advocated here. For as we have noted in section 5.2, all classical tautologies, including the law of non-contradiction, are semantically valid. Even if assertion does presuppose the law of non-contradiction, therefore (which I am not conceding), this fact can be faced with equanimity.

A much more cogent argument against dialetheism, and one that can also be read into parts of *Metaphysics* Γ4, is this. For an assertion to have determinate content, it must rule something out. The content is, as it were, what is left open when the possibilities ruled out by the assertion are deleted. Now, if dialetheism is true, nothing rules anything out. Certainly, α does not rule out ¬α; and, more generally, given any two sentences of any of the formal languages of the last chapter, there is an interpretation in which they are both true. Hence if dialetheism is true no assertion has any content; or, to put it more precisely, it is not possible to make an assertion, since any sentence uttered in an attempt to make one has no content.[2] This objection I will discuss. In fact, it can be dealt with very quickly. For a sentence to have content, it is not necessary for it to "rule out" anything. We can think of the content of a sentence as the information it carries. It is then quite possible for sentences α and β to have different and determinate contents (and therefore contents *simpliciter*) if α carries information that β does not, or vice versa. And this is true *even if* neither α nor β *logically* rules anything else out. For example, consider the sentences 'Pittsburgh is in Pennsylvania' and 'The Australian Labor party is left wing'. Each of these has determinate content not carried by the other. Each, for example, implies statements that the other does not. Moreover, this is the case even if it transpires that the Australian Labor Party is right wing too.

It is a straightforward matter to give a formal analysis of this notion of content. We may simply identify the content of a sentence, α, with the set of sentences it entails, or alternatively, with the ordered pair $\langle W_1, W_2 \rangle$, where W_1 is the set of worlds where α holds and W_2 is the set of worlds where its negation holds. These two characterisations are, in fact, equivalent.[3] Given these characterisations, different logical truths have, in general, different and non-trivial contents, as do different contradictions or other logical falsehoods. (The only sentence whose content is trivial is the sentence 'Everything is true', which implies everything; see section 8.5.) It is quite clear, therefore, how a sentence can have determinate content even if dialetheism is true, and how assertion (even of a contradiction) is possible.

---

[1] See Łukasiewicz (1971). Aristotle is also undone in Dancy (1975).

[2] This objection can be found in, e.g. Lear (1980) p. 112.

[3] If α and β have the same content in the first sense, then, since α → α, β → α, and conversely. But then in any world in which β is true α is true, and in any world in which α is false β is false; and vice versa. Conversely, if α and β hold in the same worlds as do their negations, then α ↔ β. Thus, by transitivity of implication, anything entailed by α is entailed by β and vice versa.

7.3 BELIEF: ACCEPTANCE AND REJECTION

In the previous section we considered the objection that a contradiction cannot be asserted. In section 4.6 I discussed assertion and gave a Gricean account of it. According to this, to assert a contradiction is to behave in such a way as to try to get an audience to believe a contradiction, or at least to believe that the speaker believes it (by recognising the speaker's intention to do just that.) But, it could be objected, it is impossible to believe a contradiction. Thus, it is impossible to intend to get someone to believe one, or to believe that one believes one. And hence it is impossible to assert one. Moreover, dialetheism entails that some contradictions are true. But if contradictions are unbelievable, then dialetheism is literally incredible. For two reasons, therefore, I need to dismantle the objection that one cannot believe a contradiction.[4]

The simple reply to this objection is that it is just plain wrong.[5] Many, in fact most, of us believe contradictions. The person who has consistent beliefs is rare. If someone has never found that their beliefs were inconsistent, this probably means that they just have not thought about them long enough (or may be suffering from Orwellian "doublethink" or Sartrian "bad faith"). It may be suggested that when one discovers that one's beliefs are inconsistent one changes them. *Maybe* so, but this is irrelevant. More to the point, it might be suggested that dialetheism requires us to have not just inconsistent beliefs, but consciously inconsistent beliefs, and that this is impossible: one cannot believe two inconsistent sentences in the same "mental" breath. Again, this is just plain false. The moment one realises that one's beliefs are inconsistent, one does not *ipso facto* cease to believe the inconsistent things: rather, it becomes a problem, and often a very difficult one, of how to revise one's beliefs to produce consistency. This, of course, takes time.

It might be argued that even in this context, although one believes α and believes $\neg\alpha$, one does not believe $\alpha \wedge \neg\alpha$, which *is* impossible, and which is what dialetheism requires us to do. Against this, it might be argued that the distinction between believing conjuncts separately and believing them conjointly is a spurious one, at least where the beliefs in question are conscious ones.[6] Even if one does not accept this (and I am inclined not to), there are many cases where people consciously believe an explicit contradiction (and with no real doubt). Leaving aside the White Queen, who boasted that she could get herself to believe six impossible things before breakfast,[7] I, for example, believe that the Russell set is both a member of itself and not a member of itself. I do not deny that it was difficult to convince myself of this, that is, to get myself to believe it. It seemed,

---

[4] One might also take issue with the claim that one cannot intend someone to do the impossible. See sect. 13.3.   [5] Much of the following material comes from Priest (1986).

[6] See Routley and Routley (1975), pp. 211–12.

[7] Lewis Carroll, *Through the Looking Glass*, ch. 5.

after all, so unlikely. But many arguments, most of which appear in this book, convinced me of it. It is difficult to come to believe something that goes against everything that you have ever been taught or accepted, in logic and philosophy as elsewhere. This is just a psychological fact about the power of received views on the human mind. People in the early seventeenth century found it difficult to believe that the earth moves, and many people found (and some still find) it difficult to believe the highly counterintuitive (at least to the Newtonian intuition) Special Theory of Relativity. Coming to believe in dialetheism is as difficult, I think, though no more so, than these. In fact, the number of philosophers who have consciously believed explicit contradictions is much larger than the contemporary teaching of philosophy would lead one to expect—there are, to name but a few, Heracleitus, Plotinus, Nicholas of Cusa, Hume, Hegel, and Engels.[8]

The obvious reply here is that neither I nor any of the others really believe contradictions: we just think (thought) we do (did). Perhaps the most plausible argument for this goes as follows.[9] Belief in something is not merely saying a mental 'yes' to yourself as you think the thought. Even though one must reject a behaviouristic analysis of belief, there must be important links between belief and action (or the notion of belief would be unlearnable). But there is no behaviour appropriate to believing a contradiction—short of some pathological behaviour such as schizophrenia (joke). Hence it is impossible to believe a contradiction.

The argument is not very plausible. If it works, it works just as much against unselfconscious belief of contradiction as against selfconscious belief. Yet, that one can believe two contradictory propositions without being aware of the fact is a datum much firmer than any proposed connection between belief and action. Still, something more about the argument should be said. It is impossible to give a complete answer to the objection without giving a satisfactory account of the exact connection between belief and action, which I do not have. However, it is clear that at least the following kinds of actions are connected with believing something: stating, or being disposed to state it; expressing agreement with someone who states it; using it as the basis of an argument to establish other things; and so on. Of course, some of the actions appropriate to believing that α may depend on the specific content of α. For example, taking an umbrella might be an action appropriate to a belief that it will rain. But many αs are so remote from practical affairs that such connections will be tenuous, if extant at all; for example, believing that the mass of an electron is 9.1084×10^{-28} gm, believing the continuum hypothesis to be false, or believing *Homo sapiens* to be more than 40 million years old have no direct practical consequences. I might write books on the subjects, make inferences from them, and try to persuade you of the truth of them. But these do not depend on the content of the belief in the sense in question.

[8] A discussion of these can be found in chs. 1, 2 of Priest and Routley (1983). Hegel we have already met in ch. 0.

[9] Other arguments are formulated and dealt with in Routley and Routley (1975).

It is now not difficult to see that there are actions that are quite happily connected with believing a contradiction: asserting a contradiction; writing a book about dialetheism; disagreeing with the adequacy of classical logic, and so on. There are even cases where the content of the contradiction is relevant to the action. For example, a set theorist may set out to argue from the existence of a set with contradictory properties to refute the continuum hypothesis; a dialetician who believes that a system (e.g. capitalism) is in a contradictory state may well prepare for the collapse of that system in a suitable way (e.g. by not keeping money in the bank); a lawyer who believes an inconsistent law may well go into court in Perth on Monday and win a case by invoking α and go into court in Sydney on Wednesday and win a case by invoking $\neg\alpha$, and so on. These sorts of examples, once seen, are obvious, and to go on would be to labour the point: there are plenty of connections between believing contradictions and acting.

Before leaving the question of belief, and for reasons that will become clear later, I want to say a little more about it. We may say of someone who believes that α, who behaves in whatever ways it is appropriate to behave in virtue of this, that they *accept* α. If someone does not accept or believe α, we may distinguish two further cases. First, they may not just fail to believe α, but may positively *refuse* to believe it; that is, they may *reject* it. On the other hand, they may neither believe it nor refuse to believe it, but remain "agnostic". In case these distinctions are not immediately clear, some examples will be helpful. Consider the statistician interested in testing certain hypotheses. First he will formulate a number of hypotheses, about all of which he is agnostic. Then he will collect statistical data and use them to test the hypotheses (with chi-squared tests, likelihood tests, etc.). On the basis of these tests he may reject some of the hypotheses, and then, possibly after further tests, he may accept one of the remaining ones, maybe because it is the only one left, maybe because of a positive test result (such as its falling within a certain confidence limit). As another example, consider a mathematical intuitionist. She accepts the statement that there are an infinite number of primes; there is a suitable proof of this fact. On the other hand, she will reject certain instances of the law of excluded middle, $\alpha \vee \neg\alpha$, where α is an undecided statement, such as that there are six consecutive zeros in the decimal expansion of π. Present her with a statement she has never thought about before, however, and she may neither accept it nor reject it, at least immediately, but remain agnostic. She will require time to consider the statement, and even then she may remain undecided.

The following facts should now be clear but are worth noting explicitly. First, acceptance and rejection are not exhaustive, but they are exclusive. They are not exhaustive since being agnostic is a third possibility. In particular, therefore, rejecting something is not the same as not believing it: it is much stronger. On the other hand, acceptance and rejection do appear to be incompatible. One can certainly believe something and believe its negation. One might even argue that one can believe something and not believe it, though this is much more dubious.

But it seems difficult to argue that one might both believe something and *refuse* to believe it. Characteristically, the behaviour patterns that go with doing X and refusing to do X cannot be displayed simultaneously.

Secondly, to reject something is not to accept its negation. One can reject something without accepting its negation. The statistician who rejects a certain hypothesis does not, thereby, accept its negation. In fact, its negation will not normally be a statistical hypothesis at all (i.e. of the form that a chance distribution is such and such). He could go through the whole business of hypothesis testing, accepting, and rejecting, even if the language he spoke did not contain negation. Similarly, the intuitionist who rejects an instance of the law of excluded middle, $\alpha \vee \neg\alpha$, does not, most emphatically, accept its negation, which implies $\neg\alpha \wedge \neg\neg\alpha$. Conversely, one may accept $\neg\alpha$ while failing to reject α. One would do this if, while being convinced that $\neg\alpha$ is true, one acknowledged the possibility that it might be a dialetheia. Until this was ruled out, one would have to remain agnostic about α. It is, perhaps, the confusion between rejecting something and accepting its negation which is at the root of the view that one cannot believe a contradiction. At any rate, the trichotomy accept/reject/be agnostic should now be clear.[10]

7.4 RATIONAL BELIEF

We saw in the last section that contradictions can be believed. The next objection is that, although they may be believed, they cannot be believed rationally: no rational person, when they find that their beliefs are contradictory, can remain content with this situation. Consequently, no one can rationally accept an inconsistent theory once they become aware of its inconsistency. (For present purposes, we need not distinguish between the conscious acceptance of a contradiction and of an inconsistent theory. I shall subsume them both under the rubric of accepting an inconsistency.) Indeed, many people have supposed that the conscious acceptance of a contradiction (or more generally of an inconsistent theory), with no attempt to change it, is the nadir of rationality.

Now in fact, the objection may be answered quite simply. I have already argued in the first part of the book that some contradictions are true, and if something can be shown to be true the rational person will believe it. Hence it is rational to believe some contradictions. The obvious counter-argument is that all inconsistencies are also false (and some may even be untrue), and are easily seen

---

[10] The trichotomy assert/deny/neither is discussed in similar terms by T. Parsons (1984), who attempts to use it to defend a Value gap solution to the semantical paradoxes against the extended liar reply. The solution does not, however, work. The Value gap theorist is committed to the claim that *some sentences are neither true nor false*. And, since the liar sentence is claimed to be one such sentence, he *is* committed to the claim that it is not true (*pace* T. Parsons, 1984, p. 144). Notice that it makes no sense to replace the negations in the italicised sentence by a force operator for denial.

to be so; and *if something is clearly false, a rational person cannot believe it.* It should not be surprising that the italicised statement is rejected by dialetheism. Truth and falsity come inextricably intermingled, like a constant boiling mixture. One cannot, therefore, accept all truths and reject all falsehoods, and truth (being the *telos* of assertion) is dominant over falsity. It is, perhaps, more surprising that the italicised statement is more than a little dubious even from a classical perspective. To see this, just consider the "paradox of the preface". A person, as a result of thorough and painstaking research, writes a book in which she claims $\alpha_1, \ldots, \alpha_n$. She has every rational reason to believe these claims. But she is aware that no factual book has ever been written which did not contain some falsehoods. The inductive evidence for this is overwhelming. Hence, quite rationally, she believes $\neg\alpha_1 \vee \ldots \vee \neg\alpha_n$ too. Clearly, her belief set is inconsistent. Yet she believes it, and is paradigmatically rational.[11]

It might be suggested that, though the author may believe each of a set of propositions such that she knows one of them to be false, there is no proposition that she believes such that she knows it to be false. She may believe $\alpha_1 \wedge \ldots \wedge \alpha_n$ and believe $\neg(\alpha_1 \wedge \ldots \wedge \alpha_n)$, but does not believe their conjunction. Again, we might query the distinction between believing conjuncts severally and conjointly. If the distinction be upheld, it remains to us to argue against the italicised claim of the previous paragraph on the ground that we have already shown some false things (viz. certain contradictions) to be rationally believable. Against this, it may be replied that this just begs the question, since it is precisely the rational acceptability of contradictions that is at issue. To avoid this charge, it is necessary to argue directly that contradictions can be rationally believed. To this I now turn.

The most satisfactory way to argue this would be to establish the correct account of the conditions of rational belief and show that these do not preclude the possibility of accepting contradictions. However, to establish a satisfactory account of the conditions of rational belief would be no mean undertaking. The issue is a complex one, and one that has been at the centre of a great deal of debate in recent philosophy of science. It would be foolish to try to solve this problem in a few pages, and I shall not try. What I will try to do instead is show, by quite general considerations, that it may be as rational to accept an inconsistency as anything else, whatever account of rational acceptance is (one hopes rationally) accepted.

Let us start by asking when it is rational to accept something as true. A sufficient condition for the rational acceptance of a belief or theory is that there are good, or very good, reasons supporting it. This condition is not also necessary. Some beliefs are so "basic" that it seems impossible (without some quite specific context of doubt) to give reasons for them. Thus, I believe quite rationally that I have a pen in my hand. The reasons that I believe this, excellent ones, are that I can see it and feel it. I accept, quite rationally, that I can see/feel a pen in my hand. I am, however, unable to offer any sensible reason why I believe

---

[11] This conclusion is drawn by Rescher and Brandom (1980) p. 47 ff., and Prior (1971), p. 85.

this. Similarly, I believe that $1 + 1 = 2$, but I would be hard pressed to give a reason for the truth of this. (I might appeal to the fact that I had been told it by a person of authority, but this is obviously not the kind of reason that is in question here.) This sort of situation notwithstanding, the possession of good reasons for believing something is a sufficient ground for rational acceptance.

This does not, unfortunately, get us very far. For we must ask what, in this context, a good reason is; and different philosophers have given different answers to this question. I will not try to produce an answer here, but just note that any or all of the following (separately or conjointly) can be good reasons for supposing something to be true: that it can be deduced from something already rationally accepted; that it has experimental support; that it has high statistical probability, when this is all the information we have; and so on. If we are in the very common context (in fact the normal one) where we are faced with a collection of rival hypotheses, then there are reasons of a more methodological nature that can be invoked: that the hypothesis is the simplest or the most fruitful one; that it solves problems better than its rivals; that the theory has successfully faced stiffer tests than its rivals; that its rivals form a degenerating research programme, and so on.[12] I do not suggest that these are the only kinds of reasons that can be offered in support of a theory or belief; but equally, I am sceptical of the attempts of philosophers of science to reduce them to a single "master reason".

Now the important point for present purposes is that an inconsistency can be supported by each and every kind of reason enunciated above, as a little thought suffices to show. It would be tedious to go through the whole list and demonstrate this; a few examples will, however, make it clear. In chapters 1 and 2, I argued that certain contradictions, viz. the logical paradoxes, are true. One argument for this was that they follow from principles (such as the T-scheme and the Abstraction scheme of set theory) that we have good reason to accept. The argument then switches to the question of why we have good reason to accept these principles. Some direct arguments were given for these (in sections 4.2 and 4.3), but important indirect ones were concerned to show that the alternatives (the Tarski hierarchy, ZF set theory) were inadequate (often by their own standards): they may not solve the problems (avoid all the paradoxes); they may not account for the data (the set theoretic constructions ZF cannot handle); they produce novel and spurious problems; they bristle with *ad hoc* protuberances; they partake in a degenerating research programme; and so on. Perhaps no *single* argument from this collection may suffice to make naive set theory and semantics acceptable in preference to their consistent rivals; but it seems to me that the combined array is quite sufficient to make the inconsistent theories rationally preferable.[13]

---

[12] *Cognoscenti* from the philosophy of science will recognise shades of logical empiricism, Kuhn, Popper, and Lakatos here.

[13] Sophisticated methodologists such as Lakatos are quite well aware that methodological considerations can be applied to compare theories, some of which are inconsistent, with the consequence that an inconsistent theory comes out as preferable. See Lakatos (1978*a*), p. 59.

The inconsistent theories I have been discussing are not, of course, open to empirical testing in any straightforward sense. Hence those reasons that concern experiment and observation are not applicable here. Still, it is easy enough to find situations where they are. It is necessary only to find inconsistent theories in the history of science. Of these there are plenty. As many writers on the history of science have observed,[14] every interesting theory in the history of science is faced with anomalies and inconsistencies. Of particular interest are Bohr's theory of the atom and Newtonian dynamics (based as it was on the inconsistent infinitesimal calculus);[15] for each of these received substantial empirical support—survived empirical tests, made predictions that were verified, and so on.

To sum up: whatever kind of argument it takes to make something rationally acceptable, an inconsistency can have it. The examples given show just that. Moreover, it is not very important if the reader is not convinced by the particular examples used (for example if she thinks that Bohr's theory was not really inconsistent, or the case for naive set theory is not yet strong enough). For it is clear that the sorts of considerations mooted in support of an inconsistent theory *could* mount to a rationally overwhelming case, and this is all that is necessary for present purposes. Thus, contradictions may be rationally acceptable. In fact, I claim that the logical paradoxes *are* rationally acceptable.

Before leaving this topic, let us look at the other side of the coin: rational rejectability. In the previous section I isolated the notion of rejecting. It is important to see that one can have rational grounds for rejecting something. The situation may be treated as the dual of that for rational belief. Thus, let us ask when a statement is rationally rejectable. A sufficient condition for the rational rejectability of a statement is that there are good, or very good, arguments against it. (The question of whether this is also a necessary condition is trickier in this case than in the case of acceptance, though we need not try to sort that out now.) What sort of arguments are good arguments against a theory or statement? As in the case of acceptance, there may be a muliplicity of different kinds. But certainly, the following (separately or in conjunction) can be good arguments: that it implies something we already have good reason to reject; that it is disconfirmed by the evidence; that it has a low statistical probability, where this is the only information we have; and so on. And if we are in the normal situation where we are faced with a number of rival hypotheses, there may be reasons of a more methodological nature: that a rival is simpler, or solves problems better; that a rival has passed stiffer tests; that the theory is embedded in a degenerating research programme; and, in general, that a rival is more rationally acceptable. (It might be thought that the very notion of theories being rivals collapses if dialetheism is correct. But for two hypotheses to be rivals it is neither necessary nor sufficient for them to be mutually inconsistent. What they need to be

<hr />

[14] e.g. Lakatos (1970); Feyerabend (1975), ch. 5; Feyerabend (1978), sect. 4.

[15] For details of these and other inconsistent theories in the history of science, see Priest and Routley (1983), ch. 5.

is different theories, neither of which reduces to the other, accounting for the same phenomena.)

Notice that arguments against a statement or theory are not simply, or even, arguments for its negation. For example, the intuitionist who argues against an instance of the law of excluded middle is certainly not arguing for its negation. Similarly, we can argue directly against a certain statistical hypothesis on the ground that it has a low likelihood without making a specific case for its negation. And clearly, when faced with a multiplicity of rival theories, the case against one of them is certainly not a case for its negation: theories do not even have negations. The case against something *may* be part of a case for its negation. But this very much depends on other things, as the above examples show. Conversely, the arguments for the negation of something are not, without some other considerations pertaining to the consistency of the situation, a complete case against the claim being negated. Hence, arguments *pro* and *contra* are *sui generis*.

Notice also that the rational acceptability and rejectability of something, though not exhaustive, are certainly incompatible. They are not exhaustive since there may be non-basic beliefs such that it is difficult (at least at the moment) to produce strong arguments either for or against them. A novel scientific hypothesis might be in this category. Here the rational position is agnosticism. To see that they are incompatible, note that what is rationally acceptable and rejectable (in a certain context of inquiry) is what the ideal rational agent (a fictitious but useful creature) accepts and rejects. But, as we saw in section 7.3, acceptance and rejection are mutually incompatible. In other words, if one is presented with a claim that is *prima facie* both rationally acceptable and rejectable, this conflict must be resolved in favour of one or other party, or of agnosticism. (This might be done by the kind of weighing procedure I shall discuss in the next section.) Since it is impossible jointly to accept and reject the same thing, it is, a *fortiori*, impossible to do this rationally. Hence rational acceptance and rejection are mutually incompatible.

7.5 RATIONAL CHANGE OF BELIEF

It might be suggested that, if dialetheism (or some particular contradiction) is rationally acceptable, then every theory is rationally acceptable. Does this follow? Of course not. The mere assumption of dialetheism, or of some particular contradiction, does not help one iota (provided, of course, that we do not use question-begging principles such as *ex contradictione quodlibet*) to produce good reasons for the hypothesis that I have three hands, that London has just disappeared from the face of the globe, or for classical logic.

It may be argued however, that, though we may still distinguish between theories that are rationally acceptable and theories that are not, dialetheism ruins another crucial aspect of rationality. For the rational person is one who not only believes the appropriate things under the appropriate circumstances, but also gives up their beliefs under the appropriate circumstances. And, it is argued, if dialetheism is true, no one could ever be rationally obliged to give up something they believe. For suppose someone believes a theory, *T*. Any impetus for giving up *T* will come from an argument or experiment which makes it reasonable to believe something inconsistent with *T*, α. But now, the argument continues, if dialetheism is correct, there is nothing to stop the person simply adding α to their belief set and believing the whole inconsistent totality. The very notions of rational criticisability and change of belief therefore disappear.[16] This is the final objection I will consider.

The objection, if it were correct, would be a telling one, providing as it does a transcendental argument against dialetheism. This just shows that it is self-refuting; for it claims that it is impossible to produce an effective objection to an inconsistent position, while trying to produce just such an objection. (Dialetheism, at least in the form advocated here, is an inconsistent position.) Exactly where, though, does the argument break down?

That a person may sometimes be able to accept a contradiction rationally, and that there is nothing in the domain of formal semantics ever to stop a person accepting a contradiction, I do not dispute. That a person can always accept a contradiction rationally is a blatant *non sequitur*, which I reject. It does not follow from the fact that some contradictions are rationally acceptable that all are, nor does it follow from the fact that there is nothing in formal semantics against it that it can be done rationally. In fact, even those who suppose consistency to be a constraint on rationality recognise that there are much stronger constraints. The belief that one is a poached egg is quite consistent. It can even be made consistent with observation if one is prepared to invoke the right auxiliary assumptions. Consistency is a very weak constraint, and much tougher ones are required to do the real work. For example, a constant resort to *ad hoc* manoeuvres (such as tacking on an extra assumption) speaks strongly against the rational acceptability of a theory, as does, more generally, the Lakatosian degeneration of the research programme in which the theory is embedded. And these constraints can and must play the same role in a dialetheic account of rationality.

So much is clear. But more can be said about how rational criticism is possible. In the previous sections I discussed the notions of rejection and rational rejection. These notions can now be applied. A view can be criticised and made untenable if it can be shown to imply something that is rationally rejectable; for anything that implies something rationally rejectable is itself rationally rejectable. This is essentially how arguments by *reductio ad absurdum* work.[17] Nor does the rationally rejectable consequence have to be a contradiction; anything that is rationally rejectable will do. For example, 'People turn into frogs when tapped on

---

[16] This argument can be found, for example, in Popper (1940), pp. 316–17 of reprint. Lewis (1982) also suggests that a consciously inconsistent position is uncriticisable.

[17] This point is taken from Priest (1989), where argument by *reductio* is discussed further.

the shoulder' is as good as most contradictions—and better than some. This is highly rationally rejectable since it is strongly disconfirmed by the data: when people are tapped on the shoulder they are not seen, by and large, to turn into frogs. It might be thought that if dialetheism is right then no contradiction is rationally rejectable. A moment's thought, however, will show that this is false; for if α is rationally rejectable so is $\alpha \wedge \neg\alpha$, since this entails α. In fact there are quite general reasons why arbitrary contradictions are rejectable. I defer discussion of these till the next chapter (see section 8.4). It suffices for the present to note how rejectable sentences form the anvil against which the hammer of a *reductio* works.

Naturally, in most situations of real interest, things are more complex than this simple sketch indicates. Suppose for example that a theory, T, is rationally acceptable but that, in virtue of some new evidence or argument, it is seen to deliver a contradiction, β, which there are general reasons to suppose to be rationally rejectable. What is to be done? Obviously there are two possibilities (assuming that the evidence or arguments are not themselves to be challenged— which is always a live possibility). The first is to continue to accept T, and to accept β on the ground that it is entailed by something rationally acceptable. The other is to continue to reject β and to reject T on the ground that it entails something rationally rejectable. Which is the rational thing to do? There is no general answer to this. Depending on the particular content of T and β, the answer *may* be obvious. (For example, β may entail things that are not acceptable at any price, such as that everything is true. This would be the case, for example, if the theory were based on classical logic.) In general, however, things will not be this straightforward, and we must determine whether the case for T outweighs that against β, vice versa, or neither.

How to cash out this metaphor of weighing is an interesting and important question. I shall not attempt a complete answer here. The important thing to note is that this is a problem that is not peculiar to dialetheism: it is a well recognised issue in the philosophy of science, which arises whenever we must choose between incompatibles, both of which have some support. For example, the problem is posed in orthodox philosophy of science when a well supported theory is faced with recalcitrant, or *prima facie* refuting, evidence. Given that we have defeasible reasons for the theory, and a defeasible observation contradicting it, which should be rejected? (Dialetheism may add a third possibility—that of accepting both and the consequent contradiction. But this is beside the point here.) In such contexts, some weighing process, possibly in the context of further investigation, experimentation and theorisation, is necessary to reach a (fallible) conclusion.

How this works is something like this. Given the incompatibles X and Y, each with some support, we formulate (at least) two hypotheses. One of these endorses X and locates some problem with the evidence for Y. The other does the symmetrical thing for Y. These rival hypotheses can then be evaluated methodologically. In the most favourable case, the diagnoses of the problem-locations will be independently testable, which will aid the process of comparison.

Applying this to our particular examples, if we have the supported theory, T, and the observation made, α, one hypothesis will endorse T but find some (preferably independently testable) reason why the observation was wrong. The other will endorse α and modify T (preferably in an independently testable way) to save its strength but avoid the embarrassing observational consequence. These two hypotheses can then be compared methodologically. In the case where the theory, T, faces the contradiction, β, one hypothesis will reject β and modify T in such a way as to retain its strength while avoiding the contradiction. The other will endorse T and the (local) contradiction, but will find some reason for revising the evidence against β. These two hypotheses can then be compared methodologically. I have already illustrated this last process with the comparisons between rival (consistent and inconsistent) set theories and semantics in previous chapters.

It will often be the case that the major reason against the contradiction is its a *priori* improbability. (I will argue that contradictions are *a priori* improbable in the next chapter; see section 8.4.) In this case, the situation will be that in which a theory implies that a certain rather unlikely event has occurred. As a more mundane example of this sort of situation, suppose I am playing cards and have some reason to believe the dealer to be honest. Despite this, at a crucial time he is dealt a perfect hand. The two hypotheses are now that (a) the dealer cheated: my belief that he was honest was wrong; and (b) the dealer is honest and the improbable has happened by sheer chance. How one might go about deciding between these hypotheses, though in practice a sensitive issue, is in principle clear enough. One may, in the end, have to accept that one was just unlucky. Similarly, if in the end there is no satisfactory way the contradiction can be avoided, one may have to accept that the domain in question contains dialetheias.

Anyway, to return to the main point of the section, we may summarise as follows. If a theory or hypothesis delivers a contradiction which there are good grounds for rejecting, this provides *prima facie* grounds for rejecting the theory. If there are no countervailing reasons, this is sufficient for rejecting the theory. If there are countervailing reasons, one must investigate further. In the end, one *may* decide to accept the inconsistency (though more likely one will not). But this is not a sign of stupidity: it is a sign that one is less narrow-minded and dogmatic than someone who rejects the inconsistency thoughtlessly and out of hand.[18]

If this is all disconcertingly non-algorithmic, that is just an unfortunate fact of life. It is presumably the desire to obtain something more algorithmic that is behind the demand that all contradictions should be rejected, or at least that dialetheism should specify, in advance, an algorithm for deciding which contradictions must be rejected. Such a demand cannot be met. Neither is there any

---

[18] In certain contexts there may be general considerations which show that the possibility of a contradiction need not be given serious consideration. For example, the domain in question may be such as to make a dialetheia there extremely unlikely.

reason why it should be.[19] These demands are just the last outpost of the "Euclidean" desire for certitude, which, while once common in the philosophy of science, can now be looked upon only with nostalgia.[20] Deciding the fate of a theory or hypothesis of any importance is likely to be a long and fallible business. There is no experiment, no proof, which is guaranteed to settle the matter. None the less, a sufficient weight of evidence may eventually work. Dialetheism just underlines this fact. Maybe a person can rationally hang on to a theory and to a contradiction to which it leads, at least for a time; but, as other evidence and arguments build up, as this particular consequence of the theory, or others, are found to be damaging, this may no longer remain rationally possible. Dialetheism disposes of the last vestiges of "instant rationality".

7.6 APPENDIX: PROBABILITY THEORY

In the previous sections I have made informal use of the notion of probability and associated notions, such as confirmation. I shall make further use of these notions in the next chapter. Much of what I have to say will make little sense if this informal notion is cashed out in terms of orthodox formal probability theory, according to which contradictions have uniform probability 0. It is therefore necessary to say what formal notion of probability my informal use answers to. Clearly, it should not be surprising that a change as fundamental as dialetheism requires some changes in formal probability theory. None the less, the changes need not be very profound. All the standard approaches to probability theory can be modified in fairly straightforward ways. The following is a dialetheic modification of the semantical approach of Carnap and others. Those wishing to take my word that dialetheism can be equipped with a suitable formal probability theory can omit this section.

Let M be a possible-world interpretation of the kind specified in the last chapter. For any sentence α, let $[\alpha]$ be the set of worlds in the interpretation at which α holds. Let μ be a normalised measure function on W. The probability of α, $\Pr(\alpha)$, is defined simply as $\mu([\alpha])$. It is now easy enough to check that all the usual Kolmogorov axioms hold for Pr, with the exception (as one would expect) of those concerning negation. In particular:

(i) $0 \leq \Pr(\alpha) \leq 1$

(ii) If α implies β (in the sense that $\alpha \Rightarrow \beta$ holds at G),
     then $\Pr(\alpha) \leq \Pr(\beta)$

(iii) $\Pr(\alpha \vee \beta) = \Pr(\alpha) + \Pr(\beta) - \Pr(\alpha \wedge \beta)$

---

[19] That real life requires "practical wisdom" rather than algorithm was noted by Aristotle. Recognition of the significance of this in epistemology is, perhaps, more recent. See Brown (1977), pp. 145–51.　　　　　　　　　　　　　　　[20] See Lakatos (1962).

and so on. What fails is, of course, that

(iv) $\Pr(\alpha) + \Pr(\neg\alpha) = 1$

(Their sum is always greater than or equal to 1.) Orthodox probability theory can now be developed in the usual way, except that we can no longer assume that $\Pr(\alpha \wedge \neg\alpha) = 0$, and this non-zero value will have to be carried around in various theorems.

A pleasant feature of this approach to probability theory is that, since every sentence holds in some worlds, by choosing our measure function appropriately, we can ensure that every sentence has non-zero probability. (For example, if W is finite, we can just let $\mu(X)$ be the cardinality of X divided by that of W.) This means that we can define conditional probability in the usual way:

$$\Pr(\alpha/\beta) = \Pr(\alpha \wedge \beta)/\Pr(\beta)$$

and be sure that it is always well-defined, since $\Pr(\beta)$ is never zero. Conditional probability therefore becomes easier to operate with.

As a simple application and illustration of the above points, let us investigate the conditions under which a hypothesis is disconfirmed (in the sense of having its probability decreased), when the negation of one of its consequences is observed. Suppose we have a theory, h, which implies some observational consequence, e, so that $\Pr(e/h) = 1$. Suppose that $\neg e$ is observed. Let us write $\Pr(h/\neg e)/\Pr(h)$ as c. By a simple application of the definition of conditional probability, we have

$$\Pr(h/\neg e) \cdot \Pr(\neg e) = \Pr(\neg e/h) \cdot \Pr(h)$$

and hence

$$c = \Pr(\neg e/h)/\Pr(\neg e) \tag{1}$$

Now by (iii),

$$\Pr(e \vee \neg e) = \Pr(e) + \Pr(\neg e) - \Pr(e \wedge \neg e) \tag{2}$$

And, since the left-hand side is 1,

$$\Pr(\neg e) = 1 - \Pr(e) + \Pr(e \wedge \neg e) \tag{3}$$

The conditionalised form of (2), easily established, gives

$$\Pr(e \vee \neg e/h) = \Pr(e/h) + \Pr(\neg e/h) - \Pr(e \wedge \neg e/h)$$

whence

$$\Pr(\neg e/h) = \Pr(e \wedge \neg e/h) \tag{4}$$

since the other two terms are equal to 1. Substituting (3) and (4) in (1) gives

$$c = \Pr(e \wedge \neg e/h)/(1 - \Pr(e) + \Pr(e \wedge \neg e))$$

Now, classically, this evaluates to zero: disconfirmation is total. Dialetheically, the expression may be non-zero, though, of course, it may still be less than 1.

In particular, suppose that e is *a priori* improbable, as it often is in a test-case situation. Then $\Pr(e)$ is approximately 0. And since $e \wedge \neg e$ implies e, $\Pr(e \wedge \neg e)$ is approximately 0 too. Thus, the denominator is approximately 1. Hence, unless something special happens to the numerator, $c < 1$ and disconfirmation occurs. If h entails $\neg e$ (so that h entails $e \wedge \neg e$), then something special does happen to the numerator: it is equal to 1. Thus $c > 1$, and confirmation actually occurs, as might be expected.

8

The Disjunctive Syllogism and Quasi-Validity

8.1 THE DISJUNCTIVE SYLLOGISM

In the preceding four chapters I have specified at least part of the logical theory (both formal and informal) of dialetheism. As one would expect, it deviates in crucial respects from classical logical theory. But considering how radical dialetheism is, perhaps the surprising thing is how *little* its logical theory differs from the classical theory. Essentially, it just generalises classical logical theory to allow it to handle a domain that was, before, beyond the pale (and therefore could not be admitted to exist in any non-trivial way)—the inconsistent. By increasing the scope of logical theory, it increases its power. However, it is clear that this gain is accompanied by a loss—at least in one sense. Specifically, certain rules of inference which were taken to be truth-preserving classically are not so dialetheically. Perhaps no one except the most hardened classicist would mourn the loss of paradoxes of implication such as *ex contradictione quodlibet*; but the loss goes beyond these. For classical principles of inference that do appear to be used quite commonly are dialetheically invalid. The most obvious of these is material detachment, or, as it is commonly called, the disjunctive syllogism (hereafter, DS):

$$\{\alpha \wedge (\neg\alpha \vee \beta)\} \vdash \beta$$

More generally, suppose we call an inference *quasi-valid* if it involves essentially only extensional connectives and quantifiers, and is classically valid but dialetheically invalid. (All inferences that are dialetheically valid are classically valid, as we noted at section 5.3, Fact 5.) Then the point can be summed up simply thus: the cost of dialetheism is that quasi-valid inferences can no longer be taken as universally valid. Actually, the loss is not as great as one might expect. In section 5.3 I noted, in effect, that dialetheic logic is at least as strong as Gentzen's *LK* minus cut. Now, it is well known that for many classical systems cut is redundant. For such systems there is therefore no loss using dialetheic logic.[1]

[1] For example, simple type theory permits cut-elimination (see e.g. Takeuti 1975, sect. 21). More interestingly, according to some unpublished work of Uwe Petersen, it is possible to prove all the Peano axioms in the Frege/Russell reduction of number theory to set theory with a naive

Still, the general point remains: there is a loss. And this fact might well be thought to pose a problem for, or even an objection to, dialetheism: we appear to use quasi-valid inferences, and particularly the disjunctive syllogism, quite commonly. For example, if I know that you have gone to either the supermarket or the bank, and I ascertain that you are not at the supermarket, I infer that you are at the bank. This inference certainly seems to have some legitimate basis. But if dialetheism is correct, it cannot be that the inference is formally valid. So what is it? If no such basis can be found, dialetheism would seem to be an inadequate explanation of the data of inference.

The first aim of this chapter is to show that this sort of inference does have a legitimate basis, and one, moreover, which is quite compatible with dialetheism. To put it summarily, quasi-valid inferences can be used in consistent situations. Building on this insight, we will then see how, in a sense to be made precise, dialetheic logical reasoning subsumes that of classical logic. This will provide the basis of another argument for dialetheism. Let us start with the usability of quasi-valid inferences, and, in particular, the DS.

8.2 WHAT IT IS NOT

In the next section I shall argue that it is quite legitimate to use the DS in consistent situations. The rationale for this claim is, *au fond*, the fairly trivial observation that, in order to get a counter-example to the DS, i.e. a sentence of the form $\alpha \wedge (\neg\alpha \vee \beta)$ that is true while β is not, α has to be a dialetheia. The explication of this claim is, however, a fairly subtle one, and not at all as straightforward as it might appear. Hence, before I try to explain what this claim comes to, it is essential to see what it does not come to.

It might be thought that, although the DS is not formally valid, if we add an extra premise expressing the consistency of α, the argument will become valid. It is clear that the obvious way of expressing the consistency of α, i.e. $\neg(\alpha \wedge \neg\alpha)$, will not do; for this is logically valid. Thus, any counter-example to the disjunctive syllogism will also be a counter-example to

$$\{\neg(\alpha \wedge \neg\alpha), \alpha \wedge (\neg\alpha \vee \beta)\} \models \beta$$

This should warn us that the idea may not be on the right lines. In fact, it is not difficult to show that there is no sentence in the intensional propositional language of section 6.3, $\gamma(p)$, whose only propositional parameter is p, such that

$$\{\gamma(p), p \wedge (\neg p \vee q)\} \models q^2$$

comprehension axiom but without cut. (Moreover, because of the cut-free nature of the system, non-triviality is provable in the usual way.) Hence this reduction is possible in naive set theory.

² Simply consider the one-world model in which p is a dialetheia and q is plain false. For any γ, $\gamma(p)$ holds in this model. The model also shows that there is no $\gamma(p)$ such that either $\models \gamma(p) \wedge (p \wedge (\neg p \vee q)) \rightarrow q$ or $\models \gamma(p) \rightarrow (p \wedge (\neg p \vee q) \rightarrow q)$.

Hence the DS can not be recovered enthymematically by adding any simple condition that *uses* the crucial formula.[3]

Perhaps, it may be thought, if we have a condition that *mentions* it we will do better. For example, could we not take as a suppressed premise $\neg T\alpha \wedge \neg\alpha$, or something similar such as $\neg(T\alpha \wedge T\neg\alpha)$, or $T\neg\alpha \rightarrow \neg T\alpha$? This will not work either. If α and $\neg\alpha$ are true, then so are $T\alpha \wedge \neg\alpha$ and $T\alpha \wedge T\neg\alpha$. But this does not rule out the truth of any of the above sentences. If we were sure that the truth predicate behaved consistently, then it would. However, as we have already noted (in section 4.9), it does not so behave. Indeed, if the exclusion principle holds, all the above formulas hold for all α. Moreover, it is not difficult to see that, in whatever natural way one tries to express the claim that α is not a dialetheia, there is nothing to prevent this claim itself from being a dialetheia, in which case both of '$\alpha \wedge \neg\alpha$' and 'α is not a dialetheia' may be true, whence the enthymematic argument will fail as before. To see that something may be both a dialetheia and not a dialetheia, merely consider

(1) is not true and not a dialetheia   (1)

(1) is either true or false. If it is true, it is not true and not a dialetheia. Hence it is both a dialetheia and not a dialetheia. If it is false, it is either true or a dialetheia. In either case it is true and so, as we have just seen, is both a dialetheia and not a dialetheia.

It seems that there is no premise which formulates the condition that α is consistent that can be added to the premise of a DS to make it enthymematically valid. In fact, there are quite general reasons for supposing that this must be so. The invalidity of the DS is shown by taking inconsistency seriously. Moreover, if a situation is inconsistent, adding an extra premise to the effect that it is consistent will not change the situation, but merely multiply the inconsistencies.[4] There is no statement that can be made which *forces* α to behave consistently. This is one of the hard facts of dialetheic life. Actually, it is one of the hard facts of life, *period*. There is nothing a classical logician can say to force consistency either, and any attempt that fails will occasion an immediate collapse into triviality, the highest degree of inconsistency, rather than merely a higher degree of inconsistency, as in dialetheism.

In virtue of the fact that it is precisely dialetheias that provide the counter-examples to the DS, it would seem, *prima facie*, that we ought to be able to prove in the "metatheory" that, if the situation is consistent, the truth of the conclusion of a DS follows from the truth of its premise. There can be no such valid proof, however. For if there were, we could simply apply the T-scheme to premise and conclusion and obtain a valid enthymematic deduction of α from $\alpha \wedge (\neg\alpha \vee \beta)$ and we have already seen that there is no such thing. None the less, it is

---

[3] The situation is different if we allow γ to contain propositional constants, as we will see in sect. 8.5.   [4] The point is made in Belnap and Dunn (1983).

illuminating to see where such a proof breaks down. Suppose we express the consistency of α by

$$T\underline{\alpha} \rightarrow \neg T\underline{\neg\alpha} \qquad (\alpha^c)$$

Then one proof[5] might go as follows:

1. $T\alpha \wedge (\neg\alpha \vee \beta)$
2. $T\underline{\alpha}$ by the truth conditions for $\wedge$
3. $\neg T\underline{\neg\alpha}$ by α^c
4. $T\underline{\neg\alpha} \vee \beta$ from 1 and the truth conditions for $\wedge$
5. $T\underline{\neg\alpha} \vee T\underline{\beta}$ by the truth conditions for $\vee$
6. $T\underline{\beta}$ from 3 and 5

The proof of course uses the DS at line 6. (And, had we chosen to represent the consistency of α as $\neg(T\underline{\alpha} \wedge T\underline{\neg\alpha})$, it would have used a variant of it at line 3 too.) Hence the above proof of the truth preservation of the DS under consistent circumstances is invalid, or at least only quasi-valid. And the same must be true of any similar proof, as we have seen. This does not show that such proofs carry no weight; I am, after all, going to claim that under certain circumstances quasi-valid proofs are acceptable. The point is that, if we have as yet reached no adequate understanding of when and how quasi-valid inferences can be legitimately used, such an argument will not provide it. If we do not understand the *modus operandi* of the DS, we had best avoid using it till we do. So far, then, in searching for this *modus operandi* we have drawn a blank.

8.3 ...WHAT IT IS

An adequate understanding of the legitimate use of DS given consistency is quite straightforward, and follows from the discussion of rejection in the previous chapter, together with one further fact about rational rejection, which I will call principle R.

Principle R
If a disjunction is rationally acceptable and one of the disjuncts is rationally rejectable, then the other is rationally acceptable.

Suppose that someone accepts a disjunction, $\alpha \vee \beta$. Then nothing, as yet, forces them to accept either disjunct: they may be agnostic about both. Let us suppose that they now come to reject one of the disjuncts, say α, while continuing to accept the disjunction. Then the person is rationally committed to accepting the

---

[5] The following proof is taken from Routley and Routley (1972), p. 349, who are, however, well aware that the proof uses the DS.

other, β. The rationale for this is precisely the truth condition for disjunction: $\alpha \vee \beta$ is true iff α is true or β is true. So if one limb of the disjunction is not on, the other must be.

It is important to see that this is not an application of the DS. The argument is not: $\alpha \vee \beta$ is true, but α is not true; therefore β is true. The justification is not a formal one but a pragmatic one: $\alpha \vee \beta$ is rationally acceptable; α is rationally rejectable; hence β is rationally acceptable. If this distinction is not clear, observe it in another context. If someone accepts that $\alpha \rightarrow \beta$ and accepts $\neg \beta$, then they ought to accept $\neg \alpha$. The rationale for this is precisely the formal validity of *modus tollens*: $\{\alpha \rightarrow \beta, \neg \beta\} \vdash \neg \alpha$. If, on the other hand, she accepts $\alpha \rightarrow \beta$ and rejects β, she had clearly better reject α. But this is not *modus tollens*. As we observed in section 7.3, there is a crucial difference between rejecting α and accepting $\neg \alpha$.

Principle R is clear enough. Still, it might be objected *ad hominem* that it is not correct, since someone might both rationally accept *and* reject α, in which case they are not committed to the acceptance of β. There are two points to be made in reply to this. The first is that joint rational acceptance and rejection are not possible, as I argued in section 7.4. The second is that even if they were, principle R would not be undercut. The argument that it would goes as follows. Suppose that a disjunction and one of its disjuncts is rationally acceptable. Then it does not follow that the other is rationally acceptable. Hence from the facts that a disjunction is rationally acceptable and that one of its disjuncts is rationally both acceptable and rejectable, it does not follow that the other is rationally acceptable. This argument is of the form: $\neg(\gamma \rightarrow \delta)$; hence $\neg(\gamma \wedge \eta \rightarrow \delta)$. Enough said. Some confusion may arise from the thought that something's being rationally acceptable (as well as rejectable) "cancels out" its rational rejectability. This is just a confusion. If something is rationally acceptable and rejectable, it is still rationally rejectable. Any consequences that this fact has, therefore, still stand.

Now, to return to the question of the DS, suppose that $\alpha \wedge (\neg \alpha \vee \beta)$ is rationally acceptable. This entails $(\alpha \wedge \neg \alpha) \vee \beta$, which is therefore rationally acceptable. But provided $\alpha \wedge \neg \alpha$ is rationally rejectable (as it often will be, as I will argue in the next section), then, by principle R, β is rationally acceptable. In other words, it is reasonable to accept the conclusion of a DS argument provided the contradiction involved is reasonably rejectable. It is crucial that we distinguish here between rejecting a sentence and accepting its negation. There is no sentence the acceptance of which will do the job, as we saw in the last section; there are ones the rejection of which will.

The generalisation of this to all quasi-valid inferences is but a slight one. Suppose that $\alpha_1 \wedge \ldots \wedge \alpha_n$ is rationally acceptable. Let us call this γ. Suppose that the inference from $\alpha_1 \wedge \ldots \wedge \alpha_n$ to β is quasi-valid. Then $\neg \gamma \vee \beta$ is a logical truth (see Fact 4, section 5.3) and, in fact, a necessary truth. Thus, $\gamma \Rightarrow \gamma \wedge (\neg \gamma \vee \beta)$. Moreover, the consequent of this implies $(\gamma \wedge \neg \gamma) \vee \beta$. Hence, since γ is rationally acceptable, so is this. Now, provided it is rational to reject $\gamma \wedge \neg \gamma$, β is rationally acceptable by principle R. Let us call $\gamma \wedge \neg \gamma$ the *crucial contradiction* of the inference. Then we may summarise as follows. A quasi-valid inference is usable in a consistent situation in the following sense: if the premises are rationally acceptable then so is the conclusion, provided the crucial contradiction is rationally rejectable.

The acceptability in consistent situations of instances of the DS and other quasi-valid inferences can be spelt out in another way if we are prepared to make the assumption that something is rationally acceptable just if its epistemic probability is sufficiently high. This assumption is almost mandatory if we take the notion of epistemic probability seriously.

As before, suppose that the inference from γ to β is quasi-valid (and hence that $\neg\gamma \vee \beta$ is a necessary truth). Then, where the probability in question is epistemic,[6]

$$\begin{aligned}\Pr(\gamma) &= \Pr(\gamma \wedge (\neg\gamma \vee \beta)) \leq \Pr((\gamma \wedge \neg\gamma) \vee \beta) \\ &= \Pr(\gamma \wedge \neg\gamma) + \Pr(\beta) - \Pr(\gamma \wedge \neg\gamma \wedge \beta)\end{aligned}$$

Thus,

$$\Pr(\beta) \geq \Pr(\gamma) - (\Pr(\gamma \wedge \neg\gamma) - \Pr(\gamma \wedge \neg\gamma \wedge \beta))$$

Now, since $\Pr(\gamma \wedge \neg\gamma \wedge \beta) \leq \Pr(\gamma \wedge \neg\gamma)$,

$$\Pr(\gamma \wedge \neg\gamma) - \Pr(\gamma \wedge \neg\gamma \wedge \beta) \leq \Pr(\gamma \wedge \neg\gamma)$$

Hence

$$\Pr(\beta) \geq \Pr(\gamma) - \Pr(\gamma \wedge \neg\gamma).$$

Suppose now that the probability of the crucial contradiction, $\gamma \wedge \neg\gamma$, is small. It follows that $\Pr(\beta) \approx \Pr(\gamma)$. Thus, if γ has a high probability, so does β. If γ is rationally acceptable, it has a high probability. So, therefore, does β. Hence it too is rationally acceptable.

8.4 THE IMPROBABILITY OF INCONSISTENCY

We have seen that we can allow ourselves the use of a quasi-valid inference provided we may reject its crucial contradiction, or assign it sufficiently low probability (which, arguably, comes to the same thing). This is, of course, what the classical logician does anyway. For him, consistency is an absolute *presupposition* of reasoning. This is precisely why the logical paradoxes have the devastating effect they do. For the classical logician, like any other person whose presuppositions disintegrate, starts to flounder. The dialetheist, on the other hand, considers the hypothesis of inconsistency or, better, local inconsistency (i.e. the truth of $\alpha \wedge \neg\alpha$ for particular α) to be no different, in principle, from any other hypothesis, and therefore to be evaluated on its merits. There are, however, certain considerations that will, other things being equal, cause her

---

[6] The following hold in virtue of principles of probability that are intuitively clear. They are also justified formally in sect. 7.6.

to reject it. The reason is a simple one: the statistical frequency of dialetheias in normal discourse is low. Dialetheias appear to occur in a quite limited number of domains: certain logico-mathematical contexts, certain legal and dialectical contexts (which I will discuss in Part Three), and maybe a few others. Moreover, even in the domains where they do occur, very few contradictions are dialetheias. Hence most contradictions one normally comes across are not dialetheic.

The claim that the frequency of dialetheias is low seems fairly obvious, but, inevitably, it will be asked how one knows this once one has conceded that there are some. The simplest argument for this is a head-count. The reader is invited to consider a random sample of the assertions he has met in the last few days and see what percentage might reasonably be thought to be dialetheic. If it is more than a handful, this probably means that the reader has been reading a book on paradoxes. (Maybe this one.)

A more general argument for the low frequency of dialetheias in ordinary discourse can be given as follows. It is a fact, to be verified by simple observation, that people do commonly use quasi-valid arguments. DS, for example, is used commonly in mathematics, as well as in more common-or-garden reasoning. Moreover, it is also a fact, to be verified in the same way, that such reasoning is by and large successful, or at least does not lead to recognisable errors. I know that you are either at home or in the supermarket. I ascertain that you are not in the supermarket. I go to your house and lo! You are there. Now if dialetheias were common, we would expect quasi-valid inferences to go wrong quite frequently. But they do not. Hence they are not common. The normal success of quasi-valid reasoning therefore provides the basis of a transcendental argument for the infrequency of dialetheias.

Given that the statistical frequency of dialetheias is low, and given a contradiction about which we have no particular information (or no time to take account of the further information there is), two things follow. First, this statistical frequency provides the epistemological probability of the contradiction. The probability that this contradiction is a dialetheia is also, therefore, low. Secondly, it is rational to reject the contradiction. (See the discussion of rational rejection in section 7.4.) We might summarise this situation in the razor: contradictions should not be multiplied beyond necessity.

Furthermore, provided, again, that there are no overriding considerations concerning the crucial contradiction of a particular quasi-valid inference, since the conditions that serve to push it through are met, the inference may be used. We can record this in the following maxim.

Methodological Maxim (M)
Unless we have specific grounds for believing that the crucial contradictions in a piece of quasi-valid reasoning are dialetheias, we may accept the reasoning.

For any particular contradiction, we may have additional information which depends specifically on the content of that sentence, and in virtue of which the default assumptions are overridden. Such is the case with the logical paradoxes. And we might well come to accept, or give high probability to, another contradiction on the basis of specific arguments and evidence that are produced. In general this will not be the case, however, as the statistical considerations indicate. Thus, it will usually be reasonable to use quasi-valid inferences. Let me not mince words. I am saying that it may be reasonable to argue invalidly. This may sound radical, but a little thought shows that the sound is misleading. For, *pace* Popper, we use inductive reasoning all the time, and the best inductive reasoning is (deductively) invalid. But, despite its being invalid, probability and other considerations may make it quite reasonable to employ it. Using quasi-valid inferences, we may be a little less sure of our conclusions than of our premises. (As we noted in section 8.3, the probability of the conclusion of a DS will generally be lower than that of the premise by the probability of the crucial contradiction.) But even this is not very radical. After all, even valid deductive inferences may be probability-decreasing. Merely consider the inference $\{\alpha, \beta\}$ $\models \alpha \wedge \beta$.

8.5 THE CLASSICAL RECAPTURE

With this machinery under our belt, let us finally confront classical reasoning. For this section and the next, all formulas are purely classical (that is, they contain only extensional connectives and quantifiers) unless otherwise stated or implied. Similarly, all sets of sentences (and so theories) are sets of classical formulas. For easier notation, let us denote the classical relation of logical consequence by $\Vdash$, and write $\alpha \wedge \neg\alpha$ as α! (! will always be taken to have narrow scope.) The following observation will also be useful:

For any set of sentences, Σ, and formula, α, $\Sigma \Vdash \alpha$ iff for some β,

$\Sigma \models \alpha \vee \beta$!

This observation is proved as Theorem 0 in the appendix to this chapter (section 8.6). Now suppose we have a theory, perhaps a mathematical theory, based on a set of axioms, T, which is developed with a conscious use of classical logic. Since it is a conscious assumption that a contradiction implies everything, it would seem only fair to make this quite explicit. Let F be a propositional constant, to be thought of informally as the conjunction of all formulas, and characterised by the scheme $F \rightarrow \alpha$.[7] Let T^+ be T together with the axiom scheme β! $\rightarrow F$. (Let us call this the *classical postulate*.) Then any classical consequence of T is a dialetheic

---

[7] Semantically, F takes the value $\{0\}$ at every world. If the language contains its own truth predicate then F may be defined as $\forall x T x$. The T-scheme then gives the characteristic principle.

consequence of T^+. For if $T \Vdash \alpha$ then, by the above observation, $T \models \alpha \vee \beta!$ for some β. Hence, using the classical postulate and the properties of F, α is a dialetheic consequence of T^+.[8] Thus, this sort of classical reasoning is quite intelligible dialetheically.

Most reasoning which uses quasi-valid inference is not, perhaps, of this self-consciously classical kind, and if it is not it would seem to be incorrect to impute implicit use of the classical postulate. None the less, as our discussion of quasi-valid reasoning has shown, this kind of reasoning is also quite intelligible dialetheically. Let us suppose that a classical logician and a dialetheic logician are drawing out the logical consequences of an apparently consistent set of axioms. The classical logician will use classical logic. The dialetheic logician, working on the basis of maxim M, will reason validly and quasi-validly.[9] Hence both will appear to reason in the same way.

Now suppose an inconsistency turns up. For the classical logician, disaster strikes. The theory is trivial and must be scrapped. If it is a theory that is so important that it cannot be jettisoned without replacement, then it must be reformulated, though there are no guidelines for how this is to be done, and in any interesting case there is no guarantee that the reformulated theory will not also crash. The dialetheic logician, on the other hand, is not in such an invidious position. He has the choice of scrapping the theory, and if he thinks that the contradictions in the theory are unacceptable, he will do just that; he also has other, and less nihilistic, options. The most conservative of these is to discontinue the use of quasi-valid reasoning and accept, henceforth, only those things that have been established validly. In effect, therefore, he will revert from classical reasoning to valid reasoning. There may also be more sensitive policies which reconsider the things proved quasi-validly in the light of the specific contradictions that have turned up. One such policy is described in the appendix to this chapter (section 8.6), though we do not need to go into this now. Contradictions are wont to turn up in even the best run of businesses. In classical businesses they cause bankruptcy. In dialetheic businesses they may cause voluntary liquidation, or they may merely cause a reappraisal of assets.

Suppose, on the other hand, that a contradiction never turns up. Then both the classical and the dialetheic logician can accept their (quasi-)proofs at face value. Both will accept exactly the same consequences of the theory. Thus, in consistent situations classical consequence can be understood in terms of quasi-validity: the dialetheic logician is able to reason in exactly the same way that the classical logician does. But classical logic recognises no situations other than

---

[8] We can also interpret T^+ in T, merely by mapping F to some arbitrary but fixed contradiction, and $\Rightarrow$ to material implication. In an obvious sense, therefore, classical T and dialetheic T^+ are equivalent.

[9] In other words, where the classical logician sees a classical proof of α, the dialetheic logician will see a proof of $\alpha \vee \beta!$ for some β. Then, invoking the quasi-valid inference: $\alpha \vee \beta!$; hence α, and maxim M, he will conclude that α.

consistent ones. (Or, to be precise, recognises only one other—the absolutely trivial one—which is also recognised dialetheically.) Hence dialetheism matches the power of classical logic. And dialetheic logic not only matches the power, but also, as we noted in section 8.1, extends it. For dialetheism is able to account for non-trivial reasoning in inconsistent situations. In short, dialetheic logic gives the full power of classical logic except where classical logic is demonstrably useless, and then more.

This provides us with a new argument for dialetheism. For the fact that a theory has greater power, or a wider range of applications, or, in general, subsumes a rival is a well known methodological test for that theory to be preferable to its rival. In many ways, dialetheic logic relates to classical logic, as does Special Relativity to Newtonian Dynamics. At low velocities/consistent situations, the rival theories are practically equivalent. (Though not theoretically, since the understandings the theories give of what is going on are rather different.) At high velocities/inconsistent situations, the newer theory works while the older theory crashes.

8.6 APPENDIX: *CONSEQUENCE

In the last section we considered the situation where quasi-valid reasoning is being used to determine the consequences of an apparently consistent set of (classical) axioms. We noted that if a contradiction turns up, one policy, a conservative one, is to revert to valid reasoning; we also noted the possibility of more sensitive policies which take into account not only that a contradiction has turned up, but also how that contradiction relates to the things so far established with quasi-valid reasoning. It is the purpose of this section to formulate and examine one such policy. To do this, let us start with the observation made in the last section:

Theorem 0
For any set of sentences, Σ, and formula, α, $\Sigma \Vdash \alpha$ iff for some β, $\Sigma \models \alpha \vee \beta!$

Proof
From left to right: Suppose that $\Sigma \Vdash \alpha$. Then by the compactness theorem there is a subset, $\{\beta_1, \ldots \beta_n\}$, of Σ such that $\{\beta_1, \ldots \beta_n\} \Vdash \alpha$. Let β be the conjunction of the β_is. Then by the deduction theorem, $\Vdash \neg\beta \vee \alpha$. And since all classical logical truths are dialetheic logical truths, $\models \alpha \vee \neg\beta$. But $\Sigma \models \beta$. Hence $\Sigma \models \alpha \vee \beta!$ Conversely, suppose that $\Sigma \Vdash \alpha \vee \beta!$ Then $\Sigma \models \alpha \vee \beta!$ since all dialetheic logical consequences are classical consequences. Hence, $\Sigma \Vdash \alpha$.

Now suppose we have a set of axioms, Σ, and a quasi-valid, i.e. classical, proof of α. Then by theorem 0 there is a proof of $\alpha \vee \beta!$ We will say that α is *proved with parameter* β. Then the conservative policy of the previous section amounts to this: α is acceptable provided that it is provable with a parameter, and no contradiction can be proved (with a parameter). Now, even if a formula, γ, is proved to be inconsistent, why should this affect the acceptability of something which is proved with a parameter that has nothing to do with γ? A more sensitive and liberal policy would allow α to be acceptable unless a provable contradiction really threatens the parameter in the proof of α. But how exactly is this condition to be formulated?[10]

The obvious proposal is to say that α is acceptable provided the parameter in its proof, β, is not itself provably (with a parameter) inconsistent, i.e. by Theorem 0, for no γ, $\Sigma \models \beta! \vee \gamma!$. Unfortunately, this proposal will not work. To see this, just suppose that Σ is inconsistent, $\Sigma \models \gamma!$, and that $\Sigma \models \alpha \vee \beta!$ Then since $\Sigma \models \beta! \vee \gamma!$, α cannot be accepted. Thus, nothing provable with a parameter would be acceptable, and this notion collapses back into the original conservative one.[11]

A second proposal is to say that α is acceptable provided that, for the parameter in its proof, β, $\beta!$ is not provable (*simpliciter*). This proposal is obviously not susceptible to the same objection, but it, too, will not do as it stands. Let $\Sigma = \{q! \vee r, p!\}$. Then $\Sigma \models r \vee q!$; and $q!$ is not a consequence of Σ, making r acceptable, as one would expect. Unfortunately, since $\{p!, \neg s\} \models (p \wedge \neg s)!$, $\Sigma \models s \vee (p \wedge \neg s)!$, while $(p \wedge \neg s)!$, is not a consequence of Σ, as may easily be checked. Clearly, s ought not to be an acceptable consequence of Σ. What has gone wrong? The problem is that, given any formula and arbitrary contradiction, we can manufacture new contradictions which are not forthcoming from the contradiction on its own. Hence, using the law of excluded middle, we can prove the disjunction of a formula with an unprovable contradiction. Clearly, we should accept something only if it is provable with consistent parameters of a non-manufactured kind. But how to make this precise? One could tell that the above parameter was manufactured because one could prove not only $s \vee (p \wedge \neg s)!$, but also, by working the other side of the street, $\neg s \vee (p \wedge s)!$ This suggests the following condition: α is an acceptable consequence of Σ iff:

$\Sigma \models \alpha$ or for some β, $\Sigma \models \alpha \vee \beta!$

where neither $\beta!$ nor $\neg \alpha \vee \beta!(\alpha/\neg \alpha)$ is a consequence of Σ.

We will write this as $\Sigma \models {}^*\alpha$. (The first disjunct needs to be stated explicitly since it does not imply the second disjunct.) Whether this is exactly the right way of

---

[10] The following material is heavily indebted to Batens (1989). Batens's account depends on features of the underlying paraconsistent logic he uses, features not shared by Δ. Hence my account is somewhat different.

[11] Batens's proposal is, in effect, to modify the condition to rule out this sort of situation. He suggests that α is acceptable if $\Sigma \models \alpha \vee \beta!$, where if $\Sigma \models \beta! \vee \gamma!$, $\Sigma \models \gamma!$ This will not work here. Let $\Sigma = \{p!, q! \vee r\}$. Clearly, r should be acceptable on the basis of the fact that $\Sigma \models r \vee q!$ But it is not difficult to see that $\Sigma \models q! \vee (r \wedge p)!$, while $(r \wedge p)!$ is not a consequence of Σ.

formulating the more liberal policy, I am not sure. At least, *consequence has the right kind of properties, as the following theorems show.[12]

Theorem 1
If $\Sigma \models \alpha$, then $\Sigma \models {}^*\alpha$.

Proof. The proof of this is trivial.

Theorem 2
If $\Sigma \models {}^*\alpha$, then $\Sigma \Vdash \alpha$.

Proof. If $\Sigma \models {}^*\alpha$, then either $\Sigma \models \alpha$, in which case the result follows, or $\Sigma \models \alpha \vee \beta!$ for some β. In this case, $\Sigma \Vdash \alpha \vee \beta!$ since all dialetheic consequences are classical consequences. Hence $\Sigma \Vdash \alpha$.

Theorem 3
$\Sigma \models \alpha!$ iff $\Sigma \models {}^*\alpha!$

Proof. From left to right, the result holds by Theorem 1. From right to left, suppose that $\Sigma \models {}^*\alpha!$ Then either $\Sigma \models \alpha!$ and we are home, or for some β, $\Sigma \models \alpha! \vee \beta!$ where $\neg(\alpha!) \vee \beta!(\alpha!/\neg(\alpha!))$ is not a consequence of Σ. But this is impossible, since $\Sigma \models \neg(\alpha!)$

Theorem 4
The set of semantic consequences of Σ is trivial iff the set of *consequences of Σ is trivial.

Proof. From left to right, the theorem follows by Theorem 1. From right to left the theorem follows by Theorem 3.

Theorem 5
There are sets Σ, and formulas α and β, such that (i) $\Sigma \models {}^*\alpha$ though α is not a consequence of Σ, and (ii) $\Sigma \Vdash \beta$ though β is not a *consequence of Σ.

Proof. Let Σ, $\{p!,\ q! \vee r\}$, and α be r. A simple counter-model shows that α is not a consequence of Σ. To see that $\Sigma \models {}^*\alpha$, note that $\Sigma \models r \vee q!$, but neither $\neg r \vee q!$, nor $q!$ is a consequence of Σ, as, again, simple counter-models show.

---

[12] Another interesting definition of a notion of validity intermediate between dialetheic and classical validity, which also captures an idea of reasoning under the supposition of minimal inconsistency is given in Batens (1986). Let the set of sentences α, such that $\alpha!$ is true in an interpretation M be $M!$ Call an interpretation, M, a *minimally inconsistent* (m.i.) model of a set of sentences, T, if M is a model of T, and for any interpretation, M', if $M'!$ is strictly included in $M!$ then M' is not a model of T. Call α a *m.i.- consequence* of Σ iff α is true in all m.i. models of Σ. This definition turns out to be equivalent to Batens's earlier definition (see above) for the propositional logic he considers.

Now, since Σ is inconsistent, its set of classical consequences is trivial. However, since its set of semantic consequences is non-trivial, its set of *consequences is non-trivial by Theorem 4. Hence there are βs which witness the rest of the theorem.

Theorem 6
If Σ is classically consistent (i.e. for no β, $\Sigma \Vdash \beta!$) then if $\Sigma \Vdash \alpha$, $\Sigma \models {}^*\alpha$.

Proof. Suppose $\Sigma \Vdash \alpha$. Then by Theorem 0, for some β, $\Sigma \vdash \alpha \vee \beta!$ Now $\beta!$ is not a consequence of Σ, since Σ is classically, and hence dialetheically, consistent. Suppose that $\Sigma \models \neg\alpha \vee \beta!(\alpha/\neg\alpha)$. Then $\Sigma \Vdash \neg\alpha \vee \beta!(\alpha/\neg\alpha)$, whence, since $\Sigma \Vdash \alpha$, $\Sigma \Vdash \alpha! \vee \beta!(\alpha/\neg\alpha)$. But this is impossible since Σ is classically consistent. Hence $\Sigma \models {}^*\alpha$.

We may summarise the import of the theorems thus. Let Σ be some non-trivial but possibly inconsistent set of formulas. The set of *consequences of Σ is a non-trivial set of sentences sandwiched between its set of semantic consequences and its set of classical consequences. In general it is properly sandwiched, but if Σ is (classically) consistent, it is identical with the set of classical consequences.

*Consequence therefore seems a plausible candidate for the analysis of the notion of acceptable consequence. In practice it may be difficult to determine whether something is a *consequence of a set of axioms or not. *Consequence is a highly non-effective notion. Assuming $\Vdash$ to be a Σ_1 relation in the arithmetic hierarchy, $\models^*$ is Σ_2. If α is proved (without a parameter), then, of course, it is a *consequence. If it is proved with a parameter, β, then we may be able to find a metatheoretic proof that the parameter is secure in the required sense (i.e. that there is neither a proof of $\beta!$ nor a proof of $\neg\alpha \vee \beta!(\alpha/\neg\alpha)$). If we can find no such proof, then we will have to assess, on the basis of the evidence at hand, how likely the parameters are to be secure. (For example, if, after trying, we are unable to find a proof of $\beta!$ we will have some evidence that there is no such proof.) The evidence will be fallible and inductive; but inductive grounds have their place, even in mathematics,[13] when suitable deductive grounds are not available.

---

[13] See e.g. Steiner (1975), pp. 102–8.

PART III

APPLICATIONS

Two gardeners were working in Nasr al-Din's garden. One of them was tending Nasr al-Din's cabbages and, finding snails, he began to kill them and throw them over the wall of the garden. The second gardener approached and asked 'What are you doing?' to which the first gardener replied 'Killing these snails.' 'Why are you killing them?' asked the second gardener, and the first gardener answered 'Because they are eating Nasr al-Din's cabbages.' But the second gardener said 'Let them be; they're not doing much harm, and, after all, they have their needs too.' The gardeners continued arguing and began to fight. Nasr al-Din approached, accompanied by his wife. 'What are you fighting about?' Nasr al-Din asked the gardeners, 'Tell me and I shall give my judgement.' The first gardener said 'I say that these snails should be destroyed because they are eating your cabbages.' And Nasr al-Din replied 'You are right.' But the second gardener said 'I say that the snails should be let be, and allowed to meet their needs.' And Nasr al-Din replied 'You are right'. Then Nasr al-Din's wife said to Nasr al-Din 'But Nasr al-Din, they cannot both be right.' And Nasr al-Din replied 'You are right.'

Trad., arr. Goldstein

9

Semantic Closure and the Philosophy of Language

9.1 APPLICATIONS OF DIALETHEISM

In the first part of the book I argued for dialetheism. In the second part I set out its logical theory (in a fairly generous sense of the phrase). In this part of the book I wish to chart some of its applications. Dialetheism has a number of applications. The variety of these, and the fact that the theory holds a key that unlocks many problems, provide further vindications of dialetheism. In discussing the possible applications I shall not try to be comprehensive. For example, it may be argued that dialetheism can be applied in quantum mechanics, or to the theories of vagueness, of infinitesimals, and of non-existent objects; but I shall make no further mention of these.[1] One important family of applications concerns various modalities, such as the temporal and deontic ones. I will discuss these later, and relate them to change and to the philosophy of law, respectively. The most obvious applications of the theory are to set theory and to semantics. Hence the first thing I will do is to return to these topics. We will see that dialetheism is not without relevance to the philosophy of language and the philosophy of mathematics. Let us start, in this chapter, with semantics.

9.2 A SEMANTICALLY CLOSED THEORY

In chapter 1 I argued that a natural language such as English is semantically closed, and in particular that it satisfies the Tarski closure conditions. Can we produce a theory in a formal language that models (in the sense of section 5.1) this phenomenon? The answer is 'yes', as I will now show. How to do this is, in essence, very easy; using the language of section 6.7, we merely designate one of the two-place predicates as the satisfaction predicate, give recursive satisfaction conditions, and prove the T-scheme in the usual way. It might be thought that difficulties lurk in some unsuspected place in this enterprise. To allay these fears,

---

[1] Some details of these can be found in Priest and Routley (1983), ch. 4.

I shall spell out the construction in some detail. First of all, I will allow the construction to use the exclusion principle. (In effect, this principle will be just half of the truth conditions for negation.) I will then indicate the modifications that permit it to go through without this principle.

Let L be the language of section 6.7, a first order language with identity and an implication operator. For reasons that will become clear later, we will take this to be the $\Rightarrow$ of section 6.5, and consider $\rightarrow$ to be defined in terms of it, as indicated there. $\leftrightarrow$, $\vee$ and $\forall$ are also thought of as defined in the usual way. It will be useful to suppose that the variables are indexed by the natural numbers, N, and the constants are indexed by a subset of the natural numbers, K. So the variables are $\{v_n \mid n \in N\}$ and the constants are $\{c_k \mid k \in K\}$. We might consider the variables and constants to be generated from a finite stock of symbols in the usual way. Informally, we consider the variables to range over numbers, sequences, formulas, and maybe other objects too. It would be possible to use a many-sorted language with different variables for each kind of entity. None the less, as we shall see, this is unnecessary, and it is simpler to stick with a single-sorted language. As a purely mnemonic device, I will use three distinct sorts of syntactic variable for variables: $x, y, x_1, \ldots$; $a, a_1, \ldots$; $s, s_1, \ldots$ The official language is, however, single-sorted.

Some of the predicates, functions, and constant symbols of L will have special uses; hence we will use special notations for them. Thus, we will write one of the two-place predicates as 'Sat' and think of this as the satisfaction predicate. Normally, to make sense of the notion of satisfaction we would need to suppose the first argument to be a sequence and the second a formula. However, we may suppose that nothing satisfies a non-formula, and, as we shall see below, by defining the notion of functional application sufficiently generally, we can make sense of the notion of satisfaction even when the first argument is not a sequence. We will also write three of the one-place predicates as 'Nat', 'Form', and 'Term', and think of these as denoting the set of natural numbers, the set of formulas, and terms of L, respectively. Among the constants, we must suppose that, for each logical constant, bracket, predicate, and function symbol, there is a constant that is its name. If α is one of these symbols, I will write its name as $\underline{\alpha}$, though underlining is not itself a symbol of L; and for typographical reasons I will write the names of (and) as [and], respectively. We will also need a constant to denote 0. With crushing originality, we will let that be $\underline{0}$. Among the function symbols, we will need to distinguish the following:

1. A one-place function symbol, Suc. Suc denotes the successor function. For the numeral $\underline{0}$ followed by n 'Suc's, we will write $\underline{n}$ in the usual way. Since we are working with a single sorted theory, the value of the denotation of Suc needs to be defined at arguments other than numbers. It does not really matter how this is done, but the simplest thing is to take the successor of every non-number to be itself.

2. Two one-place function symbols, Const and Var. Intuitively, the denotation of Var is a function that maps each number, n, to v_n. We may suppose that it maps non-numbers to v_0. Similarly, the denotation of Const is a function that maps k to c_k if $k \in K$, and an arbitrary but fixed constant symbol otherwise.

3. A two-place function symbol, Conc. Conc is the concatenation function. If we identify each object with its unit sequence, then Conc denotes a function that elides a pair of sequences into a single sequence. We will write Conc $x\,y$ as $x + y$ and, since concatenation is associative, omit parentheses. The concatenation function allows us to specify a canonical name, $\underline{\alpha}$, which is itself a closed term of L, for each term and formula, α, of L, thus:

$\underline{v}_n$ is Var $\underline{n}$ for $n \in N$

$\underline{c}_k$ is Const $\underline{k}$ for $k \in K$

These, with the names of the logical constants, function and predicate symbols, give a name for each symbol of L. For any string of symbols $s = s_1 \ldots s_m$:

$\underline{s}$ is $\underline{s}_1 + \ldots + \underline{s}_m$

4. A two-place function symbol, Ap, and a three-place function symbol, Sub. Intuitively, Ap $t\,t_1$ denotes the value of the function (denoted by) t at the argument (denoted by) t_1, and Sub $t\,t_1\,t_2$ denotes the function that is the same as (that denoted by) t except that its value at the argument (denoted by) t_1 is (denoted by) t_2. However, since t may not be a function—or, if it is, t_1 may not be in its range—we need to give a slightly more general informal interpretation. This we do as follows. The interpretations of Ap and Sub are, respectively, the functions g and h defined by:

$$g(x, y) = z, \text{ if } z \text{ is the unique } w \text{ such that } <y, w> \in x$$
$$= y, \text{ otherwise}$$
$$h(x, y, z) = x - \{w \mid \text{ for some } u, w = <y, u>\} \cup \{<y, z>\}$$

For ease of notation, I will write Ap $t\,t_1$ as $t(t_1)$ and Sub $t\,t_1 t_2$ as $t(t_1/t_2)$.

5. A two-place function symbol, Den. Intuitively, if t is a term of L, Den $s\,t$ is the denotation of t when its free variables are assigned denotations as *per s*. Otherwise we may think of Den $s\,t$ as fixed but arbitrary. We will write Den $s\,t$ as Den$_s(t)$.

Having looked at the language L and its informal interpretation, we can now specify the axioms of the truth theory. I will separate those that concern the mathematical machinery (group I), from those that concern the syntactic machinery (group II), from those that concern denotation (group III), from those that concern satisfaction (group IV).

Group I

1. (a) Suc $x \neq \underline{0}$
   (b) Suc $x =$ Suc $y \rightarrow x = y$
   (c) Nat $\underline{0}$
   (d) Nat $x \rightarrow$ Nat Suc x
2. $a =$ Ap $s(x/a)\, x$
3. $x \neq y \rightarrow$ Ap $s y =$ Ap $s(x/a)\, y$

A few comments: It is easy enough to check that all these axioms are true in the informal interpretation I have sketched. The fragment of Peano arithmetic in 1 suffices to prove Nat $\underline{n}$ for every natural number n, and $\underline{n} \neq \underline{m}$ for every pair of distinct numbers n and m. Simple informal inductions suffice to show these facts. All the axioms of group I would be provable in the more general context of (dialetheic) set theory/number theory. For present purposes, it is not necessary to be that general. There is also some independent interest in isolating exactly the arithmetic and set theoretic principles necessary for the construction.

Group II

1. Associativity for concatenation, $+$.
2. (a) Term Var x
   (b) Term Const x
   (c) Term $x_1 \wedge \ldots \wedge$ Term $x_n \rightarrow$ Term $f + x_1 + \ldots + x_n$ for every n-place function symbol, f.
3. (a) Term $x_1 \wedge \ldots \wedge$ Term $x_n \rightarrow$ Form $\underline{P} + x_1 + \ldots + x_n$ for every n-place predicate, P
   (b) Form $x \wedge$ Form $y \rightarrow$ Form $[+x + \underline{\wedge} + y+] \wedge$ Form $[+x+ \underline{\Rightarrow} +y+]$
   $\wedge$ Form $\underline{\neg} + x$
   (c) Form $y \rightarrow$ Form $\underline{\exists} +$ Var $x + y$

Group III

1. Nat $x \rightarrow$ Den$_s$ (Var x) $= s(x)$
2. Den$_s$(Const $\underline{k}$) $= c_k$ for $k \in K$
3. Term $x_1 \wedge \ldots \wedge$ Term $x_n \rightarrow$ Den$_s(f + x_1 + \ldots + x_n) = f$ Den$_s(x_1) \ldots$ Den$_s(x_n)$ for all n-place function symbols, f.

All the axioms in groups II and III are true in the informal interpretation indicated. Finally, for satisfaction, we could take the satisfaction scheme itself, but it is more illuminating to take the axioms for satisfaction to be as follows:

Group IV

1. Term $x_1 \wedge \ldots \wedge$ Term $x_n \rightarrow$ (Sat s $\underline{P} + x_1 + \ldots + x_n \leftrightarrow P$ Den$_s(x_1) \ldots$ Den$_s(x_n)$) for all n-place predicates, P.

2. Form x ∧ Form $y \rightarrow$ (Sat s [$+x+\underline{\wedge}+y+$] $\leftrightarrow$ Sat $s x$ ∧ Sat $s y$)
3. Form $x \rightarrow$ (Sat $s \underline{\neg}+x \leftrightarrow \neg$Sat $s x$)
4. Form x ∧ Form $y \rightarrow$ (Sat s [$+x+\underline{\Rightarrow}+y+$] $\leftrightarrow$ (Sat $s x \Rightarrow$ Sat $s y$)))
5. Form x ∧ Nat $y \rightarrow$ (Sat $s \underline{\exists}+$Var $y+x \leftrightarrow \exists b$ Sat $s(y/b) x$), where b is a variable distinct from x, y, and s.

Again, all these axioms are true in the given interpretation. Perhaps one should just note that particular instances of 1 are:

Term x_1 ∧ Term $x_2 \rightarrow$ (Sat s $\underline{\text{Sat}}+x_1+x_2 \leftrightarrow$ Sat Den$_s(x_1)$ Den$_s(x_2)$))

Term x_1 ∧ Term $x_2 \rightarrow$ (Sat $s \equiv +x_1+x_2 \leftrightarrow$ Den$_s(x_1) =$ Den$_s(x_2)$))

One might also note that, provided the collection of non-logical symbols of L is finite, so is the axiomatisation.

It is now an orthodox matter to prove the T-scheme for L. If we define Tx, as usual, as $\forall s$ Sat $s x$, then we have the following theorem, whose proof can be found in the appendix to this chapter (section 9.5).

Theorem
For every closed formula, β, of L, $T\underline{\beta} \leftrightarrow \beta$ is provable.

The construction may be performed without the exclusion principle by making the following modifications. The T-scheme can now no longer be taken to be a bi-entailment, as we saw in section 4.9. Instead, we must formulate it in terms of a non-contraposible implication, $\Rightarrow$. All the bi-conditionals of the axioms in Group IV are therefore replaced by $\Leftrightarrow$. (But note that one-way entailments may be left alone.)

So far, this is all straightforward. Since $\Rightarrow$ does not contrapose, however, the induction step for negation in the proof of the satisfaction scheme now breaks down. To get around this problem, we need to introduce a new predicate, Asat (antisatisfaction), which is to falsity what satisfaction is to truth. Axiom 3 of Group IV is now replaced by

3'. Form $x \rightarrow$ (Sat $s \underline{\neg}+x \Leftrightarrow$ Asat $s x$)

We also need to add a group of axioms which state the recursive antisatisfaction conditions of formulas. By and large, these are obvious in virtue of the discussion of falsity conditions in chapters 5 and 6, and require little comment. It should be noted that, to state the antisatisfaction conditions of $\Rightarrow$, it is necessary to employ the possibility operator, M, of section 6.6. The employment is an entirely natural one, given the falsity conditions of implication. Let us call the antisatisfaction axioms Group V.

Group V

1. Term x_1 ∧ ... ∧ Term $x_n \rightarrow$ (Asat $s \underline{P}+x_1+...+x_n \Leftrightarrow \neg P$ Den$_s(x_1)$ ... Den$_s(x_n)$)) for all n-place predicates, P.

2. Form $x \wedge$ Form $y \rightarrow$ (Asat $s\ [\,+x+\underline{\wedge}+y+\,] \Leftrightarrow$ Asat $s\ x \vee$ Asat $s\ y$)
3. Form $x \rightarrow$ (Asat $s\ \underline{\neg}+x \Leftrightarrow$ Sat $s\ x$)
4. Form $x\ \wedge$ Form $y \rightarrow$ (Asat $s\ [\,+x+\underline{\Rightarrow}+y+\,] \Leftrightarrow$ M(Sat $s\ x\ \wedge$ Asat $s\ y$))
5. Form $x\ \wedge$ Nat $y \rightarrow$ (Asat $s\ \underline{\exists}+$ Var $y+x \Leftrightarrow \forall b$ Asat $s(y/b)\ x$), where b is a variable distinct from x, y, and s.

With these new axioms, the T-scheme can be proved much as before, though the proof now requires us to prove not only the satisfaction scheme, but its dual, the antisatisfaction scheme. Full details can be found in the appendix to the chapter (section 9.5).

9.3 COMMENTS ON THE CONSTRUCTION

There are a couple of points concerning the constructions of the previous section that are worth airing. First, there is the question of the consistency of the truth theories produced (the one with the exclusion principle and the other without). To be honest, whether or not they are inconsistent I do not know. This may seem surprising, since I showed in section 1.2 that any theory which contains its own satisfaction predicate is inconsistent. However, the notion of satisfaction employed there was that of a formula with one free variable by an object. The notion of satisfaction used in the above constructions is the slightly more general one of an (arbitrary) formula by a sequence. We can define the more restricted notion in a fairly obvious way, but it would appear that the appropriate satisfaction scheme for it is not forthcoming, at least not as the theories stand, and I know of no other way in which the theories can be shown to be inconsistent. None the less, if the theories are consistent, they are so for the purely accidental reason that to show the appropriate form of the satisfaction scheme requires some principles about the existence of sequences over and above those so far required; and these principles are entirely unproblematic. The following will, for example, do:

$$\text{Nat } y \rightarrow \exists s\ s(y) = x \qquad \text{(Seq)}$$

Every object is the yth member of some sequence. Once this is added to the theory and, for technical reasons, we strengthen Axiom I, 1(c) to Axiom I, 1(c'): L Nat $\underline{0}$, the expected inconsistency is forthcoming. The proof can, again, be found in the appendix to this chapter, section 9.5.

There are also other natural ways in which the theory will become inconsistent if it is not already so. One of these is by the addition of an "empirical" premise of the form:

$$c = \underline{\neg Tc}$$

the liar sentence. Another is by extending the arithmetic axioms of Group I to contain more of Peano arithmetic. In this way we can prove the diagonal lemma (as in section 3.5) and use it to produce the necessary measure of self reference.

A harder question than that of the inconsistency of the theories, or rather the theories augmented by (Seq), is their triviality. Can everything be proved in them? I do not know the answer to this. Certainly the swift arguments to triviality, such as Curry's, fail. In the absence of a proof of non-triviality, however, there may be others, and a proof of triviality would be a knock-down argument against the acceptability of the theories. The techniques for proving non-triviality are still in their infancy, and I do not yet know of any that can be shown to solve the problem for the above theories. For what it is worth, the limited evidence that there is suggests that they are non-trivial. In particular, theories that are structurally similar, such as set theory, have been shown to be non-trivial, as I will discuss in section 10.1. Still, the question remains to be settled.

The next comment is that the constructions provide much more sophisticated examples of the sort of situation that we noted in section 4.3, where truth conditions loop. In particular, there is no question of turning either theory of truth into a second order explicit definition of truth in the usual way. For, as we noted in section 9.2, the notion of satisfaction itself occurs on the righthand side of some of the axioms stating satisfaction conditions. This does not matter. The aim of the enterprise was not to formulate a definition of truth. (An account of truth was given in chapter 4.) The aim was to show how it is possible for a theory to give the truth conditions of the sentences of its own language. And it does not matter for this that the truth conditions (or, actually, satisfaction conditions) of some of the sentences employ the notion of satisfaction itself. If one were trying to state the truth conditions of all sentences in a way which employs no semantic notions, and hence to *reduce* semantic notions to non-semantic ones, this would of course, show that the construction fails; but such an attempt, like so many reductionist ones, would appear to be quixotic. It is really no surprise if the truth conditions of semantic sentences need to contain semantic notions, just as it is no surprise if the truth conditions of set theoretic sentences need to contain set theoretic notions. Certainly this fact does not, *per se*, show that these sentences have no determinate truth conditions or truth value, as we noted in section 4.3.

None the less, the fact that semantic notions are not eliminable from the truth conditions of certain sentences, that their truth conditions are not "well founded", is important. For it allows for the possibility of "fixed points", that is, sentences whose truth (or satisfaction) conditions are the very sentences quoted on the lefthand side of the truth (or satisfaction) scheme. Thus, by numerous processes of self reference we can find a formula α, of the form $T\underline{\alpha}$. For such an α, the statement of truth conditions seems doomed to take the unilluminating form $T\underline{\alpha} \Leftrightarrow T\underline{\alpha}$. This may be harmless enough. But, of course, sometimes the situation may arise with a not-so-subtle twist. For we may find a sentence whose truth (or satisfaction) condition is the negation of the sentence quoted on the lefthand side of the biconditional. Such an example is given in the proof of inconsistency in section 9.5. A simpler example is provided if we can find, by a suitable process of self reference, a sentence, α, of the form $\neg T\underline{\alpha}$. In such cases the statement of truth conditions is of the form $\beta \Leftrightarrow \neg\beta$, and paradox is the result.

9.4 TRUTH AND MEANING

We have seen that it is quite possible for a theory to satisfy the Tarski closure conditions, and hence to be semantically closed. In this section, we will see how this fact solves a pressing problem for the theory of meaning. Central to any acceptable theory of meaning is a theory of truth. For every sentence of the language in question, the theory of truth spells out the truth conditions, or, possibly, truth-in-a-possible-world conditions, for that sentence. These truth conditions state the meaning of the sentence. Moreover, a suitable truth theory spells out how the truth[2] (in-a-possible-world) conditions of sentences are dependent upon those of their parts. In this way the theory shows how the meanings of wholes are determined by those of their parts, and thus explains how it is that we can understand the meanings of wholes we have never heard before, given that we understand the meanings of their parts and how they are put together. The reasons for the above facts are well known and have already been rehearsed, at least in part, in section 4.3. I will not, therefore, repeat them.

Now, these facts pose a problem, at least if we adopt the orthodox view that inconsistencies are intolerable, and in particular that truth is consistent. For let us suppose that we are interested in a theory of meaning for a natural language such as English. Each meaningful sentence of the language (without indexicals) must have its meaning stated in the theory, which means that it must participate in an instance of the T-scheme (or possibly its generalisation to possible worlds). Yet, as we saw in chapter 1, any theory in which the T-scheme holds for all the sentences of its own language is inconsistent.

It is clear that this is no problem for the dialetheist. We have seen in section 9.2 how it is possible to give a theory of truth for the language in which the theory is couched. All instances of the T-scheme are provable, as are the semantic paradoxes. This does not matter, at least as long as inconsistency does not spread to triviality, which we may reasonably assume to be the case. Nor is there any particular reason why, if a truth theory is to be used as the base for a theory of meaning, the theory needs to be consistent. For example, it does not wreck the theory as a theory of meaning even if an instance of the T-scheme, $T\underline{\alpha} \Leftrightarrow \alpha'$, is both provable and refutable.[3] All that is necessary is that the theory produce a determinate instance of the T-scheme for each sentence, and do this in a way that exposes the

---

[2] Or, at least, satisfaction. In this section the distinction is unimportant and I shall ignore it.

[3] Nor would this necessarily mean that α both means that α' and does not mean that α'. We can consider α' to state the meaning of α without supposing that 'is true iff' is to be read as 'means that'. Moreover, if we do insist that it is to be read this way, this hardly seems intolerable. Why should the theory of meaning not have singularities in it too? Is it not quite plausible that the liar sentence both means the same as itself and, since it means the same as its negation, does not mean the same as itself?

connection between truth conditions of sentences and those of their sub-formulas. Moreover, if one thinks that it should be a theory of truth-in-a-possible-world (and not a theory of truth *simpliciter*) that is at the heart of a theory of meaning, it is clear, in principle, how dialetheism allows for this possibility too.[4] Dialetheism therefore solves a fundamental problem of semantics.[5]

Orthodox semanticists have been aware of this problem for semantics and the theory of meaning as long as the formal semantics of natural language have been on the agenda. By and large, the problem has been avoided rather than faced. In practical terms, this has meant concentrating on giving the formal semantics of languages (or fragments of natural language) which do not themselves contain semantic notions. The sentences of such languages have well founded truth conditions, and hence no problems arise. However, the problem cannot be ignored once we wish to give the semantics of languages that themselves contain semantic notions, and in particular if we wish to give a reasonably comprehensive semantics for a natural language such as English.

A few half-hearted indications of how a more orthodox solution to the problem might go have been given. For example, it has been suggested that a language must be incapable of giving its own semantical theory, and hence that the semantics of English cannot be given in English.[6] The unsatisfactoriness of this need hardly be stressed. First, it leaves the semantics of the English predicate 'is true' a complete mystery. And if this does not mean what we think it means, then we cannot be sure that the claim that truth conditions state meaning is correct. Secondly, if someone knows the meanings of sentences of a language, it would seem to follow that he knows the propositions expressed by the T-sentences to be true. Yet if the inexpressibility thesis is right, this is not something that he can express. Now, while it may be all right to attribute very simple beliefs to a creature that cannot express them, there are obviously problems about supposing that a person has inexpressible beliefs of the degree of abstraction and logical complexity of the T-scheme.[7] But apart from anything else, the inexpressibility thesis is just obviously false, or as obviously false as anything can be in philosophy. There is, perhaps, no way of proving this until we have an adequate formal account of

---

[4] I leave the construction of a semantically closed truth-in-a-possible-world theory as a distinctly non-trivial exercise. I note, however, that there are reasons for supposing that it is a truth (*simpliciter*) theory and not a truth-in-a-possible-world theory that is at the heart of a theory of meaning, even if the language involved is a modal one, as it (effectively) is in this case; see Davies (1981), pp. 193–201. The theory of truth required for an account of validity is, of course, a different matter.

[5] An anonymous referee once quipped that the problem is solved in the same way that calling cancer healthy solves the problem of cancer. It is certainly true that I am recommending that we solve a problem by accepting what was hitherto thought of as unacceptable: some contradictions. And if this were all there were to the suggestion it would indeed be silly. But it is not. I have tried to show how contradictions can be accepted without the disastrous effects they are normally taken to have, and even with, perhaps, some beneficial effects. If a way could be found of preventing cancers from having their unfortunate effects, and even of making them beneficial, the problem of cancer would indeed be solved. [6] See Davidson (1967), p. 314.

[7] This argument is discussed further in Priest and Crosthwaite (1988).

English grammar and semantics. But give me any formal language that is supposed to be a (perhaps crude) model of (parts of) English, together with semantics for that language, and I will give you a semantics for that language in English. Of course, I will use a bit of jargon, some technicalities, and a bit of mathematics, but this is no more than is granted to any English-speaking scientist.

The point is that to suppose a natural language to be incapable of providing its own semantics flies in the face of what Tarski called the universality of natural language:[8] anything that can be said can be said in English. *Maybe* it can be argued that the thesis of the universality of natural language is false on the grounds of conceptual relativism or incommensurability. But it is hardly arguable that the notion *true sentence of English* is incommensurable with the English vernacular when the phrase 'is a true sentence of English' is part of that very vernacular.[9] And, of course, semanticists do not really believe that the semantics of English are expressible only in another language. At least, I have not noticed classes of Hindi, Urdu, and Mandarin swelled by the ranks of semanticists keen to see whether these languages contain the key to the ineffable.

As we saw in chapter 1, perhaps the major suggestion for solving the paradoxes, certainly for someone who wishes to preserve classical logic, is the rejection of the T-scheme. Whatever the merits of this suggestion as a solution to the semantic paradoxes (and, as we saw, it has few enough), this is not a move that is open to someone who requires a theory of truth as the core of a theory of meaning. For, as we noted in section 4.3, it is precisely the T-scheme (or its generalisation to possible worlds) which plays the role of stating the meaning of a sentence. Someone might note that what chapter 1 showed was that it is the homophonic T-scheme that leads to contradiction, and suggest that if we take it in a non-homophonic form, the problem may be avoided. In its non-homophonic form, the T-scheme reads:

$$T\underline{\alpha} \Leftrightarrow \alpha'$$

Where α' means the same as α, but is not α itself. (For example, if α is a modal sentence, α' might be some possible-worlds translation; or if α contains a definite description, α' might be its Russellean paraphrase.) Now, indeed, the immediate proof of contradiction is blocked, at least until we spell out the details of α' further; but the suggestion will not avoid the problem: it is clear that a necessary (though perhaps not sufficient) condition for α' to be a translation of α is that these be logically equivalent. (If it were possible for one to hold when the other did not, they could not even convey the same information.) Hence

$$\alpha' \Leftrightarrow \alpha.$$

But in this case, the homophonic version of the T-scheme is quickly forthcoming again.

---

[8] Tarski (1936), p. 164 of reprint.

[9] One might also note that Davidson himself has rejected the whole notion of conceptual relativism; see Davidson (1973).

Another response that the meaning-theorist might make is to suggest that a suitable theory of truth should not be required to prove every instance of the T-scheme, but only those instances for sentences, α that are meaningful. If a paradoxical sentence is meaningless (as, of course, many people have suggested), then its T-sentence need not be forthcoming. Indeed, we may take the fact that an appropriate T-sentence is not forthcoming as a precise way of spelling out the claim that the sentence has no truth conditions, and thus no meaning. In chapter 1 I discussed the possibility of solving the paradoxes by supposing them to be meaningless (Valueless), and showed it not to work. For example, such suggestions fall foul of the extended paradoxes. More importantly in the present context, there are good reasons why, if a theory of meaning is to be based on the theory of truth, this suggestion will not work. For, as has been stressed by Davidson, if a truth theory is to be the basis of an adequate theory of meaning for a language, it must be axiomatisable,[10] that is, recursively enumerable (r.e.). Unless it is r.e. it does not explain how it is that a person can grasp the meanings of a potentially infinite number of sentences on the basis of a finite (or at least decidable) amount of information. Unfortunately, as we shall now see, a truth theory for any sufficiently rich language, of the kind required by this suggestion, cannot be r.e. if it is consistent; as the following proof shows, it cannot even be arithmetic.

Consider a language, L, which contains that of Peano arithmetic, together with a truth predicate, T. English, for example, is such a language. Via the usual Gödelisation, we can take the truth predicate to be a predicate of natural numbers. Now a theory of truth for L is not required to prove all instances of the T-scheme. It is required to prove those and only those for which the sentence in question is meaningful, that is, on this model, those and only those for which the T-sentence is true (on some understanding of truth, the onus for the production of which is on the proponent). Let S be a semantic theory which does this, and suppose that S is r.e. Since we can effectively tell a homophonic T-sentence when we see one, and then effectively determine which sentence it is the T-sentence for, it follows that the set of meaningful sentences (that is, sentences for which the T-scheme holds) is r.e. too. Hence there is a formula of the language of arithmetic, $\alpha(x)$, such that $\alpha(\underline{m})$ is true iff m is (the code of) a meaningful formula. By the usual diagonal construction, we can find a sentence,$\neg\alpha(\underline{n}) \vee \neg T\underline{n}$, whose code number is n. Let us call this β. If $\alpha(\underline{n})$ is true, then the T-scheme holds for β. Thus:

$$\alpha(\underline{n}) \supset (T\underline{n} \equiv \neg\alpha(\underline{n}) \vee \neg T\underline{n})$$

whence $\neg\alpha(\underline{n})$. Thus $\neg\alpha(\underline{n}) \vee \neg T\underline{n}$, i.e., β. But if β is true, then β is certainly meaningful. That is, the T-scheme holds for β i.e., $\alpha(\underline{n})$.[11] Contradiction. Hence, by *reductio*, S is not r.e.

---

[10] Davidson (1965). In fact, he claims that it must be finitely axiomatisable. But this seems to me not to be right.

[11] The last inference proceeds in virtue of the principle: β; hence α $(\underline{m})$ (where m is the code of β), which is clearly truth-preserving in the intended intepretation.

A desperate way of blocking a couple of steps in the argument is to say that, if *m* is the code of a meaningless sentence, ¬T*m* is itself meaningless, and that the meaninglessness of a part spreads to the meaninglessness of the whole. This line cannot be maintained: if *m* is the code of a meaningless sentence, then, since it is not true, ¬T*m* is *true* in the intended interpretation, not meaningless.[12]

The preceding application of the extended liar paradox (for indeed it is he) shows that the theory of meaning cannot reject those instances of the T-scheme that lead to contradiction on the ground that the sentences involved are meaningless. Hence the theory of meaning requires us to accept the T-scheme, and therefore blocks the main avenue for solving the semantical paradoxes.

There therefore seems no orthodox solution to this problem for semantics. Even if there were, it would be clear from the above considerations that it would have to be a fairly tortured one, compared with which the dialetheic position is so simple and natural that one would have to be singularly perverse to choose the consistent solution. An honest approach to the theory of meaning for natural language requires dialetheism; and dialetheism solves a central problem for the philosophy of language.

9.5 APPENDIX: PROOFS OF THEOREMS

In this appendix I will prove the facts claimed in sections 9.2 and 9.3. I will prove the T-scheme first for the theory with the exclusion principle, and then for the theory without it (but with the notion of antisatisfaction). Finally, I will show how the truth theories, together with the sequence principle, (Seq), are inconsistent.

The proof of the T-scheme for the first theory proceeds in a series of lemmas.

Lemma 1
If t is a term of L, we can prove Term $\underline{t}$.

Proof. By an informal induction, if t is v_k, then by II, 2(a), Term Var $\underline{k}$, i.e. Term $\underline{v_k}$. If t is c_k, then by II, 2(b), Term Const $\underline{k}$, i.e. Term $\underline{c_k}$. If t is $ft_1 \ldots t_n$ and we have proved Term $\underline{t_1} \wedge \ldots \wedge$ Term $\underline{t_n}$, then by II, 2(c), we prove Term $\underline{ft_1 \ldots t_n}$.

Lemma 2
If α is a formula of L, we can prove Form $\underline{\alpha}$.

Proof. Again, the proof is by an informal induction. If $t_1, \ldots, t_n$ are terms and α is $Pt_1 \ldots t_n$, then by lemma 1 we have proved Term $\underline{t_1} \wedge \ldots \wedge$ Term $\underline{t_n}$. Hence by II, 3(a), we prove Form $\underline{Pt_1 \ldots t_n}$. Suppose that β and δ are formulas, that α is $(\beta \wedge \delta)$, and that we have proved Form $\underline{\beta} \wedge$ Form $\underline{\delta}$. Then by II, 3(b), we prove

---

[12] Against this suggestion see also ch. 1, fn. 15, and the text thereto.

Form $(\beta \wedge \delta)$ i.e. Form $\underline{\alpha}$. The cases when α is $\neg\beta$ or $(\beta \Rightarrow \delta)$ are similar, using the rest of II, 3(b). If α is $\exists v_k\beta$, and we have proved Form $\underline{\beta}$, then by II, 3(c) we prove Form $\underline{\exists v_k\beta}$.

Definition

To state subsequent lemmas we need the notion of relativisation. If α is any formula *or* term of L, and t is any term of L, α_t (α relativised to t) is α with every free variable 'v_k' replaced by '$t(\underline{k})$' (i.e. 'Ap t $\underline{k}$').

Lemma 3

For any term t of L, we can prove $\text{Den}_s(\underline{t}) = t_s$.

Proof. The proof is by an informal induction. If t is a variable, v_n, we can prove Nat $\underline{n}$; so by III, 1, Den_s (Var $\underline{n}$) $= s(\underline{n})$, i.e., $\text{Den}_s(\underline{v_n}) = t_s$. If t is a constant, c_k, III, 2 gives us that Den_s (Const $\underline{k}$) $= c_k$, i.e. $\text{Den}_s(\underline{c_k}) = t_s$. If t is $f t_1 \ldots t_m$, and we have proved $\text{Den}_s(\underline{t_i}) - t_{is}$ for $1 \leq i \leq n$, then, since we have proved Term $\underline{t_1} \wedge \ldots \wedge$ Term $\underline{t_n}$ by lemma 1, it follows by III, 3 that $\text{Den}_s(\underline{f\, t_1 \ldots t_n}) = f\, \text{Den}_s(\underline{t_1})$ $\ldots \text{Den}_s(\underline{t_n})$. Hence by the substitutivity of identicals $\text{Den}_s(\underline{f\, t_1 \ldots t_n}) = f\, t_{1s}$ $\ldots t_{ns} = (f t_1 \ldots t_n)_s$.

Lemma 4

If α is any formula of L, we can prove Sat s $\underline{\alpha} \leftrightarrow \alpha_s$.

Proof. The proof is by an informal induction: If $t_1, \ldots, t_n$ are terms and α is $Pt_1 \ldots t_m$ we know we can prove Term $\underline{t_1} \wedge \ldots \wedge$ Term $\underline{t_n}$ by Lemma 1. So by IV, 1,

$$\text{Sat } s\ \underline{Pt_1 \ldots t_n} \leftrightarrow P\ \text{Den}_s(\underline{t_1}) \ldots \text{Den}_s(\underline{t_n})$$

Hence by Lemma 3 and the substitutivity of identicals,

$$\text{Sat } s\ \underline{Pt_1 \ldots t_n} \leftrightarrow P\, t_{1s} \ldots t_{ns} \leftrightarrow (Pt_1 \ldots t_n)_s$$

Now suppose that α is $(\beta \wedge \delta)$ where β and δ are formulas for which we have proved the result. We can prove Form $\underline{\beta} \wedge$ Form $\underline{\delta}$ by Lemma 2. Hence by IV, 2 we prove

$$\text{Sat } s\ \underline{(\beta \wedge \delta)} \leftrightarrow (\text{Sat } s\ \underline{\beta} \wedge \text{Sat } s\ \underline{\delta})$$

By the induction hypothesis and the substitutivity of bientailments (see section 6.4),

$$\text{Sat } s\ \underline{(\beta \wedge \delta)} \leftrightarrow (\beta_s \wedge \delta_s) \leftrightarrow (\beta \wedge \delta)_s$$

The cases when α is $(\beta \Rightarrow \delta)$ or $\neg\beta$ are similar using IV, 3 and 4.

Suppose that α is $\exists v_k\beta$, where β is a formula of L, and where we have proved Form $\underline{\beta}$ by Lemma 2, and Nat $\underline{k}$. IV, 5 gives us that

$$\forall s\ \forall y\ \forall x\ (\text{From } x \wedge \text{Nat } y \rightarrow (\text{Sat } s\ \underline{\exists} + \text{Var } y + x \leftrightarrow \exists b\ \text{Sat } s(y/b)\ x))$$

Relabelling bound variables if necessary, we can take it that s is distinct from the variables in β and from v_k, and that b is v_k. Now instantiating x and y, and detaching, we get

$$\text{Sat } s \; \underline{\exists} + \text{Var } \underline{k} + \underline{\beta} \leftrightarrow \exists v_k \text{Sat } s(\underline{k}/v_k) \, \underline{\beta}$$

and so, by induction hypothesis,

$$\text{Sat } s \; \underline{\exists v_k \beta} \leftrightarrow \exists v_k (\beta_{s(\underline{k}/v_k)})$$

If we can prove $\exists v_k(\beta_{s(\underline{k}/v_k)}) \leftrightarrow (\exists v_k \beta)_s$, we are home. Now $(\exists v_k \beta)_s$ is of the form $\exists v_k \beta'$ where β' is the same as β except that, where

   (i) β contains 'v_k' free, β' contains 'v_k' free;
   (ii) if $i \neq k$ and β contains 'v_i' free, β' contains '$s(\underline{i})$'.

Hence, since 's' is distinct from 'v_k' and from all the variables in β, β' and $\beta_s(\underline{k}/v_k)$ are the same except that

   (i) where the former contains 'v_k' free the latter contains '$s(\underline{k}/v_k)(\underline{k})$'
   (ii) where the former contains '$s(\underline{i})$' $(i \neq k)$ the latter contains '$s(\underline{k}/v_k)(\underline{i})$'.

But by I, 2, $v_k = s(\underline{k}/v_k)(\underline{k})$, and if $i \neq k$ then, since we can prove that $\underline{i} \neq \underline{k}$, by I, 3, $s(\underline{i}) = s(\underline{k}/v_k)(\underline{i})$. Thus, by repeated applications of the substitutivity of identicals, we can prove

$$\beta' \leftrightarrow \beta_s(\underline{k}/v_k)$$

whence what we need follows by simple existential generalisation of both sides. This completes the induction.

The scheme proved in lemma 4 is Tarski's satisfaction scheme. With truth defined as in section 9.1, we can now prove the main theorem.

Theorem
For any closed formula β of L, we can prove $T\underline{\beta} \leftrightarrow \beta$.

Proof. By the satisfaction scheme,

$$\text{Sat } s \; \underline{\beta} \leftrightarrow \beta_s$$

where we may suppose s not to occur in β. Hence

$$T\underline{\beta} \leftrightarrow \forall s(\beta_s)$$

But β is closed. Hence β_s is simply β, and s does not occur free in β. Thus,

$$T\underline{\beta} \leftrightarrow \beta$$

* * *

The modification to the proof required by the introduction of the notion of antisatisfaction affects only lemma 4 essentially. First, we formulate the satisfaction scheme with $\Leftrightarrow$ instead of $\leftrightarrow$. The new satisfaction scheme is entailed by, but does not entail, the old one. Next, we formulate the antisatisfaction scheme:

$$\text{Asat } s \; \underline{\alpha} \Leftrightarrow \neg\alpha_s$$

The new lemma 4 states that both the satisfaction and the antisatisfaction schemes hold. The proof of this proceeds by a joint induction. The steps of the proof for the satisfaction scheme are as before, except that the case for negation now goes as follows:

$$\text{Sat } s \; \underline{\neg} + \underline{\alpha} \Leftrightarrow \text{Asat } s \; \underline{\alpha} \Leftrightarrow \neg\alpha_s$$

by IV, 3′ (with appropriate instantiations and detachments) and the antisatisfaction scheme, used as an induction hypothesis.

For the antisatisfaction scheme, the basis of the induction is provided by V, 1. The induction step for $\wedge$ goes:

$$
\begin{aligned}
\text{Asat } s \; (\underline{\beta \wedge \delta}) &\Leftrightarrow (\text{Asat } s \; \underline{\beta} \vee \text{Asat } s \; \underline{\delta}) && \text{by V, 2.}\\
&\Leftrightarrow \neg\beta_s \vee \neg\delta_s && \text{by induction hypothesis}\\
&\Leftrightarrow \neg(\beta \wedge \delta)_s && \text{by de Morgan laws}
\end{aligned}
$$

The step for $\neg$ goes:

$$
\begin{aligned}
\text{Asat } s \; \underline{\neg\beta} &\Leftrightarrow \text{Sat } s \; \underline{\beta} && \text{by V, 3.}\\
&\Leftrightarrow \beta_s && \text{by induction hypothesis.}\\
&\Leftrightarrow \neg\neg\beta_s && \text{by double negation}
\end{aligned}
$$

The step for $\exists$ goes:

$$
\begin{aligned}
\text{Asat } s \; \underline{\exists v_k \beta} &\Leftrightarrow \forall v_k \; \text{Asat } s(\underline{k}/v_k) \; \underline{\beta} && \text{by V, 5}\\
&\Leftrightarrow \forall v_k (\neg\beta_{s(\underline{k}/v_k)}) && \text{by induction hypothesis}\\
&\Leftrightarrow \neg\exists v_k (\beta_{s(\underline{k}/v_k)}) && \text{by quantifier rules}
\end{aligned}
$$

Now, as in the corresponding case for the satisfaction scheme,

$$\exists v_k (\beta_{s(\underline{k}/v_k)}) \leftrightarrow (\exists v_k \beta)_s$$

The result follows by contraposition (which is legitimate since this is an entailment).

Finally, the case for $\Rightarrow$ goes as follows:

$$\text{Asat } s \; (\underline{\beta \Rightarrow \delta}) \Leftrightarrow M(\text{Sat } s \; \underline{\beta} \wedge \text{Asat } s \, \underline{\delta}) \quad \text{by V, 4}$$

By induction hypothesis,

$$\text{Sat } s \; \underline{\beta} \wedge \text{Asat } s \, \underline{\delta} \Leftrightarrow \beta_s \wedge \neg\delta_s$$

and since $\{ \eta \Leftrightarrow \xi \} \models M\eta \Leftrightarrow M\xi$, as may easily be checked:

$$\text{Asat } s \; (\underline{\beta \Rightarrow \delta}) \Leftrightarrow M(\beta_s \wedge \neg\delta_s)$$

Now, $\models M(\eta \wedge \neg \, \xi) \Leftrightarrow \neg(\eta \Rightarrow \xi)$ as, again, may easily be checked. Hence

Asat s $\underline{(\beta \Rightarrow \delta)} \Leftrightarrow \neg(\beta_s \Rightarrow \delta_s) \Leftrightarrow \neg\underline{(\beta \Rightarrow \delta)_s}$

This completes the induction, and hence the proof of the new lemma 4. The T-scheme now follows from the satisfaction scheme as before, except that this time it is formulated with $\Leftrightarrow$. Note also that, if we define Fx (x is false) as $\forall s$ Asat s x, then the F-scheme $F\underline{\beta} \Leftrightarrow \neg\beta$ (for all closed β) follows from the antisatisfaction scheme in the same way.

* * *

The last thing to be shown in this section is that the theories plus (Seq) lead to a contradiction. Define

$\text{Sat}_1(x \; y)$ as $\exists s(s(\underline{i}) = x \wedge \text{Sat } s \, y)$

for some fixed i. Now, suppose α is any formula with the one free variable, v_i, for which x is freely substitutable:

$\text{Sat}_1(x \; \underline{\alpha}) \Rightarrow \exists s(s(\underline{i}) = x \wedge \text{Sat } s \; \underline{\alpha})$

$\qquad\qquad \Rightarrow \exists s(s(\underline{i}) = x \wedge \alpha(v_i/s(\underline{i})\,))$ by the satisfaction scheme

$\qquad\qquad \Rightarrow \alpha(v_i /x)$ by identity principles

Conversely, from (the strengthened) I, 1(c) and I, 1(d), we prove L Nat $\underline{i}$. Hence, by (Seq) and the fact that $\Rightarrow$ requires only truth preservation,

$\alpha(v_i/x) \Rightarrow \alpha(v_i/x) \wedge \exists s \, s(\underline{i}) = x$

$\qquad\qquad \Rightarrow \exists s(x = s(\underline{i}) \wedge \alpha(v_i/s(\underline{i})\,))$ by identity principles

$\qquad\qquad \Rightarrow \exists s(x = s(\underline{i}) \wedge \text{Sat} s \, \underline{\alpha})$ by the satisfaction scheme

$\qquad\qquad \Rightarrow \text{Sat}_1(x \, \underline{\alpha})$

Hence $\text{Sat}_1(x \, \underline{\alpha}) \Leftrightarrow \alpha(v_i/x)$.

Now, as in 1.2, take $\neg\text{Sat}_1(v_i \; v_i)$ for α and instantiate x with $\neg\underline{\text{Sat}}_1(\underline{v_i} \; \underline{v_i})$ to get a formula equivalent to its negation, and hence a contradiction.

10

Set Theory and The Philosophy of Mathematics

10.1 NAIVE SET THEORY

In the last chapter I discussed "naive" semantics, semantics in which the T-scheme holds for all sentences of the language of the semantic theory, and its relationship to the theory of meaning. Semantics was one of the two theories that played a major role in Part One of the book. The other was set theory. In this chapter I will discuss certain aspects of naive set theory, that is, set theory in which the abstraction scheme holds for all formulas of the language of set theory, and some of its implications for the philosophy of mathematics.

The aspects of the philosophy of mathematics I will discuss are not new—far from it. It is worth reappraising issues in the philosophy of mathematics in the light of dialetheism, however. For all modern discussions, assume that the logic of informal mathematics is classical, or at least intuitionist. More traditional discussions, while hardly based on this assumption, assume, at least, that mathematics is consistent. Since dialetheism suspends both of these assumptions, it is bound to give a new perspective. There are a number of places in the philosophy of mathematics where this perspective is illuminating, but I shall discuss only one in detail: mathematical realism.[1] My discussion throughout will be restricted to pure mathematics. References to mathematics should be understood in this way.

Let us start with a formulation of axiomatic naive set theory, N. The theory is a theory in the first order language of section 6.7, with only one non-logical predicate, $\in$. The axiom schemes of the theory are:

(Abs) $\exists z \forall y (y \in z \leftrightarrow \beta)$

(Ext) $\forall z (z \in x \leftrightarrow z \in y) \rightarrow x = y$

where in (Abs) z does not occur free in β. As I argued in chapter 2, these axioms characterise our intuitive notion of set. Sets just are the extensions of arbitrary predicates.[2]

---

[1] For a number of the others, see Priest and Routley (1983), ch. 5.

[2] In ch. 2 I formulated these principles using $\rightarrow$, which was, at that stage, a generic implication operator. The question now arises as to whether this should be the arrow of entailment or the

The following is a brief survey of the properties of N. As will be clear, there is still much about it that is unknown. One can define standard set theoretical objects (the empty set, the universal set) and operations (union, intersection, complementation, sum set, power set, ordered n-tuples, etc.) in much the same way as usual, and prove that they have the right properties.[3] Using the notion of an ordered pair, one can define relations, functions, injections, etc., and establish their usual properties.[4] This is as much set theory as the working mathematician (including, *nota bene*, the category theorist), who uses set theory only as a tool, needs. Beyond this, things are somewhat less clear. One can prove the existence of infinite sets, as, essentially, did Dedekind. (The map that maps x to $\{x\}$ is an injection of V to itself.) Von Neumann ordinals can be defined in the usual way, as can associated notions such as limit ordinal, cardinal, etc.; but it is not clear that an appropriate version of Cantor's theorem can be proved, since the standard proof of this uses $\rightarrow$ principles not available in Δ. It is also not known whether the novel sets whose existence N allows us to prove can be shown to have important properties. For example, it may be that the category of all categories (of which it, itself, is a member) has interesting category-theoretic properties, or even that N can show the existence of inaccessible cardinals. But these are open questions. One might note that, if we strengthen (*Abs*) to allow z to occur in the formula β, the (global) axiom of choice is provable.[5]

So much for what can be proved. Let us turn to the other side of the coin, what cannot be proved; specifically, what contradictions cannot be proved? It is clear that N is inconsistent: Russell's paradox is forthcoming in the usual way. The triviality of N is, at the present, an open question. Still, there are good reasons for supposing N to be non-trivial. For suppose that we take N to be based not on Δ, but on the relevant logic DK; then the theory is provably non-trivial.[6] Now Δ is very close to DK in logical strength. Very roughly, Δ is DK shorn of a few irrelevancies. Hence it is very likely that N is non-trivial. Non-triviality puts some bounds on what cannot be proved, but only very loose ones. Just how far the contradictions in N spread, or even how this idea can be formulated precisely, is an open problem, even when the theory is formulated with DK as the underlying logic.

non-contraposible $\Rightarrow$. The parallel between the abstraction scheme and the T-scheme *suggests* that the arrow of the abstraction scheme, at least, should be $\Rightarrow$. On the other hand, it seems impossible to raise doubts concerning the contraposibility of the abstraction scheme parallel to those raised against the contraposibility of the T-scheme in sect. 5.4. For the rest of chapter, then, I will assume that the set theoretic principles are formulated in terms of entailment, though I accept that this may be moot.

[3] A certain amount of care does have to be taken. For example, if we define ϕ as $\{x \mid x \neq x\}$ then $x \supseteq \phi$ cannot be proved, since this uses properties of material implication. But if we define it as $\{z \mid \forall x \, z \in x\}$, we can prove that $\neg \exists y \, y \in \phi$, and $x \supseteq \phi$. One cannot, however, prove that $\phi \supseteq x \cap x'$ (where x' is the complement of x), though one can prove $\neg \exists z \, z \in x \cap x'$.

[4] Further details of all these matters can be found in Routley (1977).

[5] See Routley (1977).

[6] See Brady (1989). The proof also shows that the theory is non-trivial even if the variable z is allowed to occur in the formula β in (*Abs*).

It is clear that N raises many interesting and important problems, and that a lot of work is going to be required to solve them. Let me finish this section with a final one. So far I have talked only about the semantic consequences of N. But we saw in section 8.6 that there is a more generous notion of consequence, i.e. *consequence. Exactly what are the *consequences of N? By the theorems of sections 8.6, they must include the semantical consequences of N and be non-trivial if N is. It may be that some of the theorems of ZF, though not theorems of N, are *consequences of N. This remains to be investigated.

10.2 SUBSTITUTIONAL SEMANTICS

So much for what can (and cannot) be proved in N. Let us now turn from proof theory to semantics, where it is possible to be somewhat more definite. It is easy enough to give N a semantics. In the last chapter we saw, in effect, how a semantically closed theory could be given for any language, possibly augmented by certain syntactico-semantic vocabulary. All we need to do, therefore, is to plug the language of N into that construction. These semantics, though technically adequate, have certain drawbacks. First, the truth conditions of sentences are given in terms of satisfaction, and satisfaction is a relation between sentences and extra-linguistic objects. *Prima facie*, therefore, such semantics commit us to mathematical realism. They therefore inherit any problems that mathematical realism has. I will return to this matter in section 10.4. Secondly, though the semantics may give truth conditions for sentences of the language of set theory, there is no way that the theory, as it stands, can prove that the axioms of the theory are true. This, of course, has nothing to do with semantic closure. Given a theory that gives the truth conditions for sentences of a language, extra principles will be required, in general, to prove that some of those conditions obtain. This situation can always be rectified by the addition of those principles to the theory. The T-scheme will then do the required job. However, this way of proceeding is rather trivial, and, just because it is trivial, it is not particularly informative. Sometimes it may be the only way of proceeding; but if a way can be found of giving the truth conditions which itself shows the axioms of a certain theory to be true, this is an important bonus, with philosophical implications that I will return to in section 10.3. Finally, on this construction there is no more connection between set theory and semantics than between any other theory and semantics. *Maybe*, in the end, this is right. But, if for no other reason than the structural similarity between the set theoretic and semantic paradoxes, we have a sneaking suspicion that the connection ought to be closer than this. A semantics for the language of set theory that exposes the connection would, therefore, be highly welcome. These reasons suggest that another approach, if one could be found, might be better. And, as we shall now see, one can be found.

On this alternative approach, the semantics proceed by a judicious use of substitutional quantification. A number of people have noted that a substitutional semantics can be given for the language of arithmetic.[7] The substitution class for the quantifiers is the class of all numerals, and, because every member of the standard model has a canonical name, a sentence is true under these truth conditions just if it is true under the truth conditions generated by satisfaction conditions in the standard model of arithmetic. Turning from arithmetic to set theory, many have felt that we have here a theory for whose language substitutional semantics cannot be given. Why this is, I will return to in the next section. Let us, first, see how they can be given. (As in the previous chapter, I will show how to do this using the exclusion principle; then I will indicate the changes that avoid this.)

To give substitutional truth conditions, we need to have an appropriate substitution class of terms in the language. To this end, we augment the language with a term-forming functor, $\{ \mid \}$, such that, if x is any variable and α is any formula of the language $\{x \mid \alpha\}$ is a term. Using these abstract terms, we can formulate the Abstraction Scheme slightly differently as:

$$(Abs') \quad ©\Pi y(y \in \{x \mid \alpha\} \leftrightarrow \alpha(x/y))$$

where α does not contain y, and where I write the universal quantifier as Π to indicate that it is a substitutional quantifier. I will write the existential substitutional quantifier as Σ.[8] We will take the substitution class of the quantifiers to be the closed set abstracts. The symbol © is of widest scope and indicates universal closure. That is, $©\beta$ is β prefixed by Πx for every variable, x, free in β. (Abs') clearly implies (the universal closure of) (Abs).

Using substitutional quantification, we can give recursive truth conditions for the *closed* formulas of the language, which do not detour through the notion of satisfaction. Supposing that we have given the truth conditions for closed atomic formulas, we can give the recursive truth conditions for compound closed formulas thus:

($\wedge$) $\alpha \wedge \beta$ is true iff α is true and β is true.

($\neg$) $\neg\alpha$ is true iff α is not true.

($\rightarrow$) $\alpha \rightarrow \beta$ is true iff (if α is true then β is true).

(Π) $\Pi y\alpha$ is true iff, for every closed term, t, $\alpha(y/t)$ is true.

The other logical constants can be thought of as defined in the usual ways.

What of the truth conditions of closed atomic sentences? Atomic sentences are of two kinds: $t_1 = t_2$, $t_1 \in t_2$. We could give the obvious homophonic

---

[7] e.g., C. Parsons (1971), Kripke (1976), and Priest (1983a) in which much of the material in this chapter first appeared. [8] This follows the practice of Kripke (1976).

truth-conditions:

$t_1 = t_2$ is true iff $t_1 = t_2$.

$t_1 \in t_2$ is true iff $t_1 \in t_2$.

where the *t*s are schematic for closed terms; but we may give the truth conditions in a more illuminating way thus:

(=) $\{x \mid \alpha\} = \{x \mid \beta\}$ is true iff for all closed terms, t, $\alpha(x/t)$

is true iff $\beta(x/t)$ is true.

(∈) $t \in \{x \mid \beta\}$ is true iff $\beta(x/t)$ is true.

Notice that this way of giving truth conditions for atomic sentences is open to us because we need concern ourselves only with *closed* formulas. If there were a variable in place of the abstract term in ∈, for example, we could not proceed in the same way. This way of giving truth conditions is not, therefore, open to someone who wishes to specify satisfaction conditions for all the formulas of the language.

A significant feature of these truth conditions is that from them, on their own, we may infer the truth of (*Abs'*) and (*Ext*).[9] This produces an extra argument, if one is needed, for the axioms of naive set theory. Of course, it is hardly an argument that, on its own, is likely to convince the sceptic, since the truth conditions for ∈ are so close to the abstraction scheme itself. Doubtless, it would be denied that these are the right truth conditions. However, this is a battle I have already fought in chapter 2. At any rate, the truth conditions make the idea that a set is the extension of an arbitrary predicate (that is, formula with one free variable) quite precise.

Finally, let us note that the above truth conditions can be modified (in a way similar to that in which those of section 9.2 were) to avoid the exclusion principle. Crucially, we treat truth and falsity independently. (¬) is replaced by

(¬') ¬β is true iff β is false

and the falsity conditions are

(∧F) $\alpha \wedge \beta$ is false iff α is false or β is false.

(¬F) ¬α is false iff α is true.

(→F) $\alpha \rightarrow \beta$ is false iff it is possible that (α is true and β is false)

---

[9] The proofs are fairly obvious. Here is the proof for (Abs'). Let α contain $x, y_1, \ldots y_n$, free. Let $t_1, \ldots t_n$ be closed terms. Let us write β for $\alpha(y_1/t_1 \ldots y_n/t_n)$. Then $\{x \mid \beta\}$ is a closed term. Consequently, by ∈, for any closed term t: $t \in \{x \mid \beta\}$ is true iff $\beta(x/t)$ is true.

By(∧) and (→): $t \in \{x \mid \beta\} \leftrightarrow \beta(x/t)$ is true.

Hence by (Π): $\Pi z(z \in \{x \mid \beta\} \leftrightarrow \beta(x/z))$ is true.

A number of further applications of Π now deliver (*Abs'*). The proof of (*Ext*) is similar.

(ΠF) Πxα is false iff for some closed term, $t, \alpha(x/t)$ is false.

(= F) $\{x|\alpha\} = \{x|\beta\}$ is false iff for some closed term,

$$t, \alpha(x/t) \text{ is true and } \beta(x/t) \text{ is false, or vice versa.}$$

(∈F) $t \in \{x|\beta\}$ is false iff $\beta(x/t)$ is false.

The proof of the truth of the axioms of naive set theory still goes through in the same way.

10.3 ANALYTICITY AND PARADOXICALITY

With the above construction under our belt, let us return to the issues raised at the beginning of the previous section and, leaving the question of realism for the next section, address the other two issues raised there, starting with the fact that these semantics can show the truth of the axioms of naive set theory.

As we saw in the last section, the truth of the axioms follows from the truth conditions of the predicates and logical constants alone. This can be seen as showing that the axioms of set theory, and therefore, presumably, all the theorems of set theory, are analytic. The dominant notion of analyticity this century is that according to which a sentence is analytic if it is true merely in virtue of the meanings of the words involved. This notion has been considered highly suspect since the 1950s because of the attacks of Quine *et al*.[10] But, as we noted in the last chapter (section 9.3), to give the meaning of a sentence is to give its truth conditions. And the axioms of the truth theory can be seen as spelling out the meanings of the predicates and logical constants involved in the individual axioms. This gives us a natural and unproblematic way of understanding the notion of analyticity. A sufficient condition for something to be true merely in virtue of the meanings of its parts is for its truth to follow logically from the axioms of the truth theory for the language, with no other axioms added. It is for just this reason that tautologies, for example, are thought of as analytic: their truth follows merely from the truth conditions of the connectives; no extra information supplied by "the world" is necessary. Whether this condition is also necessary for analyticity is a moot point. It might for example be argued that, for certain words, meaning-postulates need to be added to the truth theory in order for it to capture all facts about meaning; but this need not concern us here. That it is a sufficient condition will be quite sufficient. And what it is sufficient for is showing that set theory is analytic.[11]

---

[10] Though their success has been over-rated: see Priest (1979*b*).

[11] This account of analyticity is quite compatible with the account of analyticity given in Priest (1979*b*). There, I suggested that something is analytic if it follows from true logical conditionals (which themselves hold in virtue of the rules of inference in force). Now, truth conditions are (conjunctions of) logical conditionals, and the present account can therefore be subsumed by that account.

Let us turn to the question of the logical paradoxes. It will have been clear to the reader that the truth conditions for sentences of set theory that I have given do not ground out in non-semantic language. If we take any sentence and work out its truth conditions by applying the recursive clauses in the usual way, we will never eliminate reference to truth (or falsity), simply because each sentence has its truth conditions given in terms of the truth (or falsity) of sub-sentences. Consider, for example, the sentence $t \in \{x \mid \Sigma y \, x \in y\}$. This is true iff $\Sigma y \, t \in y$ is true; iff for some term, t', $t \in t'$ is true; iff for some formula, β, with one free variable, z, $\beta(z/t)$ is true. And our original formula is one such β.

Some would suggest that this makes the truth conditions unacceptable. Indeed, this looping is the reason that some have given for supposing that a substitutional semantics cannot be produced for an impredicative set theory.[12] In reply to this, I need only reiterate the points made in section 9.3. If we were trying to give a definition of truth, this would indeed show the attempt to be a failure. If our aim is not this, but to give a theory of the conditions under which sentences of the language of set theory are true, the failure of the truth conditions to ground out is immaterial. Nor does this make the truth conditions impotent. One might worry that the non-wellfoundedness would prevent the conditions from determining anything to be true. But we have already seen that the truth conditions show the axioms of naive set theory to be true. Nor does it necessarily make the truth conditions omnipotent. One might worry that they determine everything to be true, but there is no reason to suppose that they do. A formal proof of this would require a formalisation of the metatheory and a proof that for some α 'α is true' is not provable. I have little doubt that this is possible.[13]

Though the non-wellfoundedness of truth conditions may not be a problem, it is important. For (as in section 9.3) it allows for the possibility of "fixed points". Consider the term $\{x \mid x \in x\}$. Call this t. Then by ($\in$), $t \in t$ is true iff $t \in t$ is true, a very tight loop indeed. And if the loop gets twisted like a Möbius strip . . . : let r be $\{x \mid x \notin x\}$; then $r \in r$ is true iff $\neg r \in r$ is true iff $r \in r$ is not true (or, in the alternative construction, false). Hence, paradox results. In section 9.3 we saw that the possibility of semantic paradox arises because of non-wellfounded truth

---

[12] For example Quine (1973), p. 112. It is perhaps worth noting that, more recently, Quine has said that the 'only remaining cause for hesitation over the substitutional version [of quantification in set theory] is impredicativity' (Quine 1976, p. 504). It is, of course, always possible to avoid the impredicativity artificially by adding an infinite number of predicate constants to the language, as in Henkin (1953).

[13] If it is not necessary for truth conditions to ground out in non-semantic language, why not simply state the truth condition of any sentence, α, simply as: α is true? Though such truth conditions are trivially correct, since they *are* trivial they are uninformative. Such conditions do not allow us to show that the principles of naive set theory are true; nor do they expose the connection between the truth conditions of wholes and those of their parts, so important if an account of meaning is to be based on that of truth. And, most importantly in the context of the next section, for a theory of truth to be of use in determining ontological commitment, it must spell out the truth (or satisfaction) conditions of quantified formulas in terms of those of their subformulas. Such a trivial truth theory is useless for this purpose.

conditions. It now appears that the same is true of the set theoretic paradoxes; not because set theoretic terms are covertly semantic (they are not), but because the set abstraction operator itself gives rise to a regress of truth conditions. It is the fact that semantic regress is at the base of both the semantic and the set theoretic paradoxes which informs, I suggest, our feeling that the logical paradoxes form a single family.[14] In section 2.5 we saw that there was a sense in which both the semantic and the set theoretic paradoxes spring from the same root. We have now found a way of making this idea quite precise.

10.4 MATHEMATICAL REALISM

A perennial problem in the philosophy of mathematics concerns the existence and nature of mathematical objects, such as numbers, categories, etc. In fact, this is arguably the most central question, from which all others derive and to which they all return. Now, in one sense, there is no problem about mathematical objects and their properties. There is, after all, a number between 5 and 7; it has two prime factors, is perfect, etc. However, this will hardly seem to get very far to someone bothered by the issue: she will say 'Yes, but are there *really* any numbers with properties?' But exactly what does this mean? As usual, a large part of the philosophical problem is getting the question right, or at least getting it in a concrete enough form to say something intelligent about it. So let us see if we can tighten the question up.

We use language with which we can, *prima facie*, refer to certain mathematical objects, ascribe certain properties to them, and so on. Moreover, a number of the assertions we make are undoubtedly true. It would therefore seem that there is a realm of objects to which we refer when we talk mathematics. These objects are obviously not physical objects. That is, they are not actual, do not enter into causual chains. So let us call them 'abstract'. (Though this term has, perhaps, little content other than "non-physical".) Hence it would appear that an adequate semantics for the language of mathematics is—indeed, must be—the usual domain-and-satisfaction semantics, familiar from model theory, which relates language to a domain of non-linguistic objects. The domain in question, in which all terms find their referents, and over which referential quantifiers range, is a set of abstract objects.

Let us call such a view 'realism'. Note that there are important differences in the realist camp. An important one is between neo-Platonists (such as Quine and Gödel[15]), who take the objects in the domain to exist, and neo-Meinongians (such as Routley[16]), who do not. Exactly what this issue amounts to is a sensitive question which, fortunately, we do not have to face. Realism, as I have defined it,

---

[14] It also distinguishes them from pseudo-paradoxes such as the barber. The barber does not arise because of a regress of truth conditions.   [15] See Smart (1963) and Gödel (1947).
[16] See Routley (1980), especially ch. 11.

is neutral on this issue. A second important point to note is that the realist is not (*pace* Dummett) required to endorse the law of excluded middle. A neo-Meinongian may well argue that non-existent objects violate this law. A realist is simply someone who espouses domain-and-satisfaction semantics for the language of mathematics. Our original question of whether there are mathematical objects can now be put simply as 'Are such semantics correct?'

Many have answered this question affirmatively (or, to avoid an anachronism, did so implicitly in the terms of their day). The strength of this answer is that it is *prima facie* right. The onus is therefore on non-realists to make their point. Moreover, domain-and-satisfaction semantics are technically unproblematic: thanks to modern model theory we know exactly what they are like. In fact, I suspect that much of the modern appeal of realism comes from the enormous success of model theory. For model theory, at least in its obvious interpretation, just is the study of the relationship between language, especially mathematical language, and extra-linguistic reality. Some have even gone as far as to suggest that the notion of truth is so closely tied to this kind of correspondence theory that the mere fact that someone makes true mathematical assertions entails that realism is correct. In virtue of the discussion of truth in chapter 4, this claim can be seen to be incorrect. None the less, realism possesses the field, and it is up to non-realism to dislodge it.

The non-realist may attribute the presupposition of the correctness of mathematical realism to an illicit projection. The most adequate semantics for empirical discourse, concerning tables, people, and stars, would seem to be of the domain-and-satisfaction kind. The realist, according to the non-realist, merely transfers this picture automatically, and without justification, to mathematical discourse. Furthermore, it is not difficult to find damaging objections to realism. Since they are well known, it is not my intention to rehearse them at length here; let us look briefly at a couple.

First, if mathematical realism is correct, mathematical assertions make *de facto* claims about the world, the non-physical world to be sure, but *de facto* none the less. But mathematical statements would appear to have a necessity akin to that of logical truths, which purely descriptive statements lack. Even though a law of nature may have a necessity of a certain kind, it is possible that it could be violated in a way that it is not possible that mathematical laws might be violated. Now, if mathematical truths were merely *de facto* statements about certain objects, the source of this necessity would be totally obscure. We could say that such necessity is *sui generis* to statements about such objects. This would, however, just label the problem, not solve it.

One realist solution is to suggest that the purported necessity of mathematical statements is illusory (a standard ploy for disposing of awkward facts). Primarily, this is done by attacking the analytic/synthetic distinction. These attacks notwithstanding, it is possible to make perfectly good sense of this distinction (as I discussed in the previous section). Indeed, it it not really possible to maintain that the distinction is illusory. We have a perfectly good grasp of what it would be like for a law of nature to fail. By contrast, the idea of a possible world where $1 + 1 = 3$ (and not just where '3' means 2, or where pairs of objects sponta- neously reproduce) beggars the imagination. The suggestion that this distinction can be explained in terms of degrees of centrality to our conceptual scheme just does not work. Not only is the content of the metaphor unclear, but physical theories, however well entrenched, retain their contingency, while even novel and highly esoteric mathematical theories (such as category theory) possess this necessity. No relief for realism is to be found here. Necessity is a genuine problem for realism.

A second problem for realism is the epistemological one of how we come to know about abstract objects. (How we come to know about physical objects is, in principle, quite clear—though the details may be contentious—for the causal interaction between such objects and our sense-organs provides suitable knowledge- input.) Plato supposed us to be directly acquainted with abstract objects before birth; in this life it was necessary only to remember them. Plato's solution is so full of conceptual tangles, it is now difficult to take it seriously. Yet I fear that any solution the realist suggests will ultimately be as far-fetched. We may posit a faculty of "mathematical intuition",[17] analogous to sensory perception, but for the perception of abstract objects. But on every substantial point the analogy breaks down: there are no physical receptor organs; there is no causal chain between subject and object; there is no theory of the operation of this mech- anism; there is no independent check on whether the mechanism is working, and so no substance to the notion of making a mistake; and so on. Mathematical intuition becomes a "something I know not what", which permits the appre- hension of abstract objects. As such it is just another label for a problem, and not a solution. Another suggestion[18] is that our mathematics is epistemologically no different from our global physical theories. Both are free creations and, intertwined, are tested holistically against low-level data. This may be right for applied mathematical theories, but will not do for pure mathematical theories. Many such theories are not intertwined with physical theories. Notoriously, pure mathematics produces theories that have no application, or at least none for a long time. We know quite a lot about category theory, the intuitionist con- tinuum, transfinite arithmetic, but none of these has ever been connected with a physical theory. There is, therefore, a real difficulty for realism here.

In fact, it is just a special case of the most general flaw in realism: the fact that realism makes it impossible for there to be any truck between the source of mathematics on the one hand, and people and their practices on the other. As hardly needs to be emphasised since Wittgenstein, language is inextricably bound up with human activity. Meaningful language must play some role in human practice. Hence, any elements that are integral to the meaning of a language must

---

[17] As in Gödel (1947).   [18] Quine's; see Smart (1963).

interact with human activity somewhere. But this is precisely what is impossible on the realist view. For, by definition, abstract mathematical objects cannot causally interact with human practice—or anything else. Abstract mathematical objects, even if there were any, would be *completely irrelevant* to mathematical activity, and hence to the meaning and truth of mathematical assertions.[19] Suppose, for example, that we got rid of all abstract objects by burning them in a big Platonic (or Meinongian) incinerator. Would this destroy the meaning of '3'? Would it make '1 + 2 = 3' false? Not as long as we continue to compute in the same way. Notice that the dislocation between object and practice cannot be raised as an objection against the empirical realist. For the objects of physical realism do causally interact with us, and they and their properties do play important determining roles in our activities and practices. This is obviously true in the case of common-or-garden objects, such as chairs and teaspoons. But it is equally true in the case of more recondite physical objects, in virtue of our experimental techniques, technological practices, and so on. Mathematical objects are quite devoid of the potential for this kind of interaction.

Mathematical realism is a form of mystification; and I use the word advisedly. Mystification occurs when properties that things have in virtue of their roles in social activities are reified, owing to a failure to understand how those practices function. Thus, as Marx explained,[20] the exchange value of a commodity such as a loaf of bread is something it has in virtue of its role in a human practice: production and exchange. Outwith this setting, it would have no such property. When we fail to realise this, when we do not understand how the practice works, we take value to be an abstract and intrinsic property of the object itself. Similarly, because we fail to understand mathematical language in its context of mathematical activity, the terms take on an alienated and mystified meaning in the form of the phantom objects of mathematical realism.

The point about practice can be put in another way. It has been thought by some, Frege for example, that the existence of mathematical objects is necessary to guarantee objectivity in mathematics. Hence the objectivity of mathematics can be used as an argument for the existence of mathematical objects. But the existence of such objects is neither necessary nor sufficient for objectivity. An object (such as a signpost) is never sufficient to guarantee the concurrence of individual actions. A practice regarding its use is also required. Neither is it necessary; for the norms of a well defined practice are themselves sufficient to guarantee such concurrence. Thus, the rules of chess are quite sufficient to ensure that people agree on the moves permissible in any given chess position, without there being any abstract chess objects. Indeed, the situation would be the same if there were no physical chess objects either, chess being played entirely in the head. Which brings us, of course, very close to mathematics.

[19] Wittgenstein makes the points in e.g. his (1956). For references and discussion, see Klenk (1976), pp. 8–18.   [20] *Capital*, vol. 1, ch. 1, sect. 4.

10.5 ...AND ANTI-REALISM

One can always produce objections to a theory, but they do not bite hard until a plausible rival theory has been found. The acid test for non-realism has always, therefore, been the production of an adequate semantics of some other kind. And it must be admitted that, by and large, it has not done very well at this, especially when compared with the sophistication of model theory.

One recurrent historical anti-realism is conceptualism. In its modern form this is intuitionism. The crucial idea here is that we now give not truth conditions, where truth is defined in terms of satisfaction, but proof conditions, where the proof conditions of any formula are specified in terms of the proof conditions of its sub-formulas. For example, $\exists x \beta$ is provable iff, for some term, t, there is a proof of $\beta(t)$ and a proof that t is of the correct kind.[21] Now a central question here is how the notion of proof is to be understood, and, crucially, how we are to understand an assertion of the existence of a proof. Clearly, proofs cannot be thought of as real abstract entities, or we are back with a variety of mathematical realism. Neither can 'there is a proof' mean 'we actually possess a proof' (in our pockets, as it were). For this would make mathematics much too contingent an affair. A *via media* between these two has to be found, something in the order of 'we are effectively and in principle able to produce the (concrete) proof'.

Assuming that such an interpretation, not itself tainted with realism, can be found, this approach to the issue still faces a number of problems. Though it is clear that intuitionism avoids the epistemological problem (provided we can find a way of making proof suitably immanent), it would not seem to avoid the ontological one. As just explained, whether or not something is provable is to be cashed out ultimately in terms of human abilities. However, the existence of such abilities would seem to be a contingent or, at best, physically necessary state of affairs. Whence, then, derives the necessity of mathematical assertions? The problem is well illustrated by the fact that intuitionists like to talk of mathematics as being a mental construction. But the genuine products of mental construction, such as laws, myths, and so on, do not possess this kind of necessity.

Another point is this. Much classical mathematics is incorrect by intuitionist standards. Crucially, much classical reasoning must be regarded as invalid and mistaken. (Notice how intuitionism differs from (classical) dialetheism in this respect. In section 8.5 we saw that all classical reasoning could be understood in dialetheist terms.) Now maybe, in the end, if the arguments of Dummett and others are right, we will have to come to accept this fact. Note, however, that this is certainly not the way it appears to be, particularly from a very telling perspective: that of the working mathematician. To the working mathematician, both classical and intuitionist mathematics appear of independent interest. Both produce

---

[21] See Dummett (1977), p. 24.

structures that are worthy of investigation.[22] It would seem wrong, however, to try to treat one as a failed version of the other, just as it is wrong to treat baseball as a failed version of cricket, or a donkey as a failed version of a horse. Both would appear to be *sui generis*, and as such it would not be surprising if we require a different understanding of what is going on in each enterprise. Thus, constructive semantics may provide a non-realist semantics for intuitionism, but the problem for classical mathematics remains. For a number of reasons, therefore, it is doubtful that intuitionism provides a general solution to the problem.

Historically, the other main alternative to realism has been some form of nominalism. Nominalism is the suggestion that the semantics of mathematical language should concern not a domain of extra-linguistic entities, but, in some sense, the language itself. How to make this idea acceptably precise has been a problem. The most naive suggestion is that we simply identify mathematical objects with the word tokens that, for the realist, denote them. This will obviously not do, for many reasons. Not only does it make mathematics far too contingent an affair, but it would mean that there is only a finite number of sets, categories, etc. Hardly a satisfactory situation. Naturally, one can make the suggestion more sophisticated, but it has been a recurrent feature of precise forms of nominalism that they do not provide for the conceptual resources of mathematics in just this kind of way.[23] Still, one might hope that some suitable form of nominalism could be found.

At this point the construction of section 10.2 becomes relevant. Set theory may not be the whole of mathematics, but it is certainly the most general and fundamental part, and the construction shows that a non-realist semantics can be given for the language of set theory along lines that might reasonably be construed as nominalist; in particular, domain-and-satisfaction constructions are avoided in favour of the overtly linguistic substitutional quantification. These non-realist semantics also solve the problems that beset the realist conception of set theory. First, as we saw in section 10.3, they show that the theorems of naive set theory are analytic, true merely in virtue of the meanings of their component words. In this way, they are unlike, say, the laws of physics, and like truth functional tautologies. This can plausibly be seen as explaining their necessity. Secondly, the epistemological problem is solved along with the ontological one. For set theory no longer appears to be a theory about some transcendent realm. Rather, our knowledge of set theory follows from our knowledge of the meaning of language, and specifically from the pertinent truth conditions. The problem of the knowability of set theory reduces to that of the knowability of language.[24] It would seem, therefore, that the semantics provide a nominalistically acceptable

---

[22] Indeed, it is noteworthy that intuitionist structures have recently become very interesting for classical mathematicians owing to their appearance in classical set theory (forcing) and category theory (topoi).   [23] See Fraenkel, Bar-Hillel, and Levy (1973), p. 332 ff.

[24] One can also give a generic account of how this kind of truth condition arises. See Quine (1973), sects. 22–8.

account of set theory. To the question of how far this nominalist interpretation of set theory makes possible a nominalist interpretation of classical mathematics in general, I will return briefly at the end of the chapter.

10.6 CARDINALITY AND SYNTAX

Of the objections that might be raised to the use of substitutional quantification in the above context, few have not been answered to my satisfaction by others.[25] None the less, a couple remain to be aired. One concerns cardinality. I have suggested that a set just is the extension of a predicate. It may be retorted that, since there are countably many predicates and uncountably many sets, this must be incorrect. Furthermore, since there must be many sets that are not denoted by abstracts, it is quite possible for there to be a set that satisfies $\alpha(x)$, while for no term, t, $\alpha(t)$ is true. Hence there is no guarantee that the substitutional truth conditions will turn out the right truth values.

To a set theoretic realist the argument must carry weight; but to a set theoretic realist the substitutional semantics would be wrong anyway, merely by dint of the fact that she is a realist. For a realist, set abstracts do denote, variables do range over a set of non-linguistic entities. In other words, the semantics of set theory are domain-and-satisfaction, and that's that. To an anti-realist, however, this argument will carry little weight. Since he maintains that there are no sets, he will not agree that there are uncountably many sets, or that there are sets that satisfy $\alpha(x)$ while no term denotes such a set. He will not even agree that set abstracts denote sets. Abstracts do not denote at all. Of course, he may assert the sentence of set theory which says that the universe, V, is uncountable, but he will understand this in terms of its substitutional semantics, as saying that every substitution instance of a certain formula is false. Hence there is no problem for a non-realist here.[26]

A tougher objection is the following.[27] I have argued that, using substitutional quantification, we can give the truth conditions of the language of set theory in a nominalistically acceptable way. But now consider the truth conditions themselves. These are given in a certain language. Moreover, this language seems to refer to linguistic objects. This is particularly clear in the truth conditions for quantifiers, which are of the form: 'for all set abstracts...'. Furthermore, the linguistic objects invoked must be types, not tokens; for otherwise there would not be enough to give correct truth values. But linguistic types are just as abstract as mathematical objects. Indeed, if we code syntax in the usual way, we can take

---

[25] Especially Kripke (1976).

[26] There are also some contradictions related to König's paradox which lurk in the area; see Priest (1983a), sect. 6. Obviously these do not pose a problem for dialetheic set theory.

[27] See Quine (1973), pp. 118–20; Kripke (1976), p. 385.

syntax to be a branch of number theory itself. Hence the non-realist victory is a Pyrrhic one, committing itself, as it does, to entities that are, in principle, no different from those it wishes to avoid.

Let us grant, for a second, the claim that the language used to state the truth conditions itself requires a realist interpretation. Does it follow that nothing has been gained? The answer is 'No'. For it remains true that set theory, *per se*, has no commitment to abstract objects. It is the second order discourse about the language of mathematics that is so committed. Moreover, the abstract objects to which it is committed are of a simple and perspicuous kind.

But let us examine the question of whether the use of the language in which the truth conditions are given commits us to realism. This question is just that of whether the language in which the truth conditions are given, and in particular that part of it which appears to refer to, and quantify over, linguistic entities, should itself be considered as having domain-and-satisfaction semantics. Though I did not specify this language in section 10.2, we may take it to be that of the first order theory of syntax. Now, though we *may* furnish this with domain-and-satisfaction semantics, this is by no means obligatory. Indeed, since the theory of syntax is interpretable in first-order arithmetic, and since, as I observed in section 10.2, first-order arithmetic has a substitutional semantics, we already know how to give it a non-realist semantics. Thus, realism is avoidable.

This may be seen in another way. We may take naive set theory and semantically close it without introducing referential quantifiers. This may be done in a number of ways. One way is to combine the languages of set theory and of arithmetic, add a truth predicate, and then in this language write the theory of substitutional truth conditions for that language, using the arithmetical part to express syntax. A swifter way is simply to extend the language of set theory with a truth predicate, T, and a naming functor, Q. The latter is such that if α is any formula of the language, then $Q(\alpha)$ is a term of the language. We may allow α to be open or closed. The variables free in $Q(\alpha)$ are just those free in α. If α is closed, $Q(\alpha)$ is the name of α. Quantifiers are substitutional, with the substitution class being the set of all closed terms of the language. Axioms stating truth conditions are then added to (*Abs'*) and (*Ext*) in the obvious way. For example, $\wedge$ and Π of section 10.2 are expressed in the form

© $TQ(\alpha \wedge \beta) \leftrightarrow TQ(\alpha) \wedge TQ(\beta)$

© $TQ(\Pi x \alpha) \leftrightarrow \Pi x TQ(\alpha)$

respectively, where α and β are now schematic variables for all formulas (open and closed) of the language. Note the universal closure. ($\neg$) and ($\rightarrow$) are similar. (=) and ($\in$) become

© $TQ(\{x \mid \alpha\} = \{x \mid \beta\}) \leftrightarrow \Pi x(TQ(\alpha) \leftrightarrow TQ(\beta))$

© $\Pi y(TQ(y \in \{x \mid \beta\}) \leftrightarrow TQ(\beta(x/y)))$

respectively. We also require a new clause in the theory for the predicate T. This is the obvious:

© $(TQ(TQ(\alpha)) \leftrightarrow TQ(\alpha))$

Finally, the above axioms specify no truth conditions for formulas of the form $T\{x \,|\, \beta\}$, $t \in Q\alpha$, $Q(\alpha) = Q(\beta)$ and $Q(\alpha) = \{x \,|\, \beta\}$. How these gaps are to be plugged is, to a certain extent, arbitrary. But perhaps the simplest thing is to specify the following:

© $\neg TQ(T\{x \,|\, \beta\})$

© $\Pi x \neg TQ(x \in Q(\alpha))$

© $TQ(Q(\alpha) = Q(\beta))$ just if α is β

© $\neg TQ(Q(\alpha) = \{x \,|\, \beta\})$

Thus, truth can never be predicated of set abstracts, and names behave as *Urelemente*, identical only when the things named are identical. A moment's thought shows that it is no problem to specify appropriate falsity schemes, if required.

In either of these ways, we obtain a set theory that not only has substitutional semantics, but also can state them.[28] The distinction between the language for which the semantics is given and the language in which it is given disappears (as should be the case in any sufficiently general semantical theory). This gap therefore fails to open, leaving no room for the realist objection to be inserted.

This last move may have the air of a conjuring trick, with reference to abstract entities performing some Indian rope trick: climbing up into the metalanguage, and then disappearing—and taking the rope with it. We feel that there is something dishonest going on, but cannot quite put our finger on it. Perhaps Kripke comes close to the worry when, in a similar context, he says:[29]

... the substitutional quantifiers of the metalanguage [M, the language in which truth conditions are given] have ... names of the expressions of the object language [L, the language whose truth conditions are being given] ... as substitutes. Then either the interpretation of the metalanguage is such that these terms are thought of as denoting expressions of the object language or it is not. In the former case ... [We have realism]. In the latter case ... the metalanguage may in fact carry no ontological commitment to expressions of the object language. In this case, however, what justifies us in calling the language M a *metalanguage* for the object language, L, at all? If nothing in M purports in any way to refer to, or quantify over, expressions of L, how can a formal theory phrased in M possibly say anything whatever about the semantics of L? If the ontology of M is really supposed to be the null ontology, the formula $T(x)$ can no longer be regarded as a *predicate* satisfied by exactly the true sentences of L, but it is rather a *form* of M with no

---

[28] The theories are sufficient to prove versions of a non-homophonic T-scheme. To prove the homophonic T-scheme, further axioms would be needed. This however, is a normal situation, as Kripke (1976), sect. 5, notes.   [29] Kripke (1976), p. 341; italics original.

interpretation whatsoever. How then can the theory phrased in M be said to be a theory of truth for the language L?

I think that Kripke's rhetorical questions are to be answered as follows. Let us call the semantically closed theory just sketched LM, since it is both object and metalanguage. Then what makes the theory couched in the language LM *about* the language LM is precisely that it is the formulas of LM (and not another language) which are exhibited within a quotation term, $Q(\alpha)$. Similarly, what makes it a theory of *truth* for LM is that we look to the righthand side of the canonical biconditional theorem $TQ(\alpha) \leftrightarrow \alpha'$ to state the conditions under which α conforms to the point of asserting. (See the account of truth in section 4.5.) If it is suggested that, if nothing in LM refers, then α' can *state* nothing at all, the correct reply is that this is not only question-begging, but just plain false. (Consider 'it is raining'.)

The reason why Kripke's point is persuasive is difficult to nail down, but I think that it is essentially as follows. One forgets that there are aspects of language that are not captured by formal semantics—in particular details concerning use. But, as we saw in section 4.4, even if terms of LM are taken to refer, even if T is taken to be a predicate (in the domain-and-satisfaction sense) and not a form, there is nothing in the theory itself which makes it a theory of *truth* for LM. For this, it is necessary that we know the use to which the predicate T is to be put, and, specifically, what the point of calling something 'true' is. Moreover, if nothing in LM refers, this merely means that we cannot rely on a previously understood notion of reference to grasp aspects of the use of sentences of LM. It does not follow that they have no use, nor that they cannot be used to state truth conditions. If it is suggested that using the term $Q(\alpha)$ in the way I have indicated just makes it refer to a certain abstract object, I simply deny this. There is more to refering than simply being a noun-phrase, as the *Philosophical Investigations*, if not 'On Denoting', teaches.

Thus, we see that the substitutional semantics for set theory, for naive set theory, provide the materials to formulate a viable non-realist philosophy of set theory. The question now arises as to whether this can be extended to the whole of classical mathematics. A partial answer to this question is as follows. First, since arithmetic can be given a substitutional semantics, it is clear that the previous discussion carries over, *mutatis mutandis*, to number theory. Moreover, we may pool the languages of set theory and of arithmetic, as indicated in the last section, to give a single language for which nominalist truth conditions may be given. We thereby obtain a nominalist account of arithmetic-*cum*-set theory, and hence of classical analysis and anything else that can be reduced to this basis.

One might also attempt an argument for a general non-realism as follows. It is widely agreed that set theory provides an adequate ontology for mathematics. Some doubts on the point have been raised by category theorists, but, as I argued in section 2.3, these arise only because of the inadequacies of the cumulative hierarchy as an analysis of the notion of set. If the Frege/Russell reduction of mathematics to set theory is not correct (or cannot be performed in naive set theory without making local consistency assumptions, then not all truths of (pure) mathematics are *truths* of pure set theory; none the less, set theory is a *lingua universalis* for mathematics, and can *express* all mathematical notions.[30] Thus, if set theory has a nominalist interpretation, so does all classical mathematics. To scrutinise this argument is more than the present occasion demands. I shall therefore leave it for another. At any rate, it is established that dialetheism opens up important new prespectives in the philosophy of mathematics.

[30] In terms of Quine's fortunate distinction, expressed in unfortunate language (1953, pp. 130–2), set theory may provide the ontology of mathematics without providing its ideology.

11

The Metaphysics of Change I:
The Instant of Change

11.1 CONTRADICTIONS IN THE WORLD

The main dialetheias we have discussed so far in the book arise in the relatively abstract realm of logic (set theory and semantics). It is now time to look at contradictions that arise in more concrete realms, and especially the empirical world. It is tempting to think that the realm of dialetheias is circumscribed by the realm of logic. (Indeed, at one time I did think this.) It is easy to suppose that, although our conceptual apparatus may be inconsistent, the world as such must be consistent. Of course, the world as such is not the *kind* of thing that can be consistent or inconsistent. Consistency is a property of sentences (statements, or whatever), not tables, chairs, stars, and people. However, it might be suggested, to say that the world is consistent is to say that any true purely descriptive sentence about the world is consistent. What we are to make of the notion of a purely descriptive statement is a moot point. Still, maybe it is possible to give a satisfactory sense to this notion, and to produce some transcendental argument for the consistency of the world in this sense; but I know of no way of doing this, and there are persuasive arguments against it. Certainly Hegel, for example, took the realm of dialetheias to include statements about physical change, as we shall see. Perhaps he is not a good example of a philosopher who took the empirical world to be inconsistent, since his absolute idealism debars him from making any real distinction between the conceptual and the world. Engels is a better example for this reason. In fact, dialecticians such as these two and Heracleitus took change to be a prime area for the production of contradiction.[1] Unfortunately, they rarely cared to argue the point, often doing little more than citing the authority of Zeno. In this chapter and the next I will examine some suitable arguments. We will leave Zeno and motion till the next chapter. In this chapter we will start with the issue of discrete temporal changes. As we shall see, there are, if not conclusive, then at least plausible reasons for supposing that these may produce dialetheias, especially once we have put aside the prejudice against contradictions.

[1] See Priest and Routley (1983), ch. 2.

11.2 THE INSTANT OF CHANGE

Let us start by discussing the thorny old question of the instant of change, which may be illustrated thus.[2] As I write, my pen is touching the paper. As I come to the end of a word I lift it off. At one time it is on; at another it is off (that is, not on). Since the motion is continuous, there must be an instant at which the pen leaves the paper. At that instant, is it on the paper or off? We may formulate the problem more generally. Before a time t_0, a system s is in a state s_0, described by α. After t_0 it is in a state s_1, described by $\neg\alpha$. What state is it in at t_0? *A priori*, there are four possible answers:

(A) s is in s_0 and s_0 only.

(B) s is in s_1 and s_1 only.

(Γ) s is in neither s_0 nor s_1.

(Δ) s is in both s_0 and s_1.

Of course, there may be no uniform answer. Different changes may be changes of different kinds. The crucial question I wish to ask is whether there are any changes in class Δ, that is, dialetheic changes. If classical logic is *assumed* to be correct, then all changes must be of type A or type B. Clearly, we are not making that assumption in the present context. Moreover, we can even take it that what is at issue here is the very correctness of classical logic. Hence the issue can not be (partially) settled in this way without thoroughly begging the question. I shall argue that there are some changes of type Δ.

First of all, by the analysis of negation in section 4.7 we can rule out the possibility of type Γ changes. One of α and $\neg\alpha$ must always hold. It remains to argue that not all changes are of type A or type B. Let us return to the pen. At t_0 the pen leaves the paper. Is it on or not on the paper at this instant? The trouble is that there seems to be no good reason to say one rather than the other. It seems as much on as off, and as much off as on. Thus the asymmetric answers, A and B, seem inappropriate. The symmetrical answers, Γ and Δ, would seem much more apt. There is, however, a way of breaking the asymmetry in this case. Since the motion is continuous, there is, presumably, a last instant at which the distance between the point of my pen and the paper is zero, but no first point at which it is non-zero. (Perhaps more precisely, there is a last point at which the electrical repulsion between my pen and the paper is equal to the weight of the pen, but no first point at which this is not the case.) If we identify *being on* with *being zero distance from*, this makes the change of type A. But the identification is highly suspect. An arrow is fired into the ground. At the instant of impact, before the point of the arrow penetrates the ground, is the arrow on the ground?

[2] Much of the following comes from Priest (1982).

Even if some suitable way of preserving the asymmetry can be made to work in this case, the method will not work in general. This is because, in a number of cases, there is no objective fact that can be appealed to to break the symmetry. A particularly striking example of this is a phenomenological one. For days I have been puzzling over a problem. Suddenly the solution strikes me. Now, at the instant the solution strikes me, do I or do I not know the answer? The situation is, again, symmetrical. Before, I did not know the answer; after, I did. Moreover, one cannot suppose that in this case there is some tie-breaking ulterior fact. My epistemological state is all there is, and that is symmetrical. It makes little sense to suppose that I either did or did not determinately know the answer at the instant of change, though I am unaware which. One more example will suffice. I am in a room. As I walk through the door, am I in the room or out of (not in) it? To emphasize that this is not a problem of vagueness, suppose we identify my position with that of my centre of gravity, and the door with the vertical plane passing through its centre of gravity. As I leave the room there must be an instant at which the point lies on the plane. At that instant am I in or out? Clearly, there is no reason for saying one rather than the other. It might be suggested that in this and similar cases we are free to *stipulate* that I was, say, in. Unfortunately this is not a solution, but simply underlines the problem. I am free to stipulate in this way only because neither being in nor not being in has a better claim than the other: I am neither determinately out rather than in, nor determinately in rather than out. Thus, intrinsically, the change is symmetrical, and therefore not of type A or type B.

The most plausible way, it seems to me, to attack this argument for the existence of type Δ changes is to reject the exhaustion principle (if α is not true then $\neg\alpha$ is true), and hence allow for the possibility of type Γ changes. Naturally, this can be done only if the arguments of section 4.7 for this principle can be met.[3] But the above argument at least makes it plausible to suppose that there are type Δ changes. I will return to the question of the existence of type Δ changes in section 11.5, where we will see that there are reasons for the existence of such changes which do not presuppose the exhaustion principle.

Before I leave the subject for the time being, there is one further issue worth commenting on. My discussion so far has been predicated upon the assumption that there are instants of time. If there are no instants, there are no instants of change, and the problem of the instant of change, and the conclusions I have drawn from it, are no longer available. This has led some people to suggest that time is composed of intervals rather than instants.[4]

The proposal is undoubtedly of both technical and philosophical interest, but it faces a number of problems. First, a good part of science is based on the

---

[3] It is worth noting, also, that this principle follows from the T-scheme if its contraposition be allowed, as we noted in sect. 4.9.

[4] See e.g. Hamblin (1969). The idea can be made the basis of systems of tense logic; see Humberstone (1979).

assumption that physical continua have a structure that can be represented by the real line, and therefore that we can speak of instants of time. In particular, any science that uses the differential and integral calculus presupposes this. Therefore, this proposal, if adopted, would cause the demise of a good part of science. Or, to put it more tellingly, the proposal flies in the face of well corroborated scientific theories. Its correctness is, therefore, highly suspect.

Secondly, the philosophical consequences of the theory are somewhat dubious. For suppose that during a certain time a system, s, changes discretely from state s_0 to states s_1. Then there must be two abutting intervals, X and Y, X wholly preceding Y, such that s_0 holds throughout X and s_1 holds throughtout Y. Now, given that there is no instant dividing X and Y, we cannot ask what state s is in at it. However, just because there is no such instant, there is no time at which the system is *changing*. X is before the change. Y is after it. Thus, in a sense, there is no change in the world at all, just a series of states patched together. The universe would appear to be more like a sequence of photographic stills, shown consecutively, than something in a genuine state of flux or change. We might call this the *cinematic account* of change. As we will see, it has a habit of surfacing in consistent accounts of change. I will discuss it in more detail in section 12.2. For the present, let us just note that the cinematic account is highly counter-intuitive.

Finally, it is not even clear that dialetheism can be avoided by eschewing instants of time in favour of intervals; for, unless there are atomic intervals, a possibility that raises the shades of Zeno and exacerbates both the previous problems, intervals must be indefinitely subdivisible. Now, note that the fact that α holds at an interval, X, does not necessarily imply that it holds at every subinterval of X (or else the sun's shining on a certain day would imply that it shone during every part of the day). There is therefore nothing, in principle, to rule out the possibility of an interval such that every subinterval where α holds has a subinterval where $\neg\alpha$ holds and vice versa. What holds at this interval? What could it be but $\alpha \wedge \neg\alpha$?[5]

11.3 DIALECTICAL TENSE LOGIC

I have tried to make plausible the dialectical idea that contradictions may be realised in a process of change. An accurate development of these ideas requires a suitable logical vehicle, and the obvious one is tense logic. Equally obviously, such a logic cannot be based on classical or intuitionist logic. In this section I will show that it can be satisfactorily based on the dialetheic logic of chapters 5 and 6. Specifically, I will show how the semantics given there can be extended to those for a tense logic. First I will show how this is to be done for the extensional language of chapter 5. I will then indicate how this can be extended to the

---

[5] A similar kind of situation, with a similar conclusion, is considered by von Wright (1969), sect. 15 ff.

intensional language of chapter 6. The discussion will be restricted to propositional languages. This is not because the extension to first order languages is problematic. Rather, it is because it is clear that it is quite unproblematic. And because it appears to raise no new issues, and since it is not necessary for a further discussion of the issues so far raised, I will not pursue the matter here.

Let L be the set of formulas of the extensional language of section 5.2 augmented by the two monadic tense operators P and F, thought of as meaning 'it was the case that' and 'it will be the case that', respectively. The operators H and G ('it was always the case that' and 'it will always be the case that') are thought of as defined in the usual ways as $\neg P \neg$ and $\neg F \neg$, respectively. As before, let π be the set of truth values $\{\{0\}, \{1\}, \{0, 1\}\}$. An interpretation for the language is a triple $< W, <, v >$, where W is a set of temporal instants, $<$ is a relation on W and, for any $x \in W$, $v(x)$ (v_x) is a map from propositional parameters to π. $<$ is thought of as a relation of temporal precedence and, despite the notation, need not be an order, though this is a very natural further condition to put on it. For the present, we will impose no requirements on $<$. The converse relation of $<$ will be written as $>$. For any $x \in W$ we can extend v_x recursively to an evaluation of all formulas of L. The recursive clauses for $\wedge$, $\vee$, and $\neg$ are as in section 5.2, where v is now appropriately relativised to x. The additional clauses required for the tense operators are:

(Pa) $1 \in v_x(P\alpha)$ iff for some $y < x, 1 \in v_y(\alpha)$

(Pb) $0 \in v_x(P\alpha)$ iff for all $y < x, 0 \in v_y(\alpha)$

(Fa) $1 \in v_x(F\alpha)$ iff for some $y > x, 1 \in v_y(\alpha)$

(Fb) $0 \in v_x(F\alpha)$ iff for all $y > x, 0 \in v_y(\alpha)$

As in the non-tense logical case, the truth conditions are exactly the orthodox ones except that in the orthodox case (b) of each pair is redundant. Thus, $P\alpha$ is true just if at some past time α was true, false if at all past times α was false, and so on. It is easily checked that, for all α in L and all $x \in W$, $v_x(\alpha) \in \pi$, and that the derived truth conditions for H and G are:

(Ha) $1 \in v_x(H\alpha)$ iff for all $y < x, 1 \in v_y(\alpha)$

(Hb) $0 \in v_x(H\alpha)$ iff for some $y < x, 0 \in v_y(\alpha)$

(Ga) $1 \in v_x(G\alpha)$ iff for all $y > x, 1 \in v_y(\alpha)$

(Gb) $0 \in v_x(G\alpha)$ iff for some $y > x, 0 \in v_y(\alpha)$

Semantic consequence can be defined, in the usual way, in terms of truth preservation in all worlds in all interpretations. It is not difficult to define a sound and complete proof theory for these semantics, though I will not give details here.[6]

[6] They can be found in Priest (1982).

As might be expected, the consequence relation is similar to its orthodox cousin. In particular, we have standard valid principles of inference such as $\{ \alpha \} \models HF\alpha$, $\{ G\alpha \wedge F\beta \} \models F(\alpha \wedge \beta)$, and so on. The only real differences between this tense logic and its classical counterpart are those inherited from the differences in the underlying propositional logics.

These semantics permit a formal modelling of type Δ changes. For example, suppose b is in a room before time t_0 but leaves it at that time, henceforth remaining outside. This corresponds to the interpretation $< W, <, v >$, where W is the real line, $<$ is the usual ordering on W, and p is thought of as the sentence 'b is in the room':

$$v_x(p) = \{1\} \text{ if } x < t_0$$
$$v_x(p) = \{0\} \text{ if } x > t_0$$
$$v_x(p) = \{0, 1\} \text{ if } x = t_0$$

At $x = t_0$, $1 \in v_x(p \wedge \neg p)$, showing the contradiction realised in this type Δ change.

The above semantics display most of the important features of dialetheic tense logic. However, since the language contains no entailment operator, it is unable to express important conditions, such as that there is no last time at which α holds: $\alpha \rightarrow F\alpha$. I therefore need to indicate how the semantics are to be extended to those for a language that contains an entailment operator. Let L' be the set of formulas of the language of L augmented by $\rightarrow$ (that is, the intensional language of section 6.3 augmented by the tense operators). A semantics for this language is just a fusion of the tense semantics just described and the modal semantics of section 6.3. More precisely, an interpretation is a quintuple $< g, W, R, <, v >$, where W is the index set of possible worlds at particular times, $g \in W$ is the "base world" (which for this chapter, and this chapter only, I write in lower case to distinguish from the tense-logical operator), R is the modal accessibility relation, omniscient with respect to g, and $<$ and v are as before. The truth conditions for the extensional connectives and tense operators, too, are as before, and those for the entailment operator are as in section 6.3. Semantic consequence is also defined as in section 6.3. It is easy to check that these semantics deliver expected principles relating tense and entailment, such as $\{ \alpha \rightarrow \beta \} \models F\alpha \rightarrow F\beta$, $\{ \alpha \rightarrow \beta \} \models G\alpha \rightarrow G\beta$, $\models \alpha \rightarrow HF\alpha$, and so on. The details of a proof theory suitable for the above semantics need not be discussed here.

As specified, these semantics allow $<$ to be arbitrary. They are, therefore, the dialetheic analogue of Lemmon's K_t.[7] A standard and natural way of extending such basic tense logics is by imposing constraints on $<$ to make it, e.g., an order, dense, etc. In cases such as the above, where we have two modal operators, we may also wish to consider constraints in the form of relationships between R and $<$. Both kinds of constraint will, of course, increase the inferences that are

---

[7] For details of the classical systems referred to, see any text on tense logic, e.g. Rescher and Urquhart (1971).

semantically valid. I will not attempt a comprehensive review of these extensions here. In general, the situations, at least as far as soundness goes, are very similar to the corresponding classical situations. For example, the transitivity of $<$ is sufficient to verify $FF\alpha \rightarrow F\alpha$ and $PP\alpha \rightarrow P\alpha$. If $<$ satisfies the "forward linearity" condition—if $x < y$ and $x < z$ then $z = y$ or $y < z$ or $z < y$—this is sufficient to verify $PF\alpha \rightarrow \alpha \vee P\alpha \vee F\alpha$, and so on. Details of complete proof theoretic characterisations for most of the conditions are, however, still an open question at the moment.[8]

Another way of extending the basic tense logic is by placing constraints not on $<$ and R, but on v. For example, suppose one held that not just some, but all, changes from p to $\neg p$ realise a contradiction at the nodal point. Then it is very natural to require the following of an interpretation:

If $x < y$ and $v_x(p) \neq v_y(p)$, then there is a z such that $x \leq z \leq y$ and $v_z(p) = \{0, 1\}$

This condition is sufficient to verify what we might call 'Zeno's principle':

$$\{p \wedge P\neg p\} \models (p \wedge \neg p) \vee P(p \wedge \neg p)$$

We will now look at a more sophisticated and important example of a condition that might naturally be placed on v.

11.4 THE LEIBNIZ CONTINUITY CONDITION

The example in question incorporates a certain continuity principle into the semantics. Before looking at the exact details of this, let us consider its historical background and philosophical plausibility. The principle in question is a Leibnizian one. It may have been endorsed by others before him, though I am not aware of this. His most explicit statement of it is as follows.[9]

When the difference between two instances in a given series or that which is presupposed can be diminished until it becomes smaller than any given quantity whatever, the corresponding difference in what is sought or in their results must of necessity also be diminished or become less than any given quantity whatever. Or to put it more commonly, when two instances or data approach each other continuously, so that one at last passes over into the other, it is necessary for their consequences or results (or the unknown) to do so also.

Now, with some three hundred years of mathematical hindsight, it is easy enough to think that Leibniz is just saying that, for two mathematical sequences, (s_n) and (t_n), if

$$\lim_{n \to \infty} s_n - t_n = 0 \text{ then } \lim_{n \to \infty} s_n = \lim_{n \to \infty} t_n$$

---

[8] Some further details of the extensional case can be found in Priest (1982), sect. 3.5.
[9] Leibniz (1687), p. 351 of translation.

And no doubt Leibniz would have taken his principle to imply this. But the principle is intended to have a much wider scope than this, as the variety of applications that Leibniz goes on to give makes clear. It is intended to apply to all limiting processes—not just arithmetic, but geometric, physical, temporal, and so on. In virtue of this, we might state the principle thus: given any limiting process, whatever holds up to the limit holds at the limit; or, as L'Huilier, who, like most eighteenth-century mathematicians, endorsed the principle, put it: if a variable quantity at all stages enjoys a certain property, its limit will enjoy the same property.[10]

This continuity principle must be treated with some care. For, using it carelessly, one could prove all sorts of undesirable things, such as that every real number is rational (since it is the limit of a sequence of rationals), that the limit of every sequence of continuous functions is continuous, and so on. It is quite clear, however, that Leibniz must have held there to be some bounds on the applicability of the principle. For example, it is not the case that every parabola is a closed and bounded figure, even though every ellipse is closed and bounded and 'every geometric theorem established for an arbitrary ellipse can be applied to a parabola'.[11] And this must have been obvious to Leibniz. What, exactly, he took these bounds to be I do not know, and since my aim is not historical exegesis this is not important. What is important is that we can fix on one particular kind of application of the principle, which can be stated precisely, is very plausible, and has some interesting consequences.

Let us fix on the principle as applying to changes in physical states of affairs over time. Its content is then as follows: any state of affairs that holds at any continuous set of times holds at any temporal limit of those times. Clearly, this principle cannot be applied to give the unfortunate sorts of consequence we have just noted. Although I have stated the principle in terms of states of affairs, it could equally well have been stated in terms of events thus: any event that is occurring at a continuous set of times is occurring at any limit of those times. An event occurring can be thought of as a state of affairs, and, conversely, a state of affairs obtaining can be taken as an event for present purposes. Hence the two formulations of the principle are equivalent. Finally, we might dispense with the 'limit' jargon altogether, and put the principle simply thus: anything going on arbitrarily close to a certain time is going on at that time too. Let us call this, in honour of Leibniz, the *Leibniz Continuity Condition*, LCC for short.

The LCC has a good deal of plausibility, though why is less clear. *Au fond*, there is a feeling that, if something violated this principle, the behaviour at the limit would be, in some sense, capricious. Leibniz interprets this observation quite literally. Such a situation would show an act of caprice on the part of God the designer.[12] Since God would not behave in this way, there can be no such violation. This interpretation may strike the contemporary mind as

---

[10] See Boyer (1949), p. 256.   [11] Leibniz (1687), p. 352 of translation.
[12] Leibniz (1687), pp. 352–3 of translation.

somewhat whimsical. The problem, then, is to explain the intuition in a non-anthropomorphic way.

I will return to this problem in a moment. Let us approach it via another question. How might one establish the LCC? Clearly there is no possibility of verifying the principle by experiment. No measuring instrument, particularly no clock, is accurate to more than a finite number of decimal places. There is therefore no way in which we might hope to observe the situation at a certain time to the exclusion of states at arbitrarily close times. Neither is there any question of proving the principle by pure mathematics. There is nothing mathematically impossible in such capricious behaviour. This is because the mathematical representation of states of affairs is quite atomistic. The value at some argument of a mathematical function in extension is logically independent of its value at all others. But it is precisely here that nature may plausibly be thought to differ from such a representation. For succeeding states of affairs in nature are not atomistic: there are connections. This would be denied by a Humean. For her, if the principle held it could only be by a global accident. I therefore see no possibility of convincing a Humean of the plausibility of the principle. But of course, for a Humean, *every* sequence of events is a global accident; hence there is no possibility of convincing her of anything. Let us therefore leave this scepticism aside. For the non-sceptic there are nexuses that serve to make the state of affairs at a certain time dependent on those at other times.

Now to return to the question of the LCC and its rationale. I suspect that a change which violates the LCC is capricious in the sense that it is incompatible with the existence of some of these nexuses. How does this work exactly? There is, I think, a good deal to be said about this, and the following is at least part of it. A change that violated the LCC would be unintelligible because of the following sorts of considerations. Let us suppose that a state of affairs, s, holds before, and all the way up to, a limit time, t, but fails at t. Then, clearly, a change has occurred. But when did this change occur? It cannot occur before t, since at any time before t there are later times at which s held; but it cannot occur at t (or at any subsequent time), because at this time the change is all over: s is already terminated! We can reason similarly if the state holds after, and at all times down to, a prior limit time, t, but not at t. When did the change occur? It cannot happen after t—that is too late: at any time after t there are prior times at which s already holds; but it cannot happen at t (or at any prior time), because at that time the change has not yet started: the old state is still in place. It therefore seems, in either case, that something, namely a change, has occurred, but that it took place at no time. But this is very strange. We may countenance things that happen very quickly, but if something happens it must take *some* time, if only an instant. (For just this reason, theories of action at a distance, which require something to happen in no time, namely the transmission of an effect, have always been felt philosophically puzzling.) A possible response to this train of thought is simply to deny that there is any such thing as change itself. A change occurs when one state is replaced by another, and that's that. This response just endorses the cinematic account of change, which we met in section 11.2. As we noted there, it, too, is highly counter-intuitive.

I will return to the cinematic account in section 12.2. Let us leave the issue there for the time being and move on to the question of how the LCC is to be incorporated into the semantics of tense logic. How this is to be done is quite straightforward. In fact, there are several ways in which one might go about it. The notions of continuity and limit are topological ones. Thus, the most general approach would be to suppose that the indices, W, come with a topology, which can be employed in the stating of the condition.[13] Still, we can get a reasonable formulation without bringing in a topology, once we notice that in the real line (which is the paradigm representation of time), with the usual ordering and topology, the (open) continuous intervals are just sets of the form $\{x \mid r < x < s\}$ for real numbers r and s; and r and s are the only limits of the interval that are not already in it. It is therefore reasonable to formulate the LCC as a condition on a semantic interpretation (which I shall also refer to as the LCC—context sufficing to disambiguate) as follows:

For every propositional parameter, p, and every x, $y \in W$, if $1[0] \in v_z(p)$
for every z such that $x < z < y$, then $1[0] \in v_x(p)$ and $1[0] \in v_y(p)$.

It may seem arbitrary at first glance to impose the condition on only propositional parameters. A little thought, however, shows that the condition should not be extended to arbitrary formulas. For example, assuming that there is no such thing as a disjunctive state of affairs *per se*, a disjunction may hold all the way up to a limit without there being any single state that does so (the disjuncts, as it were, alternating). Hence there is no reason to suppose that the disjunction holds at the limit. Conceivably, one might argue for the existence of disjunctive states *per se*, in which case it would be reasonable to take steps to extend LCC to all extensional formulas; but under no circumstances should it be extended to tensed formulas. For suppose the LCC did apply to tensed formulas, and consider the moments of someone's life. Being alive is certainly a continuous state of affairs, and so we can apply the LCC to conclude that this set contains all its limit points. In particular, it has a last moment, assuming, of course, that it does not go on for ever.[14] Call this z. At any point prior to z, 'There will be a (later) time of life' is true. If we could apply the LCC to tensed sentences we could apply it to this one to conclude that it is true at z, which, manifestly, it is not. The point, of course, is that, though 'There will be a later time of life' may be true at time t, it does not describe a state of affairs that holds at time t in the pertinent sense. Its truth-maker is a future event. Hence it describes a future state of affairs.

---

[13] This approach is followed in Priest (1982). It should be noted that the continuity principle formulated there (the LCP) differs from the LCC in not requiring a continuous approach to the limit.   [14] And that time is isomorphic to the real line with the usual order and topology.

For similar reasons, it is doubtful that the LCC carries over to sentences containing →.[15]

The LCC has an effect on the semantically valid inferences in a tense logic. A systematic study of this and the corresponding proof theory has not yet been undertaken. But as an example, it is clear that the LCC will validate the following inference:

$$\{PP(q \vee \neg q),\ Hp\} \models p \tag{1}$$

For suppose the premises hold at g. Then there is some $x < g$ such that p and $P(q \vee \neg q)$ hold at x. Hence there is some $y < x$. By the LCC, p holds at y and g. The inference holds if we replace p by its negation. The future-symmetric analogues of these inferences also hold. However, all of these inferences may break down if the LCC does not hold. In general, the effects of the LCC are not very interesting if the order is both linear and discrete. For, given any three consecutive points x, y, and z, the LCC ensures that whatever propositional parameters or their negations hold at y hold at x and z. If this does not render the evaluations at all indices identical, it does so near enough to make the situation rather uninteresting. The LCC assumes real interest mainly when the ordering is continuous, or at least dense.

11.5 THE LCC AND CONTRADICTION

So much for the LCC itself. Let us now return to the question of the existence of type Δ changes, and apply the LCC. For the LCC implies that any change from a continuous state of p to a continuous state of $\neg p$ is a type Δ change. More generally, suppose that φ and ψ are any distinct literals (propositional parameters or their negations). Suppose that prior to time t system s is in state s_0: φ is true. Posterior to time t, s is in state s_1: ψ is true. Since s_0 occurs arbitrarily close to t (and continuously), it occurs at t by the LCC. But s_1 occurs arbitrarily close to t (and continuously). Hence it too occurs at t. Thus, at t there is a nexus state at which both φ and ψ are realised. In particular, if φ is p and ψ is $\neg p$, $p \wedge \neg p$ is realised at t. The LCC therefore implies that contradictions are realised at the nodal points of certain sorts of change. We can reproduce this argument in the tense logical semantics. Suppose that W is an appropriate stretch of time and that

---

[15] In this context it is worth noting the following. Suppose we formulate the LCC such that not only if a propositional parameter or its negation *holds* at all points in a certain set it holds at its 'endpoints', but also if it *fails* at all points in a set it fails at the endpoints. This formulation of the LCC would make it impossible to assign (consistently) any semantic value in certain situations. For example, where time is the real line, and where the value of a parameter is {0} up to $t = 0$ and {1} thereafter, this formulation of the LCC would require 1 and 0 to both be members and not be members of its value at $t = 0$. Conceivably this possibility might be accommodated in an inconsistent metatheory, but it seems preferable to me to argue that the failure of something to hold at a time (as opposed to the holding of its negation) is not a state of affairs in the intended sense of the word.

g is the nodal point of a change from φ to ψ; i.e., $H\varphi \wedge G\psi$ holds at g. Then, assuming only that g is suitably distant from the ends of a $<$ chain, it follows that $FF(q \vee \neg q)$ and $PP(q \vee \neg q)$ hold at g, whence, by (1) of the previous section, $\varphi \wedge \psi$ holds at g. The dialetheia produced at a type Δ change need not be instantaneous (for all I have said so far, though this is a plausible additional constraint). For example, the interpretation with real time where $v_x(p)$ is $\{1\}$ if $x < 0$, $\{1, 0\}$ if $0 \leq x \leq 1$, and $\{0\}$ if $x > 1$, is quite compatible with the LCC. Still, there must be at least an instantaneous dialetheia.

It is not only for discrete changes that the LCC can be applied to show that contradictions arise. The LCC entails that contradictions arise in continuous change too. For example, consider a body that moves in accordance with the equation $x = kt$ $(k \neq 0)$, where x is its position and t is the time, both with respect to some suitable coordinate system. Consider a point t_0. At t_0, $x = kt_0$. But for all points after (and before) t_0, $x \neq kt_0$. Hence, by the LCC, at t_0, $x \neq kt_0$. Thus at t_0, $x = kt_0$ and $x \neq kt_0$. And since t_0 was arbitrary, we see that motion produces a continuous state of contradiction. What this might possibly mean I will return to in a moment; we can at least see it as vindicating dialecticians, such as Hegel, who claimed that change would be impossible without contradiction. As he put it,[16]

... contradiction is the root of all movement and vitality; and it is only in so far as something contains a contradiction within it that it moves, has an urge and activity.

The thesis that contradictions arise at the nodal points of certain transitions can also be used to free the mind of a certain mental cramp that often arises when people consider dialetheism. A commonly heard complaint is as follows (said with an air of puzzlement): 'I just cannot see what it would be like for a contradiction to be true, what it would be like, for example, for something to be a cup and not a cup, or for a person to be in a room and not in a room.' The answer to this (objection?) should now be obvious: something is a cup and not a cup the instant it breaks into pieces. Someone is in and out of the room the instant they leave. Contradictions occur at the nodal points of certain transitions and, as such, are perfectly familiar.

We have seen that a certain kind of change from α holding to β holding, produces a nexus state where $\alpha \wedge \beta$ holds. We may, however, go a step further. We may take the nexus state produced to be the state of change itself. The state described by $\alpha \wedge \neg\alpha$ just is the state described by α changing into the state described by $\neg\alpha$. Thus, there is such a thing as a state of change, and it does take time, if only an instant. Notice how this relates to the discussion of the LCC in section 11.4. Not only is there a state of change that takes time, but it commences while the prior state obtains and terminates only after the posterior state has begun.[17]

[16] Hegel (1812), p. 439 of translation. It is worth noting that even some non-dialecticians thought that the instant of change might give rise to contradictions; see Knuuttila and Lehtinen (1979).

[17] If we suppose there to be states of change, does this not start an infinite regress? For what of the change between, e.g. the prior state, described by α, and the state of change, described by $\alpha \wedge \neg\alpha$?

The notion that a contradictory state is a state of change also starts to make sense of the fact that motion is a continuous state of contradiction. For the contradictory state of the body at t_0 in the above example, $x = kt_0 \wedge x \neq kt_0$, is then indicative of the fact that the body is not only occupying the spot kt_0, but, since its occupation is instantaneous, is at the same time both entering and leaving the spot. All this suggests that the thesis that certain kinds of contradictory state are states of change should be investigated further. To this I turn in the next chapter.

There is no infinite regress. The nexus state between these two states is described by $\alpha \wedge (\alpha \wedge \neg\alpha)$, i.e. $\alpha \wedge \neg\alpha$, which is the original nexus state. Thus, to be changing into a state of change is already to be in that state of change, as one might expect.

12

The Metaphysics of Change II: Motion

12.1 CHANGE AND MOTION

At the end of the last chapter I floated the idea that contradictions not only occur in certain sorts of change but actually are the states of change themselves. In this chapter I want to explore this possibility further. I will not discuss all types of change. I shall restrict myself to one particular kind, change of place with respect to time: motion. I do this mainly because it will allow the discussion a concreteness and precision it would otherwise lack. Moreover, at least arguably, motion is the most fundamental kind of change, all other kinds involving motion of some sort. At any rate, it will be clear that similar considerations apply to other kinds of change, and I will say a little about the flux of time itself in the final section of the chapter. I will always speak of a body in motion, rather than the, more accurate, pair of bodies in relative motion; this is merely a matter of keeping the discussion simple; it does not affect the conclusions reached. In particular, what follows is in no way committed to an absolute view of space and time.

The nature of change in general, and of motion in particular, is not a novel issue. Indeed, it is one of the oldest parts of philosophy. Nor is the idea that contradiction and change are integrally related a novel one, as we noted at the end of the last chapter. I shall therefore approach the issue by first considering the orthodox, Russellean, account of change (motion), and then comparing it with the Hegelean account. This approach will pick up the threads left hanging in the last chapter.

12.2 THE ORTHODOX ACCOUNT OF MOTION

Let us start with the orthodox account of motion.[1] This account is not orthodox in the sense that most philosophers have endorsed it. The history of philosophy shows little consensus on the issue. It is orthodox in the sense that it is now the received view. It was formulated clearly and precisely by Russell, according to

---

[1] Much of the following comes from Priest (1985).

whom motion consists *merely* in the occupation of different places at different times. As he puts it,[2]

Motion consists in the fact that, by the occupation of a place at a time, a correlation is established between places and times; when different times, throughout any period, however short, are correlated with different places, there is motion; when different times throughout some period, however short, are all correlated with the same place, there is rest.

Thus, what it is for something to be in motion at an instant is simply that it is found at different places at arbitrarily close instants.[3]

Despite the fact that this view on the matter is now the received one, it faces some not inconsiderable objections. While none of them is a guaranteed knock-down argument, they certainly show that the orthodox account does not have it all its own way. It is certainly not the universal panacea for the discomforts people have felt about change that those such as Russell hoped it would be.

First, it follows from the definition that there is no such thing as an *intrinsic* state of motion. If one had a body in motion and took, as it were, a logical "picture" of it at an instant, the picture obtained would be no different from one of the same body at the same place, but at rest. Of course, an object in motion can have an instantaneous non-zero velocity, but it would be wrong to think that this differentiates it intrinsically from a static body. For to say that it has an instantaneous velocity at t_0 is just to say that $df/dt \neq 0$ at $t = t_0$, where f is the functional specification of position with respect to time. But this is just to say that

$$\lim_{\varepsilon \to 0} \left(f(t_0 + \varepsilon) - f(t_0) \right)/\varepsilon \neq 0$$

And the quantifier 'lim' quantifies, in effect, over all instants around t_0. Hence instantaneous velocity is essentially relational. Russell, in fact, points out that there is no such thing as an intrinsic state of change, and even revels in it:[4]

[Zeno's arrow argument] denies that there is such a thing as a *state* of motion ...

This has usually been thought so monstrous a paradox as scarcely to deserve serious attention. To my mind, I confess, it seems a very plain statement of a very elementary fact, and its neglect has, I think, caused the quagmire in which the philosophy of change has long been immersed ...

Change does not involve a state of change.

What we have here, as the last sentence makes plain, is just the cinematic account of change, where the change in question is motion. And this particular

---

[2] Russell (1903), sect. 447.

[3] Russell is actually inconsistent since, after giving this definition, he allows that something may be momentarily at rest if its positional derivative with respect to time is zero at that instant. This is quite compatible with its being in motion in the official sense. This minor inconsistency in Russell is not important here.

[4] Russell *op. cit.*, pp. 351, 350, xxxiii. I have spliced the quotations together without, I think, doing an injustice to Russell. The italics are original.

case of the account is no more plausible than the general form. A sequence of states, even a dense and continuous one, indistinguishable from corresponding rest-states, does not seem to be a state of motion. If God were to take temporal slices of an object at rest in different places and string them together in a continuous fashion, he would not make the object move.

One way of bringing this home[5] is as follows. Suppose that the universe were a Laplacean one, in which the state at any time is determined by the state at any (prior) time. Then the orthodox account of change would be impossible. For the instantaneous state of an object (or of all objects) cannot even determine whether it is at the same or at a different place at subsequent times. (Recall that the velocity—or momentum—of an object is not determined by its intrinsic instantaneous state.) Now I am certainly not insisting that the universe is Laplacean. It is not. But it is a curious theory that rules this out *a priori*.

We might summarise the above objection by saying that a journey is not a series of states indistinguishable from states of rest, even a lot of them close together. This leads us to a second objection to this account of change, which comes, as might be expected, from Zeno. Zeno's paradoxes have long plagued accounts of change. Of the four usually cited, I think that that of the arrow is, perhaps, the most profound. Certainly it is that which is relevant here.

Consider a point-object in uniform motion from x to y, say the tip of an arrow. And consider an instant of its motion, t_0. At t_0 the arrow advances not on its journey to y. (If it did make some headway, this would take time. The temporal stretch involved would not, therefore, be an instant.) Thus, at $t = t_0$, total progress made equals zero. But a temporal interval, $[x, y]$, is made up of such points. It would therefore seem that, since no progress is made in any basic part of the interval $[x, y]$, no progress can be made in the whole. That is, the arrow never makes any progress on its journey at all. This is absurd.

The received answer to this one of Zeno's paradoxes is closely connected with the orthodox account of change.[6] In fact, the orthodox account leaves very little room in which to manoeuvre. For, up until the very last step, the conclusion of the reasoning is in agreement with this account. At each instant of the motion the arrow does make no advance on its journey: it is qualitatively indistinguishable from a body at rest. The only possibility for avoiding the paradox is a denial of the final step. Even given that at each instant the arrow makes no progress on its journey, in the sum of all instants it does. The whole is greater than the sum of its parts. Technically, though the measure (= length) of the points traversed in an instant is zero, the measure of points traversed in a sum of instants may be nonzero (provided there are sufficiently, i.e. uncountably, many points). To deny this step is to say where the argument fails, but it is hardly to solve the paradox. For the denial of the principle involved in the final step of the argument seems just as

---

[5] For which I am grateful to Michael Tooley.   [6] It is given by Russell (1903), sect. 332.

puzzling as the conclusion of the paradox. How can going somewhere be composed of an aggregate of going nowheres?

One should separate here a technical mathematical question from a philosophical one. We can represent the length of a certain set of points by a measure function, σ. If we define a measure function on the real line in one of the standard ways, we can show that if Z is a finite (or even a countable) set of points, $\sigma(Z) = 0$; while if Z is an interval, $[x, y]$, $\sigma(Z) = y - x$. Thus, the length of the set of points occupied at an instant (which is a singleton set) is zero; but the length of the set of points occupied in an interval of time (which is itself an interval) has non-zero measure. That one can prove a small mathematical theorem or two is one thing; but it does not ease the discomfort that one finds (or at least, that I find) when one tries to understand what is going on physically, when one tries to understand how the arrow actually achieves its motion. At any point in its motion it advances not at all. Yet in some apparently magical way, in a collection of these it advances. Now a sum of nothings, even infinitely many nothings, is nothing. So how does it do it?

12.3 THE HEGELEAN ACCOUNT OF MOTION

In virtue of the above problems, it is not at all foolish to consider alternative accounts of change. An important one such is that produced by Hegel, though similar ideas can be found in many dialecticians. The basic idea goes back to Heracleitus.[7] Hegel himself attributes it to Zeno;[8] but let us stick with Hegel's formulation. Unlike Russell, Hegel did hold a state of motion to be intrinsic: there *is* an instantaneous difference between a moving body and a stationary one. As Hegel himself puts it,[9]

[M]otion itself is contradiction's immediate existence. Something moves not because at one moment of time it is here and at another there, but because at one and the same moment it is here and not here . . .

Hegel is not denying that if something is in motion it will be in different places at different times. Rather, the point is that this is not *sufficient* for it to be in motion. It would not distinguish it, for example, from a body occupying different places at different times, but at *rest* at each of these instants. What is required for it to be in motion at a certain time is for it both to occupy and not to occupy a certain place at that time.

Put this bluntly, Hegel's account of motion would not seem to have a lot going for it. The fact that it endorses inconsistency has been sufficient to put most

---

[7] Who certainly influenced Hegel: see Hegel (1840), vol. 1, ch. 1, sect. D.

[8] Hegel (1840), vol. 1, ch. 1, sect. C4. Historically, the attribution is undoubtedly problematic. Zeno's paradoxes played an important role in Hegel's thought on the matter, however.

[9] Hegel (1812), p. 440 of translation.

modern philosophers (both East and West) off it (at least as interpreted literally). More worrying in the present context is that the account is rather cryptic. Crucially, it is not clear how the theory is meant to relate to more familiar aspects of motion, such as change of place. In particular, it does not seem to relate in any way to the canonical representation of motion by functional equations in science and applied mathematics. I (like Russell) am enough of a holist to think that our philosophical understanding of motion and our scientific understanding must be compatible. For change is, and always has been, a single problem with both philosophical and scientific aspects. One cannot divide them. It is the great strength of the orthodox account that it coheres with the canonical representation of motion. Thus, an equation of motion, $x = f(t)$, just seems to encode the idea of the occupation of different places at different times: it merely records the correlation. By contrast, Hegel's view seems to have no bearing on the matter.

Be that as it may, the considerations concerning change and contradiction in the last chapter are enough to make one suspect that Hegel is on to something here, and that that something might well solve the problems of the cinematic account of motion. So let us inquire why, exactly, Hegel held this view of motion. The reason is roughly as follows. Consider a body in motion—say, a point particle. At a certain instant of time, t, it occupies a certain point of space, x, and, since it is there, it is not anywhere else. But now consider a time very, very close to t, t'. Let us suppose that over such small intervals of time as that between t and t' it is impossible to localise a body. Thus, the body is equally at the place it occupies at t', x' ($\neq x$). Hence, at this instant the body is both at x and at x' and, equally, not at either. This is essentially why Hegel thought that motion realises a contradiction.

Of course, there is more to the story than this. For Hegel gives a reason why a moving body cannot be localised. The reason derives from his view of the continuum. Essentially, it is that in a continuum distinct points themselves merge. Thus, the reason why we cannot localise a body to t is just that t itself is not "localisable". As he puts it,[10]

[W]hen . . . we admit that time and space are continuous, so that two periods of time or points of space are related to one another as continuous, they are, while being two, not two, but identical . . . [M]ovement means to be in this place and not to be in it, and thus to be in both alike; this is the continuity of space and time which first make motion possible.

And again:[11]

[When a body is moving] there are three different places: the present place, the place about to be occupied and the place that has just been vacated; the vanishing of the dimension of time is paralysed. But at the same time there is only *one* place, a universal of

---

[10] Hegel (1840), vol. I, pp. 273, 273–4 of the translation.
[11] Hegel (1830), p. 43 of the translation. The italics are original.

these places, which remains unchanged throughout all the changes; it is duration existing immediately in accordance with its Notion, and as such it is Motion.

Hegel's view of the continuum is a fascinating one involving a number of issues. One is the notion of a variable point as it was conceived of in eighteenth-century calculus. Another is Hegel's view that such a point is the contradictory unity of the discrete and the continuous.[12] However, we need not go into these issues now. Nor do we need to endorse the Hegelean view of the continuum. Let us just accept, tentatively—say, as a speculative hypothesis—that the localisation of an object is impossible over very small times; or, to be a bit more precise, let us accept the following principle.

Spread Hypothesis
A body cannot be localised to a point it is occupying at an instant of time, but only to those points it occupies in a small neighbourhood of that time.

This is not yet completely precise, but I will give a more rigorous interpretation of it in a moment. The spread hypothesis may be strange. Yet we are now accustomed to the idea that very strange things happen at small orders of spatio-temporal magnitude, say in the order of Planck's constant. And the spread hypothesis is no stranger than many such things.

To develop the Hegelean idea further, we need to make the spread principle more precise. The obvious vehicle for this is the tense-logical semantics of the previous chapter. To keep matters simple we will, in this chapter, restrict ourselves to structures where time is represented by the real line with the usual order. I am well aware that one might find this philosophically problematic, but it is not at issue (at the moment) scientifically.

Now, consider a body, b, in motion. Again to keep things simple, let us suppose that it is moving along a one dimensional continuum, also represented by the real line. Let us write Bx for 'b is at point x'. Let us also suppose that each real, r, has a name, $\underline{r}$. This assumption is innocuous. It could be avoided by talking in terms of satisfaction rather than truth. I make it only to keep the discussion at the propositional level. Let the motion of b be represented by the equation $x = f(t)$. Then the evaluation, v, which corresponds to this motion according to the Russellean account, is just that given by the conditions:

(1a) $1 \in v_t(B\underline{r})$ iff $r = f(t)$

(1b) $0 \in v_t(B\underline{r})$ iff $r \neq f(t)$

---

[12] 'To us there is no contradiction in the idea that the here of space and the now of time [i.e., variable points in a continuum] are considered as a continuity or length; but their notion is self contradictory. Self-identity or continuity is absolute cohesion, the destruction of all difference, of all negation, of all being for self; the point, on the contrary, is pure being-for-self, absolute self-distinction and the destruction of all identity and all connection with what is different.' Hegel (1840), vol. I, p. 268 of translation.

Let us call this the *Russellean state description* of the motion. We might depict it thus:

$$v_t : \qquad \neg B\underline{r} \qquad\qquad B\underline{r} \qquad \neg B\underline{r}$$

$$\text{<- - - - - - - - - - - -)(- - - - - - - - - - - - ->}$$

$$r : \qquad\qquad\qquad f(t)$$

The appropriate state description for the Hegelean account will, of course, be different, incorporating, as it does, the spread hypothesis. In accordance with the hypothesis, there is an interval containing t, θ_t (which may depend not only on t but also on f) such that, in some sense, if $t' \in \theta_t$, b's occupation of its location at t' is reproduced at t. I suggest that a plausible formal interpretation of this is that the state description of b at t is just the "superposition" of all the Russellean state descriptions, $v_{t'}$, where $t' \in \theta_t$. More precisely, it is the evaluation, v, given by the conditions

(2a) $1 \in v_t(B\underline{r})$ iff, for some $t' \in \theta_t, r = f(t')$

(2b) $0 \in v_t(B\underline{r})$ iff, for some $t' \in \theta_t, r \neq f(t')$

Let us call this the *Hegelean state description* of the motion. Suppose we write Σ_t for the *spread* of all the points occupied at t, i.e., for $\{f(t') \mid t' \in \theta_t\}$. If Σ_t is degenerate, that is if $\Sigma_t = \{f(t)\}$, then the Hegelean state description is identical with the Russellean one. If it is not, then, as may easily be seen, the condition on the righthand side of (2b) is satisfied by all r, and we may depict the Hegelean state description as follows:[13]

$$\qquad\qquad\qquad\qquad B\underline{r}$$

$$v_t : \qquad \neg B\underline{r} \qquad (- - - - - - - - - -)$$

$$\text{<- ->}$$

$$r : \qquad\qquad\qquad f(t)$$

$$(- - - - - - - - - -)$$

$$\Sigma_t$$

As the picture shows, if Σ_t is not degenerate, then at t a number of contradictions are realised. For all $r \in \Sigma_t$, $1 \in v_t(B\underline{r} \wedge \neg B\underline{r})$. Σ_t may be degenerate for one of two reasons. The first is that θ_t may itself be degenerate. That is, $\theta_t = \{t\}$. The other is that, though θ_t is not degenerate, f is constant over it. Now θ_t is not, in general, degenerate (or the Hegelean account collapses into the Russellean one). It is quite plausible to suppose that its length depends on the velocity of b, so that the faster b is going the more difficult it is to "pin it down". At any rate, provided θ_t is non-degenerate, if b satisfies the Russellean conditions of motion at

---

[13] A more extended graphical representation is given in Priest (1985).

t (namely that at arbitrarily close points of time it is to be found elsewhere), then contradictions will be realised at *t*.[14] If, on the other hand, a body occupies the same spot at all times in 0_t, Σ_t will be degenerate and no contradiction will be realised. It is possible (for all I have said so far) for a body to satisfy the Russellean conditions for rest, that is, to occupy the same place over a period of time, and yet for a contradiction to be realised during that time. This will happen at *t* if 0_t extends beyond this period of constant position. But since 0_t is very small (maybe in the order of Planck's constant?) this unstable state of affairs can never last for very long. We might even suppose that if $df/dt = 0$ then 0_t is degenerate. Now, if *f* is constant for a period around *t*, then $df/dt = 0$ at *t*. In this case, therefore, no contradiction is realised at *t*.

There is more that might be said about 0_t. One important question is whether, in general, 0_t extends on both sides of *t*. There is, in fact, reason for supposing that it does not, but that *t* is the least upper bound of 0_t. The reason is that, if 0_t extends beyond *t* into later times, we would appear to have backward causation. For the state description at *t* will depend upon the values of *f* at times after *t*. The reason is not conclusive. The dependence need not be a causal one. Indeed, the causal dependence may go in the other direction. (So that the position at a later time causally depends on the spread at an earlier time.) However, we can rework the point. Suppose we launch two objects on exactly the same trajectories and subject to exactly the same forces. At time *t* we subject one of the objects, but not the other, to a certain force, and their trajectories become different. Now, take a point of time, *t'*, prior to *t* but very close to it. Then, unless $0_{t'}$ decreases in length as *t'* approaches *t*, which there is no reason to suppose must happen in general, we can find a *t'* such that $0_{t'}$ extends past *t*. Since the trajectories of the two objects change after *t*, their state descriptions at *t'* will differ, and this is so even though their causal histories up to and including *t'* are identical. Here, therefore, we would seem to have a case of backward causation. If one thinks that backward causation is outrageous, then this will show that 0_t must end at *t*. I, however, do not think that it is *a priori* impossible for backward causation to occur. It may even be at the root of some interesting physical phenomena. But it seems to me that appealing to backward causation in the present context has little to recommend it. Accordingly, it would seem reasonable to suppose that 0_t is all past of *t*.

12.4 ...AND ITS CONSEQUENCES

The Hegelean state description of a body in motion, with its notion of the spread of locations at any time, makes quite precise Hegel's claim that to be in motion is

---

[14] We might note that the spread principle makes the situation more inconsistent than the LCC, which generates at most the contradiction $B\,\underline{f(t)} \wedge \neg B\,\underline{f(t)}$ at *t*.

to occupy more than one place (in fact a continuum of places) at the same time, and hence both to be and not to be in some place. It therefore renders quite rigorous his account of change. Moreover, the important defect of the account that I mentioned at the start of the last section, namely that it is unclear how the account relates to the canonical mathematical representation of motion, is clearly overcome. An equation of motion, $x = f(t)$, still captures the idea that at time t the object is at $f(t)$. It is just that there is more to change than this. It might be elsewhere too!

It is also not difficult to see that this account of motion solves the problems I mentioned that beset the orthodox account. The first problem concerned the counter-intuitiveness of the claim that there is no such thing as an intrinsic state of motion. This is obviously no problem for the Hegelean account. For it, there is an intrinsic state of motion: a certain inconsistent state. The difference between a body genuinely in motion and one changing place but at rest each instant is exactly that between a Hegelean state description and the corresponding Russellean one. Provided that there is an asymmetry in θ_t, such as its being skewed to the past of t, the direction of motion is intrinsic too.

The second objection to the orthodox account was that concerning Zeno's arrow. The Hegelean account of motion may be taken to locate a fault in the argument, but at a point different from that upon which Russell lights. For, according to Zeno's argument, at a particular point in time the object occupies only a single point in space, whence it follows that it advances not on its journey during that instant, i.e. that the measure of the set of points occupied at that instant is zero. Given the spread hypothesis, however, it is not true that the moving body occupies only a single point. At an instant, t, it occupies all the points in Σ_t, which is, in general, not a singleton. Indeed, provided the function of motion, f, is continuous, Σ_t is an interval, and therefore has non-zero measure. Thus, advance *is* made during a single instant, and hence during the aggregate of instants.

We see that the Hegelean account of motion has advantages over the Russellean one. Further research may be required to investigate the account. But the above strongly suggests that the Hegelean account is to be preferred to the Russellean one. To the same extent, the spread hypothesis is confirmed. One further area of research concerns θ_t. For example, how does this depend on f, and what is its physical significance? Though I do not know the answers to these questions, I cannot resist a (perhaps rather fanciful) speculation. According to quantum theory, given any particle, there is a certain uncertainty in its location at a time, t. This is not surprising if the particle is not located at a single point, but is "spread out" over the whole interval Σ_t. Perhaps the measure of Σ_t, $\sigma(\Sigma_t)$, just is the uncertainty in the location of the object at t. Perhaps quantum mechanical indeterminacies are fundamentally the result of inconsistencies in motion, and in particular in the spread postulated by the spread hypothesis. This suggestion at least allows us to give physical significance to the spread. For, in general, the momentum, p, of an object is in a continuous state of change too; hence, by exactly the same considerations, it is spread out at t over a range Π_t. Heisenberg's uncertainty principle then gives us that:

$$\sigma(\Sigma_t) \times \sigma(\Pi_t) \geq h/2\pi.$$

Let me end this chapter with one final application of the Hegelean account of change, where the change in question this time is not motion. Take any point of time, say, midnight on 1/1/2000. Then at this time 'It is midnight on 1/1/2000' is true. For a continuous period before and up to this time 'It is not midnight on 1/1/2000' is true. Hence by the LCC, this is true at midnight too. Thus, at this time it is both midnight on 1/1/2000 and not midnight on 1/1/2000. This application of the LCC is somewhat moot. It is not completely clear that 'It is midnight' and similar temporal claims describe states of affairs in the required sense of the word. But assuming that they do, the fact that such contradictions are produced, together with the Hegelean account of change, gives an exact and plausible sense to the obviously true and non-trivial claim that time itself is in a state of change or flux. This commonsense view has given all sorts of problems to the Russellean account of change. For, on the orthodox account, the view that time is itself in a state of change amounts to the banality that at one time it is one time, and at another, another. This has prompted a variety of responses of varying degrees of incredibility, from the view that time is not in a state of flux, to the view that there are "hypertimes". The contradiction theory of change solves the problem cleanly and swiftly.[15]

Even given that "B series" (that is, non-indexical temporal) predicates, such as 'is midnight on 1/1/2000', describe genuine states of affairs, it is another question whether "A series" (that is, indexical temporal) predicates, and especially 'is past', 'is future', and 'is present', refer to states of affairs within the meaning of the LCC act. This is a rather thorny issue which I do not intend to discuss here. But if they do, and assuming that the present is the instant where the past changes into the future, applications of the LCC give the result that the present is the time when things are both future and past, past and not past, future and not future. The instantaneous present is well known for producing philosophical perplexities. If it is a contradictory object, this is hardly surprising.

A number of people have argued that time in itself is inconsistent. Many of these, such as the idealists Bradley and McTaggart, thought that for this reason it should be consigned to the realm of appearances, or of non-existence—though exactly what this means is not so clear. Dialetheism allows time to be both inconsistent and real.

---

[15] This issue is taken further in Priest (1992). More orthodox discussions of the problem can be found in Gale (1967), pt 2.

13

Norms and the Philosophy of Law

13.1 INCONSISTENT OBLIGATIONS

The last two chapters have been devoted to empirical dialetheias produced by the natural world. In this chapter I wish to discuss some produced by the social world. In particular, I wish to discuss dialetheias that are produced by systems of norms or rules. For the sake of concreteness I will discuss in detail one kind of system, which, however, I take to be fairly representative: systems of law. In section 13.5 I will broaden the discussion to encompass other kinds of normative system. For the present, let us concentrate on systems of law.[1]

Before looking at legal dialetheias as such, I wish to prepare the ground by discussing a lesser form of contradiction: inconsistent obligations, that is, situations where someone is obliged both to do *x* and not to do *x*. Though some have been tempted to deny it, that there can be—indeed, are—such situations is beyond doubt. Take a very simple case. I contract with party *X* to be present at a certain spot at a certain time. Separately, I contract with party *Y* not to be present at that spot at that time. Both contracts are validated in the usual way, by witnessing, etc. I may do this with or without ill intention. It may be my intention to deceive one of the parties. On the other hand, I may just be absent-minded. In such circumstances I am legally obliged both to be and not to be at this spot at this time. (And if it be suggested that this is not a case of inconsistent obligations *simpliciter*, since I am obliged to *X* to be at that spot and obliged to *Y* not to be, just take *X* and *Y* to be the same person.)

How can one be sure that I am committed to inconsistent obligations in the situation described? The answer is simple. If, after the event, I am sued by the party of whichever contract I do not comply with, the court will hold me in breach of obligation and award damages appropriately. Having committed myself to do something different is no defence. This is an important test, so let me spell it out clearly. A sufficient condition for my being legally obliged to do something is that the court of appropriate jurisdiction (and in the last instance the ultimate appellate court) would hold me in default were I not to do it. I will call this the *default test*.

---

[1] I am grateful to Val Kerruish for discussions on the issues of this section and the next.

The source of contradictory obligations need not be different contracts, but may be one and the same contract. Of course, in practice it is rare for a contract *per se* to be blatantly inconsistent, but it is not unusual for a contract plus contingent circumstances to give someone inconsistent obligations. Suppose, for example, that I contract to do z under condition X, but refrain from doing z under condition Y. We may suppose that X and Y are events not under the control of the parties of the contract, and that there is no *reasonable* likelihood of X and Y both occurring. Suppose that, despite this, both do occur. Can I then be held in breach for whichever of the actions I do not perform? Courts being what they are, the answer is not as determinate as one might wish. None the less, the answer is a qualified 'yes'. The qualification is due to the legal doctrine of discharge by frustration. A court may resolve that the contract has been frustrated by unforeseen circumstances and render any *prima facie* obligations void. However, frustration is not always invoked. Indeed, the precise circumstances of when it is appropriate to invoke it seem somewhat moot. Therefore, a conditionally inconsistent contract may pass the default test. It should also be pointed out that the doctrine of discharge by frustration is a relatively recent one. Until 1863 frustration was not a ground for discharge. Courts acted on the ruling of Paradine *v.* Jane (1647) that,[2]

when a party by his own contract creates a duty or charge upon himself, he is bound to make it good, if he may, notwithstanding any accident by inevitable necessity, because it might have provided against it by his contract. And therefore if the lessee covenant to repair a house, though it be burnt by lightning, or thrown down by enemies, yet he ought to repair it.

It might be granted that the above shows that someone may be legally obliged to do x and legally obliged not to do x, but not that someone can be legally obliged to do and not to do x. (In the notation of section 13.3, $O\alpha$ and $O\neg\alpha$, but not $O(\alpha \wedge \neg\alpha)$.) I shall reject this distinction in section 13.3. But is it, in any case, possible to produce an example of a collectively inconsistent obligation? The answer is, again, a qualified 'yes'. Suppose that someone contracts to bring it about that $\alpha \wedge \neg\alpha$. If they do not fulfil this, would the *prima facie* obligation pass the default test? The answer to this is unclear. Courts have a number of ways of defusing unconditional inconsistencies in contracts, from striking out minor clauses to ruling the whole thing void for uncertainty. The situation becomes clearer, for once, if we move to something less simplistic. Suppose that someone contracts to bring about a more complex inconsistency, say, the squaring of the circle. Suppose that they contracted to do this before it was known to be impossible, and that they failed to fulfil the contract. Would a court hold them in default? The answer is 'yes'. Suppose it were proved to be impossible after signing the contract but before the court hearing? The answer is still 'yes'. Suppose that it were proved to be impossible before signing the contract, but that the contractor

---

[2] Guest (1969), p. 454, where a further discussion of frustration can also be found.

took on the contract believing the proof to be wrong. The answer is still 'yes'. Hence, under many conditions one can have collectively inconsistent obligations that pass the default test.

We see that it is quite possible to be legally obliged to do the inconsistent, both distributively and collectively. To conclude this section, it is perhaps worth noting that some philosophers, such as Aquinas, were quite happy with the idea that one could have inconsistent obligations, but thought that these could arise only if one had done something improper to get oneself into this situation in the first place, for example making a promise (contract) that one ought not to have done. But even this is arguably wrong, at least in the case of legal obligation. Inconsistent legislation may well put an otherwise law-abiding citizen in this unfortunate state. For example, suppose that there is a pair of statutes, one of which requires a car owner to change registration plates on January 1st, and the other of which forbids working on a Sunday. About every seven years the average law-abiding citizen is embarrassed.[3] The possibility of inconsistent legislation produces far bigger fish to fry, however.

13.2 LEGAL DIALETHEIAS

It is important to distinguish inconsistent obligations from legal dialetheias. That one is obliged both to do x and not to do x is not itself a contradiction. I now wish to argue that legal systems are wont to produce not only inconsistent obligations but also dialetheias. A simple way of arguing this would be to endorse the principle that if one is obliged not to do x then one is not obliged to do x. (In the symbolism of section 13.3, $O\neg\alpha \rightarrow \neg O\alpha$.) This transforms any inconsistent obligation ($O\alpha \wedge O\neg\alpha$) into an outright contradiction ($O\alpha \wedge \neg O\alpha$). But as I shall argue in section 13.4, this principle is not correct; so one cannot argue in this way. The most cogent way of showing that there are legal dialetheias, and the way I shall adopt, is to produce *prima facie* examples, and then argue that they are what, *prima facie*, they appear to be. Though one might cite actual historical examples, this would not be best for my purposes. The niceties of interpretation and scholarship tend to cloak the essential issue. And since my intention is to establish only the possibility of the production of legal dialetheias, I will use hypothetical examples.

Suppose that there is a certain country which has a constitutional parliamentary system of government. And suppose that its constitution contains the following clauses:

In a parliamentary election:

(1) no person of the female sex shall have the right to vote;
(2) all property holders shall have the right to vote.

---

[3] Fuller (1969), pp. 65–6.

We may also suppose that it is part of common law that women may not legally possess property. As enlightenment creeps over the country, this part of common law is revised to allow women to hold property. We may suppose that a *de facto* right is eventually recognised as a *de jure* one. Inevitably, sooner or later, a woman, whom we will call 'Jan', turns up at a polling booth for a parliamentary election claiming the right to vote on the ground that she is a property holder. A test case ensues. Patently, the law is inconsistent. Jan, it would seem, both does and does not have the right to vote in this election.

In this example, changes in one part of the law produced contradiction in another. Change is inessential, as the next example shows. Many countries have traffic priority laws to determine which vehicle shall proceed first at an unmarked junction. Let us suppose that the priority law of a certain state is as follows:

At an unmarked junction at which two vehicles arrive simultaneously:

(1) any female driver shall have priority over any male driver;
(2) any older person shall have priority over any younger person.

We may suppose that the absent-minded legislator who made the law added clause (2) because clause (1) is not always sufficient to determine priority, but failed to realise that, if it were not made subordinate to clause (1), it could in certain cases conflict with it.

The priority law determines a unique priority in three out of four cases. It could even work in practice—if, for example, there were no, or at least very few, female drivers younger than any male driver. Yet if an occasion does arise when Mr X, of age 40, meets Ms Y, of age 30, at a junction, we have both:

Ms Y has priority   by (1)

Mr X has priority   by (2)

Consequently, Ms Y does not have priority, by the second of these and the meaning of 'priority'.[4] So Y (and, of course, X) both has and does not have priority. (It is also clear that we have a counter-example to *ex contradictione quodlibet*. It does not follow from this contradiction that the law is consistent!)

Naturally, it is possible to raise certain objections to these *prima facie* dialetheias.[5] The contradictions in question follow simply from a few contingent

---

[4] This is an internal relation in the sense of sect. 4.8. Appeal to it could be avoided by spelling out, in the priority law itself, what it is to have priority. Thus, it may be said of the relevant party that they may go first and that no other party may go first.

[5] There are many other examples of *prima facie* dialetheias. One of these, which may or may not be purely hypothetical, is the traditional one of Protagoras and Euathlus. Protagoras taught Euathlus law on the condition that Protagoras' fee should be paid when Euathlus won his first case. When the tuition was complete and Euathlus showed no sign of practising law, Protagoras sued for his fee. Whatever the judgment of the court, we have a contradiction. For (as Protagoras reasoned) Euathlus will be obliged to pay him, either in virtue of the judgment of the court (if Protagoras is successful) or by the contract (if he is not). And (as Euathlus reasoned) he is not legally obliged to pay Protagoras, either in virtue of the judgment of the court (if Euathlus is successful) or by the contract (if he is not). Many have noted that legislation may be self referential, and hence may

facts and certain statements of legal obligation, right, etc. Given that the contingent facts are not at issue, and that the reasoning is valid, the only way to reject the truth of the contradiction is to reject the truth of the statements of legal obligation, right, etc.

There are a number of ways that one might do this. The crudest is to deny that any statement of legal right, obligation, and so on, is true/false. Thus, as many of the positivists held to be correct, we might interpret a sentence such as 'Jan has the right to vote' as a covert command, i.e. 'Do not stop Jan voting!', or as an expression of attitude: 'Jan voting? OK'. This view, scarcely credible at the best of times, would find few adherents now. The verification theory of meaningfulness is, fortunately, dead. And since it was a major rationale for the non-statemental theory of norms, this view now finds itself on a branch of which the tree has been felled. There are also numerous arguments against the view.[6] Quite crucially, this account of norms makes it semantically impossible for them to be embedded in longer sentences in sentential places, which they obviously can be. Thus, it may not be the case that Jan has the right to vote, or John may believe that Jan has the right to vote. However, *'It is not the case that do not prevent Jan from voting' and *'John believes that do not prevent Jan from voting' are clearly nonsense. If more arguments are needed, then it is easy enough to derive one from the theory of truth given in chapter 4. It is uncontentious that statements of legal obligation, right, etc. (or at least many of them) have clear and objective conditions under which it is correct to assert them. (For example, it is without doubt that I presently have the right—indeed, the obligation—to vote in an Australian federal election, while my son does not.) And this is all that is necessary for the truth of such claims according to the teleological account of truth (see section 4.5). For, provided these conditions obtain, an utterance of the claim will meet the point of assertion, and so be true. Whether a statement of right/duty corresponds to some metaphysical fact is of no relevance. The point is that such statements are used, endorsed, rejected, conveyed, reasoned from/to, under substantially determinate conditions of correctness, which is sufficient warrant for calling them true/false.[7]

Once it is granted that statements of legal right/obligation are, in general, true/false, the only way out of the view that there are legal dialetheias is to deny that the (hypothetical) laws used in the examples are (hypothetically) true. This is a tough task. For we may suppose that the laws were made by duly constituted bodies in the appropriate fashion, and this would seem to be what it takes to be a law. Though legislatures may not be able to make the earth go round the moon,

---

produce situations that are paradoxical. (See Goldstein (1979) for references and discussion.) A paradigm example of this is as follows. Take the sovereign body of a State. This sovereign passes a law which contains a clause to the effect that the law cannot be repealed. Now, since it is the sovereign body, it can repeal this law. But equally, since it is sovereign, the law stands and is therefore irrepealable. It is not clear to me that these two contradictions can be shown to be more than *prima facie* dialetheias, and I will not discuss them further.

[6] See e.g. Brandt (1959), ch. 9; Forrester (1982).
[7] This is broadly in line with Hart's conception of law; see e.g. Hart (1954).

or make π equal to 3 by fiat, they would certainly seem to be able to produce legal obligations and rights by fiat. It is this that must be contested. In fact, such simple voluntarism is false. There is more to the law than the simple wording of statutes. There is also a complex process of judicial interpretation and application. The literal say-so of a statute is the law only *ceteris paribus*. It is on this fact that an objector to dialetheism must attempt to capitalise. I shall argue that this is a bad investment.

The obvious, and most plausible, way to pursue this line of objection is this. In virtue of the process of the interpretation of law, the law itself, as opposed to the literal statement of statute, must be considered to have exceptive clauses which operate under the conditions that would otherwise produce inconsistency, in such a way as to prevent it. There are a number of ways we can make good sense of this idea. For example, not all laws are of equal rank. Laws go in increasing order of strength from customary law, through case law, to legislation. Thus, it is reasonable to suppose that, if a lower ranking law contradicts a higher ranking law in a particular case, it ceases, *ipso facto*, to be applicable. Another way of making sense of the idea that a law has implicit exceptive clauses is as follows. There is a well established legal principle, *lex posterior*, to the effect that a later law always takes precedence over an earlier law when these come into conflict. Thus, an earlier law which contradicts a later law in a particular case is not applicable. Yet a third way of making sense of the existence of implicit exceptive clauses is this: The preamble of the bill that contains a piece of legislation may make the intentions of the legislators quite clear. It may then be obvious that, although a particular case falls under the act as literally worded, the law was never meant to apply to this kind of case. The intentions of the legislators therefore provide the basis for the existence of an implicit exceptive clause.[8]

Now, the crucial point in the present context is this: though the claim of the existence of implicit exceptive clauses can undoubtedly be made reasonable *sometimes* by these kinds of consideration, she who rejects dialetheism must do more than claim that apparent contradictions can sometimes be resolved in this way; she must claim that this can *always* be done. And this is most unreasonable. A case may easily arise where both of the contradiction-producing laws are of equal rank, where both laws were produced at the same time, where the intentions of the legislators are lost in the mists of time, are moot, or are downright inconsistent, where there is no precedent for waiving one law rather than another, and so on. In short, there is nothing objective to underpin the claim that one law has an implicit exceptive clause in virtue of which it is not applicable. (Both of the hypothetical examples given could be of this kind if the background details are filled in carefully.) In such circumstances, to insist that, none the less, one or other of the laws has implicit exceptive clauses is mere whimsy. There may

---

[8] This case is much more problematic than the previous cases, however. For judges do sometimes uphold the letter of the law even when it is clear that they are going against the spirit of the law; see Fitzgerald (1966), p. 137.

well be more to the law than the literal wording of statute, but to suppose that something could be a fact of law when grounded in no aspect of the legal process is just mystification.

When a contradiction of the kind we are discussing becomes important, there are procedures for resolving it. The matter goes before a court where a judge makes a decision. Since there are, *ex hypothesi*, no legal grounds on which to base the decision, the judge will decide on extra-legal (socio-political) grounds. The important point here, however, is that the judge is not trying to find out what the (consistent) law is, but is himself creating law. What the judge decides just is the law (until and unless over-ruled by a higher court, or new statute law is passed). Thus, the judge, by creating law, is changing the corpus of law. His judgement provides the basis for the law to be considered, henceforth, to have an exceptive clause. Hence, *after* the ruling the law may be consistent. This does not change the fact that *before* the ruling the law was inconsistent. Indeed, this was just why the ruling was required. We see, therefore, that the fact that literal wording is only *ceteris paribus* the law does not help to avoid dialetheism. Sometimes the *cetera* are *pares*.

There is a final, desperate, move, which is to suppose that legislation comes with a global exceptive clause to the effect that it is not applicable if it is inconsistent with the rest of the corpus of law. It might even be argued that the existence of this exceptive clause can be grounded in the fact that judges always act in such a way as to resolve contradictions. Whether or not this is so, the thesis cannot be maintained without making a nonsense of the law. If this were right, then, since there is no decision procedure for consistency, there could be no effective way of telling whether or not something is the law, which is obviously absurd. If this is not clear, consider the case where the received body of law is inconsistent, but where the inconsistency is too recondite to have been noticed (yet), or where the contingent circumstances necessary for the realisation of the legal contradiction never arise. In such a case, according to the consistency-proviso suggestion, there would be no law. None the less, the courts would proceed in the normal way applying the non-existent law, each and every non-existent law. The situation would be completely indistinguishable from the present one. (In fact, it probably is the present one.) The vacuity of this suggestion is therefore established.

13.3 DEONTIC SEMANTICS

Having established the existence of inconsistent obligations and legal dialetheias, we next need to face the question of what kind of semantical account is suitable for deontic notions. The orthodox approach[9] adds deontic operators to non-deontic logical vocabulary, and states the truth conditions of sentences that contain them

---

[9] As explained, for example, in Føllesdal and Hilpinen (1971).

in terms of a suitable accessibility relation on a set of (classical) possible worlds. It will be clear from the considerations of the previous sections that this approach will not do. It cannot even cope with inconsistent obligations, let alone deontic dialetheias. Classically, it is impossible for $O\alpha$ and $O\neg\alpha$ to be true. (Actually, this isn't quite true. If (and only if) a world accesses nothing, both $O\alpha$ and $O\neg\alpha$ will hold at the world. But then so will $O\beta$ for all β. This is absurd. If I have inconsistent legal obligations, perhaps as a result of signing contracts to sell the same car to two different people, it in no way follows that I am obliged to shoot both of them and, for that matter, do everything else.) It is possible to avoid this problem by enlarging the class of possible worlds to include inconsistent ones.[10] However, it is not clear to me that this kind of approach is correct, and that the postulation of deontically ideal worlds does not mystify the matter unduly. Hence I will follow the same syntactic approach as usual, but use a different semantic approach.

We need take only one deontic operator as primitive, O. Its reading needs to be given with some care. $O\alpha$ should be understood thus: if the world were such that all extant obligations were duly fulfilled, then it would be the case that α. It is common for O to be read 'It is obligatory that'. This is surely a mistake. For one reason, α may be any sentence; yet it is not even clear that 'It is obligatory that the sun is shining' makes sense. Obligation has to do with agents. Even if we were to restrict the scope of O to sentences that made reference to agents, it would still be doubtful that this reading is correct. For let α be the sentence 'John robs the bank or he does not.' Then $O\alpha$ may come out as true in most deontic semantics, including those I shall propose; but it is doubtful that John's robbing the bank or failing to is obligatory. Conceivably, the obligation could be regarded as a degenerate one, but it seems more sensible to suppose that obligation proper is to be understood in some way such as the following: 'x is obliged to F' means '$O(x$ brings it about that x $Fs)$' (where the fact that x Fs regardless does not imply that x brings it about that x Fs). Such an analysis of obligation requires a prior analysis of *bringing about*. This lies outside the scope of the present work, so I shall not pursue the matter here. Notwithstanding any of the above, I will often gloss $O\alpha$ as 'It is obligatory that α' in lieu of its more cumbersome and precise counterpart.

Other deontic operators may be defined in terms of O in the usual way: $F\alpha$ ($O\neg\alpha$), it is forbidden that α; $P\alpha$ ($\neg F\alpha$), it is permissible that α. (These glosses should be understood in the light of the previous discussion of O.) These do not exhaust the deontic modalities. Another concerns the possession of rights, 'x has the right to F'. Perhaps the most sensible interpretation of this is something like: 'x is permitted to F and no one else is permitted to stop x F-ing', but the exact details are not relevant here.

Let us turn now to the semantics of the deontic operators. In any world, w, O will have both an extension, $\omega^+(w)$, and an anti-extension, $\omega^-(w)$ (in a sense similar to that introduced for predicates in section 5.3). $\omega^+(w)$ contains all those

---

[10] See e.g. Priest and Routley (1983), ch. 4, sect. 4, and Routley and Plumwood (1989).

sentences of which obligatoriness may be truly predicated (at world w). $\omega^-(w)$ contains all those sentences of which it may be falsely predicated (there). We need to require that $\omega^+(w)$ and $\omega^-(w)$ be exhaustive (see section 4.7), though not exclusive. What other conditions should be placed on them? It is natural to require that $\omega^+(w)$ be closed under entailment: if $\alpha \to \beta$ is true (at G), then if $\alpha \in \omega^+(w)$, $\beta \in \omega^+(w)$. If α would be true if all obligations were fulfilled then so would β, entailment preserving truth. Dually, $\omega^-(w)$ should be closed in the opposite direction: if $\alpha \to \beta$ is true (at G) and $\beta \in \omega^-(w)$, then $\alpha \in \omega^-(w)$. A second highly plausible condition is that $\omega^+(w)$ should be closed under adjunction: if $\alpha \in \omega^+(w)$ and $\beta \in \omega^+(w)$, then $\alpha \wedge \beta \in \omega^+(w)$. If α would be true if all obligations were fulfilled and so would β, then $\alpha \wedge \beta$ would be true under these conditions. Dually, $\omega^-(w)$ should be closed in the opposite direction: if $\alpha \wedge \beta \in \omega^-(w)$, then $\alpha \in \omega^-(w)$ or $\beta \in \omega^-(w)$. These are the only extra conditions we will place on $\omega^+(w)$ and $\omega^-(w)$. Concerning the question of whether or not sets of formulas with these properties can themselves be obtained by a possible-worlds construction, we may remain blissfully agnostic. Of course, it might be suggested that the conditions I am requiring are incorrect. I will defend them later in this section. Conversely, it might be suggested that further conditions are desirable. I will address this issue in the next section. For the time being, let us leave these matters there.

In virtue of these considerations and the semantics of chapter 6, it should now be reasonably clear what the semantics of a propositional language, duly expanded with the type of deontic operators explained above, will be like. An interpretation is a 6-tuple, $\langle G, W, R, \omega^+, \omega^-, v \rangle$, where $\langle G, W, R, v \rangle$ is an interpretation for the propositional language of section 6.3, and ω^+ and ω^- are functions from W whose values are sets of formulas. For any $w \in W$, $\omega^+(w)$ and $\omega^-(w)$ exhaust the set of formulas, $\omega^+(w)$ is closed under entailment and adjunction, and $\omega^-(w)$ is closed dually, as explained in the last paragraph. The only novel clauses in the statement of truth conditions are those for O, which should be obvious in virtue of the above discussion:

(Oa) $1 \in v_w(O\gamma)$ iff $\gamma \in \omega^+(w)$

(Ob) $0 \in v_w(O\gamma)$ iff $\gamma \in \omega^-(w)$

The derived truth conditions for F and P can be easily checked to be:

(Fa) $1 \in v_w(F\gamma)$ iff $\neg\gamma \in \omega^+(w)$

(Fb) $0 \in v_w(F\gamma)$ iff $\neg\gamma \in \omega^-(w)$

(Pa) $1 \in v_w(P\gamma)$ iff $\neg\gamma \in \omega^-(w)$

(Pb) $0 \in v_w(P\gamma)$ iff $\neg\gamma \in \omega^+(w)$

Semantic consequence is to be defined in terms of truth preservation at G in the usual way.

The semantics have a natural extension to quantifiers and other first-order machinery. In the predicate case, the extension of O is taken to be a set of pairs of which the first member is an evaluation of the variables and the second is a formula. (Similarly for the anti-extension of O.) This time, however, the details of the extension to the predicate case are not straightforward. Moreover, since this kind of modelling has a general application to the semantics of non-extensional operators which goes well beyond the present area of discussion, I will pursue the issue on another occasion. The propositional semantics will be adequate for present purposes.

It is not my intention to discuss the formal details of the propositional semantics either. Instead, I will discuss some of their more philosophical aspects, which might be considered to be problematic. First, I will discuss two principles which are valid but which, it might be thought, should be rejected. The first of these is that obligation is transmitted over entailment:

$$\{\alpha \to \beta\} \models O\alpha \to O\beta$$

The second is that obligations conjoin:

$$\models O\alpha \wedge O\beta \to O(\alpha \wedge \beta)$$

Both of these can easily be checked to be semantically valid in virtue of the restrictions on ω^+ and ω^-.

The transmission of obligation over entailment would seem to be fairly clear. If α holds when all obligations are fulfilled, and α entails β, then β holds when all obligations are fulfilled. The most cogent argument against the principle is the so-called "good Samaritan paradox".[11] It can be put in many forms, but all are attempts to find a case in which an obligatory α entails a non-obligatory (indeed, forbidden) β. For example:

(i) Granny pays back the loan to the man whom she is going to kill $\to$ Granny is going to kill a man.
(ii) Granny owned up after killing the vicar $\to$ Granny killed the vicar.
(iii) Granny was very sorry for killing the vicar $\to$ Granny killed the vicar.

The examples are not cogent. (i) can be handled merely by observing a simple ambiguity in the scope of the definite description in 'Granny is obliged to repay the loan to the man whom she is going to kill.' For this may mean 'There is a (unique we hope) man whom Granny is going to kill and to whom she is obliged to repay a loan (presumably first).' And this may well be true, but no awkward obligations follow. On the other hand, it may mean that there is an obligation on Granny that there be a man whom she kills and to whom she repays a loan. The untenable obligations certainly follow from this, but it is just plain false, since only the repaying, and not the killing, needs be obligatory.

---

[11] See e.g. Castañeda (1981).

(ii) cannot be handled in the same way since there is no description present. But the antecedent is equivalent to the conjunction 'Granny killed the vicar and then she owned up.' And it is clear that this is not obligatory. Again, only the owning up need be obligatory, not the killing.

(iii) is slightly less clear. The crucial question is whether the antecedent is a purely subjective description of Granny's state of mind, in which case it does not entail the consequent, since she may be living in false hopes. Alternatively, if it does also make an objective claim, it must be considered as saying something like: 'Granny killed the vicar and was then very sorry for it', in which case the situation is the same as that in (ii).

There is another, more minor, objection to the principle of the transmission of obligation. Since $\alpha \rightarrow \alpha \vee \beta$, it follows from the principle that, if Granny is obliged to give the vicar tea, she is obliged to give him tea or poison him. This is often called 'Ross's paradox', but its air of paradoxicality disappears once we recall the precise sense of O. For if it is true that if all obligations were fulfilled the vicar would be given tea by Granny, it is true that under such conditions he would *either* be given tea *or* be poisoned. And, provided we read 'or' as *or* and not as *and*, this is not problematic.[12] "Ross's paradox" also has an "infinitary" form. Since $\alpha \rightarrow \exists x\alpha$, $O\alpha \rightarrow O\exists x\alpha$ and hence $\exists xO\alpha \rightarrow O\exists x\alpha$. Hintikka has objected to this on the ground that, though there may be an act that ought to be punished, it does not follow that there ought to be an act that is punished.[13] This *does* follow however, at least on the understanding of O that I have explained. If there is something that ought to be punished (for example Granny's murder of the vicar), then it clearly ought to be the case that *something* is punished. (Hintikka points out that in a "deontically perfect world" it is false that something is punished. Whatever we are to make of the notion of perfection here, it is equally clear that in a perfect world nothing such as Granny's murder of the vicar would occur either.) The principle of the transmission of obligation is, therefore, perfectly acceptable.

The second principle, which says that obligations can be conjoined, also seems very reasonable. If α and β would both be realised if all obligations were met, then so too would their conjunction. Indeed, it is very difficult to see what there could be to being obliged to bring about a conjunction, other than being obliged to bring about both conjuncts. Of course, if we tacitly qualify our obligations according to source, so that O_a means 'It is obligatory in virtue of Australian law that' and O_b means 'It is obligatory in virtue of British law that', then we may well have $O_a\alpha$ and $O_b\beta$ without having either $O_a(\alpha \wedge \beta)$ or $O_b(\alpha \wedge \beta)$, but it is the divers relativisations that wreck the conjunction here.

Despite this, the principle has been questioned by some writers.[14] The main reason given is as follows. It is granted that there are sentences, α, such that both

---

[12] See pp. 21 ff. of Føllesdal and Hilpinen (1971).   [13] Hintikka (1971), p. 102.
[14] See e.g. Schotch and Jennings (1981).

Oα and O¬α; but, it is suggested, O(α ∧ ¬α) is never true. I have already given reasons in section 13.1 for supposing that things of the form O(α ∧ ¬α) may be true. Why should we suppose that they cannot be? Well, as long as we stick with a logic such that α ∧ ¬α → β is valid, and retain the principle of obligation transmission, a conjoined contradictory obligation is clearly unacceptable. But once we reject the principle *ex contradictione quodlibet*, as the underlying propositional logic in our case does, this reasoning carries little weight.

Another reason that might be given for supposing that O(α ∧ ¬α) must be rejected, even if Oα and O¬α have been accepted, is that, since α ∧ ¬α cannot be true, and since "ought implies can", O(α ∧ ¬α) is not true. Against this, one might question the claim that it is impossible to realise α ∧ ¬α (for the sorts of reasons given in the previous two chapters). However, I take it that, for the sorts of αs that are likely to be of serious interest in the present context, the realisation of α ∧ ¬α is not a practical possibility. It seems to me that it is the Kantian principle that ought implies can which should be met head-on. What reasons are there for it?

Kant's justification for the principle is hardly perspicuous.[15] His point would seem to be that in general the freedom to act, to do, or to refrain is a presupposition of a set of norms (in particular, moral norms) that would otherwise be pointless. Whether or not this is so, it is irrelevant to the question at hand, since it is quite compatible with the requirement that in general agents should be able to act or to refrain, that on a particular and isolated occasion the norms may impose conditions that cannot be fulfilled. The Kantian rationale is therefore beside the point.

Few philosophers other than Kant have defended the principle, though many have appealed to Kant's authority. One of the few that has is Hare.[16] Hare suggests that it is not only the existence of a system of norms that presupposes that agents have the *general* ability to act or to refrain, but also the existence of each *particular* obligation that presupposes that the agent in question has the particular ability to act or to refrain. Hare's reason is that if the agent does not have the ability to do this the question of what he *ought* to do "does not arise". The argument is, however, very weak. The assumption is that the only situation under which '*x* ought to *F*' can be appropriately (and hence truly) asserted is when someone is deciding what some agent (perhaps herself) is to do, and that such a process of deliberation will be undertaken only if the outcome is not a foregone conclusion. At most, this shows not that "ought implies can" but only that "ought implies that someone believes can". And clearly, a person may believe something to be possible when it is not, and vice versa. A more fundamental objection to Hare is that this kind of situation is not the only one in which 'ought' statements are appropriately asserted. 'Ought' statements are often

---

[15] See e.g. the initial parts of the third section of Kant's *Foundations of the Metaphysics of Morals*.
[16] Hare (1963), sect. 4.3.

appropriately asserted when there is no question of a genuine decision to be made, for example in assigning legal responsibility. And as we saw in section 13.1, despite the doctrine of discharge by frustration, it is quite possible for an agent to be held legally responsible for something, even though circumstances meant that he had no real choice in defaulting.

Another philosopher who has defended the "ought implies can" principle is von Wright.[17] He does this by assimilating obligations to commands, and then suggesting that one cannot command someone to do the impossible. The first move I have already objected to in section 13.2. But even if this were correct, the second point is wrong. Von Wright secures it only by a tendentious account of commanding. According to him, a command to do *x* is an expression of the will of the commander that *x* be done. This is wrong. Commanding someone is just telling them what they must do, or, presumably, be liable for some penalty. Willing them to do it is not involved. For example, from a position of authority I can command someone to climb the Eiffel Tower, or even to square the circle, and want them *not* to do it, maybe so that I can penalise them. Even if all else were right, von Wright's argument would work only with the additional premise that one cannot want (will) someone to do the impossible, and this is quite false. Certainly I can will someone to do the impossible if I do not believe it to be impossible. I can even want someone to do something that I believe it to be impossible (in the hope that it is not). The argument will not, therefore, work.

When all this has been said, there remains the feeling that if someone fails to meet an obligation, not for reasons of personal failing, but just because it is impossible for him to do what is required, it is not right to blame him. This is undoubtedly true, but does not support the "ought implies can" maxim either. For the existence of an obligation is quite compatible with being unblameworthy for not fulfilling it. Suppose, for example, that I incur a debt with every legitimate expectation of being able to repay it. Through no fault of my own, I am unable to repay it. (Maybe because I am made redundant.) The obligation to repay the loan still exists, as the default test shows. The court will declare me bankrupt and appoint a receiver to try to ensure that the obligation is met as far as possible. It is clear that the appropriate attitude to me should be one of pity rather than blame. "Ought implies can" therefore has little going for it.

A final, and different, putative counter-example to the conjunction principle can be manufactured as follows.[18] I contract to do *x* by midnight. Unfortunately, by 11 pm I have put myself in a position (geographical, financial or whatever) where I cannot do it. Hence it would seem that at 11.30 pm I am still obliged to do *x*, though also obliged to make reparation for not doing *x*. It is hardly the case, however, that I am obliged to both do it and make reparation for not doing it. The problem is solved by taking the temporal considerations seriously. Until

---

[17] von Wright (1963), pp. 108 ff.   [18] Thomason (1981). The solution is also his.

midnight I am obliged to do x. But even if I know beforehand that I will not be able to do x, I have not failed till midnight. Hence it is only after midnight that I am obliged to make reparation, and after midnight I am no longer obliged to do x (though it is the case that I was so obliged). The two obligations never stand together. Thus, the second deontic principle is quite acceptable.

13.4 SOME SEMANTIC INVALIDITIES

Now that I have defended the conditions I put on ω^+ and ω^-, the question arises as to whether there are other conditions that should naturally be imposed. Though I certainly do not wish to deny the possibility of this, I know of no conditions that one might reasonably defend. In this section I will consider a couple of conditions by which one might be tempted. Most orthodox deontic logics include the principle

$$O\alpha \rightarrow P\alpha$$

or its equivalent:

$$O\neg\alpha \rightarrow \neg O\alpha$$

The rationale for this is just that it appears to state, what many have taken to be correct, that one cannot have inconsistent obligations. It may therefore be a little surprising that it is quite possible to validate this principle in the above semantics while still having inconsistent obligations. If we impose the condition that, for all $w \in W$ if $\neg\alpha \in \omega^+(w)$ then $\alpha \in \omega^-(w)$, then, as may easily be checked, the above principle is validated. Moreover, this condition does not require $\omega^+(w)$ to be consistent. For example, it will be satisfied whatever $\omega^+(w)$ is if $\omega^-(w)$ contains all formulas. The effect of this condition is not, then, to rule out inconsistent obligations. Rather, it transforms any inconsistent obligation, $O\alpha \wedge \neg O\alpha$, into a dialetheia, $O\alpha \wedge \neg O\alpha$. The principle serves to rule out inconsistent obligations only if $\omega^+(w)$ and $\omega^-(w)$ are disjoint, that is, there are no deontic dialetheias. It is therefore possible, for all that has gone before, to impose this constraint on $\omega^+(w)$ and $\omega^-(w)$, and endorse the principle.

Should this be done? The answer is, I think, 'no'. First, as I have just observed, the principle serves to multiply contradictions by turning inconsistent obligations into dialetheias. Secondly, the principle seems to have no rationale. The orthodox rationale is certainly undercut by the existence of inconsistent obligations, and no other appears to take its place. Hence the principle would appear to multiply contradictions beyond necessity. It should therefore be rejected (see section 8.4). Similar considerations apply to the principle $\neg O(\alpha \wedge \neg\alpha)$, which is verified by the condition $\alpha \wedge \neg\alpha \in \omega^-(w)$. This, too, just spreads unnecessary contradictions.

Some other restrictions on ω^+ and ω^- concern iterated modalities. The principle $O\alpha \rightarrow OO\alpha$ has some initial plausibility and has been endorsed by some philosophers.[19] It can be verified in the semantics I have given by requiring that $\omega^+(w)$ be closed not only under entailment and adjunction, but also under the condition: if $\alpha \in \omega^+(w)$ then $O\alpha \in \omega^+(w)$, and dually for ω^-. In fact, I do not think that this principle is correct. An argument against it is as follows. Suppose that the vicar has been murdered. It would seem that if you murdered the vicar (β) you ought to be punished for it ($O\alpha$), and conversely, if you did not murder the vicar, you ought not to be punished for it. Hence we have a true sentence of the form $\beta \leftrightarrow O\alpha$. By the principle of obligation preservation, it follows that $O\beta \leftrightarrow OO\alpha$. Thus, by the mooted principle, $O\alpha \rightarrow O\beta$; i.e., if you ought to be punished for murdering the vicar, then you ought to have murdered the vicar. This is surely incorrect. If you have murdered the vicar then you ought to be punished. It does not follow that you ought to have murdered him.[20]

This argument is not indisputable; but before I deal with complications, let me first raise the converse principle: $OO\alpha \rightarrow O\alpha$. This is verified by closing $\omega^+(w)$ under the condition: if $O\alpha \in \omega^+(w)$ then $\alpha \in \omega^+(w)$, and dually for ω^-, as may easily be checked. This principle would seem to fall to a similar counter-example. Suppose that you ought to go to communion ($O\alpha$) if and only if you are in a state of grace (β). We have here a claim of the form $O\alpha \leftrightarrow \beta$. By the principle of obligation transmission, $OO\alpha \leftrightarrow O\beta$. Hence, by the mooted principle, $O\beta \rightarrow O\alpha$. Thus, if you ought to be in a state of grace you ought to go to communion. But this is surely false. Suppose that you skipped confession. You are not in a state of grace, though you ought to be. And it is not the case that you ought to go to communion. Indeed, you ought not to.

Now, neither of the above counter-examples is conclusive. One reason is that both turn on finding an equivalence of the form $\gamma \leftrightarrow O\delta$, where γ and δ are factual statements, and where the connection is one of bientailment. It may reasonably be suggested that in both examples the connection, though a conditional, is not an entailment. Indeed, it might be argued that no such bientailment can possibly be right, since this would violate the is/ought distinction.

I do not want to enter the is/ought debate here. So let me, at least for the sake of discussion, concede the objection. It is still the case, it seems to me, that the import of the examples can be obtained while sidestepping these considerations. What the examples show is that the obligations that one has, or fails to have, are in general contingent upon what one does (or what others do). Now it may well be the case that α is obligatory, but that β is obligatory only on condition that α. In this case it is obligatory to do something that makes α true, and hence obligatory to do something that makes $O\beta$ true, i.e. $OO\beta$. But suppose that α is,

---

[19] For example, Hintikka (1971).

[20] This argument contains a number of statements of conditional obligation: If γ, then it ought to be the case that δ. I am assuming that these have the logical form: $\gamma \rightarrow O\delta$, and not the form: $O(\gamma \rightarrow \delta)$. Though I shall not argue it here, the English is ambiguous between these two. (Part of the case is made in Hintikka 1971.) The crucial test to determine which of these forms an English conditional obligation has is simply whether or not 'It ought to be the case that δ' can be detached, given γ. Only the first reading supports detachment. In the examples I have given, detachment is supported.

in fact, false. Then the obligation to do β fails to materialise: it is not the case that β is obligatory. Similarly, suppose that α is something such that it is not the case that it ought to be true, but that the obligation to do β arises just if it is. Then it is not the case that one ought to do something that makes $O\beta$ true, i.e. $\neg OO\beta$. But suppose that α is, as a matter of fact, true. Then $O\beta$ is true anyway. Thus, there is an important conceptual distinction between $O\beta$ and $OO\beta$ which should not be collapsed by *S4*-ish principles and their converses.

In the last section I mentioned the notion of a deontically perfect world. What would such a world be like? A simple and obvious answer is that it is just a world in which all obligations are fulfilled, that is, in which all the sentences in the set $\{\alpha \mid O\alpha$ is true$\}$ are true, that is, one that is (partially) described by $\omega^+(G)$. In virtue of the fact that $OO\alpha$ does not collapse into $O\alpha$, this is not enough. For suppose that someone is obliged to bring it about that α, and that if they bring it about that α they are obliged to bring it about that β. Then, clearly, in a deontically perfect world, since all obligations are followed up, β would be true. But even if $O\alpha$ and $\alpha \to O\beta$ are true (at G), it does not follow that $\beta \in \omega^+(G)$. We can infer $OO\beta$ by obligation preservation. Hence $O\beta \in \omega^+(w)$. This suggests that we might take a deontically perfect world to be (partially) described by the set of sentences $\{\alpha \mid$ for some i, $O^i\alpha$ is true$\}$, where O^i is just O iterated i times. But even this is not enough. For suppose that $\alpha \wedge \beta \to O\gamma$ and that $O\alpha$ and $O^2\beta$. In a perfect world, γ should be realised. But from these premises we cannot infer $O\gamma$, $O^2\gamma$, or $O^i\gamma$, for any other i. The way to obtain a (partial) description of a deontically perfect world is simply to close the set of truths under not only semantic consequence, but also the rule $\{O\alpha\} \vdash \alpha$. Such a description may well be inconsistent, though it will not, in general, be trivial.

13.5 OTHER NORMS, RULES AND GAMES

Until now I have carried out my discussion of obligation in terms of legal norms. There are many other kinds: moral and rational, to name but two. I chose to discuss legal obligations/rights, etc., since it is relatively easy to establish the existence of these. As far as consistency goes, I do not think that other norms differ, in principle, from legal ones. Hence, in general, I take the above discussion to apply equally to them.

Consider moral norms. It is a commonplace that moral norms frequently conflict *prima facie*. But it is not so easy to establish that this conflict is not just *prima facie*, and that inconsistent moral obligations may indeed arise. Quite clearly, some *prima facie* conflicts can be resolved. For example, the keeping of a fairly minor promise is obviously outweighed by the need to save someone's life. It is possible to suggest that all moral conflicts can be resolved.[21] And because

---

[21] See McConnell (1978).

moral norms are more contentious, with respect to their content, their rank, and their range, and because there is nothing analogous to the legal default test that I have applied, it is less easy to be sure, given any particular case, that it cannot be. Still, many writers have recently suggested that not all *prima facie* moral conflicts can be resolved,[22] and I think that the truth lies with them.

I do not intend to argue for this now, since I think that the question presupposes deep issues in moral philosophy. In summary, though, the situation appears to be this. What the examples of *prima facie* conflicts do is place the burden of argument on those who would claim that apparent conflicts can *always* be resolved to show just cause. Now, though it may not be impossible to do this, the only promising approach is to (a) identify some transcendent standards of morality and (b) argue that these must be consistent. By 'transcendent standards' I mean standards that may hold or fail independently of what any person or group of people believes. If there are such standards, it is possible for any given belief about morality to be wrong or, perhaps, only an approximation to the truth. Hence the possibility of resolving *prima facie* conflicts.[23] A divine command theory of morality is obviously a transcendent standards theory. But equally, utilitarianism, at least in some of its forms, is: it is quite possible for a certain act to maximise utility without anyone's realising that it does. The isolation of transcendent standards is not enough, however. It must be established that there are no conflicts in these. With a theory like the divine command theory, one might argue that God, being rational and benevolent, would not issue inconsistent commands. With utilitarianism, one might argue that α and $\neg\alpha$ cannot *both* maximise utility (or at least, if their results are of equal utility, neither is obligatory). And so on. Let me now put my cards on the table. I can subscribe to neither of the moral theories I have explicitly mentioned. Though there is, I think, some hope for making sense of a transcendent morality, there is no way of doing this in such a way as to give grounds for supposing that it must be consistent.

Of course, granted that there are inconsistent moral obligations, when these arise a *practical* problem is posed with which dialetheism gives no help. Assuming that the obligations involved are not such as to be jointly realisable, one needs to decide which of them to fulfil. All that theory can say is that whichever one one fulfils some obligation will be flunked. This is a cold comfort.

From the existence of inconsistent moral obligations, the existence of moral dialetheias is obviously another step again. However, once it be granted that there are inconsistent moral obligations, and given that one cannot rule out dialetheias

[22] See e.g. Lemmon (1962); Barcan Marcus (1980); and Routley and Plumwood (1989). Other references are given in McConnell (1978).

[23] There is little hope of avoiding the conclusion if all standards of morality are "immanent". Immanent standards are all too liable to be inconsistent. It will not help just to take consistency to be a regulative principle. All that means in this context is that we revise our moral standards once we discover a contradiction; it remains true that they were inconsistent in the first place.

a priori, the legal analogy suggests that there may be moral dialetheias too. Since I have no interesting examples to offer at the moment, we need not tarry here.

Other kinds of obligation pertain to rationality: rational obligation to believe, rational obligation to do, and so on. I shall say little about these, save to point out that I have already argued in section 7.4 that it may be rational to believe both α and $\neg\alpha$. Presumably, if the evidence becomes strong enough, it may become rationally obligatory to believe that α and to believe that $\neg\alpha$, too.

Obligations, rights, etc., belong to one species of the genus *norm*. Another species of the same genus is that of *rule* (rules of games, rules of clubs, and so on). One might suppose that they are not even a different species, since many laws (such as traffic regulations) are little more than procedural rules. It is not, therefore, surprising that similar considerations apply to sets of rules. Indeed, once we consider rules, we meet perhaps the most transparent examples of inconsistencies and dialetheias.

There are many bodies that have control over a certain set of rules with an autonomy that neither a legislature nor a judiciary has with respect to laws. It is therefore the case that what that body says just is the rule, with little *ceteris paribus* about it. For example, the International Chess Federation can make it the case that something is a rule of chess, at least competitive chess, simply by saying so. Similarly, the membership of a club can make something a rule of that club merely by duly ratifying a legal constitution to that effect. There is, therefore, nothing mysterious about how a contradiction can arise in this context. If, for example, the ICF were to pass a rule to the effect that after move 100 any rook may move as a bishop, without modifying the rule according to which rooks may move along only ranks and files, then after move 100 a rook would be both allowed to move along diagonals and not allowed to move along diagonals. This particular example is an absurd one. In virtue of the blatancy of the contradiction, the ICF would never make such a rule; but in rules of high degree of complexity this *kind* of thing could easily happen unintentionally.

Some may suggest that one should not talk of truth at all here since, just because such things can be made to hold by fiat, statements of rules, such as 'a pawn shall have the power to advance one square along its file unless . . .' are neither true nor false. This takes us back to the discussion of section 13.2 concerning the truthvaluedness of norms, which I will not repeat. Since one can use such a sentence to convey (right or wrong) information, as a premise in reasoning whether or not 'mate' can be avoided, and so on, the talk of truth/falsity is quite legitimate. Moreover, it is quite clear that there can be inconsistent sets of rules actually in force. They may even work in practice, as we saw with the example of the inconsistent traffic rules in section 13.2. Nor should there be any tendency to say that inconsistent rules are, *ipso facto*, not rules. If it transpired, for example, that the rules of chess as we now know them could produce a contradiction in some circumstances that arose only after the 100th move, it would still be the case that those were the rules, and that people played by them.

It may be useful to see that certain of the transparent cases of contradiction resemble certain of the less transparent ones. This may help to demystify. For example, suppose that there is a club whose rules mimic situations that arise in the logical paradoxes, for example, the Secretaries' Lib. Club.[24] In the constitution of this club it is laid down that someone is eligible to join the club if and only if they are secretary of a club that they are not eligible to join. Everything works fine until the club appoints a secretary who, while being a secretary of no other club, applies for membership . . . [25]

It might be pointed out that the analogy with the logical paradoxes is not very good. After all, set theory and semantics are not clubs or games, and no one has ever made their "rules" true by fiat. The point is correct, but its force is misplaced. The principles of set theory and semantics are not true by any individual or group's conscious fiat. They are true in virtue of the meanings of certain words, such as 'true'. (See the discussion of analyticity in section 10.3.) These meanings are embodied in the rules of language-use, specifically, the semantic and inferential rules. These rules, like the practice they govern, were not consciously designed in any straightforward sense. Unlike the rules of most games, which are, or were, developed with an eye on, among other things, producing a consistent set of procedures, the rules of language have grown in a complex, piecemeal, and undirected fashion. There was no divine Hilbert, whose job it was to ensure consistency, around during their development. And this is just the sort of situation in which one would expect conflicts and inconsistencies to arise. Thus, we see that the fact that game rules are made up mostly by fiat serves to enforce the analogical argument for dialetheism, not weaken it.

13.6 THE RESOLUTION OF DIALETHEIAS

It might be suggested that, though the rules of language have undergone no conscious modification, they have undergone a process of evolution, and that this process is likely to have modified the rules in the direction of consistency. The point carries some weight. If it can be established that inconsistent rules are dysfunctional, then there are reasons for supposing that they will be selected out. Answering this objection will require a rather lengthy digression from the main subject of this chapter, but since the issues raised are important, this is justified.

In reply to the objection, two points are pertinent. The first is that, even if linguistic evolution has a tendency to filter out inconsistencies, there is no reason to suppose that at any stage they are totally abolished. For evolution may produce

---

[24] The example is due to Chihara (1979). He concludes, as I do, that inconsistent rules may well be workable. He even argues on the basis of this analogy that our naive concept of truth may be inconsistent. What he fails to do (and for reasons that are not so clear) is take the crucial next step. Dialetheism is rejected out of hand.

[25] Parodying Prior (see sect. 1.2, fn. 5), we might suggest that this gives us an *a priori* proof that she is, unawares, the secretary of another club.

new contradictions as well as filter out old ones. Indeed, the very process of getting rid of one contradiction may generate another, as legal reform shows.

The second, and perhaps deeper, point is that, although some dialetheias are dysfunctional, not all are; indeed, for some it is quite the reverse. It is clear that some legal dialetheias, when they come out into the open, are dysfunctional. Consider, for example, the situation where someone both has the right, and is forbidden, to vote (see section 13.2). In such a situation an important practical problem is posed: namely, whether to let this person, and so by implication a large class of people, express a view on the constitution of parliament. This is obviously an important question which needs to be resolved. The general point is this: norms have a certain purpose, namely, the regulation of behaviour; inconsistent norms may well frustrate this purpose, and this may require change. This is graphically illustrated by the inconsistent traffic laws of section 13.2. If people act in accordance with conclusions they draw from these laws, they will end up being killed or maimed. Legal dialetheias may cause important practical problems, and if they do they are dysfunctional and will be changed.

Inconsistent norms may not be the only dialetheias that cause practical problems. If our concepts relating to measurement, such as length, time, and temperature (see section 4.8) are dialetheic, this may cause practical problems, since such concepts are closely connected with action. (Imagine buying something by a quantity whose concept is dialetheic.) And if the problems are important enough, the concepts that produce them may undergo modification. Modifying our concepts of measurement to render them consistent would be rather different from modifying the law. The former (but not necessarily the latter) requires the modification of our criteria of application for various terms, or the invention of completely new terms. Hence, such modifications entail a meaning-change or a conceptual development. These things are not, of course, unknown in the historical development of science. A plausible historical case in which a concept with inconsistent criteria of application was modified concerns the notion of apparent, or angular, size in seventeenth-century optics.[26] When it was discovered that the two different methods for determining angular size, visual estimation, and geometric ray diagrams, did not necessarily give the same result, the concept split into two: optical angular size and geometric angular size, each answering to one of the criteria. Dialetheias may well be at the root of many cases of conceptual fission and other conceptual developments.[27]

We see that if dialetheias cause practical problems they may well be dysfunctional and be subject to resolution. It should be clear, however, that not all dialetheias are like this. Only some dialetheias give rise to important practical problems. Inconsistent set theory does not produce death on the roads. And, while an inconsistent theory may raise practical problems if the contradiction

[26] See Maund (1981).
[27] The conceptual development of notions connected with polyhedra discussed in Lakatos (1976) might well be looked at from this perspective.

affects practical procedures, such as measuring and classifying, if the contradiction is located deep in the heart of theory it need not. Thus, for example, quantum mechanics, if it be an inconsistent theory due to the behaviour of the Dirac δ-function,[28] is still quite workable. Another workable theory that was certainly inconsistent was the old calculus. As contemporaries of Newton pointed out,[29] in the calculation of derivatives it was necessary, at different points, to assume that an infinitesimal was both zero and non-zero. In virtue of the close connection between proof procedures and meaning, we might even take this to be a dialetheia. At any rate, the theory was quite workable. Tradition has it that the old calculus was replaced because it was inconsistent; even this is dubious, as recent historical studies show.[30]

Of course, if the dialetheias in our concepts were to spread everywhere, this would be dysfunctional. A trivial theory/language would be useless, and would frustrate any point it was supposed to have. But, given that *ex contradictione quodlibet* fails, there is no automatic move from inconsistency to triviality—quite the reverse, since triviality is a special case. Indeed, for dialetheic concepts such as truth and sethood, we can give a transcendental argument for their non-triviality. Given that these notions are actually used, and used sensibly, any conditions for their sensible use must be fulfilled. But one of these is just non-triviality.

There is no reason, then, why dialetheias must be dysfunctional. Moreover, some of the considerations of the first part of the book can be used to show that consistentising can actually be dysfunctional. First, as we saw in section 1.7, any consistentising of our semantic notions can be achieved only at the cost of a loss in expressive power. In any consistent semantics there will be things that are inexpressible. Secondly, as we saw in section 3.4, this would also lead to an impoverishment of our powers of proof. Our naive proof-procedures are inconsistent, and if we were to render them consistent there would be truths we could no longer establish. We would therefore be deliberately making a realm of truth inaccessible to our methods of discovery. Nor is this merely an academic possibility. The consistentising demands of the cumulative hierarchy have already imposed strictures on category theory which hamper the investigation of the categorial structure of various parts of mathematics. As one modern mathematician puts it,[31]

[T]he restrictions on the formation and manipulation of [large categories] imposed by the official set theoretic framework [have come] to be regarded by some category theorists as an irksome and possibly unnecessary curtailment of their mathematical activity.

The history of science is the history of the increase in power of our conceptual tools. Consistentising here would, therefore, be a retrograde and quite undesirable step. Hence dialetheias are not uniformly dysfunctional: sometimes the opposite.

---

[28] See Priest and Routley (1983), ch. 4, sect. 3.   [29] See Boyer (1949), ch. 6.

[30] Lakatos (1978a) argues that what happened was that one conception of the continuum (= set of proof procedures) was replaced by another, for reasons not to do with their consistency but to do with their "explanatory power".   [31] Bell (1981), p. 352.

13.7 LANGUAGE GAMES

So much for the digression on the resolution of contradictions. Let us return to the main subject of the chapter: inconsistent normative systems. In virtue of the fact that the rules of language-use are just one kind of rule, dialetheism is, in a sense, just a special case of the proneness of rule governed situations to produce inconsistency. I will therefore conclude this chapter with some comments on rule-following, and in particular on Wittgenstein's remarks on the subject.

Consider, for example, the rule of inference: from $T\underline{\alpha}$ infer α, and vice versa. As we know, if this rule is followed, with a suitable choice for α, α_0, we end up asserting both α_0 and $\neg\alpha_0$. Now what is it, according to Wittgenstein, that makes the rule valid? Wittgenstein's account of what it is to follow a rule is too well known to need a long explanation; according to him, one should not suppose that the rule is correct in virtue of its correspondence with some abstract logical structure. Rather, the rule is valid because it is embodied in our practice of inference. And what it is for a rule, in our case a rule of inference, to be embodied in a practice is just that, after suitable coaching, people have a natural disposition to make the particular inference involved.[32] The validity of the inference is therefore grounded ultimately in empirical facts concerning human dispositions. (Though the rules are certainly not descriptions of those dispositions.)

This account of rule following is certainly not *de rigeur* for a dialetheist. It is quite open for a dialetheist to maintain that the T-scheme inference is valid in virtue of its correspondence to some abstract logical structure. She must then, of course, maintain that that structure is intrinsically inconsistent. This can certainly be done. However, it is also true that such a "Platonistic" conception of validity puts up stiffer opposition to dialetheism than the Wittgensteinian account. For there is a tendency, deriving from Plato, to attribute to an abstract realm a perfection lacking in the concrete world. To mix metaphors, it is common to think of the abstract world as the superego of the concrete world. It is but a short step from here to supposing the abstract world to be consistent (which is precisely what Plato does: see *Parmenides*, 129 b, c). For, if we suppose that inconsistency is a mark of imperfection (which, as I discussed in section 8.4, we frequently do, and with some justice), it is natural (though incorrect) to suppose that at the ideal limit the inconsistency disappears.

Once we move to Wittgenstein's account of rule-following, this picture, which can have such a powerful hold on thought, is broken. Even if we suppose that consistency is always a perfection (which it is not), there is no temptation to suppose that human practice has it. The imperfection of man is a theme that hardly needs harping on. Wittgenstein himself was quite well aware of this aspect of his thought. In many of his later writings there are allusions to the toleration of

---

[32] For further discussion, see Priest (1979*b*).

inconsistency,[33] and it is no coincidence that the appearance of these corresponds to the dismantling of the "logical space" theory of the *Tractatus*, with its emphasis on the crystalline purity of a logically perfect language. Frequently, thereafter, Wittgenstein remarks that a language game (that is, a set of rule-following practices) may issue in inconsistency. But this may not matter: the game may still be playable—the language may still be usable. Inconsistencies, when isolated, need cause no problem. (All these themes I have already stressed in this chapter.) Indeed, Wittgenstein comes close to saying that inconsistent language games are actually played. The game that produces the liar paradox may be just such a game.

Despite all this, Wittgenstein did not, it would seem, take the final step into dialetheism. While conceding that language games could produce inconsistencies, he seemed reluctant to call them true in the normal sense. It was another philosopher who drew the logical conclusion of this line of thought: Hegel. For to say that, following the rules that govern the use of language, we may end up with contradictions is to say, in another jargon, that our concepts are inconsistent, which is what, of course, Hegel said.[34] Hegel did not carry out his discussion in terms of human practices. Indeed, his mystification of concepts was as complete as possible, since he attributed to them a completely autonomous and independent reality. It was left to thinkers such as Marx to point out that this was just a mystified discussion of human practice.[35] None the less, Hegel did draw the dialetheist conclusion: if inconsistencies are produced by the perfectly correct application of concepts/language, they are true. Quite so.

---

[33] For references and discussion, see Priest and Routley (1983), ch. 1, sect. 5.4.

[34] See ch. 0.

[35] See the section 'Critique of the Hegelean Dialectic and Philosophy as a Whole' in the *1844 Manuscripts*, and the theses on Feuerbach, especially the first. For an excellent discussion, see Ilyenkov (1977), chs. 7, 8.

CONCLUSION

'It is impossible for the same thing at the same time to belong and not to belong to the same thing and in the same respect.' ... This is the most certain of all principles.

Aristotle, *Metaphysics*, Γ3, 1005b 18–23

14

The Transconsistent

The previous chapters advocate a novel logical theory and explore its rationale and some of its applications. By implication, they are a sustained attack on the dominant logical theory of our times, the logic of Frege, Russell, and their successors, or, as it has come to be known, classical logic. It is true that this logic can be seen as a special case of dialetheic logic, and is therefore subsumed by it (see section 8.5). None the less, the claims to universality of classical logic must be rejected. Some may wonder at my temerity in criticising classical logic, especially one of its principles which has had a general (though not a universal) acceptance for two thousand years. If this is not safe from attack nothing is. Indeed so: nothing, and no one, should be placed beyond the bounds of rational criticism—and my criticism is nothing if not rational.

There is a feeling, perhaps more common among people who use classical logical theory than among logicians themselves, that logic should not, even cannot, be questioned. This attitude is more fitting for some religious dogma than for a science. And it can be maintained only by those who wear both philosophical and historical blinkers. No one needs to be told that one needs to distinguish between our theory of dynamics and moving bodies themselves. One is an attempt to provide a correct theoretical explanation for, and description of, the other, and to confuse the two is absurd. Yet a similar confusion is common in logic. The fact that we use the same word, 'logic', for both is but an effect (rather than a cause) of this. But just as with dynamics, so with logic, one needs to distinguish between reasoning or, better, the structure of norms that govern valid/good reasoning, which is the object of study, and our logical theory, which tries to give a theoretical account of this phenomenon.[1] The theoretical principles we do actually accept are not God-given and fixed for all time. Indeed, reasoning is a complex and delicate human activity, and it is unlikely that any theory we produce, at least for the present, and maybe for ever, cannot be improved. The norms themselves may also change. There may well occur a dialectical interaction, characteristic of the social sciences, between the object of the theory and the theory itself. None the less, the distinction between a science and its object remains; and once this gap is opened, it suffices for the fallibility of any theory. We are, perhaps, fortunate to have intuitionism around to remind us of this.

[1] Chomsky (1980), p. 220, notes a similar distinction (and confusion) in grammar.

The history of logic, too, bears out the fact that the fallibility of logical theory is no mere theoretical possibility. Our current logical theory has a relatively recent origin. It has been accepted for less than a century, and is very different from its predecessor, Aristotelean logic. It is not even consistent with it. (For example, the theories are inconsistent on the question of the existential import of the A form, and on their analyses of relations.²) There is no reason to suppose that the contemporary theory will not eventually go the same way as its predecessor. Perhaps there will be a time when logicians will look with incredulity at the naivety of their predecessors who thought that consistency was a *sine qua non* of reasoning, rationality, and similar notions.

But, it may be suggested, I am attacking more than just our currently accepted logical theory: I am attacking the law of non-contradiction, which has been a part of all logical theories. In a sense, this is true. I am attacking the law of non-contradiction (though I am, of course, prepared to assert it too) in a way that is unthinkable for a classical, Aristotelean, or even intuitionist logician. It is also true that this has been a part of all articulated formal logics (though there are certainly informal logical theories, such as Hegel's, for which this is not true). None the less, the substantial point remains: the fact that the law of non-contradiction has always formed part of formal logical theories does not imply that it is immune from revision. In this respect, it is illuminating to compare our attitude to it with that towards certain principles crucial in the study of infinity. Consider, for example, the Euclidean principle that the whole must be greater than the part. For centuries this was thought of as a logical truth in a general sense of that phrase, certainly as an *a priori* truth. There did appear to be exceptions to the principle. The proof that the set of natural numbers is the same size as the set of even numbers was known to Galileo and, almost certainly, to the medievals; but these facts were regarded as paradoxes which one should try to solve. However, with hindsight we can see that they pointed the way to the study of a new realm, the recognition of whose existence emerged in the nineteenth century as the result of the work of Bolzano and Dedekind. The paradoxical objects became paradigms of the behaviour of infinities, their paradoxical properties being, indeed, a definition of infinity. The Euclidean principle, it then became clear, held only for the finite, our attachment to it being explicable, perhaps, by the fact that so many of our intuitions are drawn from the finite.

It is similar, I suspect, with the law of non-contradiction (and, to a lesser extent, with the disjunctive syllogism). This, too, has traditionally been endorsed as *a priori* unassailable. Of course, apparent counter-examples to it have been known for a long time—the logical paradoxes—but they have been regarded as problems for solution. These too, I suggest, point the way to a new realm of study. The paradoxes will come to be seen as paradigms of this realm. The law of non-contradiction will then be restricted to its correct domain of validity, the

---

² For a fuller discussion of the development of modern logical theory, see Priest (1989a).

consistent, and its failure will be taken as the defining characteristic of the new domain, our attachment to it being explicable, perhaps, by the fact that many of our intuitions are drawn from the consistent.[3]

The analogy between the infinite and the inconsistent bears further weight. Before the last century, the infinite was considered to have no, or little, structure. The nineteenth-century investigations culminating in Cantor's discovery of the beautiful structure existing beyond the finite, the transfinite, was one of the most exciting steps in the development of human thought. The inconsistent, too, has been widely held to have no interesting or important structure. Perhaps the simplest way to summarise the main point of the book is this: it has. The structure is interesting since it is not the undifferentiated plenum of relations that many have taken it to be; it is important since it bears centrally on an adequate account of sets, of semantics, of time and change, of normative systems, and possibly many other things. All this I have tried to show in the foregoing pages. However, these investigations are but a start. The realm beyond the consistent is a continent on whose shore we have just alighted. This book does little more than forge some of the basic equipment required for the exploration, and test it on some important areas of the land. I do not claim that the equipment is perfect— far from it. But it at least allows us to make a start on exploring this new and unfamiliar terrain—the transconsistent.

---

[3] See sect. 8.4 for the normality of consistency. I doubt, however, that this is the only factor in the explanation, others being the atomistic tradition in English-speaking philosophy, and the sheer weight of orthodoxy. (On these see Priest and Routley 1983, ch. 5, sect. 4, and Priest 1989*a*.)

PART IV

MATERIAL NEW TO THE SECOND EDITION

An ancient buddha said, 'Mountains are mountains, waters are waters.'
These words do not mean that mountains are mountains; they mean that
mountains are mountains. Therefore investigate mountains thoroughly...

Dōgen, *Mountains and Water Sutra* (Tanahashi 1985)

15

The Metaphysics of Change III: Time

15.1 THE SPREAD HYPOTHESIS AND THE HEGELEAN DEFINITION OF CHANGE

The subject of this chapter is time—a topic that many philosophers have found enigmatic. My aim is to suggest resolutions to some of the enigmas.[1] The particular enigmas I have in mind are time's flow, its direction, and its duration. There is, it seems to me, one key that unlocks all these problems. I will attempt to explain this in the next section. But first I need some background explanations; for the key is made of a material that will be somewhat unfamiliar.[2]

Let us start with the *spread hypothesis*. Here is a rough statement of this; I will give a more precise formulation in a moment:[3]

A physical magnitude cannot be localised to its value at an instant of time, but only to those values it has at a small neighbourhoods of that time.

I do not wish to defend the spread hypothesis here. I am content for it to remain a hypothesis, to be supported by the solutions its application provides. Let me just paint a picture that goes with the hypothesis. We suppose that over small neighbourhoods of time it is impossible to pin down states of affairs. The impossibility is not merely epistemological, but ontological: nature itself is such that it is unable to localise precisely its doings. Each instant is so intimately connected with those around it that their contents cannot but encroach.

Though I do not intend to argue for the spread hypothesis here, I note that it is not a hypothesis produced solely to solve the problems of time that I shall discuss. It was proposed initially in the context of an analysis of motion: its application

---

[1] I have little of novelty to say on the problems faced by extant proposed solutions. I will therefore say little.

[2] The rest of this section summarises the relevant parts of chapter 12. For further details, see sect. 12.3.

[3] In ch. 12 the spread hypothesis is formulated for the special case where the magnitude concerned is the spatial location of an object. (The spread hypothesis then amounts to the claim that at an instant an object may be spread over a neighbourhood of locations. Hence the name.) However, as I indicate there, there is nothing particularly special about this special case, and the present statement is just the generalisation. It is worth pointing out that the hypothesis is non-committal about the extent of the non-localisation. A natural assumption, however, is that its length is proportional to the derivative of the magnitude with respect to time.

solves a number of puzzling aspects of that subject too. Only one part of that discussion is presently relevant: an explanation of the Hegelean account of change. According to this, for a quantity to be in a state of change is for it to be in a certain contradictory state. *Merely* being in different states at different times is not enough. How this idea works we can see at the same time as making the spread hypothesis more precise.

Let us take a quantity (such as the spatial location of a body), q. q may take any of a distinct set of values (say real numbers), V. To avoid talking in terms of satisfaction, we will make the harmless assumption that every member, r, of V, has a name, r. Let q be a function, v, of time; let $Q(x)$ be the predicate 'q has the value x'; and let

$$S_t = \{Q(\mathbf{r}) : r = v(t)\} \cup \{\neg Q(\mathbf{r}) : r \neq v(t)\}.$$

The members of S_t state the fact that the value of q is $v(t)$, and not some other value; and the fact that $q = v(t)$ implies that all members of S_t are true at t. The spread hypothesis can be interpreted as saying that, for any time t, there is an interval containing t, θ_t, such that the diagram (i.e. the complete description of the atomic states) at t is just the "superposition", that is, the set-theoretic union of every $S_{t'}$ for $t' \in \theta_t$. Let us call this union, $\underset{t' \in \theta_t}{\cup} S_{t'}$, the *state description* at time t.

Now suppose that q is changing in a neighbourhood of t. Then within θ_t there is a time, t', such that $r = v(t) \neq v(t') = r'$. The state description at t is therefore inconsistent. (It will contain $Q(\mathbf{r})$, $Q(\mathbf{r}')$, and their negations.) Conversely, if q is constant in a neighbourhood of t, then, provided that θ_t is small enough to lie within this neighbourhood (which it will be if its length is proportional to dv/dt), then the state description at t is consistent. Thus is the Hegelean account of change illustrated. To be in a state of change is to have an inconsistent state description.

So much for the state of change. What of the direction of change? A contradictory state is an intrinsic state of change, such as motion. And just as a state of change, when it occurs, is intrinsic, so the direction of change, if there is one, must be. The intrinsic nature of the direction of change at t corresponds to a certain asymmetry in the state at t. 'Which asymmetry?' is a question that might be answered in several ways. One that is not *ad hoc* is as follows. θ_t will not necessarily be distributed symmetrically about t. In fact, there are reasons to suppose that t is the leading edge of θ_t, so that the interval is skewed all to the past of t, at least normally. (Essentially, the reason is that, if the interval projects to the future of t, this would seem to permit backwards causation.) Now, let us call $\{v(t') : t' \in \theta_t\}$ the *spread* of q at t. Then q is intrinsically increasing at t if $v(t)$ is the upper bound of the spread at t, intrinsically decreasing if it is the lower bound, and intrinsically neither otherwise. (Drawing a few diagrams will quickly convince the reader of this.) Thus, the direction of change at t, if it exists and is not indeterminate, is from the interior of the spread to the exterior, though $v(t)$.

So much for preliminaries.

15.2 THE FLOW OF TIME

Let me now explain the application I wish to make of these ideas. The paradigm of a physical magnitude, q, is spatial location, in which case the change is motion. But it could equally well be momentum, charge, or what not. The suggestion I wish to make is that it can also be time itself. We would not normally, perhaps, think of time as a physical magnitude in the same sense as velocity and charge are. I suggest that, for the purposes of the application of the spread principle, it is. Whether this commits me to an absolute, as opposed to a relative, view of time I shall not discuss here. Henceforth, I shall use q for the state of time. V is the set of reals, and the function v is simply the identity function. Applying the above, by the spread principle, for every time t there is an interval containing t, 0_t, such that, for all $t' \in 0_t$, $Q(t')$ is true at t. So, for example, at 12 noon it is every time around 12 noon. This much is trivial. What is not so trivial is its application to the enigmas concerning time.

The first enigma I have in mind, and perhaps the most fundamental one, is the flow of time. We commonly think that time somehow flows or changes, so that events in the distant future become less future until they become present, recently past, and then remotely past. But, of course, as many have observed,[4] as soon as one tries to make sense of this idea one winds up in, if not absurdities, then at least grave difficulties. If time flows, then it would seem that it must change *with respect to* something else, but there is nothing else for it to change with respect to. Some have bitten the bullet and postulated hyper-times[5] and, pushed on by the obvious regress, even hyper-times of higher orders. But few have given this idea serious credence.

A more orthodox response[6] is simply to deny the objective reality of the flow. This, however one puts it, amounts to the claim that the flow is an illusion produced by some psychological mechanism: the flow is merely the way in which a manifold of befores and afters appears to conscious beings of a certain kind. The view is implausible. What credibility it has is due to the fact that no one, so far, has come up with a workable way of understanding the flux of time. But the present machinery can provide just that.

Given the above application of the spread principle, the state of q at any time is inconsistent, since the identity function is nowhere constant. This, according to the Hegelean account of change, is exactly what it is to be in a state of change. Thus, the reality of the flux of time does not have to be denied; neither does it have to be accommodated by the postulation of hyper-times. There is only one time, and that, being in a constantly inconsistent state, is in a state of flux.

This account of the flux of time can also be applied to solve another problem, which is particularly acute for those who have wished to deny the reality of the

---

[4] See e.g. Williams (1951); Smart (1949).   [5] e.g. J. W. Dunn (1927).
[6] See e.g. Grünbaum (1967*a*); Mellor (1984).

flow of time. This is to account for the apparent lack of symmetry between space and time. Why is it that time appears to flow and space does not? The present account suggests a simple answer to this: there is no analogue of the spread principle for space. Or, to put it another way, there is, but the interval of non-localisation about a spatial point, s, is just $\{s\}$. Why this is one might debate; I will return to the issue briefly in section 15.4. It suffices here to note that, if this is so, analogous contradictions for space do not arise. State descriptions indexed by spatial locations, rather than temporal ones, are consistent. Space, unlike time, is not in a state of flux.

15.3 THE DIRECTION AND DURATION OF TIME

So much for the flow of time. What of its direction? What accounts for the anisotropy of time? This again has been a thorny problem, particularly for those who have denied the reality of the flow of time. They have had to locate the anisotropy of time not in time itself, but in processes in time—a tall order, since apparently all causal laws are time-symmetric.[7] Again, the solution to the problem on the present approach is obvious. Since the identity function is monotonically increasing, $v(t)$ is always the upper bound of the spread of q at t. Thus, the direction of the flow of time is perpetually from past to future—which seems just about right.

We might note also that, on this account of the direction of time, it makes perfectly good sense to ask what a world would be like in which all processes went backwards in time. This makes little sense on more orthodox accounts of the direction of time; for if all physical processes go backwards, then, if the direction of time is defined by these, so too does time itself.[8] According to the Hegelean account of change, the direction of change of a quantity at t is a function of the skew in its interval of non-localisation about t. As I have noted, there are reasons to believe that the skew is normally towards the past. But the direction of time, we may now suppose, is determined by the skew in time itself. Thus, as long as the interval of non-localisation of time is skewed in the same direction as the intervals of all the other quantities, they all have the same direction. If, however, time were skewed in the *opposite* direction from all (other) quantities, their direction (relative to time) would be reversed. All processes would therefore go backwards in time, as, therefore, would causation.

The question of whether time itself could go backwards on this account is less clear. Of course, we can let t be the *trailing* edge of 0_r. But unless there is some other significance to the direction of the t-axis this would be nothing but a change of notation. One thing that would provide this significance is if tense

---

[7] Common solutions are to attribute it to either the increase of entropy or the direction of causation. See e.g. Grünbaum (1967); Gold (1966); Reichenbach (1956); Mellor (1984).

[8] See e.g. Gold (1966).

were real (as "A theorists" maintain). Then the future and past would be independent of the direction of skew, and it would make independent sense to talk of 0_t as being skewed towards the future. Since I do not wish to discuss the reality of tense here, I shall not pursue this possibility further, though I will return to the matter briefly in section 15.4.

What it would be like to *experience* any of these changes, I am not sure. However, experience brings me to the last of the enigmas of time I would discuss. The present is a durationless instant. But this fact seems to do no justice to the phenomenology of time: we experience the present not as a durationless point, but as having some little duration. This sort of present has been called by the unfortunate name of the *specious present* by some philosophers.[9] I prefer to call it the *extended present*. A graphic way of focusing attention on the extended present is by concentrating on our experience of certain sorts of motion. For example, consider an analog watch or clock, with hands for the hour, the minute, and the second. One cannot see the minute hand (and *a fortiori* the hour hand) move—unless it is of the kind that jumps occasionally. One sees it in a certain position and infers that it has moved, since one remembers its being elsewhere. The second hand, by contrast, can actually be seen to move. One does not infer its motion by comparing present position with remembered position. Its motion is part of the phenomenological furniture. It is as if one can see the whole of a short stretch of motion at once. But of course, every point of the motion occurs at a different instantaneous time. The conclusion that we experience a present extended through a certain period of time seems mandatory.

Despite this, the theory of the extended present has not found favour among the orthodox. It seems to end quickly in absurdity. How can we possibly experience two times at the same time? By the time we experience the later one, the earlier one must be over. This leaves, of course, an awkward problem about what to say about the phenomenology of our experience of the present. Let us not go into what has been said. That is unnecessary; for it is clear that the extended present is accommodated very happily by the assumption that time itself satisfies the spread hypothesis. For every t' in the spread of q at t, $Q(t')$ is true at t. There is, to put it picturesquely, some past occurring at the present. The extended present just is the spread of time around the present (or perhaps just some part of it if we do not experience it all). The third enigma of time is therefore solved.

15.4 SOME VARIATIONS AND EXTENSIONS

The main aim of the chapter, to explain a solution to some puzzles of time, has now been fulfilled. However, it will be clear that it has been fulfilled only in outline. The solution has numerous ramifications. While I cannot hope to treat

---

[9] See Mabbott (1951) for a discussion of the specious present.

them all here, I want at least to pursue some of them. I will do this by considering a possible objection, which may well have occurred to the reader already. The objection can be put in several different ways, but one reasonably perspicuous way is as a sorites.

Let us suppose, for the sake of illustration, that the duration of θ_t is one minute. Then at 12 noon it is every time in the interval around 12 noon; thus, it is also one minute to 12. But at one minute to 12 it is every time in the interval around one minute to 12. It is therefore two minutes to 12. But at two minutes to 12. . . . Hence at 12 noon it is every past time; and similarly for every other time.

Certainly, this conclusion is unacceptable: it is not all past times now. The objection may be met in a number of different ways which modify, or fill out, the basic theory differently. I will consider four.

Solution 1

The sorites argument exploits the fact that we have applied the spread hypothesis to time itself. Refrain from doing this, and apply it only to the quantities in time. Result: the flow of time itself can no longer be explained in terms of the inconsistency of the state description of time. As in orthodox accounts, time does not flow. And as in orthodox accounts, the direction of time has to be explained by the asymmetry of processes in time. However, this is neither the direction of causation, nor that of increase in entropy, but is the skew of the intervals of non-localisation of physical states of affairs. The extended present may still be accounted for in much the same way: it makes little difference to the explanation whether the past itself persists into the present, or just to past states of affairs.

This solution is perhaps the least enticing. The modified theory, while still offering *some* advantages over the more orthodox accounts, reneges on the prime advantage of the original theory: the explanation of the flow of time itself.

Solution 2

Maintain that the spread hypothesis applies to time itself, but now suppose that time is correctly represented by the non-standard real line, and that θ_t is infinitesimal. It then follows that at 12 noon it is every time infinitesimally before 12; but since adding infinitesimal to infinitesimal never gives a non-infinitesimal, the regress never gets beyond an infinitesimal distance from 12. Result: the flow and the direction of time may be accounted for as before. The extended present cannot, since this is not, presumably, infinitesimal.

At the cost of endorsing the thought that physical continua have the structure of the non-standard real line (which has some independent advantages), this is a more enticing solution. Of the three aspects of time discussed, the extended present is the one that most plausibly might be expected to have an explanation in terms of the psychology of observers.

Solution 3

Maintain that the spread hypothesis applies to time itself, and that 0_t is not infinitesimal, but draw a distinction—or, rather, enforce a distinction explicit in the representation. The distinction is between 'The time is t' being true (i.e. '$Q(t)$' being true) and t being the index of the state description. Then the sorites is broken. For when the index of the state description is 12 noon, 'It is one minute to 12' is true; but it does not follow that the index of the state description is one minute to 12, and so the argument goes no further.

This is, perhaps, the most obvious response, and the most attractive, since it sacrifices none of the explanatory power of the account. But one may be less than satisfied with it. For it would appear that we are now operating with a two-time system after all. Intuitively, we have only one way of specifying time: we say 'It is 12 noon'. Now, is this to be interpreted as ' "It is 12 noon" is true' or as 'The index of the state description is 12 noon'? And whichever it means, what exactly are we to make of the other notion, which appears to have been smuggled in under the guise of our familiar talk of time?

There is, however, a possible answer to this point: we do, in fact, have two ways of specifying time: by "A series" tensed locutions (such as 'It is now Tuesday', and by "B series" non-tensed locutions (such as '9 June 2004 falls on a Tuesday'). Could it not be the case that these two ways correspond to the distinction we have observed? The sentences in the state description give the (inconsistent) B-series descriptions of time holding; whereas the index of the state description marks the point representing the present, dividing the temporal continuum into past and future.

The reply is a tempting one. It allows us to make sense of the dual temporal scales; it sits well with the thought that 0_t marks the extended present: the real present is the punctual now, located within an extended present of clock times. Finally, it also explains why a similar construction is not to be expected for space (see section 15.2). Spatial "A series" terms, like 'here', have no independent reference in the same way that tensed terms, like 'now', do.

On the negative side, a disadvantage of this solution is its loss of neutrality on the A-series/B-series issue, that is, on the question of the reality of tense. Everything in this chapter until now could be accepted equally by someone who denied the objective reality of tense and by someone who endorsed it. Obviously, buying this interpretation of solution 3 commits us to a realist view of tense. But on the other hand, and because of its engagement, this construction may shed new light on this issue.

Solution 4

The fourth kind of solution appeals to the thought that the predicate '$x \in 0_t$' is vague. This is a natural enough thought. If someone asks the time and we say

'It is 12 noon', it does not have to be *exactly* noon for us to have spoken truly. If we take the predicate to be vague, then the argument here is simply a kind of sorites paradox; and we may then apply some of the standard techniques for defusing such paradoxes. Thus, for example, we might take θ_t to be a fuzzy set. The degree to which it is true that 'It is n minutes before noon'—and so to which $12 - n/60$ is the index of the state description—would then "fade out" as n increases. If this sort of approach can be made to work, then we can endorse all of the contents of previous sections, *and* remain neutral on the reality of tense.

It is clear that the ramifications of the approach to time countenanced in this chapter spread a great deal further than I have pursued them. But it is also clear that the application of the spread hypothesis and the Hegelean account of change provide at least *prima facie* solutions to a number of problems in the philosophy of time. And that is sufficient for the present.[10]

[10] A draft of this chapter was read at the annual meeting of the Australasian Association of Philosophy, held at the University of New South Wales in August 1985. I am grateful for comments made there by David Lewis, Hugh Mellor, and Chris Mortensen. I am also grateful to Peter Forrest and Jean Paul van Bendegem for their written comments.

16

Minimally Inconsistent *LP*

16.1 THE CLASSICAL RECAPTURE

Intuitionism is a revisionist philosophy. It sees a good part of the reasoning of classical mathematics, particularly that concerning infinite totalities, as quite fallacious. It has therefore wished to debunk it. The programme of paraconsistent logic has never been revisionist in the same sense. By and large, it has accepted that the reasoning of classical mathematics is correct. What it has wished to do is to reject the excrescence *ex contradictione quodlibet*, which does not appear to be an integral part of classical reasoning, but merely leads to trouble when reasoning ventures into the transconsistent.

Since the early days of paraconsistent logic it has, however, been clear that the rejection of *ex contradictione* is not possible without the rejection of other things which appear to be much more integral to classical reasoning. Crucially, the disjunctive syllogism is a casualty in most paraconsistent logics. The problem is therefore posed as to how to account for the apparently acceptable but invalid classical reasoning.

There are at least two strategies for trying to solve the problem.[1] The first is to note that the most crucial failures of the disjunctive syllogism appear to be those where the material conditional is attempting to play the role of a detachable conditional. One may therefore attempt to reconstruct the informal reasoning of classical mathematics (and similar areas) by producing a new account of the conditional to be grafted on to an underlying extensional paraconsistent logic (without ruining its paraconsistent properties)[2] and using this in the reconstruction.

This is the route that standard relevant paraconsistent logic has taken. Several logicians (including Brady, Meyer, Mortensen, Priest, and Routley) have attempted to reconstruct various fragments of classical reasoning in this way. While the results are not definitive, they are not terribly encouraging. There appear to be classical arguments that defy reconstruction in this way. The most ambitious project of this kind was Meyer's attempt to reconstruct the reasoning of classical number theory in the relevant theory $R^{\#}$. This project has ended in

---

[1] They are spelled out clearly in Priest (1979*a*), Sect. 4.
[2] As in ch. 6, or Priest (2002).

failure.[3] And this is so where the underlying logic, *R*, is a very strong one, much stronger than is suitable for many paraconsistent purposes. Thus, though the aim of furnishing paraconsistent logic with a detachable conditional is a highly important—indeed, essential—enterprise, it would now appear that the aim of reconstructing sensible classical reasoning in this way may not be realisable.

16.2 LIMITING THE MODELS

The other way of attempting to recapture sensible classical reasoning stems from the observation that counter-examples to inferences such as the disjunctive syllogism occur only in the transconsistent. Hence, provided we stay within the domain of the consistent, which classical reasoning of course does (by and large), classical logic is perfectly acceptable. (Similarly, for intuitionism, classical logic is perfectly acceptable provided one stays within the domain of the decidable.)

Compared with the first strategy for appropriating classical reasoning, this strategy has little that can go wrong with it: nothing has to be reconstructed; the theory just legitimises classical reasoning as it stands. The problems for this strategy are rather different. The first is to understand the exact import of the claim that, 'provided we stay within the domain of the consistent, classical logic is perfectly acceptable'. This is not as easy as it appears, but I have discussed the matter at length elsewhere[4] so will not take up the issue again. I merely report that an important upshot of that discussion is that we are justified in assuming consistency until and unless it is shown otherwise.

The second problem for this approach is to see whether it can be worked up into an interesting formal theory of reasoning. It can; and that is the main topic of this chapter.[5] The crucial insight here is due to Batens;[6] it is that, given some information from which we have to reason, we can cash out the idea that the situation is no more inconsistent than we are forced to assume by restricting ourselves to those models of the information that are, in some sense, as consistent as possible, given the information—or, as we will say, are minimally inconsistent.

How, precisely, one is to understand minimal inconsistency may depend on the underlying paraconsistent logic. For reasons I have explained elsewhere,[7] my preferred extensional paraconsistent logic is the system *LP*. Hence I shall work with this (though clearly the techniques are more generally applicable). First, I review the semantics of *LP*; then I will explain minimally inconsistent *LP*, *LPm*. I will then establish a number of its pleasing properties.

---

[3] See Friedman and Meyer (1992). [4] See ch. 8 and Priest (1989).
[5] A somewhat different approach is given in sect. 8.6; but this now strikes me as contrived in comparison with the approach of this chapter. [6] Batens (1986, 1989).
[7] Chs. 4 and 5 above, and Priest (1979*a*).

16.3 SEMANTICS FOR *LP*

The semantics for *LP* are as explained in Chapter 5; but it will make the technical material in this and subsequent chapters a bit more digestible if we make a few minor changes.

We will take the logical operators of the language to be ¬, ∧, and ∀. ∃ and ∨ can be taken as defined in the usual way. As in previous chapters, I will use lower-case Greek letters as schematic letters for formulas of the language, and upper-case Greek letters for sets of formulas. I will use lower-case Roman letters, from p on, as schematic letters for atomic formulas.

I will write a first order interpretation as $\mathcal{M} = \langle D, I \rangle$. In chapter 5 I wrote the denotation function as d; from now on I will use this letter for members of the domain. In that chapter I also wrote the denotation function as den; I will now write the denotation function for closed terms (and, as we will see in a moment, there will be no others) as I as well. Any standard classical interpretation is isomorphic to an *LP* interpretation in which all atomic formulas (and so all formulas) take the value {0} or {1}. Consequently, I will call all such interpretations *classical interpretations*.

It will also make things a bit slicker if we restrict ourselves to closed terms and formulas only. We may then dispense with the notion of satisfaction, and employ only the notion of truth (in an interpretation). Thus, in the first order case we may forget the argument s in the truth value assignment, v. To this end, given an interpretation, $\mathcal{M}$, we take the *language of* $\mathcal{M}$ to be the language augmented by a set of individual constants, one for each member of D. If $d \in D$, we will write this name as **d**. (Thus, in the language of $\mathcal{M}$, every member of the domain of $\mathcal{M}$ has at least one name.) The truth conditions for ∀ may now be given thus:[8]

$$1 \in v(\forall x \alpha) \Leftrightarrow \text{for all } d \in D, 1 \in v(\alpha(x/\mathbf{d}))$$

$$0 \in v(\forall x \alpha) \Leftrightarrow \text{for some } d \in D, 0 \in v(\alpha(x/\mathbf{d}))$$

($\alpha(x/d)$ denotes α with all free occurrences of 'x' replaced by 'd'.)

It will also be helpful to rephrase the definition of *LP* consequence in terms of models:

$\mathcal{M}$ *is a model for* α ($\mathcal{M} \Vdash \alpha$) iff $1 \in v(\alpha)$

$\mathcal{M}$ *is a model for* Σ ($\mathcal{M} \Vdash \Sigma$) iff 1 for all $\beta \in \Sigma, \mathcal{M} \Vdash \beta$

α *is an LP consequence of* Σ ($\Sigma \models \alpha$) iff every model of Σ is a model of α

One property of *LP*, not hitherto mentioned, will be useful in what follows. So I will state it now. (I relegate proofs of this and all other lemmas to a technical appendix of this chapter.)

---

[8] The ⇒ in what follows has nothing to do with the sign as used in earlier chapters. It is simply a metalinguistic conditional.

Lemma 1
Let M be any interpretation. If, for every atomic formula p, in the language for M, $v(p) = \{1, 0\}$, then for every formula α, $v(\alpha) = \{1, 0\}$.

16.4 SEMANTICS FOR *LPm*

Giving the precise definition of minimal inconsistency requires us to find some measure of degree of inconsistency, or, what comes to the same thing, a way of ordering interpretations with respect to their inconsistency. One might attempt this in a number of ways, but the one that appears to give the best result is as follows.[9] If α is a formula, recall that $\alpha!$ is $\alpha \wedge \neg\alpha$. Note that $1 \in v(\alpha!)$ iff $v(\alpha) = \{1, 0\}$. If $M = \langle D, I \rangle$ is an interpretation, define the inconsistent part of M, $M!$, to be the set of atomic facts with value $\{1, 0\}$ in M, i.e.

$$M! = \{\, p : \text{for some } P \text{ and } d_1, \ldots, d_n \in D, p = P\mathbf{d}_1 \ldots \mathbf{d}_n \text{ and } 1 \in v(p!)\}$$

$M!$ is a subset (in general, proper, since objects may have more than one name) of the true contradictory atomic sentences. (In the case of a propositional interpretation, v, $v!$ is just the set of propositional parameters taking the value $\{1, 0\}$.) $M!$ is an appropriate measure of the inconsistency of M. If M is classical, then $M!$ is clearly ϕ, which is minimal. If every atomic formula (and so every formula) is inconsistent, then $M!$ is maximal.

We can now define a consistency ordering thus:

$$M_1 < M_2 \text{ iff } M_1! \subset M_2!$$

Here $\subset$ is strict inclusion. As is easy to check, $<$ is a strict partial order. $M_1 \leq M_2$ is defined in the obvious way as: $M_1 < M_2$ or $M_1 = M_2$. We now define:

M *is a minimally inconsistent (m.i.) model of* Σ *$(\Sigma \Vdash_m \alpha)$ iff $M \Vdash \Sigma$ and if $M' < M, M' \nVdash \Sigma$.*

α *is a m.i. consequence of* Σ *$(\Sigma \models_m \alpha)$ iff every m.i. model of Σ is a model of α.*

16.5 PROPERTIES OF *LPm*

The first thing to observe about *LPm* is that it is non-monotonic. For example, let Π be $\{p, \neg p \vee q\}$. Then $\Pi \models_m q$, since the m.i. models of Π are just the classical models. But $\Pi \cup \{p!\} \nvDash_m q$, since there is an m.i. model of the premises

---

[9] For a fuller discussion, see Priest (1988).

where p has the value $\{1, 0\}$ and q has the value $\{0\}$[10]. Note however that, if r is a distinct atomic formula, $\Pi \cup \{r!\} \models_m q$, since in m.i. models of the premises only r takes the value $\{1, 0\}$ In effect, *LPm* is a logic that implements the default assumption of inconsistency.

To state some more general properties of *LPm*, we need a little notation. Let Σ^{CL}, Σ^{LP}, and Σ^m be the set of classical, *LP*, and *LPm* consequences of Σ, respectively. Then:

Fact 1
$\Sigma^{LP} \subseteq \Sigma^m \subseteq \Sigma^{CL}$, *since every classical model of Σ is an m.i. model, and every m.i. model is an LP model.*

Fact 2
In general, the inclusions in Fact 1 *are proper, since* $\Pi \not\models q$, *but* $\Pi \models_m q$ *(where Π is as above); and* $\{p!\} \not\models_m q$, *but q is a classical consequence of* $\{p!\}$.

Fact 3
If Σ is classically consistent, $\Sigma^m = \Sigma^{CL}$, since if Σ is classically consistent, its m.i. models just are its classical models.[11]

Hence *LPm* is a more generous notion of consequence than *LP*, which allows for classical inferences—such as the disjunctive syllogism—provided inconsistency does not "get in the way"; in particular, it is identical with classical logic in consistent situations. It thus gives a precise account of how it is that classical inferences are acceptable, paraconsistently, in consistent situations.

[10] And, like many non-monotonic logics, it is not closed under substitution. Thus, $\{p, \neg p \vee q!\} \not\models_m q!$, since there is an m.i. model in which $p!$ is true, but not $q!$.

[11] In the original version of this paper (Priest 1991a), an extra condition was imposed on the *definiens* of the consistency ordering: that $\mathcal{M}_1$ and $\mathcal{M}_2$ have the same domain. With this clause, Fact 3 is, in fact, false. Let $\Sigma = \{\exists x Px, \exists x \neg Px\}$. Let $\mathcal{M}$ be the interpretation where $D = I^+(P) = I^-(P) = \{a\}$, and all the other predicates behave consistently. This is an m.i. model of Σ, even though $\mathcal{M}! = \{Pa\}$ and Σ is classically consistent. (I am grateful to Diderik Batens for pointing out the mistake to me.) Without the extra clause, it is not an m.i. model, since, if $\mathcal{N}$ is any classical model of Σ, $\mathcal{N}! = \phi$. As the original paper pointed out, without this additional clause, minimising inconsistency may involve minimising the size of the domain in certain ways. Thus, let $\Sigma = \{\forall x(Px!)\}$; without the extra clause, if $\mathcal{M}$ is an m.i. model of Σ then $\mathcal{M}$ has a single-element domain. For suppose we have an m.i. model with two distinct members, a and b. $\mathcal{M}! = \{Pa, Pb\}$ (the other predicates behaving consistently). We can obtain a more consistent model simply by cutting b out of the domain. Hence $\Sigma \models_m c_1 = c_2$. At the time I wrote the paper, I thought this counter-intuitive. I have now changed my mind. If we are serious about minimising inconsistencies, then we *should* minimise the inconsistent part of the domain, which may mean contracting it. Of course, since *LPm* is non-monotonic, adding information to Σ may well take away the consequence in question. Thus, $\{\forall x(Px!), c_1 \neq c_2\} \not\models_m c_1 = c_2$. For consider the interpretation $\mathcal{M}$, where $D = I^+(P) = I^-(P) = \{a, b\}, I(c_1) = a, I(c_2) = b$, and all other predicates behave consistently. This is a model of the premises, not the conclusion. But it is minimally inconsistent. $\mathcal{M}! = \{Pa, Pb\}$; and if we try to make this smaller by cutting b from the domain, we must then have that $I(c_1) = I(c_2) = a$. Hence $\mathcal{M}!$ becomes $\{Pa, a = a\}$, and is not decreased. Similarly, $\{\forall x(Px!), Qc_1, \neg Qc_2\} \not\models_m c_1 = c_2$.

16.6 REASSURANCE: THE PROPOSITIONAL CASE

I have noted that *LPm* is a more generous inference engine than *LP*. The next question is 'How much more generous?' Can we, for example, prove more contradictions using *LPm* than using *LP*? The answer to this is 'In general, yes'. To see this, just note that $\{p!, q! \vee r\} \models_m (p \wedge r)!$ For in any m.i. model of the premises, *r* must be true. Hence $p \wedge r$ must be true; but since *p* is also false, so is $p \wedge r$. However, $\{p!, q! \vee r\} \not\models (p \wedge r)!$ as a simple counter-model demonstrates.

This raises the possibility that Σ^m might collapse into triviality when Σ^{LP} does not. This would obviously be unfortunate, since it would show that there are perfectly sensible (non-trivial) contexts where *LPm* could not be used. Its theoretical legitimacy would therefore have to be restricted, just as that of classical logic is. It would be very reassuring, therefore, if, whenever Σ^{LP} is non-trivial, so is Σ^m. Let us therefore call this property *Reassurance*.

Reassurance is not to be taken lightly. For example, suppose that we augment *LP* with propositional quantifiers and a conditional operator, $\rightarrow$, satisfying (at least) *modus ponens*. Let

$$\Sigma = \{\exists p(p!)\} \cup \{p_i! \rightarrow p_{i+1}! : i \text{ is a natural number}\}$$

(where the natural numbers index the propositional variables). From the perspective of *LP* + *modus ponens*, Σ is non-trivial. It does not entail p_0, for example. But Σ has no m.i. model. If $\mathcal{M}$ is a model of Σ, then $\mathcal{M}!$ must be non-empty. Let *n* be the least *m* such that p_m is inconsistent. Then $\mathcal{M}'$, which is exactly the same, except that $n+1$ is the least *m*, is a less inconsistent model. Hence, vacuously, Σ is trivial under m.i. consequence.

It is, therefore, a welcome result that *LPm* satisfies Reassurance (with a couple of qualifications that I will comment on in due course). For propositional *LPm* the result was proved where Σ is finite in Priest (1988). The propositional case where Σ is infinite follows from the following lemma, whose proof is due to Fangzhen Lin (in conversation).

Lemma 2 (Lin's Lemma)
If v is a model of Σ then there is an m.i. model of Σ, v', such that $v' \leq v$.

For suppose that Σ is non-trivial. Then there must be a *v* and α such that $v \Vdash \Sigma$ and $v \not\Vdash \alpha$. Hence there must be a propositional parameter, *p*, such that $v \not\Vdash p!$ by Lemma 1. By Lin's Lemma, there is a v' such that v' is an m.i. model of Σ, and $v' \not\models p!$. Hence, Σ^m is non-trivial.

16.7 REASSURANCE: THE FIRST-ORDER CASE

For the first order case, the proof of Reassurance is slightly more complicated, and depends on two more lemmas.

Lemma 3
Let the language contain a finite number of predicates, and let M be a finite interpretation such that $M \Vdash \Sigma$. Then there is an M' such that $M' \leq M$ and $M' \Vdash_m \Sigma$.

Note that this is the first order analogue of Lin's Lemma, but restricted to the finite case. Its generalisation is still open (though I conjecture that it is true). If it could be proved, Reassurance in general would follow in the way that it does in the propositional case.

To state the next lemma we need a definition. Let $M = \langle D, I \rangle$ be an interpretation. Let $\sim$ be an equivalence relation on D, which is also a congruence relation on the denotations of the function symbols in the language (i.e., if f is a function symbol, and $d_i \sim e_i$ for all $1 \leq i \leq n$, then $I(f)(d_1, \ldots, d_n) \sim I(f)(e_1, \ldots, e_n)$). If $d \in D$, let $[d]$ be the equivalence class of D under $\sim$. Let $M^\sim = \langle D^\sim, I^\sim \rangle$, the *collapsed interpretation*, be defined as follows. $D^\sim = \{[d] : d \in D\}$. If c is a constant, $I^\sim(c) = [I(c)]$; if f is an n-place function symbol,

$$I^\sim(f)([d_1], \ldots, [d_n]) = [I(f)(d_1, \ldots, d_n)]$$

(this is well defined, since $\sim$ is a congruence relation); and if $a_1, \ldots, a_n \in D^\sim$,

$$\langle a_1, \ldots, a_n \rangle \in I^{\sim +}(P) \text{ iff } \exists d_1 \in a_1, \ldots, \exists d_n \in a_n, \langle d_1, \ldots, d_n \rangle \in I^+(P)$$

$$\langle a_1, \ldots, a_n \rangle \in I^{\sim -}(P) \text{ iff } \exists d_1 \in a_1, \ldots, \exists d_n \in a_n, \langle d_1, \ldots, d_n \rangle \in I^-(P).$$

It is easy to check that $\langle I^{\sim +}(=), I^{\sim -}(=) \rangle$ satisfies the appropriate conditions. Hence the interpretation is well defined. In effect, the new interpretation identifies everything in an equivalence class, producing a composite individual with all the properties of the individuals of which it is composed.

Lemma 4 (Collapsing Lemma)
For every formula, α, in the language of M, $v^\sim(\alpha) \supseteq v(\alpha)$.

The Collapsing Lemma assures us that, if the original interpretation is a model of some set of sentences, the collapsed interpretation will also be a model.[12]
We can now prove Reassurance subject to two restrictions:

1. the number of predicates in the language is finite;
2. there are no function symbols in the language.

For suppose that Σ^{LP} is non-trivial. Then, for some α, $\Sigma \nVdash \alpha$. Hence there is an $M = \langle D, I \rangle$ such that $M \Vdash \Sigma$ and $M \nVdash \alpha$. By Lemma 1 there is some predicate,

---

[12] Note that the proof of this lemma depends heavily on the monontonicity of the connectives. That is, if truth values are added to inputs, they are never lost in outputs. This feature is not shared by so called Boolean Negation. If there were such a connective in the language, the Collapsing Lemma would therefore fail. This point is related to the argument against the meaningfulness of Boolean Negation in Priest (2006), sect. 5.1.

P, and $d_1, \ldots, d_n \in D$, such that $\mathcal{M} \not\Vdash P\mathbf{d}_1 \ldots \mathbf{d}_n$! Define the equivalence relation, $\sim$, on D as follows:

$x \sim y$ iff $x = y = d_1$ or $x = y = d_2$ or $\ldots$ or $x = y = d_n$
or $x, y \notin \{d_1, \ldots, d_n\}$

In effect, $\sim$ leaves $d_1, \ldots, d_n$ alone, but identifies all other members of D. Clearly, $D^\sim$ is finite. Moreover, by the Collapsing Lemma $\mathcal{M}^\sim \Vdash \Sigma$. Further, it is obvious that $\mathcal{M}^\sim \not\Vdash P\mathbf{d}_1 \ldots \mathbf{d}_n$!. By Lemma 3, there is an $\mathcal{M}' \leq \mathcal{M}^\sim$ such that $\mathcal{M}' \Vdash \Sigma$, and since $\mathcal{M}' \leq \mathcal{M}^\sim$, $\mathcal{M}' \not\Vdash P\mathbf{d}_1 \ldots \mathbf{d}_n$!. This is not quite what we need to show, since this sentence belongs to the language of $\mathcal{M}$, and not to the original language. But it follows that $\mathcal{M}' \not\Vdash \forall x_1 \ldots \forall x_n (Px_1 \ldots x_n)$!, a formula that is in the original language. Hence Σ^m is non-trivial.

The two restrictions on Reassurance are not significant ones in the present context. In practice, a piece of reasoning, being finitary, never uses more than a finite number of predicates. Classical reasoning certainly does use function symbols sometimes; but as is well known, these are not essential. Classically equivalent reasoning can be performed employing predicates instead of function symbols.

The Collapsing Lemma, on which the above proof of Reassurance depends, is interesting in its own right, and will come in for further use in the following chapters. It may initially be rather surprising. After all, we can, given any model of a set of formulas (without function symbols), produce a model of any smaller cardinality simply by choosing an equivalence relation that identifies the appropriate number of objects. And this is true even though the set may contain formulas that appear to constrain cardinality, e.g. $\exists x \exists y\, x \neq y$. The reason they do not do so in a paraconsistent context is, of course, that there is no guarantee that they behave consistently.

The Reassurance Theorem provides the final piece of evidence that *LPm* provides a good theoretical account of how classical reasoning is possible in consistent domains, and, in a constrained way, in the transconsistent too. The next job is to look at m.i. consequence in some interesting inconsistent theories, such as Naive Set Theory; but that is a whole new subject.

16.8 APPENDIX PROOFS OF LEMMAS

Proof of Lemma 1
The proof is by a simple recursion over the structure of formulas. Details are omitted.

Proof of Lemma 2 (Lin's Lemma)
In *LP* every formula is logically equivalent to one in disjunctive normal form. Hence, without loss of generality, we can assume that the members of Σ are of the form $\pm p_1 \vee \pm p_2 \vee \ldots \vee \pm p_n$, where $\pm$ is either $\neg$ or nothing.

Consider the set $S = \{v' : v' \leq v \text{ and } v' \Vdash \Sigma\}$. S is partially ordered by $\leq$. Let C be any chain in the ordering. We show that C is bounded below. It follows by Zorn's Lemma that C has a minimal element, which gives the result.

If C is finite, we are home; so suppose it is infinite. Let

$$C! = \cap\{\mu! : \mu \in C\}$$

Define a subset, Σ', of Σ as follows:

$\alpha \in \Sigma'$ iff $\alpha \in \Sigma$, α is $\pm p_1 \vee \pm p_2 \vee \ldots \vee \pm p_n$, and for $1 \leq i \leq n$, $p_i \notin C!$

If $\alpha \in \Sigma'$ then, for some $v \in C$, the value of each propositional parameter in v is classical, since C is a chain. Hence α has a classical model. Similarly, if Σ'' is a finite subset of Σ', Σ'' has a classical model. By the classical Compactness Theorem, Σ' has a classical model, μ.

Define a model, μ', as follows:

$$\mu'(p) = \{1,0\} \quad \text{if } p \in C!$$
$$= \mu(p) \quad \text{otherwise}$$

Clearly, $\mu' \leq v'$ for all $v' \in C$. It remains to show that $\mu' \Vdash \Sigma$. If $\alpha \subset \Sigma'$, then there is no propositional parameter in $C!$ that occurs in α. Hence $\mu' \Vdash \alpha$, since $\mu \Vdash \alpha$. If, on the other hand, $\alpha \in \Sigma - \Sigma'$, then there is a propositional parameter, p, in $C!$ that occurs in α. Hence $\mu' \Vdash \alpha$.

Proof of Lemma 3

Since there is a finite number of predicates in the language and the domain of $\mathcal{M}$ is finite, $\mathcal{M}!$ is finite. Thus, $\{\mathcal{M}' : \mathcal{M}' \leq \mathcal{M} \text{ and } \mathcal{M}' \Vdash \Sigma\}$ is a finite set partially ordered by $\leq$. Hence there is a minimal member.

Proof of Lemma 4 (Collapsing Lemma)

We first show that, for any term, t, $I^\sim(t) = [I(t)]$. This is proved by recursion on the structure of t. It is true for constants, by definition. The recursion case is as follows:

$$I^\sim(ft_1 \ldots t_n) = I^\sim(f)(I^\sim(t_1), \ldots, I^\sim(t_n))$$
$$= I^\sim(f)([I(t_1)], \ldots, [I(t_n)])$$
$$= [I(ft_1 \ldots t_n)]$$

We now prove the result by recursion on the structure of α. I will give only the truth cases; the falsity cases are similar. For atomic sentences, the argument is as follows:

$$1 \in v(Pt_1 \ldots t_n) \Rightarrow \langle I(t_1), \ldots, I(t_n)\rangle \in I^+(P)$$
$$\Rightarrow \exists d_1 \in [I(t_1)], \ldots, \exists d_n \in [I(t_n)], \langle d_1, \ldots, d_n\rangle \in I^+(P)$$
$$\Rightarrow \langle [I(t_1)], \ldots, [I(t_n)]\rangle \in I^{\sim+}(P)$$
$$\Rightarrow \langle I^\sim(t_1), \ldots, I^\sim(t_n)\rangle \in I^{\sim+}(P)$$
$$\Rightarrow 1 \in v^\sim(Pt_1 \ldots t_n)$$

The recursion case for $\wedge$ is as follows (that for $\neg$ is similar):

$$1 \in v(\alpha \wedge \beta) \Rightarrow 1 \in v(\alpha) \text{ and } 1 \in v(\beta)$$
$$\Rightarrow 1 \in v^\sim(\alpha) \text{ and } 1 \in v^\sim(\beta)$$
$$\Rightarrow 1 \in v^\sim(\alpha \wedge \beta)$$

The case for $\forall$ is as follows:

$$1 \in v(\forall x\alpha) \Rightarrow 1 \in v(\alpha(x/\mathbf{d})) \text{ for all } d \in D$$
$$\Rightarrow 1 \in v^\sim(\alpha(x/\mathbf{d})) \text{ for all } [d] \in D^\sim$$
$$\Rightarrow 1 \in v^\sim(\alpha(x/\mathbf{a})) \text{ for all } a \in D^\sim$$
$$\Rightarrow 1 \in v^\sim(\forall x\alpha)$$

17

Inconsistent Arithmetic

17.1 SOME HISTORY

The study of formal inconsistent arithmetics is relatively young, going back about twenty-five years. It has, however, already occasioned a number of interesting technical results, as well as philosophical spin-offs. In this chapter we will look at some of these. We will see how inconsistent arithmetics are delivered by certain kinds of inconsistent models, and what such models are like. We will then turn to more philosophical issues. These concern, importantly, the way that inconsistent arithmetics relate to some of the limitative results of classical metamathematics. I will bring these matters to bear on the discussion of inconsistent arithmetic of Chapter 3. An important concern will be some criticisms of Stewart Shapiro (2002).

Let us start with a little history. The first person to construct an inconsistent arithmetic (as far as I know) was Nelson (1959), who used a realisability semantics to produce an inconsistent arithmetic, based on a paraconsistent logic of an intuitionist kind. Current developments in the subject, however, trace back not to this, but to R. K. Meyer's paper, 'Relevant Arithmetic'. This paper, in an incomplete form, was circulated among relevant logicians, and was abstracted as Meyer (1976); sadly, the full version of the paper has never appeared. Meyer's concern was relevant Peano arithmetic, that is, essentially, the axiomatic arithmetic in which one takes the Peano axioms, replaces the conditionals employed with a relevant conditional, and then uses an underlying relevant logic, R in Meyer's case, to prove things about numbers. In investigating the properties of this theory, $R^\#$, Meyer noticed that it could be given a finitary consistency proof (formalisable in $R^\#$ itself—showing that Gödel's Second Incompleteness Theorem may not apply once one jettisons classical logic). Specifically, there are models with a two-element domain which verify all the theorems. The models were also models of the three-valued logic $RM3$, and they verified a lot more than the theorems of $R^\#$: they verified an inconsistent set of sentences (though $R^\#$ is itself consistent).

In Meyer and Mortensen (1984) generalisations of Meyer's model were investigated. Specifically, different finite sizes of the domain were employed, as were different many-valued semantics for the conditional. It thus became clear that there was a substantial family of inconsistent arithmetics. The models were constructed, in effect, by deploying an equivalence relation on the natural numbers which is a congruence with respect to successor, addition, and multiplication. Mortensen realised that similar techniques could be applied to the numbers in a non-standard model of arithmetic. In Mortensen (1986, 1988) he constructed many inconsistent arithmetics using this technique and investigated a number of the properties of this family.[1]

Two things had become clear by this time. The first is that the inconsistent arithmetics are very powerful. Specifically, they can be made to contain all of the sentences true in the standard model of arithmetic—as expressed using just the classical propositional connectives, $\wedge$, $\vee$, $\neg$, and $\supset$, where $\alpha \supset \beta$ is defined in the usual way as $\neg\alpha \vee \beta$. The second is that, although a lot of the initial interest in these arithmetics was occasioned by an interest in a non-material conditional, and specifically in what could be proved using such a conditional, once one moved to a model-theoretic perspective the non-material conditional did not play a large role: all of the truths of the standard model came for free anyway. This meant that one could simply forget about the non-material conditional, and investigate the structure of the theories, as expressed in the classical vocabulary (though the underlying logic could not, of course, be classical, since the interpretations model inconsistent sets of sentences). This, in turn, allowed inconsistent models to be constructed by a simple yet powerful model-theoretic construction, the Collapsing Lemma. A form of this had already been established by Dunn (1979); a version that allowed it to be immediately applicable to the construction of inconsistent models was given in Priest (1991a).

All the tools were now at hand for circumscribing an important class of inconsistent arithmetics and investigating their structure. The class was simple enough to be natural, and complex enough to be mathematically interesting. The analysis of the finite case was given in Priest (1997), and that of the general case in Priest (2000). Let us look at some of the details.

17.2 COLLAPSED MODELS OF ARITHMETIC

First, some definitions. Let L be the standard language of first-order arithmetic: one constant, **0**, function symbols for successor, addition, and multiplication (′, +, and ×, respectively), and one predicate symbol, =. We will be concerned with *LP* interpretations of this language—of which classical interpretations are

---

[1] Mortensen also observed that the techniques in question could be applied, equally, to give inconsistent theories of other sorts of mathematical theory, such as fields and rings. In his (1990) he deployed these ideas to produce inconsistent models of the differential calculus. Mortensen's work is nicely summarised in his (1995). Priest (1995), pt 4, Technical Appendix, used similar techniques to construct inconsistent set theories with various properties.

special cases.[2] Let $\mathcal{N}$ be the standard (classical) interpretation of the language; and if $\mathcal{M}$ is an interpretation, let $\text{Th}(\mathcal{M})$ (the *theory* of $\mathcal{M}$) be the set of sentences true in $\mathcal{M}$. A *model of arithmetic* is any *LP* interpretation of *L* that is a model of $\text{Th}(\mathcal{N})$. Note that, as well as $\mathcal{N}$ any classical non-standard model of arithmetic is a model of arithmetic in the sense I will use the word here. But there are many more. In particular, as we will see, there are models of arithmetic, $\mathcal{M}$, such that $\text{Th}(\mathcal{M})$ is inconsistent. I will call such models, naturally enough, *inconsistent models of arithmetic*.

Inconsistent models can be produced by applying the Collapsing Lemma.[3] Let $\mathcal{M} = \langle M, I \rangle$ be any classical model of $\text{Th}(\mathcal{N})$. Let $\sim$ be an equivalence relation on M which is also a congruence relation with respect to the interpretations of the function symbols. Then we define the collapsed interpretation, as in section 16.7, to produce a collapsed interpretation, $\mathcal{M}^{\sim}$. By the Collapsing Lemma, $\mathcal{M}^{\sim}$ is a model of arithmetic. Provided that $\sim$ is not the trivial equivalence relation, which relates each thing only to itself, then $\mathcal{M}^{\sim}$, will model inconsistencies. For suppose that $\sim$ relates the distinct members of M, n and m; then in $\mathcal{M}^{\sim}$, $[n] = [m]$ and so $\langle [n], [m] \rangle$ is in the extension of $=$. But since $n \neq m$ in $\mathcal{M}$, $\langle [n], [m] \rangle$ is in the anti-extension too. Thus, $\exists x(x = x \wedge x \neq x)$ holds in $\mathcal{M}^{\sim}$. Let me give a couple of simple examples of this.

Example 1. Let $\mathcal{M}$ be the standard model of arithmetic. $n, p \in M$ and $p > 0$. Define a relation, $\sim$, on M, thus:

$$x \sim y \text{ iff}(x, y < n \text{ and } x = y) \text{ or } (x, y \geq n \text{ and } x = y \pmod{p})$$

It is easy to check that $\sim$ is a congruence relation on M. Let $\mathcal{M}_n^p$ be the model obtained by collapsing with respect to this. The Collapsing Lemma assures us that it is a model of arithmetic. It is finite; it has an initial tail of length n that behaves consistently. The other numbers form a cycle of period p. The successor graph can be depicted as follows:

$$0 \rightarrow 1 \rightarrow \ldots \rightarrow n \rightarrow n+1$$
$$\uparrow \qquad \downarrow$$
$$n+p-1 \leftarrow \cdots$$

Example 2. Let $\mathcal{M}$ be any non-standard classical model of arithmetic. Define the relation $\sim$ as follows:

$$x \sim y \text{ iff}(x, y \text{ are standard numbers and } x = y) \text{ or } (x, y \text{ are non-standard})$$

Again, it is easy to check that $\sim$ is an equivalence relation which is also a congruence on the arithmetic operators. The model obtained by collapsing with respect to this

---

[2] The logic can also be that of First Degree Entailment. It makes no difference, since the theories with which we will be concerned are complete. For details of First Degree Entailment, see Priest (2001), ch. 8.

[3] Though at the time of writing it is not known whether all inconsistent models can be produced, essentially, by employing this construction.

equivalence relation contains the standard interpretation, plus an inconsistent "point at infinity", Ω. The successor graph can be depicted as follows:

$$0 \rightarrow 1 \rightarrow \ldots \Omega$$

$$\circlearrowleft$$

These examples give something of the flavour of inconsistent models of arithmetic. An account of the general structure of this class is unnecessary for understanding the rest of this chapter. I have therefore put it in an appendix (section 17.9).

Before we leave purely technical issues behind, one final note. First order arithmetic has many classical non-standard models, but none of them is finite. One of the intriguing features of inconsistent models of arithmetic is, as we have just seen, that it has finite models. These have a particularly notable feature: if M is finite, $\text{Th}(M)$ is decidable. For the truth value in M of an atomic sentence can be computed, since the denotations of the functions and predicates, being on a finite domain, are computable. The truth values of propositional compounds are computed by LP truth tables, and, since the domain is finite, quantified sentences are equivalent to finite conjunctions/disjunctions. Thus, $\exists x \alpha$ has the same truth value as $\alpha(x/\mathbf{d}_0) \vee \ldots \vee \alpha(x/\mathbf{d}_n)$, where $D = \{d_0, \ldots, d_n\}$. (Recall that I am using bold face as a naming device.)

17.3 CONSISTENT *v.* INCONSISTENT ARITHMETICS

We now turn to more philosophical issues.[4] If M is any model of arithmetic, $\text{Th}(M)$ is a theory, that is, a set of arithmetic sentences closed under LP consequence, and contains $\text{Th}(N)$. If M is an inconsistent model of arithmetic, $\text{Th}(M)$ is also inconsistent.[5] I will call any such theory an *inconsistent arithmetic*.

Let us ask the following question: Could it be that the correct arithmetic is one of the inconsistent ones?[6] 'Which inconsistent arithmetic?' it might well be replied. That is obviously an important question; but for the present it does not need to be addressed. (The question is discussed in the context of the finite models in Priest 1994a.) The following considerations do not depend on which inconsistent arithmetic is at issue—or if they do, I will make this explicit.

---

[4] The first person to deploy the technical material on inconsistent models in a philosophical context was van Bendegem (1993, 1994). He was particularly concerned with the finite models, and developed an argument for finitism on the basis of them. Priest (1994) took up the idea, but used the finite models in defence of inconsistent arithmetic, rather than finitism. Where van Bendegem saw a greatest number, Priest saw a least inconsistent number. The idea of a least inconsistent number was discussed further in Priest (1994a).

[5] There are, in fact, LP theories that contain all of $\text{Th}(N)$, but that are not the theory of some collapsed model. This, for example, $\bigcap_{n \in \omega} M_n^p$, being an intersection of theories, is a theory. But it contains the sentence $\exists x\, x \neq x$, while it contains nothing of the form $\mathbf{n} \neq \mathbf{n}$.

[6] A quite different question is whether it would be appropriate to *revise* our arithmetic by adopting an inconsistent one. This is discussed in Priest (2003a).

The orthodox view is certainly that the consistent Th($\mathcal{N}$) is the true arithmetic, not Th($\mathcal{M}$), where $\mathcal{M}$ is some inconsistent model of arithmetic. Of course Th($\mathcal{N}$) is true of $\mathcal{N}$, and Th($\mathcal{M}$) is true of $\mathcal{M}$. That is not contentious. The question is whether it is $\mathcal{N}$ or $\mathcal{M}$ that is the correct interpretation of the language of arithmetic. It might seem as though it is easy to resolve this issue, but it is not. A dispute between the proponent, A, of "standard arithmetic" and the proponent, B, of an inconsistent arithmetic is of a somewhat unusual kind. Anything (at least, anything arithmetic) that A endorses, B will endorse too. Thus, for example, A will insist that there is no greatest number ($\forall x \exists y\, y > x$); B will concur. The locus of disagreement will be in the fact that B will assert things that A will not wish to assent to. Why suppose A right and B wrong? A may point out that B's view of arithmetic is inconsistent; but unless they have some independent reason to suppose that inconsistency—or at least inconsistency in arithmetic—is a bad thing, this simply begs the question. A may, of course, attempt to mount a defence of consistency in general. I will not enter into that debate here. Let me just say, for the record, that I am not aware of any very persuasive—and in particular non-question-begging—arguments for that conclusion.[7]

Are there any reasons, however, that push us towards endorsing an inconsistent arithmetic? One reason is that inconsistent arithmetics avoid some of the limitative results of the classical metatheory of arithmetic, and the unhappinesses associated with these.[8] Inconsistent arithmetics can do lots of things that consistent arithmetics cannot do. Thus, for example, as I have already noted, some inconsistent arithmetics are decidable. If one of these is the correct arithmetic, then there is an algorithm for solving any arithmetical problem, which would certainly be very nice.

Another thing that inconsistent arithmetics can do is contain their own truth predicate; hence Tarski's Theorem is avoided. Tarski's Theorem shows that any theory that contains its own truth predicate is inconsistent; but this is obviously no problem in an inconsistent arithmetic! The language of arithmetic that we have been dealing with so far contains no truth predicate. However, it is well known[9] that any arithmetic based on *LP* can be extended conservatively with a truth predicate, T, satisfying the two way rule:

$$\frac{T\langle \alpha \rangle}{\alpha}$$

where $\langle \alpha \rangle$ is the numeral of the Gödel number of α.[10] (In the chapters of the first edition I used underlining to indicate an appropriate name-forming device. In this and subsequent chapters, I use angle brackets instead.)

---

[7] See e.g. Priest (1998).

[8] This matter is discussed further in Priest (1994). I am not now happy with a number of the arguments used in that paper. Some reasons why are explained in Priest (1996*a*).

[9] See e.g. Priest (2002), sect. 8.1.

[10] It is worth noting also that any finite *LP* model of arithmetic will model all instances of the Induction Schema, however the language of arithmetic is extended. The schema is of the form $(\alpha(x/\mathbf{0}) \wedge \forall x(\alpha \supset \alpha(x/x'))) \supset \forall x\alpha$. With a little massaging, this can be seen to be equivalent to

Of course, since the extension of the language with a truth predicate is conservative, if we start with a consistent arithmetic, the purely arithmetic fragment of the theory with the truth predicate will also be consistent. So the inconsistency generated by the truth predicate gives no reason, as such, to suppose that the purely arithmetic fragment is inconsistent. But if one can have a truth predicate, excluding it from "pure arithmetic" is somewhat arbitrary. Truth has just as good a claim to be considered a logical predicate as the identity predicate. It should, therefore, be a part of all "pure theories".

17.4 GÖDEL'S THEOREMS

Another thing that consistent arithmetic cannot do is provide a complete axiomatic theory. Inconsistent arithmetics can do this. As I have already noted, there are decidable complete inconsistent arithmetics; *a fortiori* they are axiomatic (and so, to point out the obvious, they can be specified by an axiom system in the usual way, quite independently of any consideration of collapsed models).[11] In virtue of the methodological importance of axiomatisability in mathematics, this is a significant plus.

Naturally, it is worth asking what happens to the "Gödel undecidable sentence" in these arithmetics. Take any axiomatisable inconsistent arithmetic, Θ. Since it is axiomatisable, its membership can be represented in the theory of the standard model, $\mathrm{Th}(\mathcal{N})$, by a formula of one free variable, $\beta(x)$.[12] ($\beta(x)$ is of the form $\exists y\, \mathrm{Prov}(y,x)$, where $\mathrm{Prov}(y,x)$ represents the proof relation of Θ.) That is, for any sentence, α,[13]

If $\alpha \in \Theta$ then $\beta\langle\alpha\rangle \in \mathrm{Th}(\mathcal{N})$.

If $\alpha \notin \Theta$ then $\neg\beta\langle\alpha\rangle \in \mathrm{Th}(\mathcal{N})$.

Since $\mathrm{Th}(\mathcal{N}) \subseteq \Theta$,

(1) If $\alpha \in \Theta$ then $\beta\langle\alpha\rangle \in \Theta$.

(2) If $\alpha \notin \Theta$ then $\neg\beta\langle\alpha\rangle \in \Theta$.

The undecidable sentence is a sentence, γ, of the form $\neg\beta\langle\gamma\rangle$. It is not difficult to see that both γ and $\neg\gamma$ are provable in Θ. For either $\gamma \in \Theta$ or $\gamma \notin \Theta$. In the first case, $\beta\langle\gamma\rangle = \neg\gamma \in \Theta$, by (1). In the second case, $\neg\gamma \in \Theta$, since Θ is complete, but $\neg\beta\langle\gamma\rangle = \gamma \in \Theta$, by (2). Either way, $\gamma \wedge \neg\gamma \in \Theta$. Note that, unlike the case

$\neg\alpha(x/0) \vee \exists x(\alpha \wedge \neg\alpha(x/x')) \vee \forall x\alpha$. Now, if the last disjunct is true, we are home. If not, there is some n such that $\alpha(x/n)$ fails, and since there is only a finite number of numbers in the domain, at least such n. Since $\alpha(x/n)$ fails, $\neg\alpha(x/n)$ holds. Thus, if $n = 0$ the first disjunct holds; if not, $n = m'$, and $\alpha(x/m)$, so the middle disjunct holds.

[11] Whether there are infinite models whose theories are axiomatic is currently an open question.
[12] $\beta(x)$ indicates that x may occur free in β. $\beta(t)$ then indicates $\beta(x/t)$.
[13] I write $\beta\langle\alpha\rangle$ instead of $\beta(\langle\alpha\rangle)$, etc., for ease of readability.

of the contradiction connected with Tarski's Theorem, γ is a purely arithmetic sentence; that is, its vocabulary is just that of the pure language of arithmetic.

Given the inconsistency of the arithmetic in question, a consistency proof for it, and *a fortiori* a consistency proof within Θ, is not to be expected. Classically, of course, consistency and non-triviality go together; but in a paraconsistent context, this is not the case. In particular, though Θ is inconsistent, it is not trivial (unless it is produced by collapsing under the degenerate equivalence relation that relates everything to everything). And the non-triviality of Θ can be proved within Θ. In this sense, Gödel's Second Incompleteness Theorem fails for inconsistent arithmetics. For take any unprovable sentence, α. Then since $\alpha \notin \Theta$, $\neg \beta\langle\alpha\rangle \in \Theta$, by (2). (Beware, however. This does not rule out $\beta\langle\alpha\rangle$ from being in Θ, too! We will return to this matter later.)

Finally, closely connected with Gödel's Second Incompleteness Theorem is Löb's Theorem, to the effect that in classical arithmetics, if $\beta\langle\alpha\rangle \supset \alpha$ is provable, so is α. It follows that not all instances of $\beta\langle\alpha\rangle \supset \alpha$ are provable. But this seems odd. All such sentences are clearly true; how is it that truths that seem as innocent as these *must* fail to be provable? In Θ, as one would expect, all instances are provable. For $\alpha \in \Theta$ or $\alpha \notin \Theta$. In the second case, $\neg\beta\langle\alpha\rangle \in \Theta$, by (2). In either case, $\neg\beta\langle\alpha\rangle \vee \alpha \in \Theta$. Note, also, that all instances of the converse are also provable. For if $\alpha \in \Theta$, then $\beta\langle\alpha\rangle \in \Theta$, by (1), so $\neg\alpha \vee \beta\langle\alpha\rangle \in \Theta$. And if $\alpha \notin \Theta$, $\neg\alpha \in \Theta$, since Θ is complete; hence $\neg\alpha \vee \beta\langle\alpha\rangle \in \Theta$. In a sense then, β is a truth predicate, since $\beta\langle\alpha\rangle \equiv \alpha \in \Theta$ (though this does not necessarily mean that $\beta\langle\alpha\rangle$ and α have the same truth values).

17.5 THE NAIVE NOTION OF PROOF

We see, then, that inconsistent arithmetics can do a lot of nice things, and can avoid a number of features that many have held to be problematic for consistent arithmetic. This does not demonstrate that true arithmetic is inconsistent, but it certainly moves us in this direction. There are considerations that drive us further.

As is clear to anyone who is familiar with Gödel's Theorem, at its heart there lies a paradox. Informally, the "undecidable" sentence is the sentence 'This sentence is not provable.' Suppose that it is provable; then, since whatever is provable is true, it is not provable. Hence it is not provable. But we have just proved this. So it is provable after all (as well).[14] Let us look at this paradox more closely.

When mathematicians establish things to be true, they give proofs. These are informal deductive arguments, appealing to things that have already been proved or, ultimately, from things that are obviously true, and so require no proof. As in section 3.2, I will call the notion of proof in question here *naive* proof. Let us

[14] The paradox is of the same kind as the "Knower Paradox"; see Priest (1995), sect. 10.5.

restrict ourselves to what can be proved naively about natural numbers. The language of naive proof about numbers is standard mathematical English (or some other natural language), but it is natural to suppose that this can be regimented into a suitable formal language, so that sentences may be assigned Gödelcodes. Let us write $\beta_N(x)$ as a predicate of natural numbers which expresses the fact that x is (the code of) a sentence that is naively provable. β_N satisfies the following principles:

(3) $\vdash_N \beta_N\langle\alpha\rangle \supset \alpha$

(4) If $\vdash_N \alpha$ then $\vdash_N \beta_N\langle\alpha\rangle$

where $\vdash_N$ records naive proof. For (3), it is analytic that whatever is naively provable is true. Naive proof just is that sort of mathematical argument that establishes something as true. And since this is analytic, it is itself naively provable. (Whether it is axiomatic or is derivable from more fundamental principles, we do not need to go into here.) For (4), if something is naively proved then this fact itself constitutes a proof that α is provable.

But from these two principles, we can show that $\vdash_N$ is inconsistent. By usual methods of self reference, we can construct a sentence that says of itself that it is not provable, i.e. a sentence γ, of the form $\neg\beta_N\langle\gamma\rangle$. Substituting in (3) gives us $\vdash_N \beta_N\langle\gamma\rangle \supset \neg\beta_N\langle\gamma\rangle$; i.e., $\vdash_N \neg\beta_N\langle\gamma\rangle \vee \neg\beta_N\langle\gamma\rangle$. Thus, $\vdash_N \neg\beta_N\langle\gamma\rangle$; that is, $\vdash_N \gamma$. By (4), $\vdash_N \beta_N\langle\gamma\rangle$ (i.e. $\vdash_N \neg\gamma$). Arithmetic is therefore inconsistent.

I have not assumed that β_N is itself a predicate that can be constructed from the usual arithmetic vocabulary $(', +, \times, =)$. But, as we saw in chapter 3, there are in fact reasons to suppose that an appropriate predicate can be so defined. It is part of the very notion of proof that a proof should be effectively recognised as such. For the very point of a proof is that it gives us a way of settling whether something is true. It is, therefore, a proof only when it is recognised as such. Dummett (1975) has stressed the point: it is part of the very notion of proof, unlike truth, that we can recognise one when we see it—at least in principle. Moreover, proof of the kind in question is a human practice. It is one that must be taught and learned. The human brain is, presumably, some sort of finite-state machine. It could not grasp the notion of proof if this were not axiomatic; if it were not, it would transcend the abilities of such a machine. For similar reasons, one must suppose that the grammar of any speakable language must be generated by a decidable set of rules. It might be pointed out that standards of proof may change over time, and that there is no reason to suppose that the change itself must occur in a rule-governed way. Indeed so. But we may take naive proof to comprise the standards of proof that are in operation here and now.[15]

So suppose that naive proof in this sense is, indeed, axiomatic. That is, there is a set of axioms, all of which are intuitively correct, and a set of rules that intuitively preserve truth. Since the theory is axiomatic, we can find a Σ_1 formula

---

[15] For further discussion, see ch. 3.

of the standard language of arithmetic, $\beta(x)$, which expresses provability. It says (in coded form) that there is a sequence of formulas such that every member is either an axiom or . . . , etc. By techniques of self reference, we can find a sentence, γ, of the form $\neg\beta\langle\gamma\rangle$. We can now reason essentially as we did for β_N. Since the axiom system is intuitively correct, we can show that all its theorems are true (as in the proof of section 3.5). That is, we can establish that $\vdash_N \beta\langle\alpha\rangle \supset \alpha$. From this, we reason as before to obtain $\vdash_N \gamma$. This shows naively that $\beta\langle\gamma\rangle$ is true. It follows that $\vdash_N \beta\langle\gamma\rangle$; i.e., $\vdash_N \neg\gamma$. As before, we have an inconsistency, but this time the inconsistent formula is one in the language of pure arithmetic. That is, arithmetic, as expressed in the usual vocabulary, is itself inconsistent.[16] Nor is this technically unfeasible. In section 17.4 we have already seen how a pure arithmetic can contain its own proof predicate and the attendant contradiction concerning its Gödel sentence.

17.6 SHAPIRO'S CRITICISMS

In the rest of this chapter, I will apply some of the topics just discussed to the critique of inconsistent arithmetics given by Shapiro (2002). Following the ideas of chapter 3, Shapiro constructs an axiomatic theory, PA*, that can prove its own Gödel sentence. The language of the theory contains a truth predicate, which is involved in the proof of the sentence; but the Gödel sentence itself, as Shapiro emphasises, is purely arithmetic, employing only the proof predicate for the theory, which, being axiomatisable, is expressible in terms of $'$, $+$, $\times$, and $=$. Actually, the exact details of PA* are left somewhat under-determined; but we need not go into that here. What I want to discuss are the unpalatable consequences that Shapiro supposes to follow from the fact that this theory can prove its own Gödel sentence. The features that Shapiro points to are possessed just as much by the axiomatisable inconsistent arithmetics that we looked at in section 17.4. We can therefore discuss his objections in this context.[17]

In the inconsistent arithmetic, Θ, of section 17.4 both γ and $\neg\gamma$ are provable, where γ is purely arithmetic and is of the form $\neg\beta\langle\gamma\rangle$. Since γ is provable, there is some number, g, which is the code of its proof. Hence, $\mathrm{Prov}(g, \langle\gamma\rangle)$ is true in the standard model, and so is provable in Θ. But $\neg\beta\langle\gamma\rangle$ is $\neg\exists y\, \mathrm{Prov}(y, \langle\gamma\rangle)$, i.e., $\forall y\neg\mathrm{Prov}(y, \langle\gamma\rangle)$. Hence $\neg\mathrm{Prov}(g, \langle\gamma\rangle)$ is provable as well. Now, $\mathrm{Prov}(x, y)$ expresses a primitive recursive relation. Hence, if Θ is the true arithmetic, we have to accept that there are inconsistencies concerning numbers that are of this

---

[16] In the original version of this paper (Priest 2003), a different version of this argument was given, which did not distinguish between β_N and β. Since these are only extensionally equivalent, one cannot simply substitute one for the other in intensional contexts (such as that provided by $\vdash_N$), which that argument effectively does. I am grateful to Albert Visser for pointing this out to me.

[17] The material in this section arose from a seminar at the University of St Andrews at the end of 2002. I am grateful to the participants, and particularly to Steward Shapiro, for their helpful comments.

very basic kind. Worse, consider the following biconditionals. From left to right, they are unproblematic. Suppose that we accept them from right to left too.

$P + m$ is the code of a proof of formula with code n iff

$\text{Prov}(\mathbf{m}, \mathbf{n}) \in \Theta$

$P - m$ is not the code of a proof of formula with code n iff

$\neg\text{Prov}(\mathbf{m}, \mathbf{n}) \in \Theta$

Then we have to accept that some number both is and is not the code of a proof, and, more generally, that something could be both provable and not provable. What could this mean?

Shapiro offers three responses to this situation.

A   Reject the soundness of Θ, on the basis of the fact that primitive recursive relationships are consistent.

B   Accept that Θ is sound, but reject the biconditionals P+ and P−, and hence, on the assumption that Θ is the true arithmetic, the isomorphism between numbers with their operations and strings with theirs.

C   Accept that Θ is sound, the biconditionals P+ and P−, and hence that something can be both provable and not provable.

All of these options, Shapiro argues, should be resisted. If one is to take seriously the idea that Θ is the true arithmetic, option **A** is obviously not the way to go. One has to accept that even primitive recursive relations may be inconsistent. But this is not news. In the finite models of arithmetic even numerical equations can be inconsistent; that is, there can be truths of the form $\mathbf{m} = \mathbf{n} \wedge \mathbf{m} \neq \mathbf{n}$. One also has to accept, more generally, that even the computational part of mathematics is inconsistent. But this is not a problem either. Θ itself tells us exactly what an inconsistent computation theory is like. The Δ_0 formulas (that is, the sentences obtainable from equations using connectives and bounded quantifiers) express the recursive properties/relations.

Option B certainly involves jettisoning a connection in terms of which logicians have become accustomed to thinking. This is certainly a loss, though I do not think it as devastating as Shapiro does. However, it seems to me that the simplest and most natural response is option C, so I will discuss this option at length. Shapiro marshals essentially two considerations against it. Let us consider these in turn.

17.7 THE INCONSISTENCY OF PEANO ARITHMETIC

Shapiro's first objection, and the quicker to deal with, is that, if one holds that primitive recursive relations are inconsistent, it follows not just that Θ is inconsistent, but that Peano arithmetic (PA) is inconsistent—which seems implausible. The reason is that all recursive relationships are known to be representable in PA.

The reply is simply that, if the recursive relationships are as specified by Θ, they are *not* all representable in PA—just because it is consistent. Where does the proof of the fact that all recursive relationships are representable in PA break down, however? The answer depends on which proof we are talking about, and on which inconsistent theory of arithmetic is correct. But let us suppose, for the sake of illustration, that Θ is $\mathrm{Th}(\mathcal{M}_{10}^{6})$. As we saw in section 17.2, the successor diagram of this is as follows:

$$0 \rightarrow \cdots \rightarrow 8 \rightarrow 9 \rightarrow 10 \rightarrow 11$$

$$\uparrow \qquad \downarrow$$

$$15 \leftarrow \cdots$$

Now let us look at a direct proof to the effect that the formula $x = y'$ represents the successor relation in PA.[18] We need to show that if $i = j'$ then $i = j' \in PA$. This is proved by induction on j. Suppose that $j = 0$. Then if $i = 0'$, $i = 1$ and $1 = 0' \in PA$. Now suppose that the result holds for j, and show it for j'. So suppose that $i = j''$. Since i is not 0, there is a k such that $i = k'$. Hence, $k' = j''$, and $k = j'$. By induction, $k = j' \in PA$; so $i = k' = j'' \in PA$.

The second part of this argument breaks down for $\mathrm{Th}(\mathcal{M}_{10}^{6})$, since a number may have multiple predecessors, some of them *greater* than itself. Thus, suppose that j is 8. If $i = 8''$ then certainly, for some k, $k' = 8''$; k can be 9 or 15. Now, $9' = 8''$, $9 = 8'$, $9 = 8' \in PA$ (by induction), and so $9' = 8'' \in PA$. But, though $15' = 8''$, it does not follow that $15 = 8'$, so the argument breaks down. Indeed, $15 = 8' \notin PA$.

Thus, and in general, if you take Θ to provide the correct account of recursive relationships, then these will be representable (trivially) in Θ; but PA will be incomplete, since it captures only a consistent fragment of the truth. Dually, of course, if you take the usual classical line on recursive relationships, PA will be complete, but Θ will give *more* than the truth, because it is inconsistent. In other words, if you match up the formal arithmetic and the theory of recursive relations properly, then you will get representability. But if you mis-match these by taking one to be consistent and the other not, then things will go wrong.

17.8 THE INCREDULOUS STARE

Shapiro's other main objection amounts to a version of the incredulous stare. Let me put it in his own words:[19]

On all accounts—including the non-dialetheic perspective—we have that g is the code of a Θ-derivation of γ. This can be verified with a painstaking, but completely effective,

---

[18] Proofs of this kind can be found in Boolos and Jeffrey (1974), ch. 14, pt III.
[19] Shapiro (2002), p. 828. I have changed the notation to bring it into line with that used in this essay. The italics are original.

check. How can the dialetheist go on to maintain that, in addition, g is *not* the code of a
Θ-derivation of γ? What does it mean to say this? Since ¬Prov is recursive predicate, we
can supposedly verify—at the same time, in almost exactly the same way—that g is not
the code of a Θ-derivation of γ. How?

Shapiro asks how we can possibly verify a sentence expressing a recursive relation
and its negation. What can this mean?

In principle, the answer is easy. Since we are endorsing P+ and P−, we are
now taking seriously the thought that metatheoretic sentences may be contradictory. If so, they must play by the same rules as those of Θ, and in particular be
based on the logic *LP*. In any theory based on *LP*, α and $\neg\alpha$ are verified by
different procedures. Thus, e.g., to determine whether $t_1 = t_2$ is true, we have to
look to see whether $\langle I(t_1), I(t_2) \rangle \in I^+ (=)$. To determine whether $t_1 \neq t_2$ is true,
we have to look to see whether $\langle I(t_1), I(t_2) \rangle \in I^- (=)$. These are separate matters.
Thus, in $\mathrm{Th}(\mathcal{M}_{10}^6)$, once we have checked to see whether $\mathbf{i} = \mathbf{j}$, the question of
whether $\mathbf{i} \neq \mathbf{j}$ is a *further* question. $0 = 0$ is true, but $0 \neq 0$ is not; $10 = 10$ is true,
but so is $10 \neq 10$.

Thus, to bring the matter to bear on proof explicitly, suppose that g is the code
of a proof of γ. Suppose, for the sake of argument, that the code is 37. Then to say
that g is the code is to say something equivalent to $g = 37$. What does it mean to say
that it is also not the code of a proof of γ? It is to say that $g \neq 37$ as well. This is the
case if $37 = 37 \wedge 37 \neq 37$, which it can be in an inconsistent arithmetic.

And what does it mean to say that γ is both provable and not? To say that it is
provable is to say that $\exists x(x$ is the code of a proof of $\gamma)$, i.e. that, on the supposition at hand, $\exists x\, x = 37$. To say that it is not provable is to say that $\neg\exists x(x$ is
the code of a proof of $\gamma)$, i.e. $\forall x \neg(x$ is the code of a proof of $\gamma)$, i.e. $\forall x \neg x = 37$,
i.e. $0 \neq 37 \wedge 1 \neq 37 \wedge \ldots \wedge 37 \neq 37 \wedge \ldots$; which is, of course, true if $37 \neq 37$.
In other words, to say that γ is not provable is to say that every number is distinct
from a code of the proof of γ. This does not rule out there being a proof of γ. (In
general, the truth of $\neg\alpha$ in a paraconsistent setting does not rule out the truth of
α.) In particular, it will hold if the proof is distinct from itself. And how can a
proof be distinct from itself? In the same way that a number can. After all, on
option C, the one at issue, we are retaining the structural identity between strings
and numbers. Both are, after all, abstract objects. And the inconsistent behaviour
of strings is just as good or bad as the inconsistent behaviour of numbers.[20]

There are, or course, concrete objects whose behaviour in some sense represents the behaviour of abstract objects. In this case there are things, such as marks
of dried ink on paper, that represent abstract proofs. But properties of abstract

---

[20] It is worth noting that, if numbers have inconsistent properties, then this will affect their
behaviour whatever theory they are taken to be coding. Thus, the Gödel codes of PA will behave just
as inconsistenly as those of Θ. In other words, if numbers are inconsistent, we may expect things to
be both provable and not provable in PA just as much as in Θ. This does not, of course, mean that
PA is itself inconsistent. As to where the inconsistency of Gödel codes arises, it might be only for
numbers so large that they are larger than anything that is humanly meaningful (see Priest 1994).

objects do not carry over of necessity to their physical representations. Thus, two tokens of one and the same proof type need not be identical. One would expect them, instead, to satisfy some sort of graphical relation, R. What of two proof tokens that represent different proof types? Arguably, they must satisfy some quite distinct relation, R', where both R and R' may consistently hold between tokens.

To illustrate, and for the sake of simplicity, consider not proofs, but letters. Let R_o be the relationship that holds between two tokens of 'o', R_c be the relationship that holds between two tokens of 'c', R be the relationship that holds between two tokens of the same letter type, and R' be the relationship that holds between two tokens of different letter types. It is natural to suppose that, whatever R and R' are, they satisfy at least the following conditions:

If $xR_o y$ then xRy

If $xR_o y$ and $zR_c w$ then $xR'z$

Now let t_1, t_2, and t_3 be three token letters such that t_1 is a clear case of an 'o', that t_3 is a clear case of a 'c', but that t_2 is slightly ill formed, and could be either an 'o' or a 'c'. Then we have $t_1 R_o t_2$ (t_1 and t_2 are both 'o's) and $t_2 R_c t_3$ (t_2 and t_3 are both 'c's). It follows that $t_1 R t_2$ and $t_1 R' t_2$.

We could also, of course, go down the dialetheic path: insist that identity is represented by the relation R and that difference is represented by its negation, $\overline{R}$, but hold that, on some occasions at least, physical reality realises both xRy and $x\overline{R}y$. Thus, for example, t_2 might be a borderline case in a sorites sequence of tokens starting with clear 'o's and ending with things that are clearly not 'o's. If borderline cases realise truth value gluts, t_2 may be both an 'o' and not an 'o'. But this is not the place to pursue such metaphysical speculations.

Shapiro's objections stem from being half-hearted about dialetheism. If one endorses an inconsistent arithmetic, but tries to hang on to either a consistent computational theory or a consistent metamathematics of proof, one is in for trouble. The solution to Shapiro's problems is therefore not to be half-hearted, and to accept that these other things are inconsistent too. Indeed, the arithmetic itself shows us how to do this: the facts about computability and provability are simply read off from the arithmetic.

Discussions in the philosophy of mathematics are always built on shaky foundations if they are not underpinned with the appropriate technical material. This is certainly true of discussions of the inconsistency of arithmetic. The inconsistent models show us exactly what can be done and how. That hardly settles many of the interesting philosophical questions. But it does put a firm skeleton below the philosophical flesh.[21]

[21] The philosophical discussion in this chapter has appealed to various metatheoretic properties of inconsistent arithmetics. How were these established? A natural assumption is that they were proved in a classical (consistent) metatheory, such as ZF. If we are now endorsing an inconsistent (meta-)arithmetic, we can no longer be working in ZF. What entitles us to be sure that we may still

17.9 APPENDIX: THE STRUCTURE OF INCONSISTENT MODELS OF ARITHMETIC

In this appendix I will indicate the general structure of models of arithmetic. Let $\mathcal{M} = \langle M, I \rangle$ be any such model. I will refer to the denotations of $'$, $+$, and $\times$ as the arithmetic operations of $\mathcal{M}$; and, since no confusion is likely, use the same signs for them. I will call the denotations of the numerals *regular* numbers.

Let $x \leq y$ be defined, in the usual way, as $\exists z\ x + z = y$. It is easy to check that $\leq$ is transitive. For if $i \leq j \leq k$, then for some x, y, $i + x = j$ and $j + y = k$. Hence $(i + x) + y = k$. But $(i + x) + y = i + (x + y)$ (since we are dealing with a model of arithmetic). The result follows.

If $i \in M$, let $N(i)$ (the *nucleus* of i) be $\{x \in M;\ i \leq x \leq i\}$. In a classical model, $N(i) = \{i\}$, but this need not be the case in an inconsistent model. For example, in any $\mathcal{M}_n^p$ (see section 17.2) the members of the cycle constitute a nucleus. If $j \in N(i)$, then $N(i) = N(j)$. For if $x \in N(j)$ then $i \leq j \leq x \leq j \leq i$, so $x \in N(i)$, and similarly in the other direction. Thus, every member of a nucleus defines the same nucleus.

Now, if N_1 and N_2 are nuclei, define $N_1 \preceq N_2$ to mean that, for some (or all, it makes no difference) $i \in N_1$ and $j \in N_2$, $i \leq j$. It is not difficult to check that $\preceq$ is a partial ordering. Moreover, since for any i and j, $i \leq j$ or $j \leq i$, it is a linear ordering. The least member of the ordering is $N(0)$. If $N(1)$ is distinct from this, it is the next (since for any x, $x \leq 0 \vee x \geq 1$), and so on for all regular numbers.

Say that $i \in M$ has *period* $p \in M$ iff $i + p = i$. In a classical model every number has period 0 and only 0. But again, this need not be the case in an inconsistent model, as the $\mathcal{M}_n^p$ demonstrate. If $i \leq j$ and i has period p, so does j. For $j = i + x$, so $p + j = p + i + x = i + x = j$. In particular, if p is a period of some member of a nucleus, it is a period of every member. We may thus say that p is a period of the nucleus itself. It also follows that, if $N_1 \preceq N_2$ and p is a period of N_1 it is a period of N_2.

If a nucleus has a regular non-zero period, m, then it must have a minimum (in the usual sense) non-zero period, since the sequence $0, 1, 2, \ldots, m$ is finite. If $N_1 \preceq N_2$ and N_1 has minimum regular non-zero period, p, then p is a period of N_2. Moreover, the minimum non-zero period of N_2, q, must be a divisor (in the usual sense) of p. For suppose that $q < p$, and that q is not a divisor of p. For some $0 < k < q$, p is some finite multiple of q plus k. So if $x \in N_2$, $x = x + q = x + p + \ldots + p + k$. Hence $x = x + k$; i.e., k is a period of N_2, which is impossible.

invoke those results? One answer goes essentially as follows. Start with a model of ZF, say (an initial segment of) the cumulative hierarchy. Then use the Collapsing Lemma to produce a collapsed model of ZF in which the structure of the numbers brings it into line with the inconsistent arithmetic we are envisaging. (For collapsed models of ZF, see Priest (1995), pt 3, tech. appx.) We can take the theory of that collapsed model to provide the metatheory in which we are working. And just as any theorem of standard arithmetic holds in the theory of a collapsed model of arithmetic, so any theorem of ZF holds in that theory.

If a nucleus has period $p \geq 1$, I will call it *proper*. Every proper nucleus is closed under successors. For suppose that $j \in N$ with period p. Then $j \leq j' \leq j + p = j$. Hence $j' \in N$. In an inconsistent model, a number may have more than one predecessor; i.e., there may be more than one x such that $x' = j$. (Although $(x' = y') \supset x = y$ holds in the model, we cannot necessarily detach to obtain $x = y$.) But if j is in a proper nucleus, N, it has a unique predecessor in N. For let the period of N be q'. Then $(j + q)' = j + q' = j$. Hence, $j + q$ is a predecessor of j; and $j \leq j + q \leq j + q' = j$. Hence, $j + q \in N$. Next, suppose that x and y are in the nucleus, and that $x' = y' = j$. We have that $x \leq y \vee y \leq x$. Suppose, without loss of generality, the first disjunct. Then for some z, $x + z = y$; so $j + z = j$, and z is a period of the nucleus. But then $x = x + z = y$. I will write the unique predecessor of j in the nucleus as $'j$.

Now let N be any proper nucleus, and $i \in N$. Consider the sequence: $\ldots, ''i, 'i, i, i', i'' \ldots$. Call this the *chromosome* of i. Note that if $i, j \in N$, the chromosomes of i and j are identical or disjoint. For if they have a common member, z, then all the finite successors of z are identical, as are all its finite predecessors (in N). Thus they are identical. Now consider the chromosome of i, and suppose that two members are identical. There must be members where the successor distance between them is a minimum. Let these be j and $j'^{\cdots '}$ where there are n primes. Then $j = j + n$, and n is a period of the nucleus—in fact, its minimum non-zero period—and the chromosome of every member of the nucleus is a successor cycle of period n.

Hence, any proper nucleus is a collection of chromosomes, all of which are either successor cycles of the same finite period, or sequences isomorphic to the integers (positive and negative). Both sorts are possible in an inconsistent model. Just consider the collapse of a non-standard model, of the kind given in section 17.2, by an equivalence relation which leaves all the standard numbers alone and identifies all the others modulo p. If p is standard, the non-standard numbers collapse into a successor cycle; if it is non-standard, the nucleus generated is of the other kind.

To summarise: the general structure of a model is a linear sequence of nuclei. There are three segments (any of which may be empty). The first contains only improper nuclei. The second contains proper nuclei with linear chromosomes. The third contains proper nuclei with cyclical chromosomes of finite period. A period of any nucleus is a period of any subsequent nucleus, and if a nucleus in the third segment has minimum non-zero period, p, the minimum non-zero period of any subsequent nucleus is a divisor of p. We might depict the general structure of a model as follows:

$$
0, 1 \ldots
\begin{array}{|c|}
\hline
\ldots a \to d \ldots \\
\ldots b \to b' \ldots \\
\vdots \\
\hline
\end{array}
\ldots
\begin{array}{|cccc|}
\hline
d_0 \to \ldots \to d_i & & e_0 \to \ldots \to e_i & \\
\uparrow & \downarrow & \uparrow & \downarrow \\
d_m \leftarrow \ldots \leftarrow d_i' & & e_m \leftarrow \ldots \leftarrow e_i' & \\
\hline
\end{array}
\ldots
$$

The structure of finite models can be inferred simply by putting the constraint of finitude on the above characterisation. In the finite case, the order type of the proper nuclei can be any finite linear ordering. In the case of infinite models, the possible order types of the proper nuclei are less clear. Some order types are known to be possible. It is not yet known whether any are impossible. There is much more to be said on all these matters, but its discussion here is not warranted. Details can be found in Priest (2002), sections 9.3 and 9.4, and especially Priest (2000).

18

Paraconsistent Set Theory

18.1 PARACONSISTENT SET THEORY: BACKGROUND

This major topic of this chapter is set theory, and specifically the shape of an acceptable paraconsistent set theory. I will review what is currently known about the matter and suggest some new ideas. There are, it must be confessed, as many questions as answers. At the end of the chapter I will apply the discussion to another important issue for paraconsistency: that concerning its metatheory—and especially the model-theoretic definition of validity. The connection is, of course, that such a metatheory is formulated within set theory.

The problem posed by Russell's Paradox and its set theoretic cousins may be thought of as generated by two factors: first, an unrestricted abstraction—or comprehension—principle of set existence, which allows an arbitrary condition to specify a set, and second, various principles of logic which allow certain instances of this (or their conjunction) to entail everything. Since the discovery of these paradoxes, the orthodox reaction has been to maintain the principles of logic in question, but reject the unrestricted comprehension principle. This strategy gives type theory, Zermelo–Fraenkel set theory, and so on.

There is, however, another possible strategy: to maintain the comprehension principle and reject, instead, some of the principles of logic in question. There are various ways one may do this, but the one that will be concern us here is the paraconsistent way. Allow for the set theory to entail contradictions, but reject the principle *ex contradictione quodlibet*, or, to give it its more colourful name, Explosion, $\{\alpha, \neg\alpha\} \vdash \beta$, and hence obtain a theory that is inconsistent but non-trivial.

How should one do this? Part of the answer is easy. A paraconsistent set theory can naturally be thought of as a theory that endorses the two axioms (or one axiom and one axiom schema):

$$\forall x(x \in y \leftrightarrow x \in z) \rightarrow y = z \qquad (Ext)$$

$$\exists x \forall y(y \in x \leftrightarrow \alpha) \qquad (Abs)$$

where x does not occur free in α.[1] The rest of the answer is not easy, however. What is the appropriate underlying logic? In particular, what notion of conditional is being employed in (*Ext*) and (*Abs*)?

Paraconsistency gives us several choices in answering this question. In making the appropriate choice, there are two constraints that need to be borne in mind. First, the resulting theory should not allow us to prove too much; second, it should not allow us to prove too little.

For the first: although using a paraconsistent logic allows isolated contradictions to be accepted, we do not want wholesale contradiction. In particular, if *everything* were provable, the theory would be quite useless. And even though contradictions do not imply everything, there may still be arguments delivering triviality. A notorious one is Curry's Paradox. Suppose that the conditional of the logic satisfies both *modus ponens* and Contraction (or Absorption): $\{\alpha \rightarrow (\alpha \rightarrow \beta)\} \vdash \alpha \rightarrow \beta$. Triviality then ensues, as we saw in section 6.2.

This fact puts fairly severe constraints on an appropriate underlying logic. In fact, it rules out very many paraconsistent logics. For example, it rules out da Costa's well known C systems. It also rules out many of the best known systems of relevant logic, such as R.[2] Not everything is ruled out, though, as we shall see.

But before we turn to this, let us consider the other constraint: not too little. It is easy enough to choose an underlying logic for paraconsistent set theory that does not give triviality. Choose the null logic (in which nothing follows from anything). This is obviously not very interesting. A minimal condition of adequacy on a paraconsistent set theory would seem to be that we can get at least a decent part of standard, orthodox, set theory out of it. We might not require everything; we might be prepared to write off various results concerning large cardinality, or peculiar consequences of the Axiom of Choice. But if we lose too much, set theory is voided of both its use and its interest.

It should be remembered here, as I noted in section 16.1, that paraconsistency, unlike intuitionism, has never been a consciously revisionist philosophy. The picture has always been that classical mathematics, and the reasoning that this embodies, is perfectly acceptable as long as it does not stray into the transconsistent. It is only there that it goes awry. So the unproblematically consistent bits of orthodox set theory, at least, ought to be delivered by a paraconsistent set theory.

The results of this second constraint are in some tension with the results of the first. Put crudely, the matter is this. If we weaken our logic in a way that is sufficient to avoid triviality, we weaken it so much that it fails to deliver much set theory that we want to keep. We will see how this tension plays out in the following discussion.

---

[1] One might also want to add an appropriate version of the Axiom of Choice to these. There are, however, ways of obtaining the axiom from unrestricted comprehension. One way is to use the machinery of Hilbert's ε-calculus (see e.g. Leisenring 1969, pp. 105–7). Another, much more radical, way is to take (*Abs*) in an absolutely unrestricted form which allows α to contain 'x' free. This delivers the Axioms of Choice (see Routley 1980, p. 924 f.) while, surprisingly enough, maintaining non-triviality (see Brady 1989).   [2] For a survey of paraconsistent logics, see Priest (2002).

18.2 THE MATERIAL STRATEGY

As we have just seen, an underlying logic for a paraconsistent set theory must invalidate either *modus ponens* or Contraction. Both are live options. Let us start with the rejection of *modus ponens*. There are various ways in which one can arrange for *modus ponens* to fail in a paraconsistent logic, but undoubtedly the most natural is to take the conditionals (and biconditionals) in (*Ext*) and (*Abs*) to be material. That is, $\alpha \rightarrow \beta$ is simply *defined* as $\neg\alpha \vee \beta$. ($\alpha \leftrightarrow \beta$ is defined in the usual way as $(\alpha \rightarrow \beta) \wedge (\beta \rightarrow \alpha)$.) In nearly every paraconsistent logic, material detachment fails: $\{\alpha, \neg\alpha \vee \beta\} \nvdash \beta$. I will call this the *material strategy*. (The strategy does not, of course, mean that the language employed does not contain different kinds of conditional. For example, it may contain a relevant and detachable conditional as well—though it need not.)

A simple and natural choice here is the logic *LP* of chapter 5. A sound and complete tableau system for this is as follows.[3] Lines are of the form $\alpha, +$ or $\alpha, -$. A tableau for the inference $\{\alpha_1, \ldots, \alpha_n\} \vdash \beta$ starts with the lines

$\alpha_1, +$
$\vdots$
$\alpha_n, +$
$\beta, -$

The rules are as follows:

$$
\begin{array}{ccc}
\alpha \wedge \beta, + & \alpha \wedge \beta, - & \neg(\alpha \wedge \beta), \pm \\
\downarrow & \swarrow \searrow & \downarrow \\
\alpha, + & \alpha, - \quad \beta, - & \neg\alpha \vee \neg\beta, \pm \\
\beta, + & &
\end{array}
$$

$$
\begin{array}{ccc}
\alpha \vee \beta, - & \alpha \vee \beta, + & \neg(\alpha \vee \beta), \pm \\
\downarrow & \swarrow \searrow & \downarrow \\
\alpha, - & \alpha, + \quad \beta, + & \neg\alpha \wedge \neg\beta, \pm \\
\beta, - & &
\end{array}
$$

$$
\neg\neg\alpha, \pm
$$
$$
\downarrow
$$
$$
\alpha, \pm
$$

---

[3] See Priest (2001), sect. 8.3.

$$\forall x\alpha, + \qquad \forall x\alpha, - \qquad \neg\forall x\alpha, \pm$$
$$\downarrow \qquad\qquad \downarrow \qquad\qquad \downarrow$$
$$\alpha(x/b), + \quad \alpha(x/a), - \quad \exists\neg x\alpha, \pm$$
$$\exists x\alpha, + \qquad \exists x\alpha, - \qquad \neg\exists x\alpha, \pm$$
$$\downarrow \qquad\qquad \downarrow \qquad\qquad \downarrow$$
$$\alpha(x/a), + \quad \alpha(x/b), - \quad \forall\neg x\alpha, \pm$$

$$\cdot$$
$$\downarrow$$

$$b = b, +$$

$$b = c, +$$
$$\alpha(x/b), \pm$$
$$\downarrow$$

$$\alpha(x/c), \pm$$

Here, b and c are any terms on the branch, a is a constant new to the branch, and '$\pm$' can be disambiguated consistently either way.[4] The closure rules for a branch are two:

$$\alpha, + \qquad \alpha, -$$
$$\alpha, - \qquad \neg\alpha, -$$
$$\times \qquad\quad \times$$

(The second of these enshrines the LEM.)

The paraconsistent set theory that this logic produces has a number of interesting features. It is provably non-trivial.[5] It validates all those axioms of ZF that are instances of (*Abs*) (of course). It validates the Axiom of Infinity, but not the Axiom of Foundation. It can also (unlike ZF) demonstrate the existence of a universal set.[6] What theorems of ZF—beyond the axioms—it can (or cannot) establish is as yet a largely unanswered question. But the failure of material detachment means that most of the natural arguments fail. While this does not mean that there are no unnatural arguments for the same conclusions, the prospects look rather bleak. The failure of detachment is a singular handicap.

---

[4] The rule for $b = b$ means that this can be introduced at any time.

[5] It might be thought that without detachment the axioms cannot be shown to be inconsistent. This is false, though. An instance of (*Abs*) is $\forall x(x \in r \leftrightarrow \neg x \in x)$; whence we have $r \in r \leftrightarrow \neg r \in r$, and cashing out the conditional in terms of negation and disjunction gives $r \in r \land \neg r \in r$. More generally, whenever α is a classical consequence of Σ, there is a β such that $\alpha \lor (\beta \land \neg\beta)$ follows from Σ (see sect. 8.6). Hence any classically inconsistent theory is inconsistent in this logic also.

[6] For details of all this, see Restall (1992). Note that he defines '$x = y$' as '$\forall z(z \in x \leftrightarrow z \in y)$'.

For the same reason, any other way of pursuing the material strategy does not look promising.

A more promising strategy is to look at the consequences of the axioms not in *LP*, but in the non-monotonic *LPm* of chapter 16. The results of this approach are presently unknown.[7]

18.3 THE RELEVANT STRATEGY

A second, and perhaps more plausible, strategy is to use a conditional in a logic that validates *modus ponens*, but not Contraction. The most plausible candidate for this is a relevant logic weaker than *R*, one of the *depth relevant* logics, as they are sometimes called. The following is a tableau system for such a logic. (A semantics with respect to which it is sound is discussed further in the next chapter, in section 19.8.) Lines are now of one of two forms. One is $\alpha, +i$ or $\alpha, -i$, where i is a natural number (thought of as representing a world). Premises and conclusion take the number 0. The other is *rijk*, where i, j, and k are natural numbers. (r represents a ternary accessibility relation, as is standard in the semantics for relevant logics.) The rules for *LP* are all present, except that a natural-number world parameter, i, is added uniformly.[8] Thus, for example, the rule for $\land +$ is

$$\alpha \land \beta, +i$$

$$\downarrow$$

$$\alpha, +i$$
$$\beta, +i$$

It is easiest to define the conditional, $\rightarrow$, in terms of a non-contraposing conditional, $\Rightarrow$. Thus, $\alpha \rightarrow \beta$ is $(\alpha \Rightarrow \beta) \land (\neg\beta \Rightarrow \neg\alpha)$. The rules for $\Rightarrow$ are as follows. When $i > 0$ (i is an impossible world),

---

[7] Adopting the material strategy in some form goes *half*way towards meeting Goodship (1996), who advocates taking the main conditional of both the Comprehension Principle and the T-schema to be material. Would treating the conditionals in the two schemas show the paradoxes of self reference to be of different kinds? No. They still all fit the Inclosure Schema (Priest 1995, pt 3), and so have the same essential structure.

[8] The rules for identity are an exception. These are:

$$b = c, +i$$
$$\alpha(x/b), \pm j$$
$$\downarrow \qquad \downarrow$$
$$b = b, +0 \qquad \alpha(x/c), \pm j$$

$$\alpha \Rightarrow \beta, + i \qquad \alpha \Rightarrow \beta, - i$$
$$rijk \qquad\qquad \downarrow$$
$$\swarrow \qquad \searrow \qquad rijk$$
$$\alpha, - j \ \ \beta, + k \qquad \alpha, + j$$
$$\beta, - k$$

$$\neg(\alpha \Rightarrow \beta), - i \quad \neg(\alpha \Rightarrow \beta), + i$$
$$rijk \qquad\qquad \downarrow$$
$$\swarrow \qquad \searrow \qquad rijk$$
$$\alpha, - j \ \ \neg\beta, - k \qquad \alpha, + j$$
$$\neg\beta, + k$$

In the lefthand rules j and k are any numbers on the branch. In the righthand rules j and k are new to the branch.

When $i = 0$ (i is a possible world), the rules simplify to

$$\alpha \Rightarrow \beta, + 0 \qquad \alpha \Rightarrow \beta, - 0$$
$$\swarrow \qquad \searrow \qquad \downarrow$$
$$\alpha, - j \ \ \beta, + j \qquad \alpha, + j$$
$$\beta, - j$$

$$\neg(\alpha \Rightarrow \beta), - 0 \quad \neg(\alpha \Rightarrow \beta), + 0$$
$$\swarrow \qquad \searrow \qquad \downarrow$$
$$\alpha, - j \ \ \neg\beta, - j \qquad \alpha, + j$$
$$\neg\beta, + j$$

In the lefthand rules j is any number on the branch. In the righthand rules j is new to the branch.

The closure rules are now

$$\alpha, + i \qquad \alpha, - 0$$
$$\alpha, - i \qquad \neg\alpha, - 0$$
$$\times \qquad\quad \times$$

(So the LEM is guaranteed only at the base world.)

Naive set theories based on relevant logics such as this are known to be inconsistent but non-trivial. Indeed, the logic may be strengthened in various ways, and this is still true—though not, of course, with Contraction.[9] Thus, this relevant set theory satisfies the first constraint. What of the second?

To answer this question (at least to the extent that the answer is known), it is useful to divide set theory into two parts. The first comprises the basic set theory

---

[9] See Brady (1989) and Priest (2002), sect. 8.

that all branches of mathematics use as a tool. The second is the more elaborate development of this, which includes transfinite set theory, as it can be established in ZF, "higher" set theory.

The theory is able to provide for virtually all of basic set theory—Boolean operations on sets, power sets, products, functions, operations on functions, etc. (I will return to the reason for the qualification 'virtually' in a moment.) Thus, for convenience, let the language be augmented with set-abstract terms. We may define the Boolean operators, $x \cap y$, $x \cup y$, and $\bar{x}$, as $\{z : z \in x \wedge z \in y\}$, $\{z : z \in x \vee z \in y\}$, and $\{z : z \notin x\}$, respectively, and $x \subseteq y$ as $\forall z(z \in x \rightarrow z \in y)$. We can then establish the usual facts concerning these notions.[10]

How much of the more elaborate development of set theory can be proved is not currently known. What can be said is that the *standard* proofs of a number of results break down. One thing we obviously lose is that kind of argument that appeals to vacuous satisfaction. Thus, for example, suppose that we wish to establish $\forall x(x < \xi \rightarrow A(x))$ by transfinite induction on the ordinal ξ. We can no longer argue in the basis case that, since $\neg x < 0$, $x < 0 \rightarrow A(x)$; but we can make the zero case explicit, and perform the induction on $\forall x(\xi = 0 \vee (x < \xi \rightarrow A(x)))$. The first disjunct must then always be considered as a special case. Things not so easy to reconstruct are arguments employing *reductio*, such as Cantor's Theorem. Where α is an assumption made for the purpose of *reductio*, we may well be able to establish that $(\alpha \wedge \beta) \rightarrow (\gamma \wedge \neg \gamma)$ for some γ, where β is the conjunction of other facts appealed to in deducing the contradiction (such as instances of (*Abs*)). But contraposing and detaching will give us only $\neg \alpha \vee \neg \beta$, and we can get no further. Even given β, the failure of the disjunctive syllogism prevents us from obtaining $\neg \alpha$.[11] Much remains to be done in investigating higher set theory in this context.

Let me now return to the qualification 'virtually'. Problems arise with the empty set. There can be no set ϕ such that, for every a and b,

(1) $a \cap \bar{a} \subseteq \phi$

(2) $\phi \subseteq b$

For let a be $\{x : \alpha\}$ and b be $\{x : \beta\}$. Then (1) and (2) together give us: $(x \in \{x : \alpha\} \wedge x \in \overline{\{x : \alpha\}}) \rightarrow x \in \{x : \beta\}$. (*Abs*) then gives $(\alpha \wedge \neg \alpha) \rightarrow \beta$, and the theory is not paraconsistent.

If we define ϕ_1 as $a \cap \bar{a}$, then this clearly satisfies (1), but it does not satisfy (2). Alternatively, if we define ϕ_2 as $\{x : \forall y \ x \in y\}$ then it is easy enough to show that this satisfies (2), but not (1). It is provably the case that both ϕ_1 and ϕ_2

---

[10] Much of this is spelled out in Routley (1980), sect. 8.

[11] This is not the only sort of problem. Various natural arguments require the use of principles that involve nested $\rightarrow$ s, such as Permutation, $\{\alpha \rightarrow (\beta \rightarrow \gamma)\} \vdash \beta \rightarrow (\alpha \rightarrow \gamma)$. The logic just described does not contain this principle. Whether it can be added while maintaining non-triviality is not known. There is certainly triviality in the area. See Slaney (1989).

have no members. One cannot, though, show that they are identical. For $\{\neg x \in y \wedge \neg x \in z\} \not\vdash x \in y \leftrightarrow x \in z$. Generally speaking, one cannot expect the global structure of the universe of sets to be a Boolean algebra, as it is classically (albeit the case that, classically, the maximum element of the algebra and some set theoretic complements are proper classes). What one will have, instead, is a De Morgan algebra.[12]

This might, perhaps, be something that can be accepted. Boolean algebras are, after all, just special cases of De Morgan algebras. But we are not finished yet. It is not only the empty set that has multiple dopplegangers; so does the universal set. In fact, all sets do. For let α be an arbitrary truth; then $x \in y \leftrightarrow (x \in y \wedge \alpha)$ is not *relevantly* valid (from left to right). Thus, even though y and $\{x : x \in y \wedge \alpha\}$ have the same members, we will not have $y = \{x : x \in y \wedge \alpha\}$. What has gone wrong at this point is clear. (*Ext*) notwithstanding, the entities in question are not extensional. Nor is this an accident; the identity conditions of the entities in question are given in terms of $\rightarrow$, and this is an intensional functor, more at home in giving the identity conditions for properties than for sets.

This suggests changing the biconditional in (*Ext*). A natural thought is to replace it with the material biconditional, $\equiv$. Natural as this thought is, the strategy does not work. For $\{\alpha \wedge \neg\alpha\} \models \beta \equiv \alpha$. Now let α be any provable contradiction. Then for any z, $x \in z \equiv \alpha$. By (*Ext*), it now follows that $z = \{x : x \in \alpha\}$; there is only one set. (Note that this argument does not go through in the material strategy because the material conditional does not detach to give the identity.)

There is another possibility. To see this, consider restricted quantification for a moment. It is natural to express 'all *A*s are *B*s' using a conditional, thus: $\forall x(Ax \rightarrow Bx)$. If $\rightarrow$ is a standard relevant conditional, then the inference

1. Everything is B; hence all *A*s are *B*s

fails, since it depends on the validity of the inference $\{B(a)\} \vdash A(a) \rightarrow B(a)$. Yet inferences of this form are frequently appealed to when employing restricted quantifiers of the kind in question. If we interpret $\rightarrow$ as $\supset$, the material conditional, the inference is valid enough. But now the inference

2. All *A*s are *B*s; a is an A; hence a is a B

fails, since it employs the Disjunctive Syllogism, $\{A(a), \neg A(a) \vee B(a)\} \vdash B(a)$. This is even worse.

A solution to this problem is to use another sort of conditional. In many formulations of relevant logics, there is a logical constant, t, which may be thought of as the conjunction of all (actual) truths.[13] (So t is true at the base

---

[12] For a more systematic discussion of the issue, see Dunn (1988).

[13] See e.g. Dunn and Restall (2002), p. 10. Sometimes, depending on the context, t gets interpreted as the conjunction of all logical truths.

world, 0, and any other world at which all the things true at the base world are true.) The appropriate tableau rules for t are:

$$\cdot \quad \alpha, +0$$
$$\downarrow \quad t, +i$$
$$t, +0 \quad \alpha, -i$$
$$\times$$

It is not difficult to check that these validate the following inferences:

$$\vdash t$$

$$\alpha \vdash t \to \alpha$$

We may now define an enthymematic conditional, $\twoheadrightarrow$, in terms of t:

$$\alpha \twoheadrightarrow \beta \text{ is } (\alpha \wedge t) \to \beta$$

and use this as the conditional involved in restricted universal quantification. Thus, 'All As are Bs' is to be understood as $\forall x(A(x) \twoheadrightarrow B(x))$. We now have

$$\{B(a)\} \vdash t \to B(a)$$
$$\{B(a)\} \vdash A(a) \twoheadrightarrow B(a)$$

Hence $\{\forall x B(x)\} \vdash \forall x(A(x) \twoheadrightarrow B(x))$. And $\{\forall x(A(x) \twoheadrightarrow B(x))\} \vdash (t \wedge A(a)) \to B(a)$. Hence $\{A(a), \forall x(A(x) \twoheadrightarrow B(x))\} \vdash B(a)$. So both the inferences 1 and 2 are valid.[14]

Now return to set theory. It is natural to hear 'y is a subset of z' as 'all members of y are members of z'; that is, on the present account, $\forall x(x \in y \twoheadrightarrow x \in z)$. Let us define $y \subseteq z$ in this way. We may now take (Ext) to be $\forall x(x \in y \rightleftarrows x \in z) \to y = z$, where $\rightleftarrows$ is the biconditional corresponding to $\twoheadrightarrow$. This is equivalent to $(y \subseteq z \wedge z \subseteq y) \to y = z$.

Using $\rightleftarrows$ instead of $\leftrightarrow$ in (Ext) overcomes many of the problems we noted. Thus, for example, there is only one set that contains everything: $\{\forall x \, x \in y\} \vdash \forall x(x \in z \twoheadrightarrow x \in y)$. So $\{\forall x \, x \in y, \forall x \, x \in z\} \vdash y = z$. Moreover, let α be any truth. Then we have $t \to \alpha$, so $x \in y \twoheadrightarrow (\alpha \wedge x \in y)$. Since $(\alpha \wedge x \in y) \twoheadrightarrow x \in y$, we have $y = \{x : x \in y \wedge \alpha\}$. The structure of sets is still not a Boolean algebra, since the empty set is still not unique.[15] We do not have $\{x \notin y\} \vdash x \in y \twoheadrightarrow x \in z$. Hence we do not have $\{\neg \exists x \, x \in y\} \vdash y \subseteq z$ or, therefore, $\{\neg \exists x \, x \in y, \neg \exists x \, x \in z\} \vdash y = z$. But the empty set is enough of an oddity that this may not matter too much. Reconstructing the reasoning of set theory using $\twoheadrightarrow$ in (Ext) and the definition of $\subseteq$ therefore looks much more promising.

---

[14] For a general discussion of restricted quantification in relevant logic, see Beall *et al.* (forthcoming), which suggests the use of a different, but closely related, kind of enthymematic conditional.

[15] Note, in particular, that $\twoheadrightarrow$ does not contrapose. So from the fact that $x = y$, we cannot infer that $\bar{x} = \bar{y}$.

18.4 THE MODEL THEORETIC STRATEGY

I have discussed the material strategy and the relevant strategy for naive set theory. These do not exhaust the possibilities. Let us return to the axiomatisation that employs a material conditional uniformly. Call this M. (And suppose that the language contains just the standard extensional connectives and quantifiers, as in the usual formulations of ZF—and no set abstracts.) This time, we will consider not what is provable in M, but what the models of M are. M has many models, many of which are clearly pathological. For example, there is the model with but a single element, which both is and is not a member of itself. (This verifies the trivial theory.)

But M has many other models. Let us use the Collapsing Lemma to construct some. Let $\mathcal{M} = \langle D, I \rangle$ be any model of ZF. Let ξ be any ordinal in $\mathcal{M}$, and a be the initial section of the cumulative hierarchy, V_ξ, in $\mathcal{M}$. (That is, the pair $\langle \xi, a \rangle$ satisfies the formula 'x is an ordinal and $y = V_x$' in $\mathcal{M}$.) Define a relation, $\sim$, on D as follows:

(x and y are in a (in $\mathcal{M}$) and $x = y$) or (x and y are not in a (in $\mathcal{M}$))

This is obviously an equivalence relation. (Since there are no function symbols, it is vacuously a congruence relation too.) It leaves all the members of V_ξ alone, but identifies all other members of D. Construct the collapsed interpretation, $\mathcal{M}^\sim = \langle D^\sim, I^\sim \rangle$, as in section 16.7. The Collapsing Lemma tells us that $\mathcal{M}^\sim$ is a model of ZF.

But something else also happens. Let me use boldfacing for names. Then 'a' refers to a in $\mathcal{M}$, and $[a]$ in $\mathcal{M}^\sim$. For all $b \in D^\sim$, the sentence $\mathbf{b} \in \mathbf{a}$ has the value $\{1,0\}$ in $\mathcal{M}^\sim$. For if (in $\mathcal{M}$) b is of rank less than ξ, $\mathbf{b} \in \mathbf{a}$ is true in $\mathcal{M}$, and so in $\mathcal{M}^\sim$; and if not, there is some x that is also not of rank less than ξ (e.g., $\{b\}$) such that b is in x. (I am not, here, assuming the Axiom of Foundation.) Since x has been identified with a in $\mathcal{M}^\sim$, $\mathbf{b} \in \mathbf{a}$, is true in $\mathcal{M}^\sim$. Whatever b is, there are elements that do not have rank less than ξ such that b is not a member of them (e.g. $\{c\}$, where c is distinct from b and has rank greater than ξ). Since these have been identified with a in $\mathcal{M}^\sim$, $\mathbf{b} \in \mathbf{a}$ is also false in $\mathcal{M}^\sim$. Now consider any sentence of the form $\mathbf{b} \in \mathbf{a} \equiv \alpha(x/\mathbf{b})$. The value of the left side is $\{1,0\}$. Hence the biconditional is true in $\mathcal{M}^\sim$ ($\{\beta \wedge \neg\beta\} \models \beta \equiv \alpha$). So $\forall x(x \in \mathbf{a} \equiv \alpha)$ is true, as is $\exists y \forall x(x \in y \equiv \alpha)$. So $\mathcal{M}^\sim$ is a model of (*Abs*). It is a model of (*Ext*) as well, of course, since this is in ZF. Hence $\mathcal{M}^\sim$ is a model of naive set theory (materially construed).[16]

In fact, we can obtain more than this. Suppose that in $\mathcal{M}$ there are inaccessible cardinals. Let ϑ_1 be the least such, and ϑ_2 be a greater one. Take ξ to be ϑ_2. Since the sets of rank less than ϑ_2, and *a fortiori* less than ϑ_1, remain unaffected in the

---

[16] The fact that $\mathcal{M}^\sim$ is a model of (*Abs*) is a special case of a more general lemma, which I prove in the appendix to this chapter.

collapse, both of these are consistent substructures of $\mathcal{M}^\sim$ which are models of ZF. Moreover, any theorem of ZF with its quantifiers relativised to V_{ϑ_1} (so that $\exists x \alpha$ becomes $\exists x \in c \; \alpha$, where c refers to V_{ϑ_1}; and similarly for $\forall$) holds consistently in $\mathcal{M}^\sim$. (This is not true of V_{ϑ_2}, since this set itself behaves inconsistently.[17]) That is, V_{ϑ_1} is a consistent inner model of ZF (which shows that the theory of $\mathcal{M}^\sim$ is highly non-trivial).

To take stock, what we have established is that there are interpretations that

- are models of (*Ext*) and (*Abs*)
- are models of ZF
- contain the cumulative hierarchy (at least up to V_{ϑ_1}) as a consistent inner model

We may therefore suppose that the true interpretation of the language of set theory has these properties. This is an appealing picture. The cumulative hierarchy (up to ϑ_1) is a perfectly good, consistent, set theoretic structure; but it does not exhaust the universe of sets. There may be non-well-founded sets (such as the set of all sets) and inconsistent sets, such as the set of all sets that are not members of themselves.[18] The universe of sets is just much richer than orthodox set theory takes it to be.

Of course, the model $\mathcal{M}^\sim$ that we actually constructed using the Collapsing Lemma is still pathological from this perspective. It contains only one inconsistent set, [*a*], which has to do duty for all inconsistent and non-well-founded sets. There are undoubtedly other models (the details of whose natures require further investigation).[19] It should be remembered that, even in classical logic, set theory—and every other theory with an infinite model but an "intended interpretation"—has an absolute infinity of pathological models. Specifying the correct interpretation is always a further issue. The model $\mathcal{M}^\sim$ at least suffices to demonstrate the possibility of interpretations of naive set theory that have the above properties.[20]

And to return, at last, to the question of what to make of the theorems of orthodox set theory, ZF, on this approach. The answer is obvious. Since the

---

[17] In fact, V_{ϑ_2} behaves just like the set of all non-well-founded sets, given Mirimanoff's Paradox. It is well founded, but it is also a member of itself, so is not well founded.)

[18] And if the arguments concerning the inconsistency of arithmetic of chs. 3 and 17 are correct, the natural numbers are too (as opposed to some consistent approximations thereto).

[19] Some of these can be obtained by other applications of the Collapsing Lemma. Different methods of constucting models of inconsistent set theory, some of which also model ZF, are discussed in Libert (2003).

[20] Criticising the strategy under discussion here, Weir (2004), p. 398, says: 'It will not do to say...that the models which...[do not have the desired properties] are "pathological" or "unintended". All the dialetheist's ZFC models are unintended in the sense that they do not capture anything like the full structure of the naive universe of sets. This compares unfavourably with the unintended models of first-order number-theory: they at least contain the "real" structure of numbers.' This is simply question-begging. The thesis is precisely that one of these models does

universe of sets is a model of ZF (as well as naive set theory), these hold in it. We may therefore establish things in ZF in the standard classical way, knowing that they are perfectly acceptable from a paraconsistent perspective.[21] We cannot, of course, require the theorems of ZF to be consistently true in that universe; but if, on an occasion, we do require a consistent interpretation of ZF, we know how to obtain this too. The universe of sets has a consistent substructure that is a model of ZF.

18.5 METATHEORY OF PARACONSISTENT LOGIC

Let us turn, finally, to the issue of paraconsistent model theory. If the paraconsistent strategy for set theory is to be anything more than an intellectual exercise, the underlying logic used must, in some sense, be the right one for reasoning about sets. Hence arise familiar debates about which logic is correct, and why. A frequent objection made against paraconsistency in this debate goes as follows. Paraconsistent logics have metatheories. In particular, they have appropriate semantics, proof systems, and corresponding soundness, and (hopefully) completeness results. Now the logic in which such proofs are carried out must be classical, non-paraconsistent, logic.[22] This shows that paraconsistent logic cannot be maintained as the correct logic.

The argument is far too swift. For a start, the logic of the metatheory of a theory need not be classical. For example, an intuitionist metatheory for intuitionist logic is well known.[23] Is there a metatheory for paraconsistent logics that is acceptable on paraconsistent terms? The answer to this question is not at all obvious. First, the standard proofs in the metatheories of paraconsistent logics are usually given, as are most mathematical proofs, in an informal way. The question, then, is how to interpret the proofs formally. A normal assumption is that the proofs are carried out using classical logic. And indeed, this would seem to be sufficient for the purpose. This point is not definitive, however. Most paraconsistent logics are generalisations of classical logic in one way or another. In particular, they coincide with classical logic in those cases (models) that are consistent (i.e. in which all formulas behave consistently). Hence, as I argued in chapter 8, if an informal argument concerns a consistent situation, and can be regimented using classical logic, it is perfectly acceptable for a paraconsistent logician. Can a

---

capture the full structure of the universe of sets. (Or, if there are many equally good models, then each captures the structure of an equally good universe.) From the dialetheic perspective, it is precisely the cumulative hierarchy that is an incomplete fragment of the universe of sets. And the models in question do contain the cumulative hierarchy as a fragment (at least up to an inaccessible cardinal).

[21] In particular, the argument constructing the interpretation $\mathcal{M}^{\sim}$ above can be carried out in ZF, and so is perfectly acceptable.

[22] Rescher (1969), p. 229, documents this claim, though he does not endorse it.

[23] See e.g. Dummett (1977), ch. 5, esp. p. 197.

paraconsistent logician, or at least one who subscribes to paraconsistent set theory, look at the metatheoretic arguments concerning paraconsistent logic in this way? The answer, unfortunately, is 'no'. For metatheoretic constructions are carried out in set theory; and paraconsistent set theory is not consistent.

In the model theory of paraconsistent logic, we must therefore use paraconsistent set theory, however that is best construed. To what extent model theory can be developed on the relevant strategy for naive set theory is still an open question. But the model-theoretic strategy for naive set theory provides a simple way of accommodating paraconsistent model theory. One may think of the metatheory of the logic, including the appropriate soundness and completeness proofs, as being carried out (as we know it can be) in ZF. According to the model-theoretic strategy, the results established in this way can perfectly well be taken to hold of the universe of sets, paraconsistently construed. The paraconsistent logician can, therefore, simply appropriate the results.

It might be thought that this approach to the metatheory of paraconsistent logic suffers from a problem. In the material and model-theoretic strategies for paraconsistent set theory, the relationship between the premises and the conclusion of a valid inference is expressed by a material conditional. Thus, simplifying to the one-premise case for perspicuity, and writing the relation 'α holds in $\mathcal{I}$' as '$\mathcal{I} \Vdash \alpha$', an inference from α to β is valid iff:

Val   for every interpretation, $\mathcal{I}(\mathcal{I} \Vdash \alpha \supset \mathcal{I} \Vdash \beta)$

Now, the material conditional does not support detachment. Hence an inference can be valid, yet this does not licence the detachment of the conclusion from the premise. Surely this deprives the notion of validity of its punch?

No. As we saw in chapter 8, the disjunctive syllogism is perfectly acceptable provided the situation is consistent. Provided we do not have $\mathcal{I} \Vdash \alpha$ and $\mathcal{I} \nVdash \alpha$, we can get from $\mathcal{I} \Vdash \alpha$ to $\mathcal{I} \Vdash \beta$. In particular, then, provided that $\mathcal{I}$ is in part of the universe of sets that is consistent (the cumulative hierarchy, or a sufficiently generous part thereof), we have business as usual. (*Note:* this does not mean that the set of things made true by $\mathcal{I}$ is consistent. '$\mathcal{I} \Vdash \alpha$ and $\mathcal{I} \nVdash \alpha$' is quite different from '$\mathcal{I} \Vdash \alpha$ and $\mathcal{I} \Vdash \neg\alpha$'.) If $\mathcal{I}$ is a set outside this part of the universe, matters are different. Thus, we may expect that there is an interpretation, $\mathcal{M}$, that is in accord with the actual, in the sense that, for any γ, γ iff $\mathcal{M} \Vdash \gamma$. One should not expect this interpretation to be in the hierarchy. Appropriate techniques of diagonalisation will give us sentences, α, such that $\mathcal{M} \Vdash \alpha$ and $\mathcal{M} \nVdash \alpha$. In such cases, even though **Val** holds, the fact that α (i.e. $\mathcal{M} \Vdash \alpha$) will not allow us to detach β (i.e. $\mathcal{M} \Vdash \beta$). However, such α's will be unusual. In standard cases **Val** will provide a licence to get from α to β.

It might still be thought odd to have the validity of a deductive inference grounded in a defeasible inference such as the disjunctive syllogism. But a little thought should assuage this worry. The difference between a material $\mathcal{I} \Vdash \alpha \supset \mathcal{I} \Vdash \beta$ and a relevant $\mathcal{I} \Vdash \alpha \rightarrow \mathcal{I} \Vdash \beta$ is not as great as might be thought in this context. Both are simply true (or false) *statements*. Inference, by contrast, is an *action*. Given the premises of an argument, an inference is a *jump* to a new state.

No number of truths is the same thing as a jump. (This is the moral of Lewis Carroll's celebrated dialogue between Achilles and the Tortoise.[24]) None the less, truths of a certain kind may *ground* the jump, in the sense of making it a reasonable action. There is no reason why a sentence of the form $\gamma \supset \delta$ may not do this just as much as one of the form $\gamma \rightarrow \delta$. It is just that one of the latter kind always does, while one of the former kind does so only sometimes.

If it is still not clear how a sentence can function in this way, consider sentences of the form

(*) You promised to do *x*

The truth of (*) normally grounds doing *x*, in the sense of making it reasonable to do it. But, to use a celebrated example, suppose that (*) is true, where the *x* in question is the returning of a weapon to a certain person. And suppose that that person comes requesting the weapon, but you know that they intend to use it to commit suicide. Then the truth of (*) does not, in this context, ground the action. Just as with validity and the material conditional, the truth of a sentence of a certain kind may ground an appropriate action in normal circumstances, but fail to do so in unusual circumstances.

This objection dealt with, there would seem nothing to prevent the paraconsistent logician from simply appropriating all the classical metatheoretic results in the way explained. The appropriation might be thought to have all the charms of theft over honest toil (as Russell said in another context); on the other hand, why reinvent the wheel?

At various times in its history, mathematics has been shocked by the discovery of new kinds of entity: irrational numbers, infinitesimals, transfinite sets, and so on. The reception by the mathematical community of these entities has often been controversial and contentious; and the discovery has always been followed by a process of rethinking mathematical reasoning in the light of these entities and their properties. The discovery of inconsistent objects, such as the Russell set—of all those sets that do not contain themselves—is the most recent, and perhaps the most contentious, episode of this kind, and we are still in the process of thinking through its ramification for mathematical reasoning. In such mathematical revolutions, it is always important to preserve the central parts of previous mathematical thought. What I have been engaged in this chapter is a contribution to this project.

18.6 TECHNICAL APPENDIX

In this appendix I will prove a result (due to Restall 1992) which provides a simple criterion that may be deployed in constructing models of (*Abs*) when the biconditional it employs is the material conditional, $\equiv$.

---

[24] Carroll (1895).

An *LP* interpretation (for the language of set theory) is a pair, $\langle D,I \rangle$, where D is the domain of quantification and I is the interpretation function. $I(\in)$ may be thought of as a pair, $\langle I^+(\in), I^-(\in) \rangle$, but it will be helpful for present purposes to think of it equivalently as a matrix, $(e_{m,n} : m,n \in D)$, that assigns each pair of objects in the domain, $\langle m,n \rangle$, a semantic value, $e_{m,n}$. (Thus, $e_{m,n} = \{1\}$ iff $\langle m,n \rangle \in I^+(\in)$ and $\langle m,n \rangle \notin I^-(\in)$; $e_{m,n} = \{1,0\}$ iff $\langle m,n \rangle \in I^+(\in)$ and $\langle m,n \rangle \in I^-(\in)$; $e_{m,n} = \{0\}$ iff $\langle m,n \rangle \notin I^+(\in)$ and $\langle m,n \rangle \in I^-(\in)$.) To make life easy, I will assume that every member, n, of D has a name, $\mathbf{n}$, in the language. Thus, $v(\mathbf{m} \in \mathbf{n}) = e_{m,n}$.

Given two vectors of *LP* values, $(g_m : m \in D)$, $(h_m : m \in D)$, the first will be said to *subsume* the second iff, for all $m \in D$, $g_m \supseteq h_m$. Now consider a matrix of such values $(e_{m,n} : m, n \in D)$. This will be said to *cover* the vector $(g_m : m \in D)$ iff, for some $n \in D$, the vector $(e_{m,n} : m \in D)$ subsumes it. A vector indexed by D is *classical* iff all its members are $\{1\}$ or $\{0\}$.

Lemma

Let $\mathcal{M} = \langle D, I \rangle$. If $I(\in)$ covers every classical vector indexed by D, $\mathcal{M}$ is a model of (Abs).

Proof

Let α be any formula not containing x, and consider the vector $(v(\alpha(y/\mathbf{m})) : m \in D)$. This certainly subsumes some classical vector; choose one such, and let this be subsumed by $(e_{m,n} : m \in D)$. Now consider any formula of the form $\mathbf{m} \in \mathbf{n} \equiv \alpha(y/\mathbf{m})$. Where the two sides differ in value, one of them has the value $\{1, 0\}$. Hence the value of the biconditional is either $\{1\}$ or $\{1, 0\}$. Thus, the same is true of $\forall y(y \in \mathbf{n} \equiv \alpha)$, and $\exists x \forall y(y \in x \equiv \alpha)$.

The construction of section 18.4 applies this lemma in the simplest possible way. The membership vector for $[a]$ in $\mathcal{M}^{\sim}$ is uniformly $\{1, 0\}$. This vector, on its own, subsumes every classical vector.

19

Autocommentary on the First Edition

19.1 TWENTY YEARS ON

Cognitive agents are fallible, both individually and collectively. One might make an exception for a god, if one believed one to exist—though such a being would hardly need to read this book! It is the rest of us to whom I refer. Human agents form beliefs. Despite the traditional definition of "man" as "rational animal", they often form beliefs in a quite irrational fashion. Even when they behave in a paradigmatically rational way, they may end up with the wrong results: in the last instance evidence is always soft, less than conclusive, etc.; and the world (part of which comprises people) has a habit of throwing up new ideas, arguments, phenomena, etc., which can undercut the most rationally grounded of beliefs. A relatively superficial knowledge of both contemporary cognitive psychology and the history of ideas is sufficient to bear all this out. As it is put at the end of chapter 7, the desire for certitude can now be looked on only with nostalgia—of a time when we knew less about both of these areas of inquiry. In a word, all beliefs, certainly all beliefs of any degree of substance, are fallible.[1] The failure of a person to revise his or her beliefs is, then, not a mark of rationality—quite the opposite: it in fact shows that the person has ceased thinking.[2]

When I wrote the first edition of *In Contradiction*, I was under no illusion that my own theorising was immune from these considerations, as its penultimate sentence shows. Indeed, a few years later, I wrote:[3]

Dialetheism is a view that has been widely (though quite incorrectly) viewed as absurd, since Aristotle stamped his magisterial authority on logic. It would be remarkable indeed, if, in crafting a case for it, one managed to get it exactly right first time.

Twenty years after the publication of the first edition, I remain committed to the book's major themes. But, as one would expect in the light of the preceding considerations, my views on many matters have shifted. There are certainly things that I didn't get right (or right enough) first time. No doubt there will be things that I don't get right this second time either!

---

[1] And, yes, that belief is fallible too.
[2] On the situated nature of belief, see Priest (2006), sect. 8.6, esp. fn. 24.
[3] Priest (1993), p. 53.

The point of this chapter is to chart some of the developments that have taken place since the first edition was published, and to indicate some places where I have changed my mind. I will proceed by giving an autocommentary on the first edition, chapter by chapter. Many of the matters are covered at length in *Beyond the Limits of Thought* (*BLT*, Priest 1995) and *Doubt Truth to be a Liar* (*DTBL*, Priest 2006)—the companion volume to the second edition of *In Contradiction*. Where this is the case, I will not go into the matters at length here.

19.2 CHAPTER 0

Chapter 0 provides an introduction to dialetheism, via a brief discussion of Kant and Hegel. The discussion of Kant and Hegel is taken up at much greater length in Part 2 of *BLT*. The dialetheic aspects of the thought of Hegel, and also of Marx, are discussed at length in Priest (1990, 1991). Incidentally, Hegel *did* know about the Liar Paradox. In his comments on Eubulides in his *Lectures on the History of Philosophy* (part 1, chapter 2, C.1.b) he says that the liar[4]

both lies and does not lie . . . For here we have a union of opposites, lying and truth, and their immediate contradiction . . .

He also berates the error of those who have tried, futilely, to give a 'one sided' answer to the question of the status of the liar.

19.3 CHAPTER 1

Chapter 1 is a case for dialetheism based on the semantic paradoxes, mainly arguing that consistent accounts of the paradoxes won't fly. The Hydra-headed monster which is the programme to give a consistent account of the paradoxes has not lain down to die since 1987. It has grown many new heads. I do not propose to discuss the new theories in detail here, since they suffer from essentially the same kinds of problem that beset earlier accounts—and, indeed, must do so.[5] In particular, they all face the dilemma of the choice between inconsistency and a self-refuting inexpressibility, as I discussed in sections 1.7, 2.5, and 3.4. This theme is pursued at much greater length in *BLT* (especially part 3), so there is no need to go into further detail here. Another thing that *BLT* does is to tie down much more precisely the claim of section 1.1 that all the paradoxes of self reference, both semantic and set theoretic, belong to a single family: they are all inclosure paradoxes, generated by the inclosure schema.

[4] Hegel (1955), p. 460.
[5] The most interesting of these are the accounts by Barwise and Etchemendy (1987), McGee (1990), and especially Field (2003). Detailed discussion of these can be found in Priest (1993, 1994*b*, and forthcoming a), respectively.

Despite the fact that all the paradoxes are of a kind, it is important to note that there are significant differences between them. (It is often startling to see how an author may suggest a solution to some version of the Liar Paradox and assume that it will generalise automatically to all the semantic paradoxes of self reference.) Thus, for example, the paradoxes of denotation, such as Berry's, have certain distinctive features. One is that they may not appeal to the Law of Excluded Middle (as discussed in sections 1.3 and 1.8), in which case they cannot be solved by denying that principle. Another is that all the paradoxes in this family deploy descriptions, or something equivalent, essentially. Any attempt to handle this sort of paradox must take cognisance of this fact.[6]

Even within versions of the Liar Paradox, there are important differences. Thus, the paradigm Liar Paradox is a sentence of the form 'This sentence is false.' Some take this sentence to be neither true nor false. This is not implausible. But consider now the "strengthened" version, 'This sentence is not true.' That is, a sentence, λ, of the form $\neg T\langle\lambda\rangle$. (Angle brackets here indicate a name-forming device.) As section 1.3 points out, it clearly cannot be maintained that this sentence is not true and not false without obvious contradiction.

In a recent note,[7] and following Parsons (1984), Restall suggests that someone who subscribes to truth value gaps need not assert/accept that the λ is not true: they may simply deny/reject it, where these are dual but *sui generis* notions. Such notions make perfectly good sense dialetheically, but such a simple fix will not work. Gap theorists typically want to do more than express the status of λ; they want to reason about its status and that of things of the same kind. Indeed, they really need to do more than this. The mere fact that *some* sentences have the appropriate status is not enough. We need reason to suppose that λ itself does. Gap theory is in trouble here. The precise details depend on the gap theory in question, but let us take a standard example to illustrate matters: Kripke's account. Kripke wants to explain how and why certain sentences, including λ, get the appropriate status. They do so since they are ungrounded. That is, a certain construction is described such that anything that comes to be ungrounded (U) in this process is neither true nor false. The Liar falls into this category. Thus, Kripke's theory entails things like

1. $\forall x(Ux \rightarrow (\neg Tx \wedge \neg T\mathrm{Neg}(x)))$

(where Neg is a function that maps a sentence to its negation). The theory itself, then, *entails* that λ is not true; so we *should* assert this. We might want to deny that λ is true too, but this is beside the point. Note that the negations in 1 cannot be replaced by a force-operator for denial. Such operators attach to whole sentences. If the ability to express the status of λ were restricted to the use of a force-operator, reasoning of the sort in which the gap theorist engages would be crippled.[8]

---

[6] The matter is discussed further in Priest (forthcoming c).   [7] Restall (2004).

[8] See sect. 7.3, fn. 10.

In some ways, the situation is not unlike that in negative theology. In official negative theology, one cannot assert anything about God. All one can do is deny any claim made. All well and good. But negative theologians also try to explain why statements about God have the status they do. In the process, they typically have to reason about God in a way that goes beyond making denials.

Note that none of this is a problem for the dialetheist. It is certainly true that asserting a negation and denying come apart for a glut theorist as much as for a gap theorist. But the glut theorist does not need to use denial to express the status of λ and reason about it. The status of λ is that it is both true and false:

2. $T\langle\lambda\rangle \wedge T\langle\neg\lambda\rangle$

This content can be grammatically embedded in other sentences as one wishes. It might be pointed out that the dialetheist cannot rule out the possibility that the statement concerning the status of λ may itself behave inconsistently. Indeed so. It could turn out that $(T\langle\lambda\rangle \wedge T\langle\neg\lambda\rangle) \wedge \neg(T\langle\lambda\rangle \wedge T\langle\neg\lambda\rangle)$. But this is beside the point. It does not mean that 2 does not express the status of λ: just that that status is itself inconsistent.

Finally in connection with λ, note that this version of the paradox has features that make it special even in a dialetheic context. All paradoxes of self reference are both true and false, but this one is also both true and untrue. Assuming that one ought to assert what is known to be true, and to deny what is known to be untrue, this version of the paradox gives rise to a rational dilemma: one ought both to assert it and to deny it (though one can't do both). This is discussed further in *DTBL*, chapter 6.

19.4 CHAPTER 2

Chapter 2 is a case for dialetheism based on the set theoretic paradoxes of self reference. Much of this is an attack on the claim of the cumulative hierarchy to exhaust the domain of sets. Twenty years on, the thought that the hierarchy exhausts all sets looks even more suspect than it did then, since we have seen both the development and significant applications of non-well-founded set theory, e.g. by Aczel (1988). Of course, Aczel's sets are quite consistent, but there would seem to be lots of non-well-founded sets that are not consistent (the Russell set, the set of all sets, all ordinals, all non-well-founded sets, and so on).

The case of the set theoretic paradoxes is also high on the agenda in *BLT* (especially chapter 11). The arguments concerning proper classes of section 2.3 and the relationship between semantics and set theory of section 2.4 are discussed further there.

One place where I think I did overplay my hand is in the critique of large cardinal postulates in section 2.3. It is in the spirit of paraconsistent set theory to be as generous as possible about the universe of sets. The universe contains sets consistent and inconsistent, well founded and non-well-founded, and—it is natural to suppose—very large and very small. From this perspective, large cardinal postulates look very natural. At any rate, mathematical orthodoxy is now pretty firmly on the side of such postulates—at least for such small cardinals as the strongly inaccessibles; and I am happy to go along with this.[9]

There is more to be said about set theory, but this can wait till the auto-commentary on chapter 10.

19.5 CHAPTER 3

Chapter 3 is a case for dialetheism based on Gödel's first Incompleteness Theorem, arguing that true arithmetic is inconsistent. The thought that arithmetic might be inconsistent must have seemed particularly outrageous in 1987. Set theory, with its large infinities and well known paradoxes, is one thing; arithmetic seems quite a different kettle of fish. (As a friend once said to me, you can do arithmetic with match-sticks.) Of course, once the notion of proof, with its attendant paradoxes, gets in on the act, this is not so clear.

At any rate, there have been significant developments in the theory of inconsistent arithmetics over the last twenty years, and we now have a very clear idea of what inconsistent arithmetics are like. The formal developments have made it possible to treat the arguments for the inconsistent arithmetics more firmly, and to reply to some interesting criticisms (essentially along the lines: How could match-sticks be inconsistent?). All this is spelled out in chapter 17.[10]

Chapter 3 ends:

We might think of the cumulative hierarchy or the Tarski hierarchy as latterday Kantian attempts to retain a certain control over conceptual production. But as we have seen, such constraints are ultimately of no avail: dialetheism is inherent in thought.

This is exactly the *leitmotif* of *BLT*.

19.6 CHAPTER 4

Chapter 4 is a discussion of truth and various of its connections with dialetheism. As section 4.1 says, any account of truth would seem to be compatible with dialetheism. (This point is taken further in chapter 2 of *DTBL*.) The chapter argues for what it calls the teleological account of truth (which I still find

[9] Another place where I got it wrong was in sect. 2.1. Cantor's later distinction between consistent and inconsistent totalities was not, it would appear, motivated simply by the paradoxes. See Hallett (1984), p. xiii.

[10] The connection between Gödel's Theorem, inconsistency, and the anti-mechanist case, mentioned briefly in sect. 3.2, is discussed further in Priest (1994c).

plausible). Just as winning is the generic aim of playing a game, so speaking truly is the generic aim of assertion (and, we might add, related cognitive states such as believing/accepting). Since 1987 deflationary accounts of truth have become popular (starting with Horwich 1990). A number of dialetheists, in particular, have subscribed to such a view (e.g. Beall and Armour-Garb[11]). Section 4.4 contains an argument against deflationism which I still find persuasive. This assumes that meaning is to be given in terms of truth conditions, which assumption may, of course, be rejected (as it is by Horwich); but I know of no other approach to meaning that I find very satisfactory.

In Contradiction argues for a number of counter-examples to the "Law of Non-Contradiction" (LNC)—at least in one understanding of that notion.[12] If this "Law" fails, it is natural to suppose that the "Law of Excluded Middle" (LEM) may fail too. *In Contradiction* takes the position that it does not. In section 4.7 the teleological account of truth is used to argue for the LEM. Essentially, the argument is to the effect that, since assertion is a one-player game, anything less than truth is falsity: there is no middle ground—such as drawing, in a two-player game. This argument was criticised by Terry Parsons (1990), who argues that falsity here needs to be understood as *untruth*. Anything that fails to live up to the aim of assertion is, *ipso facto*, not true (and so should be denied).[13] To get from this to any substantive claim about negation, one needs to relate untruth to falsity, e.g. with the principle that $\neg T\langle\alpha\rangle \rightarrow T\langle\neg\alpha\rangle$, which the argument does not establish, and which in this context would clearly beg the question. I think that Parson's critique of the argument is right.

The argument of section 4.7 is not without significance, however. It still shows that, as far as the linguistic act of assertion goes, there is nothing to distinguish between different ways in which an utterance may fail to meet its end—and so for the distinction between α being false and α being neither true nor false to get a grip on. It therefore (at the very least) raises a challenge for the gappist to find some other ground. (This is the value of the game analogy. In a multiple-player game there is a natural distinction between losing and drawing; in a one-player game there is not. In the game of asserting, there is no other player.)

If a distinction is not to be found in language, as it were, the only other place, I guess, is in the world. The major strategy here, it seems to me, is to appeal to

---

[11] See Armour-Garb and Beall (2001); Beall and Armour-Garb (2003); see also Beall (2005).

[12] Apart from the ones dealt with at length in the first edition, fn. 24 of sect. 4.8 mentions three others: vagueness, infinitesimals, and non-existent objects (see also sect. 9.1, fn. 1). The topic of non-existent objects is dealt with at length in Priest (2005). Generally speaking, it is argued there that to handle non-existent objects one needs to suppose that some worlds are inconsistent, but not necessarily the actual one—though the final chaper of the book does make a case for this. Infinitesimals, I think, are best handled by the Chunk and Permeate mechanism (see Brown and Priest 2004), which is not dialetheic. And as far as vagueness goes—all bets are currently off.

[13] Note that this conclusion, on its own, is not without its sting. It establishes, even if one denies the Law of Excluded Middle in general, that particular instances of the form $T\langle\alpha\rangle \vee \neg T\langle\alpha\rangle$ still hold. These are precisely the ones that give the "strengthened liar" its punch, as I noted in discussing ch. 1.

some sort of correspondence/truthmaker theory. Within the class of assertion failures there may then be cases where there are facts that make ¬α true and those where there is not. Thus, for example, someone may claim that a future-contingent, β, is neither true nor false, on the ground that there is (as yet) no fact that makes either β or ¬β true. But as section 4.7 argues, if there is no fact that makes β true, there is a fact that can be thought of as making ¬β true, namely the fact that there is no fact that makes β true. Perhaps it could be argued that there are no facts of this form. But I can't see why not; somehow there have to be facts of the form (or truth makers for sentences of the form): there is nothing of such and such a kind.[14]

The argument, then, puts the onus on those who would attack the LEM to draw an appropriate distinction and establish that it is semantically significant. There are also other arguments for the LEM. One of these is based on the fact that negation is a contradictory-forming (and not a contrary-forming) operator. This argument is spelled out in detail in *DTBL*, chapter 4, so I will pursue it no further here, except for one comment.

In a discussion of my defence of the LEM ($\Box(\alpha \lor \neg\alpha)$), Restall (2004) introduces the notion $\Gamma \vdash \Delta$, where Γ and Δ are sets of sentences, as meaning that it is logically incoherent to accept every member of Γ and reject every member of Δ. When one of these sets is empty (and ignoring set braces), $\vdash \alpha$ then means that it is logically incoherent to deny α; and $\alpha \vdash$ means that it is logically incoherent to assert α. He goes on to suggest that the LEM need not be formulated as

1. $\vdash \alpha \lor \neg\alpha$

but may, with equal justice, be formulated as

2. $\neg(\alpha \lor \neg\alpha) \vdash$

In fact, neither of these formulations—or even both together—has the force of the LEM in the sense required to define a contradictory-forming operator. 1 says that it is incoherent to deny $\alpha \lor \neg\alpha$. Maybe so. It does not follow that one ought to assert it—let alone that it is true. 2 says that it is incoherent to assert $\neg(\alpha \lor \neg\alpha)$. Again, this does not entail that $\alpha \lor \neg\alpha$ is true. Even intuitionists think that it is incoherent to assert $\neg(\alpha \lor \neg\alpha)$, since this entails $\neg(\alpha \land \neg\neg\alpha)$.

Finally, section 4.9 deals with the principles of Exhaustion and Exclusion, and endorses the first, but not the second. Together, these amount to the full contraposability of the T-schema. Arguments against the contraposability of the schema are given in section 5.4. They are not ungainsayable, but I still find them persuasive. They can be gainsaid by those who take α and $T\langle\alpha\rangle$ to have identical content. This is the line run by the dialetheic deflationists Beall and

---

[14] As noted in sect. 4.7, an intuitionist may argue that, if there are such facts, some of these at least are verification-transcendent, and so cannot be semantically significant. A criticism of this view is provided in *DTBL*, sect. 4.4.

Armour-Garb, mentioned above. As I have already observed, I am not a deflationist (though I would not go to the wall over the matter). But it is not clear to me that even deflationists need to subscribe to the T-schema in a contraposable form. Deflationism may be thought of as the view that α and $T\langle\alpha\rangle$ have the same *truth content*. That leaves it entirely open, it seems to me, as to whether they have the same *falsity content*.[15]

19.7 CHAPTER 5

Chapter 5 specifies the semantics of a language with extensional connectives and quantifiers. The study of paraconsistent logics has gone much further since 1987.[16] However, I would make no changes of substance to this chapter. The only change that I would make if I were to write the chapter now is to take semantic evaluations as relations between formulas and truth values (rather than as functions to sets of truth values), as mooted in section 5.2.[17] Thus, the expressions $x \in v(\alpha)$ would be replaced by $\alpha\rho x$. With no particular restrictions on ρ, this gives the semantics of first degree entailment (section 5.2, fn. 3), in which the LEM fails. In *LP* we require that every propositional parameter, p (and so every formula), relates to *at least* one truth value. Adding the further constraint that every parameter (and so every formula) relates to *at most* one value makes all evaluations classical. Thus, it becomes absolutely obvious that classical evaluations are special cases of *LP* evaluations.

19.8 CHAPTER 6

Chapter 6 extends the semantics of chapter 5 to a language that contains an intensional conditional operator, $\rightarrow$. What inferences concerning $\rightarrow$ are valid is, of course, a major concern of the chapter. But what inferences are invalid is also important. In particular, as the chapter explains, if Curry-style triviality is to be avoided, the principle of absorption (or, as I have come to refer to it more usually since, contraction) must be invalid.[18] The semantics should provide a plausible

---

[15] Sect. 4.2 provides an argument for the T-schema based on the unmentioning function of truth. To endorse what Yasuo said (when we do not know what he said), we say 'What Yasuo said is true.' Suppose that what Yasuo said was that Kyoto is beautiful. We are then committed to the claim that 'Kyoto is beautiful' is true. But if this were not to imply that Kyoto is beautiful, we would not have endorsed this claim. As JC Beall pointed out to me, this inference requires only the T-schema from left to right. However, the use of the truth predicate in this way requires more than this. When we endorse Yasuo's words, we wish to endorse what he said, no more, no less. This requires that 'Kyoto is beautiful' and ' "Kyoto is beautiful" is true' have the same truth content. This is the biconditional in both directions.

[16] Perhaps the best place to find a survey of the subject now is Priest (2002).

[17] And as spelled out in Priest (2001), sect. 8.2.

[18] Exactly why triviality is to be avoided is discussed at length in *DTBL*, ch. 3.

justification for this. The conditional, →, of chapter 6 is a strict conditional, defined in terms of a binary accessibility relation, R. The failure of contraction arises because of the failure of R to be reflexive. An account of why this is plausible is offered in section 6.4.

Since 1987, the semantics of relevant logics have been improved substantially. In particular, the notion of an impossible world is much better understood.[19] I now think it better to give a relevant account of the conditional, deploying the notion of an impossible world to explain the failure of contraction.

In the appropriate semantics for the logic,[20] an interpretation contains two disjoint classes of worlds: the logically possible, P, and logically impossible, I. Let us write W for $P \cup I$. The actual world (G), we may suppose, is one of the possible worlds. A possible world may be physically impossible. That is, the laws of physics may be different at it. But just as the laws of physics may be different at a world, so may the laws of logic. The logically impossible worlds are the worlds in which they are different.[21] In particular, then, validity needs to be defined in terms of truth preservation at just the possible worlds.[22] (What is preserved in worlds where logic is different is clearly another matter.)

The truth and falsity conditions of the extensional connectives (at *all* worlds, w) are those of chapter 5, relativised to the appropriate world. Thus, for example,

$$(\alpha \wedge \beta)\rho_w 1 \text{ iff } \alpha\rho_w 1 \text{ and } \beta\rho_w 1$$

$$(\alpha \wedge \beta)\rho_w 0 \text{ iff } \alpha\rho_w 0 \text{ or } \beta\rho_w 0$$

Since the laws of logic hold at possible worlds, and the LEM is a law of logic, we need to add the constraint that

(*) For all $w \in P, p\rho_w 1$ or $p\rho_w 0$

The law may, of course, fail at logically impossible worlds, so the constraint is not imposed on worlds in I.

The appropriate conditional operator represents a conditional that may be expressed by 'if... then it follows logically that...'. As chapter 6 argues, this is most naturally understood in terms of truth preservation at all worlds. Thus, where $w \in P$, the truth and falsity conditions for ⇒ are [23]

$$(\alpha \Rightarrow \beta)\rho_w 1 \text{ iff for all } x \in W, \text{ if } \alpha\rho_x 1 \text{ then } \beta\rho_x 1$$

$$(\alpha \Rightarrow \beta)\rho_w 0 \text{ iff for some } x \in W, \alpha\rho_x 1 \text{ and } \beta\rho_x 0$$

---

[19] See Priest (2001), sect. 9.7.

[20] A tableau system that is sound with respect to the semantics can be found in sect. 18.3.

[21] This still leaves the nature of worlds an open question. It seems to me that any standard answer to the question may be maintained. In Priest (2005), ch. 7, a noneist answer is given.

[22] Or just G, but in these semantics G has no special properties relevant to validity, so we may omit it.

[23] Chapter 6 deploys a conditional, →, that also preserves falsity backwards. But as I observed there, $\alpha \to \beta$ may be defined as $(\alpha \Rightarrow \beta) \wedge (\neg\beta \Rightarrow \neg\alpha)$. So I will just concern myself with the simpler connective here.

Clearly, this makes, e.g., $p \Rightarrow p$ logically true. At logically impossible worlds, the conditional, expressing as it does a fact of logic, may behave quite differently.[24] In particular, sentences such as $p \Rightarrow p$ may fail. Technically, this may be achieved in various ways, but perhaps the most versatile mechanism is that used in Routley/Meyer semantics, namely, the deployment of a ternary relation, R, on worlds. If $w \in I$, the truth/falsity conditions are then[25]

$$(\alpha \Rightarrow \beta)\rho_w 1 \text{ iff for all } x, y \in W \text{ such that } Rwxy, \text{ if } \alpha\rho_x 1 \text{ then } \beta\rho_y 1$$

$$(\alpha \Rightarrow \beta)\rho_w 0 \text{ iff for some } x, y \in W \text{ such that } Rwxy, \ \alpha\rho_x 1 \text{ and } \beta\rho_y 0$$

It is now clear how $p \Rightarrow p$ may fail at an impossible world, w: we simply have $Rwxy$ where p holds at x but fails at y. It is also clear that, and why, contraction may fail. Suppose that $w \in P$ and $p \Rightarrow (p \Rightarrow q)$ holds at w. Let x be any world such that p holds there; it follows that $p \Rightarrow q$ holds there. But it does not follow that q holds there: x may be a logically impossible world, so *modus ponens* may fail. Hence $p \Rightarrow q$ may not be true at w.[26]

A natural question at this point is what, exactly, the ternary relation R means. Various suggestions concerning this have been made, though none of them is entirely satisfactory.[27] But this is perhaps not so important. If w is a logically impossible world, then $\Rightarrow$ may behave in pretty much any way one likes. If $Rwxy$, then y just records whatever you can get from a conditional, $\alpha \Rightarrow \beta$, given the information, α, contained in x.

The account of the conditional just given is essentially that of the relevant logic B, and it verifies all the principles listed in sections 6.3 and 6.4. It is not quite B, though, since the standard semantics for B handles negation using the Routley *, while the present approach uses a many-valued approach to negation. Thus, it validates the inference $\{\alpha \wedge \neg\beta\} \models \neg (\alpha \Rightarrow \beta)$, which is not valid in B. In virtue of the constraint on propositional parameters, it also verifies the LEM: $\models \alpha \vee \neg\alpha$, which is also not valid in B unless some further constraint is added. It has no standard name in the literature.

Actually, this is not quite right. The constraint (*) ensures that all propositional parameters, and so all formulas built up from them using extensional connectives, satisfy the LEM. But this need not be true of conditional formulas. To see this, suppose that there are two worlds: G, and an impossible world, w.

---

[24] It might be asked why the truth conditions of conjunction and disjunction don't have different truth/falsity conditions at impossible worlds. It is because they don't express logical facts in the way that $\Rightarrow$ does.

[25] Actually, we can give the truth/falsity conditions for $\Rightarrow$ uniformly (that is, at all worlds) by these conditions. We simply add the constraint that, if $w \in P$, $Rwxy$ iff $x = y$. This gives the possible-world conditions above.

[26] The semantics of ch. 6 can be seen as a special case of these semantics. The ternary relation, R, is collapsed into a binary relation by the condition: if $Rwxy$ then $x = y$. (The binary relation is actually the *converse* of that used in ch. 6, which reverses the more usual order of the arguments.) The possible worlds are all those, including G, that are omniscient. And gaps are closed at all worlds, not just the possible ones.   [27] See the discussion in Priest (2001), sect. 10.6.

At G, p and q are simply true; at w, p is simply true and q is neither true nor false. Then $p \Rightarrow q$ is neither true nor false at G. If conditionals are to satisfy the LEM at G and other possible worlds, something more needs to be done.

One possibility is to modify the falsity conditions for conditionals at possible worlds, w, to the following:

$(\alpha \Rightarrow \beta)\rho_w 0$ iff (it is not the case that $(\alpha \Rightarrow \beta)\rho_w 1$) or (for some $w' \in W$,

$\quad \alpha \rho_{w'} 1$ and $\beta \rho_{w'} 0$)

This simply closes the gaps for conditionals.

There are advantages to maintaining the falsity conditions of $\Rightarrow$ as they are, however. This may be achieved in another way. Suppose that there is a world with a gap in it; that is, some sentence, α, is neither true nor false. It is natural to suppose that there are worlds that are essentially the same, except that that gap is filled; indeed, there are worlds of this kind where it is true, and worlds where it is false (and maybe worlds where it is both). Let us write the set of things true at world w as $[w]$. Then, more precisely, the condition is that, for any α and w,

AC: if α is neither true nor false at w, there are worlds, w_0 and w_1,

such that $[w] \subseteq [w_0]$, $[w] \subseteq [w_1]$, α is false at w_0, and true at w_1

The rationale for AC is that, given an ontological gap at w, its metaphysical structure could be augmented a little to fill it. If, for the sake of illustration, there are worlds where, as Aristotle claimed, 'There will be a sea battle tomorrow' is neither true nor false—because it is as yet undetermined—then there are worlds that are the same, except that there are *additional* laws of nature which determine the event either one way or the other, and so in which the statement is true/false. In *DTBL* (section 5.2) AC is called the *Augmentation Constraint* (and further of its consequences are discussed).

If we restrict ourselves to interpretations where the Augmentation Constraint is satisfied, then all conditionals are either true or false at possible worlds. For suppose that at such a world, w, $\alpha \rightarrow \beta$ were neither true nor false; then there would be a world, x, where α is true and β is neither true nor false. Now consider x_0, guaranteed by the Augmentation Constraint. At x_0, α is true and β is false. Hence $\alpha \rightarrow \beta$ is, in fact, false at w.

Given the specification of an arbitrary interpretation, whether it satisfies the Augmentation Constraint is not, in general, effectively checkable.[28] (Whether there are conditions on the components of an interpretation that are necessary and sufficient to realise the Constraint, and which can be effectively checked, is not, at the time of writing, known.) However, something that is sufficient, and that can often be used in practice, is the presence of the trivial world, $w_\perp$. This is

---

[28] It is worth noting, however, that the constraint is satisfied in canonical models (in the model-theoretic sense). If w is any world, that is, set of sentences, then $w \cup \{\alpha\}$ and $w \cup \{\neg\alpha\}$ can each be extended to prime theories, which are worlds in the model. In particular, then, a proof theory without the LEM is not complete with respect to canonical models.

a world at which every propositional parameter is both true and false, and the only instance of the ternary relation that $w_\perp$ enters into is $Rw_\perp w_\perp w_\perp$. It is not difficult to establish that everything is true and false at $w_\perp$. For any w and α, then, $w_\perp$ plays the role of both w_0 and w_1. The presence of $w_\perp$ has a very strong effect on conditionals at possible worlds: they are all at least false; but the behaviour of negated conditionals is often not very important.

This deals with the conditional connective.[29] The details of the other logical machinery in the new setting are routine. Thus, constant-domain quantifiers can be added to the semantics as in section 6.7. What corresponds to the condition (*) in the predicate context is (in the notation of chapter 6)

For all $w \in P, d_w^+(P) \cup d_w^-(P) = D^n$

where P is an n-place predicate, $d_w^+(P)$ and $d_w^-(P)$ are the extension and anti-extension of P at w, and D is the domain of quantification.

The identity predicate, like all predicates, has an extension and anti-extension at every world. For it to function as identity, it needs to satisfy the condition

For all $w \in P, d_w^+(=) = \{\langle a, a \rangle : a \in D\}$

This ensures that $x = x$ is a logical truth. (Clearly, one should not expect this constraint to extend to impossible worlds as well. In such worlds, $x = x$ may fail.) It is also not difficult to check that $\{x = y\} \models \beta \leftrightarrow \beta(x/y)$ (where y is free when substituted for x).[30]

Finally, as in section 6.6, we can define $L\alpha$ as $\neg\alpha \Rightarrow \alpha$. It is not now true that $L\alpha$ holds at a possible world if α holds at all worlds. It may hold even though α has no truth value at some (impossible) worlds. The dual of $L\alpha$, $M\alpha$, is $\neg L\neg\alpha$, i.e. $\neg(\alpha \Rightarrow \neg\alpha)$. It is easy to check that $M\alpha$ *does* hold at a possible world iff there is some world—possible or impossible—where α holds. For this reason, M should not be thought of as a possibility operator. (We could, of course, add such an operator, $\Diamond$, to the language. The appropriate truth conditions for this at possible worlds, w, are: $\Diamond\alpha\rho_w 1$ iff for some $w' \in P, \alpha\rho_{w'} 1$.)

19.9 CHAPTER 7

Chapter 7 contains a discussion of rationality and related notions. These matters are taken up at much greater length in *DTBL*. The critique of Aristotle on the LNC referred to in section 7.2 is provided at length in chapter 1 of that book; the

---

[29] Sect. 6.5 raises the issue of the connection between logical conditionals of this kind and ordinary English conditionals, 'if...then...'. I now think that these are best conceived of as relevant *ceteris paribus* conditionals of the kind given in Priest (2001), sect. 10.7. For further discussion of the matter, see Priest (forthcoming c).

[30] Note that this condition does not deliver the validity of $(x = y \wedge \beta) \rightarrow \beta(x/y)$. If $x = y$ holds at an impossible world, it is not guaranteed that x and y have the same denotation. The validity of this principle can be obtained by adding the further constraint that at impossible worlds, $w, d_w^+(-) \subseteq \{\langle a, a \rangle : a \in D\}$.

notions of acceptance and rejection in section 7.3 are discussed in chapter 6;[31] section 7.4, on rationality, is much expanded in chapter 7; and the comments there on rationality and inconsistent theories are taken up in chapter 9.[32] The issue of belief revision in section 7.5 is explored in greater detail in chapter 8. (The details in that chapter concerning rational choice, and the rationality index of a theory, can be thought of as spelling out the notion of the methodological comparison of theories discussed.) Finally, the account of probability theory in section 7.6 is applicable just as much to the semantics I specified in connection with the autocommentary on the last chapter.[33]

The only place where I would take something back concerns the argument of section 7.4 to the effect that you cannot be rationally obliged to both accept and reject something. As *DTBL*, section 6.5, explains, I now think you can be: you can have a rational dilemma of this kind. The argument against the possibility of this in section 7.4 is to the effect that, since acceptance and rejection are incompatible, the ideal rational agent cannot accept and reject something. Since what is rationally acceptable or rejectable is what the ideal rational agent actually accepts or rejects, it follows that rational acceptability and rejectability are also incompatible. The trouble with this argument is that the ideal rational agent may be an impossible object! Rationality may impose incompatible constraints. In this case, they can be satisfied only by performing incompatible actions.[34]

This matter is relevant to an objection put to dialetheism by Weir (2004). His argument is long, but the crucial claim (p. 414) is that, for a rational agent, x,

A/R: if x accepts $\neg\alpha$ then x rejects α

Hence, if x accepts α and $\neg\alpha$, x both accepts α and rejects α, which is impossible. The argument obviously requires that rationality cannot put impossible constraints on an agent—which, as I have just indicated, I think it can. But the problems with Weir's argument run much deeper than this.

By 'accept' and 'reject' Weir does not mean quite what I mean by those words. To accept something is to act as if one believes it; to reject something is to act as if one 'disbelieves' it (pp. 403 f.). Weir never says explicitly what he means by 'disbelieve'. Generally speaking, the notion is susceptible to at least three interpretations. To disbelieve α might be:

1. to believe $\neg\alpha$
2. not to believe α
3. to refuse to believe α

---

[31] The history of dialetheism mentioned on p. 120, fn. 8, is covered in much more detail in Priest (forthcoming *d*), sect. 3.

[32] I now think that the Bohr theory of the atom is not a good example of a potentially dialetheic theory. It is best handled by a paraconsistent mechanism that is not dialetheic. See Brown and Priest (2004).

[33] One thing to note. To ensure that all logical truths, such as the LEM, take unit probability, one should require, as one would expect, that the measure, μ, is on the set of *possible* worlds.

[34] See the critique of the position adopted in the first edition by Goodship (1996).

So let me cover all the bases. (If Weir means something different from all of these, the meaning eludes me.)

In case 1, there is nothing impossible about accepting something and rejecting it. One can quite easily behave as if one believes α and $\neg\alpha$. For many αs I behave in exactly that way.

It is much less clear that one can behave as if one believes and does not believe α, or believes α and refuses to believe α. The question, then, is why one should endorse **A/R** under these interpretations. Weir's answer is that, if one is using negation with the correct meaning, one's acceptance and rejection patterns should mirror one's belief/disbelief patterns, and

B/D: if x believes $\neg\alpha$ then x disbelieves α

Now, what the correct meaning of negation is, is a crucial part of the dispute between classical and dialetheist logicians. But we can sidestep that issue.[35] In case 1 **B/D** is a simple tautology, and all may agree on it. In case 2 the crucial claim is that, if someone believes $\neg\alpha$ and believes α, then they do not use negation with its proper meaning. This is just false. Many of us—including classical logicians—believe contradictions, wittingly or unwittingly. This does not betray a misunderstanding of negation, just (perhaps) imperfect beliefs. Indeed, quite independently of dialetheism, inconsistent beliefs are arguably quite rational. (On all this, see section 7.4.) In case 3 the crucial claim is that, if someone believes $\neg\alpha$ and does not refuse to believe α, then they do not use negation with its proper meaning. We have just noted that someone can believe $\neg\alpha$ and α without misunderstanding negation. And in that case they believe $\neg\alpha$ and do not refuse to believe α (since, if one does refuse to believe α, one does not believe α). So the argument still fails.

19.10 CHAPTER 8

Chapter 8 gives an account of how a dialetheic logician can appropriate normal classical reasoning: the classical recapture. I would make two changes to this now.

First, and most importantly, I would replace the construction concerning *consequence ($\models^*$) in section 8.6 with that of minimally inconsistent (m.i.) consequence ($\models_m$) in chapter 16. The notion of *consequence always struck me as a bit artificial. By contrast, the notion of m.i. consequence, which has the same important properties, seems to me to be both simple and natural.[36]

---

[35] It is discussed at length in *DTBL*, pt 2.

[36] Weir (2004), pp. 399 ff., objects that employing *LPm* (as well as *LP*) violates the 'universality of logic'. I do not think so. When viewed as I suggested, *LPm* is the "universal" logic; *LP* is its monotonic fragment; and classical consequence is the result if the premises are consistent. According to Weir (p. 403, fn. 18) non-monotonic logics are 'not genuine logics'. I don't know what 'genuine' means in this context, but since a uniform model-theoretic account of validity

Second, I now no longer endorse principle *R* of section 8.3. (If a disjunction is rationally acceptable and one of the disjuncts is rationally rejectable, then the other is rationally acceptable.) If there are rational dilemmas, as I argue in *DTBL*, section 6.5, this principle cannot be correct. Let α be something that is both rationally acceptable and rejectable. For any β, α entails $\alpha \vee \beta$, so this is rationally acceptable too. By principle *R*, β is rationally acceptable.[37]

In reply to an objection against principal *R* in section 8.3, I argued that, if one accepts a disjunction and rejects one of the disjuncts, one is still committed to accepting the other, even if one also accepts the disjunct. This, it now seems to me, is just wrong. Arguably, the situation is exactly the same as that concerning the disjunctive syllogism (DS). Given $\alpha \vee \beta$, $\neg\alpha$ delivers β only if one does not also have α. Similarly, if one accepts $\alpha \vee \beta$, rejecting α delivers β only if one does not also accept α.[38]

Section 8.3 uses principle *R* as part of a justification for the use of quasi-valid inferences in consistent situations. If principle *R* cannot be sustained, then neither can this justification. Note, however, that the probability considerations of section 8.3 still stand. Thus, one can employ quasi-valid inferences to take one from things with a high probability to other things with a high probability. This, still, therefore, provides a justification for their use in appropriate contexts. More importantly, the probability considerations of section 8.4 also stand. The low *a priori* probability of contradictions can therefore be taken to justify taking consistency to be a default assumption, in the way required for m.i. consequence, which, then, justifies the use of classically valid inferences in consistent situations.[39]

19.11 CHAPTER 9

Chapter 9 shows how to construct a semantically closed theory. The language of the theory contains its own truth predicate, and the theory establishes all instances of the T-schema. The construction and proof goes through in exactly the same way using the logic whose semantics are specified in the commentary on chapter 6. (To perform the construction in the non-contraposible case, this requires us to maintain the falsity conditions of $\Rightarrow$ as before.) Moreover, the

that covers both monotonic and non-monotonic cases can be given (see *DTBL*, ch. 11), I see little substance to the claim.

[37] For this argument, see Smiley (1993).

[38] See the critique of the position adopted in the first edition by Goodship (1996). As she points out, principle *R* can still hold in the form of a defeasible conditional.

[39] Olin (2003), p. 32, challenges the argument for the statistical infrequency of contradictions given in sect. 8.4 to the effect that we rarely go wrong in applying the disjunctive syllogism, on the ground that, when we apply the syllogism and obtain a result that does not check out, we backtrack and reject one of our premises. Perhaps so. But the point is that, when the premises of the reasoning are well grounded, we rarely have to back-track in that way.

non-triviality of semantically closed theories based on relevant logics of this kind is well established.[40]

The inconsistency proof given at the very end of the chapter does not go through as it stands, since the inference $\{L\alpha\} \vdash \beta \Rightarrow \alpha$ is not valid in the semantics. However, it is easy enough to repair the argument. As before, we establish (in the notation of chapter 6) that $\text{Sat}_1\,(x, \underline{\alpha}) \Rightarrow \alpha(v_i/x)$. Now let α be $\neg\text{Sat}_1(v_i, v_i)$, and x be $\underline{\alpha}$ to get

$$\text{Sat}_1(\underline{\alpha}, \underline{\alpha}) \Rightarrow \neg\text{Sat}_1(\underline{\alpha}, \underline{\alpha})$$

It follows that $\neg\text{Sat}_1(\underline{\alpha}, \underline{\alpha})$. By the axiom that guarantees the existence of appropriate sequences, we have: $\exists s\, s(i) = \underline{\alpha}$. Hence

$$\exists s(\neg\text{Sat}_1(\underline{\alpha}, \underline{\alpha}) \wedge s(i) = \underline{\alpha})$$

By identity principles, $\exists s(\neg\text{Sat}_1(s(i), s(i)) \wedge s(i) = \underline{\alpha})$; and so $\exists s(s(i) = \underline{\alpha} \wedge \text{Sat}(s, \underline{\alpha})$, by the satisfaction schema. That is, $\text{Sat}_1(\underline{\alpha}, \underline{\alpha})$.

19.12 CHAPTER 10

Chapter 10 discusses the properties of a dialetheic set theory, the semantics of the language of set theory, and applies all this to argue for a nominalistic philosophy of mathematics (or, at least, of set theory). The current situation with respect to paraconsistent set theory is spelled out in detail in chapter 17, so I need say nothing more about it here. As that chapter indicates, there is a close connection between the topic of paraconsistent set theory and the topic of the semantics of paraconsistent logics (that is, the model theoretic definition of validity, together with standard properties of this, such as soundness and completeness). Chapters 6 and 7 specify such a semantics, but do so in an informal way. No attempt is made there—or anywhere else in the first edition—to say how one might formalise these informal proceedings. An account of this is provided by the model theoretic strategy of section 18.4. One can think of the metatheory as being carried out within ZF set theory, and then simply appropriate the results.

Given chapter 9, it is natural to ask whether this procedure can be semantically closed. Can the theory give an account of the validity of inferences in its own language? In one sense, this is very easy. Accounts of validity define the notion for an arbitrary language of a certain kind, and are given in the language of set theory. The language of set theory *is* (normally) a language of the kind in question. One does not need a paraconsistent logic or set theory for semantic closure in this sense: classical ZF can do it.

Of course, what classical ZF cannot do (if it is consistent) is define an interpretation for the language of set theory and show that it is a model for ZF.

---

[40] See Priest (2002), sect. 8.5.

Something like this can be done in naive set theory, at least on the model theoretic strategy. Let $\mathcal{M}$ be the intended interpretation (or one of the intended interpretations) for the language of set theory. $\mathcal{M}$ is a model of ZF. Now, within ZF we can define the notions of interpretation and truth in an interpretation ($\Vdash$). We may suppose that the latter notion is defined in such a way as to make sense when the lefthand side of the relation is not an interpretation—say, by making it vacuously true. We can also define the theory of an interpretation, Th (that is, the set of sentences true in the interpretation), in the usual way, and prove within ZF that

For all $x, x \Vdash \text{Th}(x)$

This, then, holds in $\mathcal{M}$.

Now, within $\mathcal{M}$ we can, as we cannot in ZF, establish the existence of the intended interpretation, that is, a pair $\langle D, I \rangle$ where D is the universal set and $\langle x, y \rangle \in I$ iff $x \in y$. Let this interpretation be m. Thus, we have an instance of the Comprehension Principle of the form

$$x \in m$$
$$\equiv \exists y \exists z (x = \langle y, z \rangle \wedge \forall u\, u \in y \wedge \forall w (w \in z \equiv \exists u \exists v (w = \langle u, v \rangle \wedge u \in v)))$$

Given this, we may then conclude, in $\mathcal{M}$, that $m \Vdash \text{Th}(m)$. This is a version of semantic closure. (Of course, it does not follow from this that $\text{Th}(m)$ is consistent.)

Let us turn now to the philosophy of mathematics. My metaphysical dispositions are those of a materialist. It has always struck me as highly counterintuitive that there should exist objects of a non-physical kind, and in particular that there should exist abstract objects. Chapter 10 gives a nominalist account of, at least, sets. The account turns on giving (in section 10.2) a semantics for the language of set theory which employs only substitutional quantification.

I have now become dissatisfied with this view. For a start, if one adopts the model theoretic strategy for set theory, one can no longer give the truth conditions of identity statements by ($=$) (in section 10.2). To do so would result in the conclusion that all sets are identical (as section 18.3 points out). More importantly, as section 10.6 points out, it is not clear to what extent the nominalist account of arithmetic and set theory given in that chapter generalises to the whole of mathematics. It now seems to me that a noneist account of mathematics provides a better materialist account of mathematics. According to this, only material objects exist; abstract objects are one (important) class of non-existent objects. Crucial to the view is that objects (existent and non-existent) can be characterised in certain ways, and that the objects characterised have their characterising properties—though not necessarily at this world: at worlds that realise the appropriate representation. This is the Characterisation Principle (CP). The view is set out in detail in *Towards Non-Being*.[41]

---

[41] Priest, (2005), especially ch. 7.

In the terms of section 10.4, this is a realist (though not a platonist) view. It behoves me, then, to say something about what I think is wrong with the arguments against realism in that section. Essentially three are marshalled. The replies to all involve the CP essentially (which is why the traditional platonist, who does not accept this principle, does not have similar replies).[42]

The first argument is to the effect that true statements of mathematics would seem to have a status quite different from those about the physical world. True mathematical statements, it is claimed, are necessarily true; true physical statements are contingent. Now it is not true that all statements about physical objects are contingent. Assuming the necessity of true identities, the following is a necessary truth: if the Morning Star ceased to exist, so would the Evening Star. Conversely, at least on the account given in *Towards Non-Being*, some statements about mathematical objects are contingent. They are guaranteed to be true only in those worlds that realise the appropriate representation—indeed, they may not be *actually* true at all. The axioms of naive set theory may well be true (and even analytic), but the statements that describe, e.g., the intuitionist continuum, are not: they hold only at those worlds where the continuum actually does behave like that.[43]

But, clearly, there does appear to be a difference in status of some kind between standard statements about mathematical objects and those concerning physical objects. What explains this? It is not the modal status of the two kinds of statement, but their epistemic status. The truth of 'The Morning Star is the Evening Star' cannot be determined without empirical observation. Hence it is *a posteriori*. By contrast, the CP is *a priori*. Hence we can know that mathematical objects have their properties (at the appropriate worlds) without any empirical observation. This explains the difference we feel between the two kinds of statement.

The second objection is a standard one, to the effect that, since non-existent objects have no causal efficacy, it is impossible to know anything about them. The reply to this is essentially that we know the CP *a priori*. This tells us about certain characterising properties of mathematical objects, and we infer others from these.

The final objection is a challenge to realism to pin down the connection between mathematical objects and human practices, especially those of counting, etc. If there is no such connection, the view is simply a form of mystification. The connection can be specified very simply, though—and again the CP is the key. We have a practice of characterising things in certain ways, of representing them in our subjective imagination and our objective language. This is what ties the objects to our activities. In the case of the most fundamental parts of

---

[42] Most of the following points are discussed at greater length in Priest, (2005), ch. 7.

[43] Not that locating an inconsistent theory at a possible world protects the actual world from contradiction. If $\alpha \wedge \neg\alpha$ is true at a possible world, $\Diamond(\alpha \wedge \neg\alpha)$ is true at the actual world. $\neg\Diamond(\alpha \wedge \neg\alpha)$ is a logical truth.

mathematics, such as number theory and set theory, this characterisation is not an overt one. It is implicit in our practices of counting, grouping, etc. (Indeed, in the case of numbers, it took thousands of years to figure out, in the form of the Dedekind/Peano axioms, the explicit form of the characterisation implicit in our practice of counting.) In such cases, then, the connection lies invisible, below the surface of our practice.

Section 10.4 puts the challenge in a picturesque way. Mathematical objects are irrelevant to mathematics, it is claimed, since if all were destroyed mathematics would be unaffected (as long as we continue to practice it in the same way). What is the noneist to say about this conditional? The important question to ask is how this conditional is to be expressed. The first natural thought is to express it as:

If mathematical objects were not to exist, mathematics would be the same (as it is now).

But this is something a noneist will agree with: mathematical objects *do not* exist! For the question to make any sense, it must be framed in terms of neutral quantifiers, thus:

$\neg \mathfrak{S} x(x$ is a mathematical object$) >$ mathematics is the same (as it is).

Here, $\mathfrak{S}$ is the particular quantifier ('something is such that') and $>$ is the appropriate conditional. To evaluate this conditional, we need to look at the "nearest" worlds where $\neg \mathfrak{S} x(x$ is a mathematical object$)$. In these, something like 3 would not be a mathematical object; it would be a table, a tiger, a tree… The world would clearly not be one in which 3 has its characterising properties. In such a world, mathematics *would* be different. (Or, at least, there is no reason why it should be the same.) Again, then, the noneist will agree with the conditional.

The version of noneist realism provided in *Towards Non-Being* does not, then, seem to fall to the objections marshalled in chapter 10. A final natural question is to what extent the view of sets as non-existent objects counts as a change on the view, expressed in section 2.1, that sets 'just are the extensions of arbitrary conditions'. That view can be thought of as the conjunction of two: (1) every condition has a set as extension; (2) every set is the extension of some condition. The important part, at least for dialetheic purposes, is (1). It is this (in conjunction with the abstraction principle) that gives rise to dialetheias. Nothing I have said reneges on this in any way. The converse principle, (2), is anodyne for everyone, at least in one sense. Given any set, a, the condition '$x \in a$' defines it. But one might interpret (2) more strongly as something like: every set is the extension of some condition that does not presuppose a prior grasp of the set itself. This is, of course, a very vague way of putting matters; but it will do for here. When I wrote the first edition I did subscribe to some view of this kind—at least implicitly. Given my current views, I now feel no such compulsion.

19.13 CHAPTER 11

Chapter 11 goes together with Chapter 12 and the new Chapter 15 to provide an essay on the metaphysics of change. Chapter 11 itself deals with the simplest case, discrete changes.[44]

The only comment about that chapter that needs to be made concerns the changes to the tense-logical semantics required by the propositional semantics described in the autocommentary on chapter 6. These are relatively minor (and do not affect the extensional part at all). The truth and falsity conditions given in the chapter remain the same. In particular, they are the same at both possible and impossible worlds. Since we are now in a context where we have both temporal and modal operators, the members of W must be thought of as instantaneous states of worlds. Thus, the members of P are instantaneous states of worlds that have the actual laws of logic; while the members of I are instantaneous states of worlds in which logic may be different. It would seem natural, then, to require that, if $x < w$ or $w < x$, and $w \in P$, then $x \in P$. The laws of logic are time-invariant. Given that the non-tensed formulas satisfy the LEM at possible worlds, this condition ensures that tensed formulas (and so all formulas) do so too.

19.14 CHAPTER 12

Chapter 12 criticises the orthodox, Russellian, account of motion, and advocates an alternative, Hegelean, account. Essentially two sorts of objections are urged against the orthodox account. The first is to the effect that, according to it, there is no instantaneous state of change: we have only "cinematic" change. This has various counter-intuitive consequences. The second is that the account falls prey to Zeno's Arrow Paradox. According to the alternative account, to be in motion is to be in a certain instantaneous inconsistent state. The account deploys the Spread Hypothesis to explain how and why this occurs. Further criticisms of the orthodox account are given in Tooley (1988) and Priest (forthcoming e), the latter of which also contains further discussion of Hegel on the continuum.[45] The chapter ends with an application of the LCC to time. The new chapter 15 extends this thought by applying the Spread Hypothesis to it.

[44] The problems to which this gives rise, though they have not exercised philosophers much in the last one hundred years or so, are of venerable lineage. On medieval discussions of the issues, see Kretzmann (1982) and Spade (1982). Interestingly, as Koji Tanaka pointed out to me, a view similar to the one expressed in the chapter can be found in later Mohist logic. At the moment something ceases to be an ox, both 'ox' and 'non-ox' refer to it. See Graham (1978), sect. A50, p. 298. Mortensen (1997) models the inconsistencies generated at the instant of change (especially in the context of quantum transitions) using inconsistent arithmetic.

[45] Tooley also criticises some other accounts of motion. One of these is in terms of infinitesimals (p. 232), but it is too swift. Even if there are infinitesimal times, it is quite possible to hold that an object moves an infinitesimal amount in an *instant*.

19.15 CHAPTER 13

Chapter 13 is a discussion of normative dilemmas and dialetheias. The major part of the chapter concerns legal norms, but the discussion is widened towards the end of the chapter, and the matter is brought to bear on the issue of dialetheism in general, via a discussion of human practice.[46]

Section 13.3 gives a semantics for a deontic logic with an obligation operator, O. When I wrote the first edition, I was somewhat half-hearted about the use of worlds in semantics for logics. I therefore gave an unusual non-world semantics for O. My attitude has now changed. Writing *Introduction to Non-Classical Logic* (Priest 2001) convinced me of the power and versatility of the notion of a world; and interpreting worlds (or at least worlds other than the actual) as kinds of nonexistent object (as is done in Priest (2005, section 7.3)) assuaged my ontological scruples. I would therefore now prefer an appropriate world-semantics for O.[47]

We suppose that the semantics I described in connection with chapter 6 are augmented with a binary accessibility relation, S, on worlds. Intuitively, wSw' iff w' is a world where all the obligations that obtain at w are fulfilled. If w is a possible world, the truth/falsity conditions for O are

$O\alpha\rho_w 1$ iff for all w' such that wSw', $\alpha\rho_{w'} 1$

$O\alpha\rho_w 0$ iff for some w' such that wSw', $\alpha\rho_{w'} 0$, or it is not the case that

$O\alpha\rho_w 1$

The second disjunct in the falsity conditions provides a simple way of ensuring that all sentences of the form $O\alpha$ (and so all sentences constructed using sentences of this form) satisfy the LEM. The truth/falsity conditions for O at impossible worlds are the same, except that the second disjunct in the falsity conditions is dropped.

In these semantics, S is an arbitrary relation, but this suffices to validate the following inferences:[48]

$\{\alpha \Rightarrow \beta\} \vdash O\alpha \Rightarrow O\beta$

$\vdash (O\alpha \wedge O\beta) \Rightarrow O(\alpha \wedge \beta)$

as may easily be checked.

---

[46] Page 189 refers to the notion of *bringing it about that*. This notion has been much investigated since in so-called STIT logics (see e.g. Belnap 1991; Belnap and Perloff 1990; Xu 1994.) Page 186 claims that the verification theory of meaning is dead. Whether fortunately or otherwise, it seems to have come back to life since the first edition was written. On this matter see the beginning of the Preface of Priest (2005).

[47] Page 191 notes that semantics of the kind I give have applications to other sorts of operators. I make great use of them, in effect, to give a semantics for intentional operators in Priest (2005).

[48] Note that the principle of necessitation for O is not validated. The fact that α holds at all possible worlds does not entail that it holds at all worlds accessible via S, since some of these may be impossible.

If desired, further constraints can be imposed on S, generating further valid inferences. For example, the conditions in the lefthand column of the following table validate the corresponding inference in the righthand column:

$\forall w \exists w' \, wSw'$	$\vdash O\neg\alpha \Rightarrow \neg O\alpha$
$\forall x, y, z$ (if xSy and ySz then xSz)	$\vdash O\alpha \Rightarrow OO\alpha$
$\forall x, z$ (if xSz then $\exists y(xSy$ and $ySz))$	$\vdash OO\alpha \Rightarrow O\alpha$

but these extra conditions should be resisted, as section 13.4 explains.[49]

Finally, on a more general issue, section 13.5 flags the possibility that the considerations of the chapter may apply to the norms of rationality. That point is pursued much further in *DTBL*, chapter 6.[50]

19.16 CHAPTER 14

Chapter 14 draws the crucial distinction between the truths of logic and our theories thereof, and makes some remarks on the historical evolution and fallibility of the latter. These matters are pursued at length in chapters 10–12 of *DTBL*.[51]

The chapter ends by pursuing an analogy between the transfinite and the transconsistent. I have not made much explicit use of the notion of the transconsistent since writing the first edition, but the analogy with the transfinite strikes me as being as close and as suggestive as it did then.

---

[49] A denotically perfect world, w, of the kind described at the end of sect. 13.4, is simply one such that wSw.

[50] Tidying up a couple of other matters: p. 202 moots the possibility that the Newton/Leibniz version of the calculus might be thought of as a case of dialetheism. This I now think false. See Brown and Priest (2004). Page 203 cites a passage from the *Parmenides* to show that Plato was prepared to accept the possibility that the world of flux (though not the world of forms) might be inconsistent. It is worth noting that at the end of that most puzzling dialogue he seems pushed into the view that the world of forms is inconsistent too. Finally, I discuss Wittgenstein's preparedness to accept contradictions further, and especially in the context of his remarks on Gödel's first Incompleteness Theorem, in Priest (2004).

[51] The brief comment about Aristotelian logic is expanded in sect. 10.8 of that book.

20

Comments on Some Critics

20.1 THE EMPIRE STRIKES BACK

If one attacks a view that constitutes an entrenched orthodoxy, it would be naive to expect the orthodox simply to agree—just like that. Strategically, if it can be made to work, the best response to a heresy is to ignore it. There is nothing like trying to crush a heresy to spread it. Contemporary dialetheism often did meet with this reaction in its early years. The view was taken to be so bizarre that if any notice at all was taken of it, it was with the attitude of meeting a philosopher's party-trick.[1] But turning one's back is not always an option; and another is to fight back. This is exactly what some of those of the orthodox persuasion have done.[2] This is entirely proper. New ideas should be tested in the hard light of intellectual day. Some of the criticism has indeed occasioned me to revise my views concerning dialetheism. Exactly how, I explained in the last chapter. But by much of the criticism—especially of the more fundamental kind—I have been unpersuaded. The main point of this final chapter is to discuss some of the criticisms that have been made and explain why. To respond to all the criticisms would be prolix and tiresome, and fortunately many of them have been taken up in other chapters of the second edition, in *Doubt Truth to be a Liar* (*DTBL*), and elsewhere, including the second edition of *Beyond the Limits of Thought* (*BLT*), section 17.1. I select, therefore, only those that have not been commented on in one of those places, and, among those, the ones that are most interesting and/or persistent.

20.2 DIALETHEIC LOGIC

One of the major things that critics have commented on is the logic of dialetheism itself. Let us start with this.

[1] A friend, and influential philosopher, in the UK told me recently that it was not until the debate with Timothy Smiley at the joint session of the Mind Association and the Aristotelian Society in 1993 that he 'realised I was serious'.
[2] Some of the critics, with appropriate replies, are as follows: Denyer (1989), Priest (1989*b*); T. Parsons (1990), Priest (1995); Smiley (1993), Priest (1993a); Everett (1993, 1994, 1996), Priest

The dialetheic notion of logical consequence is criticised by Tennant (2004), especially on grounds concerning its proof theory. Specifically, he suggests that the following questions can be answered only negatively (p. 367):

1. Are the logical reforms of the dialetheist able to accommodate the great bulk of ordinary reasoning in mathematics and the natural sciences?
2. Does the dialetheist's 'logic of paradox' have a satisfying proof theory?
3. Does it do justice to logic as a science of *inference* (as opposed to providing a fancy deviant model of semantic evaluations)?
4. Does it accommodate the very arguments that the dialetheist uses when trying to show that certain propositions are indeed dialetheias?

I beg to differ.

Re question 1: It is standardly assumed that classical logic can make a good fist of the task in question. (If there are problems, they are to the effect that it makes too much valid, not an insufficient amount.) But anything a classical logician can do, a dialetheic logician can do too (see section 8.5). In particular, if Σ is consistent and α follows from Σ classically, then $\Sigma \models_m \alpha$ too (see chapter 16). If Σ is inconsistent, all that one can do with it in classical logic is show it to be so, that is, show that Σ entails some explicit contradiction. Dialetheic logic can do that too (see section 8.6, theorem 0).[3]

Re question 2: Whether or not *LP* has a satisfying proof theory depends, of course, on what satisfies you. It certainly has proof procedures that are demonstrably sound and complete. (One is given in section 18.1.) Tennant subscribes to a proof-theoretic account of validity and meaning. A proof theory suitable for this end must have a very specific form (namely, one in some kind of natural deduction system, where the logical operators have introduction and elimination rules that are appropriately "balanced"). Whether or not dialetheic logic has such a proof procedure I do not know. But I do not, myself, subscribe to a proof theoretic account of validity. (See *DTBL*, section 11.3, for a critique of this, and an endorsement of a model theoretic account.) And I am not persuaded by the verificationist arguments to the effect that we need a proof theoretic account of meaning (see *DTBL*, section 4.4). I endorse the more usual truth-conditional account of meaning (as in Chapter 9).[4]

(1996); Denyer (1995), Priest (1996*a*); Eklund (2002), Beall and Priest (forthcoming); Shapiro (2002), Priest (2003); Field (2005), Priest (2005*a*); Beall and Ripley (2004), Armour-Garb and Priest (2005); Slater (2005), Priest (forthcoming g). See also Goodship (1996), Bromand (2002), and the essays in pt V of Priest, Beall, and Armour-Garb (2004).

[3] Tennant appears to cast doubt on this result (p. 374). But, as best I can understand his comments, they are to the effect that, when we can deduce from $\alpha \lor \beta$! from Σ, we have no way, in general, of knowing which limb of the disjunction obtains. This is true, but not relevant to the present issue.

[4] Indeed, there is a well known argument (due to Fitch) which appears to show that the verificationist principle that whatever is true is knowable entails that whatever is true is known—which would appear to be a *reductio* of verificationism. The only plausible way I know of avoiding the force of this argument is to be a dialetheist! (See Priest (forthcoming f).)

Re question 3: I am not entirely sure that I understand what this is supposed to mean. But I presume that the italicised 'inference' indicates an insistence on a proof theoretic, as opposed to a model theoretic, account of validity. I have already addressed this in the previous point.

Re question 4: Again, I am not entirely sure what Tennant has in mind here. As far as I am aware, all the arguments for contradictions in *In Contradiction* are dialetheically valid. In any case, even if they are not, they are classically valid; and any classically valid argument for a contradiction translates into a dialetheically valid one (section 8.6, theorem 0).[5]

I do not find Tennant's questions worrying, therefore.[6]

Next, the definition of validity of chapter 5 is criticised by Weir (2004), section 4, for being "one-sided", that is, for requiring only truth-preservation forwards. I do not find this a particularly telling point. If one is in a context where one wishes falsity to be preserved backwards, one can simply look at arguments, $\alpha_1, \ldots, \alpha_n/\beta$, where $\neg\beta \models \neg(\alpha_1 \wedge \ldots \wedge \alpha_n)$. More generally, one can define a stronger notion of logical consequence, $\Sigma \models' \alpha$, as follows:

$$\text{(if } \beta\rho 1 \text{ for all } \beta \in \Sigma \text{ then } \alpha\rho 1) \text{ and (if } \alpha\rho 0 \text{ then } \beta\rho 0 \text{ for some } \beta \in \Sigma)$$

Weir claims that the resulting notion of logical consequence is 'hopelessly restricted'. In fact, it is hardly weaker than *LP*. The main difference is that it is no longer the case that $\models' \alpha \vee \neg\alpha$; instead we have $\beta \wedge \neg\beta \models' \alpha \vee \neg\alpha$. Indeed, there are now no logical truths, but this can be rectified in various ways. The simplest is just to define $\models' \alpha$ not as $\phi \models' \alpha$ but as: for all ρ, $\alpha\rho 1$.

Finally, it has been pointed out that one can endorse the logic *LP* without being committed to its dialetheic semantics. In particular, one can give a semantics in which sentences may be ambiguous, defining validity in terms of disambiguations.[7] This may indeed be true; it is true; but this goes nowhere towards meeting the arguments for dialetheism. In any case, there seems to be little reason to believe, for most of the contradictions to which *In Contradiction* points, that they arise because of ambiguity. 'This sentence is false' for example, is

---

[5] Tennant indicated (in correspondence) that this is just a reference to sect. 7.3 of his paper, where he points out that the proof procedure given in the reference he cites is purely propositional. Quantifier tableau rules are given in sect. 18.1, and natural deduction rules are given in Priest (2002), sect. 6.4.

[6] Tennant has a variety of other arguments in his paper. The first concerns the logical absurdity constant. I am quite happy that there is a constant, $\perp$, such that $\perp \models \alpha$ for arbitrary α (see sect. 8.5). I just do not think that $\neg\alpha$ is equivalent to $\alpha \to \perp$ (see *DTBL*, sect. 4.7). (For a more detailed discussion of Tennant's critique here, see the 2nd edn of *BLT*, sect. 17.1.) In the final section of his paper, Tennant also criticises my account of the paradoxes of self reference by giving his own. But he does not address the arguments of the 1st edn that would appear to apply to his account. For example, he says that the liar sentence is 'radically truth-valueless' (p. 378), but he does not address the extended version of the paradox: this sentence is false or radically truth-valueless (sect. 1.3). Nor does he address the paradoxes that do not use the LEM, such as Berry's. Similarly, he claims that the "Gödel Paradox" shows that the notion of naive proof cannot be formalised. He does not address the considerations of sect. 3.2 as to why this is false or irrelevant.

[7] Variations on this theme can be found in Lewis (1982), Batens (2002), and Brown (2004).

hardly ambiguous in the way that 'He was hit by a bat' is. But even if it were, if there is no hope of disambiguating in practice, which would seem to be the case for such contradictions, there is effectively very little difference between such a view and dialetheism.[8]

20.3 THE EXTENDED LIAR PARADOX

Perhaps the topic related to dialetheism that has occasioned most flak is the Extended Liar Paradox. Let us now turn to this.

Chapter 1 argues against attempted consistent approaches to the Liar Paradox that they fall foul of versions of the paradox shaped specifically to take account of whatever consistent approach is advocated, by employing the very notions of that approach. (Thus, if one takes a paradoxical sentence to be neither true nor false, the appropriate version is the sentence 'This sentence is false or neither true nor false.') This invites a *tu quoque*, to the effect that a dialetheic solution falls to the same point.[9]

The thought is to concentrate on a sentence that says of itself that it is false and not true, false only. Let ξ be a sentence of the form[10]

$$F\langle\xi\rangle \wedge \neg T\langle\xi\rangle$$

ξ is either true or false, $T\langle\xi\rangle \vee F\langle\xi\rangle$. If ξ is true then, by the T-scheme, it is false and not true. So $T\langle\xi\rangle \wedge F\langle\xi\rangle \wedge \neg T\langle\xi\rangle$. If it is false, its negation is true, so $\neg F\langle\xi\rangle \vee T\langle\xi\rangle$. But by the exhaustion principle $\neg F\langle\xi\rangle \rightarrow T\langle\xi\rangle$. So in either case $T\langle\xi\rangle$, and so, as we have seen, $T\langle\xi\rangle \wedge F\langle\xi\rangle \wedge \neg T\langle\xi\rangle$ (and in the second case, $\neg F\langle\xi\rangle$ as well). This is a contradiction of the kind that will sink any consistent solution, but it obviously does not sink a dialetheic solution. The contradiction is exactly what one should expect to get in the context.

One may attempt to reformulate the situation in a more damaging way. Instead of talking of ξ as being true or false, we may talk of its semantic value. So let us write 'the value of $\langle\beta\rangle$' as $\mathrm{Val}\langle\beta\rangle$. Given $T\langle\alpha\rangle \vee F\langle\alpha\rangle$ and the LEM, it is not difficult to show that

Trichotomy $(T\langle\alpha\rangle \wedge \neg F\langle\alpha\rangle) \vee (T\langle\alpha\rangle \wedge F\langle\alpha\rangle) \vee (\neg T\langle\alpha\rangle \wedge F\langle\alpha\rangle)$

This suggests defining 'Val' as follows:

1. $\mathrm{Val}\langle\alpha\rangle = \{1\}$ iff $T\langle\alpha\rangle \wedge \neg F\langle\alpha\rangle$
2. $\mathrm{Val}\langle\alpha\rangle = \{1,0\}$ iff $T\langle\alpha\rangle \wedge F\langle\alpha\rangle$
3. $\mathrm{Val}\langle\alpha\rangle = \{0\}$ if $\neg T\langle\alpha\rangle \wedge F\langle\alpha\rangle$

---

[8] For further discussion, see Priest (1995b).

[9] In various forms, the argument is attempted by Smiley (1993), Everett (1993), Bromand (2002), and Littman and Simmons (2004).

[10] Angle brackets here are a name-forming device.

Now let ξ be

$$\text{Val}\langle\xi\rangle = \{0\}$$

$\text{Val}\langle\xi\rangle = \{1\} \vee \text{Val}\langle\xi\rangle = \{1,0\} \vee \text{Val}\langle\xi\rangle = \{0\}$. In the first two cases $T\langle\xi\rangle$, so by the T-schema $\text{Val}\langle\xi\rangle = \{0\}$. So either $\{0\} = \text{Val}\langle\xi\rangle = \{1\}$ or $\{0\} = \text{Val}\langle\xi\rangle = \{1,0\}$. In either case, $0 = 1$. So far all α, $\text{Val}\langle\alpha\rangle = \{1\}$, and everything is true. In the third case, $T\langle\xi\rangle$, by the T-schema, so $\text{Val}\langle\xi\rangle = \{1\}$ or $\text{Val}\langle\xi\rangle = \{1,0\}$. The result is the same.[11]

The conclusion of this argument is not just an inconsistency, but a triviality: everything is true. This is unacceptable to any rational dialetheist. But the problem with the argument is easy to see. Bearing in mind the original version of the argument, we should expect to have $T\langle\xi\rangle \wedge F\langle\xi\rangle \wedge \neg T\langle\xi\rangle$, and so both of $T\langle\xi\rangle \wedge F\langle\xi\rangle$ and $\neg T\langle\xi\rangle \wedge F\langle\xi\rangle$. That is, cases 2 and 3 of the definition of Val overlap. This is not, therefore, a good definition (any more than is a definition of a numerical function, f, such that $f(n) = 1$ if $n \leq 5$ and $f(n) = 0$ if $n \geq 5$).

Littman and Simmons (2004) give a twist to the argument by taking semantic values to be diagrams, not numbers. In particular, corresponding to the three cases of **Trichotomy**, we have the values $\boxed{T}$, $\boxed{F}$, and $\boxed{T \quad F}$, which they call E_1, E_2, and E_3, respectively. They then invite us to consider the sentence, ξ: $\langle\xi\rangle$ is completely and correctly evaluated by E_2.[12] That is, I take it, ξ is $\text{Val}\langle\xi\rangle = E_2$. The reply is exactly the same: the cases are not mutually exclusive. Changing the values from numbers to pictures changes nothing essential.[13]

Handling functions in a logic that admits contradictions is a sensitive matter. A way to sidestep their use is to employ relations instead of functions. Thus, in the case of semantic values, we can eschew the function Val in favour of the relation, Rel, so that[14]

$$\text{Rel}(\langle\alpha\rangle, 1) \text{ iff } T\langle\alpha\rangle$$

$$\text{Rel}(\langle\alpha\rangle, 0) \text{ iff } F\langle\alpha\rangle$$

[11] This is the way the argument is formulated by Smiley (1993). He takes 'Val' to be truth-in-an-interpretation, rather than truth *simpliciter*. This raises extra, and irrelevant, complexities.

[12] I change their notation to bring it into line with that used in this essay.

[13] In the first part of their paper, Littman and Simmons marshal some other objections against a dialetheic solution to the semantic paradoxes. One of these concerns pragmatic versions of the Liar, such as 'This sentence is not acceptable.' This sort of case is dealt with in *DTBL*, ch. 5. Their other main complaint is that an inconsistent semantic theory is 'unintelligible'. It may be fine to say, for example, that ξ is both true and false, but to say that ξ is both true and not true tells us nothing about its status, since the second conjunct 'takes back' what the first one says (p. 319). It does not: negation is not cancellation (see *DTBL*, sect. 1.13). The second conjunct adds *more* information. And if it be retorted that such a contradiction cannot be understood, then all I can say is: get your understander a new logic-processor. (The joke is an old one. In the early days of the Mind/Brain identity theory, J. J. C. Smart is reputed to have said, to a critic who claimed that he just could not undertand what it would be for a mental state to have a physical location, 'Get your understander rewired.')

[14] Littman and Simmons (2004) construct a whole ingenious hierarchy of graphical truth values, corresponding to contradictory sentences of various kinds. Putting the matter as follows makes it clear that there are only two truth values: true and false. Different sentences just relate to these in different (consistent and inconsistent) ways.

ξ now becomes a sentence of the form $\text{Rel}(\langle\xi\rangle, 0) \land \neg\text{Rel}(\langle\xi\rangle, 1)$, from which we can infer $\text{Rel}(\langle\xi\rangle, 1) \land \text{Rel}(\langle\xi\rangle, 0) \land \neg\text{Rel}(\langle\xi\rangle, 1)$—as one would expect—but go no further.[15]

A natural thought at this point is as follows. If we have set abstracts at our disposal, we can obtain an appropriate function by invoking these, since we can define $\text{Val}\langle\alpha\rangle$ as $\{x\colon \text{Rel}(\langle\alpha\rangle, x)\}$. But, as should be expected, the same problem now emerges at a different point. We have

$$(\text{Rel}(\langle\alpha\rangle, 1) \land \neg\text{Rel}(\langle\alpha\rangle, 0)) \lor (\text{Rel}(\langle\alpha\rangle, 1) \land \text{Rel}(\langle\alpha\rangle, 0))$$
$$\lor (\neg\text{Rel}(\langle\alpha\rangle, 1) \land \text{Rel}(\langle\alpha\rangle, 0))$$

And 1 and 0 are the only values:

$$(*) \quad \forall x(\text{Rel}(\langle\alpha\rangle, x) \to (x = 1 \lor x = 0)),$$

In the third case of the paradoxical reasoning,

$$\neg\text{Rel}(\langle\alpha\rangle, 1) \land \text{Rel}(\langle\alpha\rangle, 0)),$$

we need to establish that $\text{Val}\langle\xi\rangle = \{0\}$, i.e. $\{x\colon \text{Rel}(\langle\xi\rangle, x)\} = \{0\}$, so that we can apply the T-schema. Thus, we have to prove that

1. $x = 0 \to \text{Rel}(\langle\xi\rangle, x)$
2. $\text{Rel}(\langle\xi\rangle, x) \to x = 0$

What happens now depends on what we take the conditional employed in 1 and 2 to be. (This is inherited from the appropriate conditional in a paraconsistent set theory.) But whatever it is, the reasoning does not go through. Thus, for example, with respect to 2: given (*), however the conditional is interpreted, we can infer that $\text{Rel}(\langle\xi\rangle, x) \to (x = 0 \lor (\text{Rel}(\langle\xi\rangle, x) \land x = 1))$ and so $\text{Rel}(\langle\xi\rangle, x) \to (x = 0 \lor \text{Rel}(\langle\xi\rangle, 1))$. We may even be able to get to $\text{Rel}(\langle\xi\rangle, x) \to (x = 0 \lor \text{Rel}(\langle\xi\rangle, 1)) \land \neg\text{Rel}(\langle\xi\rangle, 1))$. But there is no way of getting to $\text{Rel}(\langle\xi\rangle, x) \to x = 0$ without the disjunctive syllogism. Since $\text{Rel}(\langle\xi\rangle, 1) \land \neg\text{Rel}(\langle\xi\rangle, 1)$, this is hopeless.[16]

A final suggestion at this point is that formulating the troublesome sentence as $\text{Rel}(\langle\xi\rangle, 0) \land \neg\text{Rel}(\langle\xi\rangle, 1)$ is too weak, since it does not *require* ξ to take only the value 0. What we need, it might be thought, is a sentence, ξ, of the form $\text{Rel}(\langle\xi\rangle, 0) \land \forall x(\text{Rel}(\langle\xi\rangle, x) \to x = 0)$. But now, in the crucial case of the reasoning (the third, where $\text{Rel}(\langle\xi\rangle, 0) \land \neg\text{Rel}(\langle\xi\rangle, 1)$), we again have to prove that $\text{Rel}(\langle\xi\rangle, x) \to x = 0$; and this is impossible for the same reasons as before.

[15] One can, in fact, show that a theory with a truth predicate and the relation Rel is non-trivial. The construction mirrors the non-triviality construction for the T-schema, as given in Priest (2002), sects. 8.1 and 8.2. We dispense with a truth predicate in favour of the binary relation $\text{Rel}(x, y)$. In the iterative construction, the extension of this predicate remains constant unless x is a closed sentence and y is 0 or 1. We put $\langle\langle\alpha\rangle, 1\rangle$ in the extension of Rel at level k if α is eventually true by k, and $\langle\langle\alpha\rangle, 0\rangle$ in the anti-extension if $\langle\alpha\rangle$ is eventually false by k. The fixed point is then constructed in the usual way. Tx can be defined as $\text{Rel}(x, 1)$, and Fx as $\text{Rel}(x, 0)$.

[16] Nor will it help to point out that the reasoning is valid in ZF (see sect. 18.4): Rel is not in the language of ZF.

This is the version of the argument given by Bromand (2002). To overcome the problem, he simply helps himself to the required principle, taking it (or, more accurately, its generalisation to the three cases) as an axiom. Specifically, he endorses (**):

$$(\mathrm{Rel}(\langle\alpha\rangle, 1) \wedge \forall x(\mathrm{Rel}(\langle\alpha\rangle, x) \rightarrow x = 1))\vee$$

$$(\mathrm{Rel}(\langle\alpha\rangle, 1) \wedge \mathrm{Rel}(\langle\alpha\rangle, 0) \wedge \forall x(\mathrm{Rel}(\langle\alpha\rangle, x) \rightarrow (x = 1 \vee x = 0)))\vee$$

$$(\mathrm{Rel}(\langle\alpha\rangle, 0) \wedge \forall x(\mathrm{Rel}(\langle\alpha\rangle, x) \rightarrow x = 0))$$

If one does this, then the argument of course goes through; but there is no reason why one should endorse such an axiom. Bromand notes that dialetheists are committed to the claim that every sentence is true only, false only, or both true and false; and he suggests that this is what (**) expresses. It does not; it is **Trichotomy** that expresses this fact. True, it does not express the fact that the only candidates for the value of α are 1 and 0. But this is what (*) expresses.

Bromand is unhappy with this; he thinks that (*) is not strong enough. He illustrates his worry with respect to the first case of the trichotomy:[17]

[A]ccording to

$$\mathrm{Rel}(\langle\alpha\rangle, 1) \wedge \neg\mathrm{Rel}(\langle\alpha\rangle, 0) \wedge \forall x(\mathrm{Rel}(\langle\alpha\rangle, x) \rightarrow (x = 1 \vee x = 0))$$

α is true, not false, and either true or false. Unfortunately, 'α is only true' does not follow from this.

By 'α is only true', here, he means $\forall x(\mathrm{Rel}(\langle\alpha\rangle, x) \rightarrow x = 0)$. Quite so. If that is what you mean by 'true only', it does not. Use the words in that way if you wish, but this is not something to which dialetheism is committed. Indeed, it is not true for ξ by dialetheic lights. Since $\mathrm{Rel}(\langle\xi\rangle, 1)$ is true and $1 = 0$ is not, the conditional $\mathrm{Rel}(\langle\xi\rangle, 1) \rightarrow 1 = 0$, and so $\forall x(\mathrm{Rel}(\langle\xi\rangle, x) \rightarrow x = 0)$, is not true. Of course, in a dialetheic context this does not rule out its being true as well, but it does show that there is no legitimate presumption of this.

20.4 EXPRESSABILITY

This brings us to another objection to dialetheism that has been made by several writers.[18] The thought here is that the dialetheist has no way of expressing the claim that α really isn't true. For whatever they say, it is *logically* compatible with this that α *is* true, so they may subscribe to that too. The point is sometimes made in terms of communication. Suppose that you say α. I cannot say anything, be it $\neg\alpha$ or anything else, that indicates disagreement with you. For I might subscribe

---

[17] Page 746; I change his notation to bring it into line with that used here.
[18] Among others: T. Parsons (1990), Everett (1996), Olin (2003), pp. 35 f., and Shapiro (2004).

to these *and* α. Thus, it is useless to add 'I am expressing disagreement with you'; for I might agree with you too.[19]

The challenge is a quite general one, but it assumes a particular significance in the context of the semantic paradoxes. As chapter 1 argues, the only way that various consistent accounts of the paradoxes can be maintained is by taking some notion, to the legitimacy of which the proponent of the solution is committed, not to be expressible in the language of the paradox. Were it present, contradiction would ensue. It might well be thought that dialetheists are in the same boat. If they could express the thought that something is not ("*really* is not") true, unacceptable consequences might be expected to follow, as we have just been discussing in the previous section.

The objection is misguided, however. A dialetheist can express the claim that something, α, is not true—in those very words, $\neg T\langle \alpha \rangle$. What she cannot do is ensure that the words she utters behave consistently: even if $\neg T\langle \alpha \rangle$ holds, $\alpha \wedge \neg T\langle \alpha \rangle$ may yet hold. But in fact, a classical logician (or anyone else who subscribes to the validity of Explosion) can do no better. He can endorse $\neg T\langle \alpha \rangle$, but this does not prevent his endorsing α as well. Of course, if he does (and assuming the T-schema), he will be committed to everything. But classical logic, as such, is no guard against this. What this shows is that all the classical logician can do by way of saying something to indicate that α is not to be accepted is to assert something that will collapse things into triviality if he does accept α. But the dialetheist can do this too. She can assert $\alpha \rightarrow \perp$ (or $\alpha \rightarrow F$, as this is written in section 8.5).

But, it will be pointed out, dialetheists, like everybody else, do often communicate the fact that they don't accept something, α, and they do not do this by asserting $\alpha \rightarrow \perp$. How is this possible? It can be done in two ways. The first is by the employment of conversational implicatures of the Gricean kind. One of the conventions that governs conversation is to give all the relevant information. Suppose you say to me 'How many siblings do you have' and I reply 'I have two brothers.' This may be true, but the answer is definitely misleading if the whole truth is that I have two brothers and one sister. In virtue of my answer, you may reasonably infer that I have no sisters. In the same way, suppose you ask me whether α and I aver that ¬α. If I believed $\alpha \wedge \neg\alpha$, the answer would be decidedly incomplete. You may reasonably infer, therefore, that I do not accept α, though what I say does not entail this.[20]

The other way a difference of views about α may be communicated is as follows. Suppose that you assert α. There is nothing I can *assert* that entails

---

[19] A naive person might argue against the possibility of irony, in a similar way, on the ground that it would make it impossible to convey agreement with somebody. Suppose you assert α, and I utter 'Indeed, α'. This need not express agreement, since my words may be ironical. And adding 'I wasn't being ironical' does not help: that may be even more ironical. Despite this, expressing agreement obviously is compatible with the possibility of irony. Expressing disagreement is compatible with the possibility of dialetheism—and ultimately for much the same reasons.

[20] As Shapiro (2004), p. 339, observes, this does not entail that I reject α; I might simply be undecided.

disagreement (as opposed to conversationally implicating it). But I can *deny* α, which will do the trick. Denial is a speech act distinct from asserting (like commanding or questioning); and, post-Fregean wisdom to the contrary, it is *sui generis*, not to be reduced to asserting the negation of α. The matter is discussed more fully in *DTBL*, chapter 6, so I need say no more about it here.

The most recent episode in the debate about expressability is Shapiro (2004).[21] After rehearsing some of the above considerations, he observes, quite correctly, that neither implicature nor denial can act on embedded sentences. He says (pp. 339 f.):

> Suppose that Karl says 'β', and his dialetheist friend Seymore does not want to disagree (yet), but he wonders if Karl is mistaken. Seymore might want to assert a conditional: 'if Karl is mistaken then φ'. How can Seymore express this? ... The dialetheist just does not have a statement equivalent to 'Karl is mistaken in asserting β.'

But this is just wrong. The dialetheist has a statement exactly equivalent to 'Karl is mistaken in asserting β', namely that very sentence. As Shapiro notes, this does not rule out logically Karl's not being mistaken, too. As I have already noted, nothing that *anyone*—even a classical logician—does can enforce consistency; but that is a different point. The question was which sentence has the propositional content that Karl is mistaken. Exactly that one.

Appearing to concede this point (perhaps), Shapiro asks exactly what one ought to do if one takes it that Karl is both mistaken and not mistaken about β— that he is right and wrong about β. Since he is right, one ought to assert β; since he is wrong, one ought to deny it; one cannot do both. We have a dilemma. Well, such is life sometimes. (The matter is discussed at length in *DTBL*, chapter 6, so again I need discuss it no further here.) Admitting this possibility, Shapiro says (p. 341) 'Such may be life, but I hope not.' You can, of course, always hope.

Shapiro goes on to worry about the notions of 'simple truth and simple falsehood', that is, by definition, being true but not false, or false but not true ($T\langle\alpha\rangle \wedge \neg F\langle\alpha\rangle$ and $F\langle\alpha\rangle \wedge \neg T\langle\alpha\rangle$). He says (p. 341) that to express the notions in those very words will 'not do the required work'. Exactly what the required work is supposed to be is not stated, and is unclear to me. But the problem he foresees is clear enough. Something (as we already noted in the last section) can be simply false and true as well (and vice versa): $F\langle\alpha\rangle \wedge \neg T\langle\alpha\rangle \wedge T\langle\alpha\rangle$. Well, nothing can force consistency; we have already been over that ground.

Shapiro points out that, if one subscribes to the exclusion schema, $F\langle\alpha\rangle \rightarrow \neg T\langle\alpha\rangle$, then to say that something is simply false is equivalent just to saying that it is false. Hence the notions of simple truth and falsehood (p. 342)

> ...do not do their work. They do not distinguish *any* dialetheias from those sentences that we would like to say are false but not true, or true but not false.

It seems to me that this objection is entirely question-begging. If one does subscribe to the exclusion scheme, there *is* no distinction—nor, therefore any

---

[21] In what follows, page references are to this. All italics in quotations are original.

work to be done to draw it. (One should note, here, that we are talking about truth/falsity *simpliciter*, not truth/falsity in an interpretation. Truth/falsity in an interpretation is quite different. Even if one endorses the exclusion schema, this does not entail that, for any given interpretation, ρ, $\langle\alpha\rangle\rho 0 \rightarrow \neg\langle\alpha\rangle\rho 1$.)

In any case, I do not accept the exclusion schema (section 4.9), and I do not think that $F\langle\alpha\rangle$ entails $F\langle\alpha\rangle \wedge \neg T\langle\alpha\rangle$. In considering this possibility, Shapiro notes that for a liar sentence in the form $\xi: \neg T\langle\xi\rangle$ we have $T\langle\xi\rangle \wedge \neg T\langle\xi\rangle$, and by the exhaustion principle $(\neg T\langle\xi\rangle \rightarrow F\langle\xi\rangle)$, $T\langle\xi\rangle \wedge \neg T\langle\xi\rangle \wedge F\langle\xi\rangle$. This particular sentence is therefore simply false and true. He then says (p. 342):

I would have thought that the dialetheist would want to *deny* that the Original Liar is simply false. The point of introducing the notion of simple falsehood in the first place was to *distinguish* some falsehoods from at least *paradigm* dialetheias. The notion of simple falsehood fails to do this.

I am not sure what the first place was in this case, nor, therefore, what its point was. But since $F\langle\alpha\rangle$ and $F\langle\alpha\rangle \wedge \neg T\langle\alpha\rangle$ are not logically equivalent, there is a distinction between being false and being simply false. The fact that some sentences (be they paradigm dialetheias or anything else) may be in both camps is just one of those contradictory facts of life that populate the dialetheic landscape. ξ is simply false—and it is true as well. But as we have already noted, asserting merely the first conjunct of this is misleading.[22]

Similar issues arise concerning the notion of being a dialetheia, of being both true and false, $T\langle\alpha\rangle \wedge F\langle\alpha\rangle$, and Shapiro goes on the discuss these. To say that something is not a dialetheia is to say that $\neg(T\langle\alpha\rangle \wedge F\langle\alpha\rangle)$, that is, $\neg T\langle\alpha\rangle \vee \neg F\langle\alpha\rangle$. This follows from the exclusion schema (and the LEM). If one subscribes to the schema, then one has to accept that there are no dialetheias. Since there are, this is, of course, a contradiction. It is not clear to me why this is supposed to be a worse contradiction than that engendered by any contradiction, $\alpha \wedge \neg\alpha$, in the light of the logical truth of $\neg(\alpha \wedge \neg\alpha)$. (Recall, again, that we are talking about truth, not truth in an interpretation.) But, as before, I do not accept the exclusion principle (nor, therefore, the claim that there are no dialetheias). $\neg(Tx \wedge Fx)$ expresses (non-vacuously) the claim that x is not a dialetheia. Some dialetheias *will* satisfy it; but this is just to say that we cannot force the predicate to behave consistently. By now this is very old news.[23] Shapiro tries to put a new spin on it (p. 344):

Priest might protest that I am demanding a *consistent* use of the property of not being a dialetheia, and then add that this is not possible, nor is it desirable... Fair enough (at least for the sake of argument). The classes of dialetheias, simple truths and simple falsehoods will overlap in any case. But we have just seen that... the overlap is too

---

[22] Shapiro continues (p. 342): 'The point is general. Let α be any sentence that is not true, so that $\neg T\langle\alpha\rangle$. Then it follows that is false. So α is false and not true, so is *simply* false. And this holds whether or not is also true... The dialetheist must hold that every dialetheia that is not true is simply false'. Indeed so.   [23] As old as sect. 8.2.

extensive for the distinction to be useful . . . [T]he notion is all but useless if we have to say that every untruth is also a non-dialetheia, including the Original Liar and nearly every other dialetheia that we run across in the course of thinking about this stuff . . . I would have thought that Priest would deny that the Original Liar is a non-dialetheia, rather than asserting that it is one.

Shapiro overplays his hand here. There is indeed an overlap in the categories of being and not being a dialetheia. But the only denizen of the overlap we have on the table is $\xi \ (\neg T\langle \xi \rangle)$. And this is very special. By its particular properties, it is true and it is not true—and so not (true and false). But the same is not the case for any other of the standard paradoxes of self reference (including the liar in the form 'this sentence is false'). (See the comments on chapter 1 in section 19.3.) And I am quite happy to assert that ξ is a non-dialetheia, provided that I can add that it is as well.

Shapiro has one last crack at the thought that $\neg(T\langle \alpha \rangle \wedge F\langle \alpha \rangle)$ expresses the claim that α is not a dialetheia. If so, $\neg \exists x(Tx \wedge Fx)$ expresses the claim that there are no dialetheias. But this (p. 345) 'is equivalent to the equivalence of untruth and falsehood', which would appear to mean something quite different. Indeed it does. Given the LEM, $\forall x(\neg Tx \leftrightarrow Fx)$ entails $\neg \exists x(Tx \wedge Fx)$; but the entailment does not go in the other direction. (Given the world-semantics for $\rightarrow$, $\forall x(\neg Tx \leftrightarrow Fx)$, tells you something about all worlds; $\neg \exists x(Tx \wedge Fx)$ tells you something about only one of them.)

In the final part of his paper, Shapiro transplants the thoughts above into a model theoretic context, where what is at issue is truth in an interpretation. I do not contest the mathematical results he argues for; the material raises only one novel philosophical point. The model theoretic truth/falsity conditions for negation are

$\langle \neg \alpha \rangle \rho 1$ iff $\langle \alpha \rangle \rho 0$

$\langle \neg \alpha \rangle \rho 0$ iff $\langle \alpha \rangle \rho 1$

Suppose one accepts the model theoretic analogue of the exclusion principle as well:

$(*)\langle \neg \alpha \rangle \rho 1 \rightarrow \neg \langle \alpha \rangle \rho 1$

(the converse is granted). It follows that every theory is consistent (p. 351). The notion of consistency therefore becomes vacuous.

All very well, but from a dialetheic perspective $(*)$ would seem to be entirely unmotivated. Shapiro disagrees. Its absence is simply 'an artefact of the formalism' (p. 350). Specifically (p. 352),

> The classical logician has a well-developed, coherent, and powerful homophonic model-theory, but this is denied to the dialetheist. The dialetheist needs to show that the clauses for '¬' really do reflect the essential properties of *negation*. Otherwise the semantics is artificial.

Now, model theory is certainly not denied to the dialetheist; what is doing all the work here is the word 'homophonic'. The point therefore simply reduces to the claim that paraconsistent negation is not *really* negation. But in a debate between a paraconsistent logician and a classical logician, it is exactly the correct semantic conditions for negation that are at issue. And the onus is just as much on the classical logician to argue that the truth conditions they prefer are correct as it is on the dialetheist to do the same.[24] Moreover, once we are countenancing truth value gaps or gluts, homophonic truth conditions would seem to have little appeal. If α is a gap, it is not true, but $\neg\alpha$ is not true either. If α is a glut, $\neg\alpha$ is true, but α is *also* true. Of course, this does not settle the matter in a dialetheic context. But one can hardly claim that the rejection of the homophonic conditions is simply an artefact. In this context, it is enforcing homophony which is patently artifactual.

20.5 MOTION

Much of the criticism of dialetheism has fallen on a dialetheic account of the paradoxes of self reference—and especially the Liar Paradox. Indeed, in the minds of some critics, dialetheism just is dialetheism about these paradoxes. The paradoxes certainly make a strong case for the position, but dialetheism is a quite general logical/metaphysical view, and not to be identified with any one of its possible applications. Several more of its applications are rehearsed in *BLT*, and these hardly exhaust the possibilities. (The area of aesthetics, for example, where we are wont to make inconsistent judgements concerning art works, would seem to be a fruitful ground for dialetheism.[25] There are also numerous issues in the Asian philosophical traditions that beg to be considered in the light of it.)

Of the applications of dialetheism discussed in the first edition of *In Contradiction*, other than the paradoxes of self reference, the one that has drawn the most comment is the account of motion in chapter 12. In particular, this has been criticised by Tooley (1988) and Mortensen (2004), each of whom espouses a consistent but non-orthodox account of motion.[26]

Tooley takes motion to be an instantaneous theoretical (= unobservable) property of a moving object. The state of the object at any time is consistent, however. In section 2.3 of his paper he levels seven(!) criticisms against the Hegelean account. These do not strike me as persuasive, for the following reasons.

1. The first objection is that the account is committed to dialetheism. In the present context, this clearly carries little weight.

2. The second is that the account is incomplete, since it fails to specify what, exactly, the area of indeterminacy at t, θ_t, is. This detail can be filled in in numerous different ways. A plausible one is to take θ_t to be an interval whose right-hand endpoint is t, and whose length is $k.|dx/dt|$ (or zero if the derivative is not defined), where we may take k to be a fundamental constant, like Planck's constant.

[24] For my attempt to discharge the obligation, see *DTBL*, ch. 4.
[25] See Cooke (forthcoming).
[26] Some of Mortensen's criticisms are raised in a different context in Mortensen (1997).

3. Tooley's third objection goes as follows. '[C]onsider two objects that have the same velocity at some instant, and that do not differ with respect to their intrinsic properties. It would seem that their instantaneous states should be qualitatively indistinguishable at the time in question.' But they need not be, since, though they have the same velocity at the instant, t, they may yet be at different points at times within θ_r. Hence their state descriptions as t will be different. This argument simply begs the question. In the example given, just because the two objects have different state descriptions at t, they precisely do not have the same intrinsic properties at that instant.

4. The fourth objection is to the effect that the account 'does not explain what it is for an object to have a certain velocity'. Now, it is true that the velocity of an object cannot be read off from its instantaneous state description. But neither is the state description meant to fill this role. If the equation of motion of the object is given by $x = f(t)$, the velocity of the object is, as usual, $df(t)/dt$. As chapter 12 makes clear, the Hegelean representation of motion does not abolish the standard representation: it adds to it.

5. The fifth objection goes as follows. Consider an object which moves according to the equation $x = f(t)$. Consider some time, t_0. It is possible for the object to have been at rest and in motion at different times in θ_{t_0}, at the point $f(t_0)$. When this is the case, 'information about the points that it has occupied during the relevant interval will not suffice to determine whether the particle is at rest, or moving, at the time in question'. The sort of situation that Tooley envisages can be illustrated by a particle that moves in accord with the equation $x = t^2(t-1)$, where, we may suppose, $\theta_0 = \{0\}$ and $\theta_1 = [0, 1]$. At $t = 0$, $x = 0$, $dx/dt = 0$, and the state description of the particle is consistent. At $t = 1$, $x = 0$, $dx/dt \neq 0$, and the state description is inconsistent. Hence, according to the Hegelean account, the particle is in motion at $t = 1$, The fact that it was at rest at $x = 0$, when $t = 0$ and $0 \in \theta_1$, is completely irrelevant. Neither would there seem to be anything counter-intuitive about this state of affairs.

6. The sixth objection invites us to consider a particle that moves according to the equation

$x = 0$ if $t < 0$

$x = t$ if $t \geq 0$

The orthodox account cannot answer the question of whether or not the particle is in motion at $x = 0$, since its derivative is not defined there. Can the Hegelean account do better? It can. Assuming that θ_t is all to the past of t, the state description at $t = 0$ is consistent. Hence the particle is at rest—which is what Tooley himself argues it to be. Tooley also asks us to consider a possible world where a force is applied before $t = 0$ but acceleration commences only at $t = 0$. He concludes that in such worlds the velocity of the object at $t = 0$ is what it is after $t = 0$, namely 1. I think this is a complete non sequitur. The fact that the object has non-zero acceleration at $t = 0$ entails nothing about its velocity at that time.

7. The final objection is to the effect that any account of motion that is an alternative to the orthodox account must explain why the orthodox account 'works as well as it does'. In the case of the Hegelean account, this is easy. As I have already noted in connection with objection 4, the Hegelean account incorporates the functional descriptions of motion, and the corresponding computation of derivatives. (It just adds to these.) Thus, it incorporates anything that can be achieved therewith.

Turning to Tooley's own account, he offers (in section 4 of his paper) six arguments. Since he takes himself to have disposed of the Hegelean account at this point, his arguments target the orthodox account. In fact, all the arguments attack, in one way or another, the thought that the state of motion is relational, and so is not intrinsic to the instant. This is all grist to the Hegelean mill. The arguments therefore provide no reason to prefer Tooley's account to the Hegelean account.

What Tooley does not discuss is Zeno's Arrow Paradox. This is one of the major arguments for the Hegelean account. Does Tooley's account fare any better than the orthodox account on this matter? No. Even though it takes motion to be intrinsic to an instant, it is still the case, for him, that no advance on the journey is made at an instant. How it advances at all is, therefore, just as puzzling as before. In fact, if anything, Tooley's account is in worse shape than the orthodox account. As we saw in section 12.2, Russell, rightly or wrongly, took the paradox to be solved by rejecting instantaneous states of motion. Even this step is not open to Tooley.

Mortensen's account and criticisms are quite different. He contrasts the Hegelean account of motion with that of the great seventh-century Buddhist logician Dharmakīrti, and comes down on the side of Dharmakīrti. Central to Dharmakīrti's account is the claim that all things that exist, exist for only an instant. But in the world of change each existent thing behaves consistently at any instant.

The most important thing to note here is that the contrast between the two accounts (mine and Dharmakīrti's) is ill posed. There are two quite distinct issues here. The first is whether reality is composed of instantaneous things or continua. The second is whether or not the state of an object in motion—whether that object persists through time or is composed of instantaneous parts—is consistent. There are, therefore, four possibilities concerning theories of objects in motion:

State Object	Consistent	Inconsistent
Persistent	A	B
Instantaneous	C	D

The orthodox Russellean account is of type A. The Hegelean account is of type B. Dharmakīrti's account is of type C. As far as I know, nobody has espoused a theory of type D, but it is certainly quite possible. According to such an account, all objects are instantaneous, but those that constitute a body at rest have consistent states at an instant, while those that constitute a body in motion have inconsistent states at that instant.

Now the important thing, as far as I am concerned, is whether we should be in the first or the second column. The metaphysics that goes with the bottom row is quite different from the metaphysics that goes with the top row; but as far as the accounts of motion go, this is not particularly important.

Dharmakīrti certainly has arguments to the effect that we ought to be in the bottom row;[27] but he does not, as far as I am aware, have any arguments to the effect that we ought to be in the lefthand column, other than a general adherence to the LNC, which counts for little in the present context.[28] Moreover, the considerations marshalled in chapter 12 that push us towards the righthand column are independent of which row we are in. The theories in the lefthand column, since they deny an intrinsic state of change, produce versions of the cinematic account of change, with its counter-intuitive consequences. Indeed, Dharmakīrti's account is an extreme form of the cinematic account. Each state of the world is replaced by an absolutely distinct one—not even any of the objects are the same.

And Mortensen, like Tooley, does not discuss the Arrow Paradox. But unless we apply something like the Spread Hypothesis, which will generate inconsistencies, and so push us into the second column, we have no solution to this. An object in motion must make some progress in an instant. Hence at each instant something, be it a continuant or an instantaneous part of an object, must occupy more than one place, and so be in a contradictory state. In fact, elsewhere Mortensen has actually strengthened the Arrow argument.[29] He points out that, since at each instant the object in motion makes no advance, its advance is non-existent. It follows that its advance at the totality of instants is also non-existent. Even an infinite number of non-existents cannot add up to an existent! Hence it does not move.

Mortensen raises one further objection to the Hegelean account in the third main section of his paper. He argues that since, in Relativity Theory, whether or

---

[27] Not that I find the argument cited by Mortensen in the second main section of his paper persuasive. This is as follows. Let a_1 and a_2 be the (parts of) an object in motion at t_1 and t_2, respectively. Then a_1 is at x_1 and a_2 is at x_2, and so not at x_1. Since a_1 is at x_1 and a_2 is not, a_1 and a_2 are distinct. From a dialetheic perspective, the argument is fallacious. We certainly have $\{a = b, Pa\} \models Pb$, but we don't have the contraposed form: $\{Pa, \neg Pb\} \not\models a \neq b$. (To see this, just take a model with one world, where 'a' and 'b' both denote the same object, which satisfies P and its negation, and where identity behaves consistently.) Even from a non-dialetheic perspective, the argument is dubious, however. a_1 and a_2 *both* have the properties of of being-at-x_1-at-t_1 and being-at-x_2-at-t_2. Mortensen himself raises problems for the bottom row in the later part of his paper.

[28] Mortensen has an argument, in the second main section of his paper, based on the assumption that, for me, non-zero velocity is not sufficient for motion. But this appears to be based on a misunderstanding. I do think that non-zero velocity is sufficient for motion (though zero-velocity is not sufficient for rest). If $dx/dt \neq 0$ at t_0, then the state description of the object at t_0 is inconsistent, so it is in motion. It is on the Russellean account of motion that non-zero velocity is not sufficient for (an intrinsic state of) motion.   [29] Mortensen (2002), sect. 6.

not something is in motion is frame-relative, 'Priest's theory is not relativistically invariant'. This is not true. All that follows is that the interval 0_p and so the state description of the object, is frame dependent. This is no more surprising than that velocity itself is frame dependent.

I conclude that neither Tooley's nor Mortensen's critique of the Hegelean account of motion succeeds.

20.6 CONTRADICTIONS IN THE WORLD

Let me finish by commenting on one final matter. Dialetheism is simply the view that some contradictions are true. That is, there are some sentences (statements, propositions, or whatever one takes truth-bearers to be), α, such that both α and $\neg\alpha$ are true. This is a view about language (or language-like entities). One may therefore ask 'does it follow that there are contradictions in the world'? In one quite unproblematic sense it does. If something is true, there must be something that makes it so. Call this the world. If some contradictions are true, then the world must be such as to make this the case. In this sense, the world is contradictory.

What it is in the world that makes something true is another matter. It might be just that our concepts have such and such a structure, or that our words have such and such a meaning. It is natural to suppose that the truth of a paradox of self reference is determined in this way (provided that it has no contingent premises). This might not be the only thing, however. The contradictions of motion are due, no doubt, to our concept of motion, but there would be no contradictions unless things in the world moved. In a world where everything was frozen there would be none. Similarly, if there are laws of the form 'no person in category A is obliged to do X' and 'every person in category B must do X', whether or not there is a person who is in both category A and category B may be a quite contingent matter. The world, then, may be the world of spatio-temporal objects and their physical properties. But whatever it is, if dialetheism is true, the world is such as to make it so. In this sense, the world is contradictory.

Whether the world is contradictory in any more profound sense is not such a straightforward matter. Indeed, beyond the sense I have given to it, it is not even clear what the claim means. It is not uncommon to hear it said, though, that reality itself is consistent; if there are dialetheias, these arise only because our language/concepts engage with it in an inconsistent way. (Compare this with the view that there is no vagueness in reality; vagueness arises only because of a certain indeterminacy in our language.) Mares (2004) distinguishes between *metaphysical* dialetheism and *semantic* dialetheism. Metaphysical dialetheism holds that 'there are things in the world that are actually inconsistent'; semantic dialetheism holds that 'there are no inconsistencies in things but . . . inconsistencies arise because of the relationship between language and the world' (p. 265). Mares endorses semantic dialetheism,[30] and cites me as a metaphysical dialetheist.

To illustrate further the distinction he has in mind, he cites accounts of each kind. First, metaphysical dialetheism: suppose that one is a traditional correspondence theorist. Then the truth of α and $\neg\alpha$ will correspond to facts in extra-linguistic reality. In particular, then, there must be "negative facts"—facts that make negated sentences true—which may operate independently of the corresponding "positive fact". (A detailed articulation of such a theory can be found in *DTBL*, section 2.7.) Next, semantic dialetheism: one may note that a dialetheia will arise if a notion is over-defined. Thus, suppose that we define the predicate '*x* is an Adult' to be true of persons iff they are 16 or over, and to be false of persons iff they are 18 or under. Then, though the facts about people and their ages are consistent enough, a 17-year-old will be both an Adult and not an Adult. One might hold that all dialetheias arise because of (implicit) definitions of this kind.

Drawing the distinction between metaphysical and semantic dialetheism in general terms, however, is not so straightforward. Let me do what I can.

To be a metaphysical dialetheist, one must suppose that it makes sense to talk about reality itself, as opposed to what is said about it. That is, one must suppose that

1. There is an extra-linguistic reality

Next, this reality must comprise things that are propositional in some sense, or the talk of its being consistent or inconsistent would make no sense. (Thus, if reality were just constituted by objects such as tables and chairs, saying that it was consistent or inconsistent would be a simple category mistake; see section 11.1.) So we must have that

2. Reality is constituted by facts

or by fact-like entities such as objects-cum-properties. Even given 2, there is still nothing consistent or inconsistent simply in a bunch of facts. There must therefore be more to the matter than this; there must be something within the structure of facts that corresponds to negation in language. It must be the case that

3. There are polarities within facts

That is, if f^+ is a possible fact, say one that would make α true, there must be a corresponding one, f^-, that would make $\neg\alpha$ true.

Given all these conditions, metaphysical dialetheism makes sense, and is the view that for some f both f^+ and f^- obtain/exist/are actual, or however one wishes to phrase the matter.

Semantic dialetheism, as defined by Mares, says that 'there are no inconsistencies in things'. This can be interpreted in different ways. One is to the effect

---

[30] Versions of semantic dialetheism are also held by Beall (2004) and Kroon (2004).

that talk of inconsistencies in things makes sense, but that there aren't any: there are no actual f^+ and f^- of the required kind. But one can take it, more strongly, to be to the effect that the very claim that there are inconsistencies in things makes no sense. That is, it may be a rejection of 1, 2, or 3 above. One may be some kind of anti-realist: there is no language-independent reality. One may be a realist, but hold that reality is not propositional. One may hold that it is, but that there is nothing in reality that corresponds, intrinsically, to negation in language.

The sorts of considerations that might lead us to accept (or reject) 1 and 2 are familiar from standard discussions in metaphysics. What sort of consideration might lead us to accept 3 is less familiar, but here is one. Consider for a moment not negative facts, but general facts (corresponding to sentences of the form 'All *A*s are *B*s'). In his lectures on logical atomism, Bertrand Russell argued as follows:[31]

> It is perfectly clear, I think, that when you have enumerated all the atomic facts in the world, it is a further fact about the world that those are all the atomic facts there are about the world, and that is just as much an objective fact about the world as any of them are. It is clear, I think, that you must admit general facts as distinct from and over and above particular facts. The same applies to 'All men are mortal.' When you have taken all the particular men that there are, and found each one of them severally to be mortal, it is definitely a new fact that all men are mortal; how new a fact, appears from ... [my observation that] it could not be inferred from the mortality of the several men that there are in the world.

Russell's point is clear. Suppose that you have two worlds, w_1 and w_2, whose distinct atomic facts are as follows:

In some sense, it is clearly a fact about w_1, in a way that it is not about w_2, that *every fact is one of* $f_1, \ldots, f_n$. Such a fact is irredeemably general. There must, therefore, be facts parts of the internal structure of which correspond to a universal quantifier.

But if this argument is good, it would seem to work just as well for negation. It is clearly a fact about w_1, in a way that it is not about w_2. That f_{n+1} *is not a fact*. Such a fact is irredeemably negative. There must, therefore, be facts parts of the internal structure of which correspond to negation. (In a lecture earlier than the one from which I have just quoted, Russell, in fact, endorses the existence of negative facts, though not on these grounds.)

[31] Pears (1972), pp. 93–4.

Anyway, and to return to Mares, the kind of semantic dialetheist he is, particularly with respect to 1, 2, and 3, is not clear (to me, anyway). So I will leave him to explain his own position, and turn to my own. Mares takes me to be a metaphysical dialetheist,[32] but *In Contradiction* is, in fact largely neutral on most of the relevant issues. The account of truth offered in chapter 4 is not a correspondence theory; but it is quite compatible with giving a truth-conditional semantics for languages. Such semantics are, in fact, given at various points in the book. If the domain of quantification involved in these semantics is taken to comprise language-independent objects, then we certainly have realism of some kind; so we have 1. In the truth-conditional semantics, predicates have extensions and anti-extensions. If these report a structure that pre-exists in the objects (so providing not just the appropriate factual structure, but also the polarities within it), we have 2 and 3. If, on the other hand, these are a structure that language simply imposes on them, then not. But that is an issue on which *In Contradiction* is silent.

For what it is worth, there may well be no uniform answer to the issue of metaphysical dialetheism. Metaphysical dialetheism is simply a consequence of dialetheism plus the appropriate form of metaphysical realism, and will stand or fall with this. It is natural to suppose that in some areas of concern to dialetheism one should be a realist, and in some one should not (see section 4.3). Thus, in the legal cases (discussed in chapter 13) it is natural to suppose that what is the case about rights, etc., and so about legal dialetheias, is the result of simple say-so. There is no language-independent reality in the appropriate sense. In the case of motion (discussed in chapter 12) it is more natural to suppose that whatever is happening is doing so completely independently of us and what we say. (The earth would have gone around the sun, even had we never evolved.) This is certainly realism of some kind, though further steps are necessary to take us to the appropriate metaphysical realism, as we have already seen. The case of mathematics (discussed in chapter 10)[33] seems delicately poised between these two, objectivity pulling one way, abstractness pulling the other.

As hardly needs to be said, for each of the areas at issue, the question of whether or not these natural suppositions are correct—and, indeed, of whether or not metaphysical realism is correct—is a hard issue, and not one that it is appropriate to try to adjudicate here. As the Preface of the first edition notes, there are many issues related to dialetheism that the book makes no attempt to resolve. It fights just one battle. Trying to overturn what has been the received wisdom on a topic so central to Western philosophy for over two thousand years is battle enough for one book.

---

[32] So does Bobenrieth (2005), who also espouses some kind of semantic dialetheism.

[33] And of other abstract objects, such as those that may be concerned in the paradoxes of self-reference.

Bibliography

Aczel, P.
(1988) *Non-Well-Founded Sets* (CSLI Lecture Notes), University of Chicago Press.
Anderson, A. and Belnap, N.
(1975) *Entailment*, Princeton University Press.
Armour-Garb, B.
(2004) 'Minimalism, the Generalization Problem, and the Liar', *Synthese* 139, 491–512.
Armour-Garb, B. and Beall, JC
(2001) 'Can Deflationists be Dialetheists?' *Journal of Philosophical Logic* 30, 593–608.
Armour-Garb, B. and Priest, G.
(2005) 'Analetheism: a phyrric victory', *Analysis*, 65, 167–73.
Arnold, J. and Shapiro, S.
(forthcoming) 'Where in the (World Wide) Web of Belief is the Law of Non-Contradiction?', *Noûs*.
Barcan Marcus, R.
(1980) 'Moral Dilemmas and Consistency', *Journal of Philosophy* 77, 121–36.
Barwise, J. and Etchemendy, J.
(1987) *The Liar: an essay on truth and circularity*, Oxford University Press.
Bar-Hillel, Y.
(1957) 'New Light on the Liar', *Analysis* 18, 1–6.
Batens, D.
(1986) 'Dialectical Dynamics within Formal Logics', *Logique et Analyse* 114, 161–73.
(1989) 'Dynamic Dialectical Logic', in Priest, Routley, and Norman (1989).
(2002) 'On Some Remarkable Relations between Paraconsistent Logics, Modal Logics and Ambiguity Logics', pp. 275–93 of W. Carnielli, M. Coniglio, and I. D'Ottaviano (eds.), *Paraconsistency: the logical way to be inconsistent*, Marcel Dekker.
Beall, JC
(1999) 'From Full Blooded Platonism to Really Full Blooded Platonism', *Philosophia Mathematica* 7, 322–5.
(2004) 'True and False—As If', chapter 12 of Priest, Beall, and Armour-Garb (2004).
(2005) 'Transparent Disquotationalism', chapter 1 of Beall and Armour-Garb (2005).
Beall, JC and Armour-Garb, B.
(2003) 'Should Deflationists be Dialetheists?' *Noûs* 37, 303–24.
Beall, JC and Armour-Garb, B. (eds.)
(2005) *Deflationism and Paradox*, Oxford University Press.
Beall, JC, Brady, R., Hazen, A., Priest, G., and Restall, G.
(forthcoming) 'Restricted Quantification in Relevant Logics', *Journal of Philosophical Logic*.
Beall, JC and Priest, G.
(forthcoming) 'Not So Deep Consistency: a reply to Eklund', *Australasian Journal of Logic*.
Beall, JC and Ripley, D.
(2004) 'Analetheism and Dialetheism', *Analysis* 64, 30–5.

Bell, J.
(1981) 'Category Theory and the Foundations of Mathematics', *British Journal for the Philosophy of Science* 32, 349–58.

Belnap, N. D.
(1991) 'Before Refraining: concepts of agency', *Erkenntnis* 34, 137–69.

Belnap, N. D. and Dunn, J. M.
(1983) 'Entailment and the Disjunctive Syllogism', in G. Fløistad (ed.), *Contemporary Philosophy*, Vol. 1, Nijhoff.

Belnap, N. D. and Perloff, M.
(1990) 'Seeing To It That: a canonical form for agentives', pp. 167–90 of H. E. Kyburg, R. P. Loui, and G. N. Carlson (eds.), *Knowledge Representation and Defeasible Reasoning*, Kluwer Academic.

Bobenrieth, A.
(forthcoming) 'Paraconsistency and the Consistency or Inconsistency of the World', to appear in Carnielli *et al.* (forthcoming).

Boolos, G. and Jeffrey, R.
(1974) *Computability and Logic*, Cambridge University Press.

Boyer, C.
(1949) *Concepts of the Calculus*, Dover.

Brady, R.
(1984) 'Reply to Priest on Berry's Paradox', *Philosophical Quarterly* 34, 157–63.
(1989) 'The Non-Triviality of Dialectical Set Theory', in Priest, Routley, and Norman (1989).

Brandt, R.
(1959) *Ethical Theory*, Prentice Hall.

Bromand, J.
(2002) 'Why Paraconsistent Logic Can Only Tell Half the Truth', *Mind* 111, 741–9.

Brown, B.
(2004) 'Knowledge and Non-Contradiction', chapter 8 of Priest, Beall, and Armour-Garb (2004).

Brown, B. and Priest, G.
(2004) 'Chunk and Permeate I: the infinitesimal calculus', *Journal of Philosophical Logic* 33, 379–88.

Brown, H.
(1977) *Perception, Theory and Commitment*, Chicago University Press.

Burge, T.
(1979) 'Semantical Paradox', *Journal of Philosophy* 76, 169–98.

Cantor, G.
(1895) '*Beiträge zur Begründung der transfiniten Mengenlehre*', *Mathematische Annalen* 46, 481–512. Reprinted in English in *Contributions to the Founding of the Theory of Transfinite Numbers*, ed. P. Jourdain, Dover, 1955.
(1899) Letter to Dedekind. Published in English in J. van Heijenoort (ed.), *From Frege to Goedel*, Harvard University Press, 1967.

Cargile, J.
(1989) Review of *In Contradiction*, *Canadian Philosophical Review* 9, 243–9.

Carnielli, W. *et al.*
(forthcoming) *Proceedings of the Third World Congress on Paraconsistency*, Marcel Dekker.

Carroll, L.

(1895) 'What the Tortoise Said to Achilles', *Mind* 4, 278–80.

Castañeda, H.

(1981) 'Paradoxes of Deontic Logic: the solution to them all in one fell swoop', in Hilpinen (1981).

Chihara, C.

(1979) 'The Semantic Paradoxes: a diagnostic investigation', *Philosophical Review* 88, 590–618.

(1984) 'Priest, the Liar, and Gödel', *Journal of Philosophical Logic* 13, 117–24.

Chomsky, N.

(1980) *Rules and Representations*, Columbia University Press.

Church, A.

(1956) *Introduction to Mathematical Logic*, Princeton University Press.

Cooke, B.

(forthcoming) 'Art-Critical Contradictions'.

Curry, H.

(1942) 'The Inconsistency of Certain Formal Logics', *Journal of Symbolic Logic* 7, 115–17.

da Costa, N. and French, S.

(1988) Review of *In Contradiction*, *History and Philosophy of Logic* 10, 115–20.

Dancy, R.

(1975) *Sense and Contradiction: a study in Aristotle*, Reidel.

Davidson, D.

(1965) 'Theories of Meaning in Learnable Languages', in Y. Bar-Hillel (ed.), *Logic, Methodology and Philosophy of Science*, North-Holland.

(1967) 'Truth and Meaning', *Synthèse* 17, 304–23.

(1973) 'On the Very Idea of a Conceptual Scheme', *Proceedings and Addresses of the American Philosophical Association* 47, 5–20.

Davidson, D. and Harman, G. (eds.)

(1972) *Semantics of Natural Language*, Reidel.

Davies, M.

(1981) *Meaning, Quantification and Necessity*, Routledge & Kegan Paul.

Dedekind, R.

(1888) '*Was sind und was sollen die Zahlen*', reprinted in English in *Essays in the Theory of Numbers*, Dover, 1963.

Denyer, N.

(1989) 'Dialetheism and Trivialisation', *Mind* 98, 259–63.

(1995) 'Priest's Paraconsistent Arithmetic', *Mind* 104, 567–75.

Devlin, K.

(1980) *Fundamentals of Contemporary Set Theory*, Springer-Verlag.

Dowden, B.

(1984) 'Accepting Inconsistencies from the Paradoxes', *Journal of Philosophical Logic* 13, 125–30.

Drake, F.

(1974) *Set Theory: an introduction to large cardinals*, North-Holland.

Dummett, M.

(1959) 'Wittgenstein's Philosophy of Mathematics', *Philosophical Review* 68, 324–48. Reprinted in Dummett (1978).

(1959a) 'Truth', *Proceedings of the Aristotelian Society* 59, 141–62. Reprinted in Dummett (1978).

(1963) 'The Philosophical Significance of Gödel's Theorem', *Ratio* 5, 140–55. Reprinted in Dummett (1978).

(1973) *Frege*, Duckworth.

(1975) 'The Philosophical Basis of Intuitionist Logic', in H. Rose and J. Shepherdson (eds.), *Logic Colloquium '73*, North-Holland. Reprinted in Dummett (1978).

(1977) *Elements of Intuitionism*, Oxford University Press.

(1978) *Truth and Other Enigmas*, Duckworth.

Dunn, J. M.

(1976) 'Intuitive Semantics for First-Degree Entailments, and "Coupled Trees"', *Philosophical Studies* 29, 149–68.

(1979) 'A Theorem of 3-Valued Model Theory with Connections to Number Theory, Type Theory and Relevance', *Studia Logica* 38, 149–69.

(1988) 'The Impossibility of Certain Second-Order Non-Classical Logics with Extensionality', pp. 261–79 of D. F. Austin (ed.), *Philosophical Analysis*, Kluwer Academic.

Dunn, J. M. and Restall, G.

(2002) 'Relevance Logic', pp. 1–128, vol. 6, of D. Gabby and F. Guenthner (eds.), *Handbook of Philosophical Logic*, 2nd edn, Kluwer Academic.

Dunn, J. W.

(1926) *An Experiment with Time*, Faber.

Eklund, M.

(2002) 'Deep Inconsistency', *Australasian Journal of Philosophy* 80, 321–31.

Engels, F.

(1894) *Anti-Dühring*, 3rd edn. Page references to the English translation, Progress Publishers, 1975.

Everett, A.

(1993) 'A Note on Priest's Hypercontradictions', *Logique et Analyse* 36, 39–43.

(1994) 'Absorbing Dialetheias', *Mind* 103, 414–19.

(1996) 'A Dilemma for Priest's Dialetheism?' *Australasian Journal of Philosophy* 74, 657–68.

Feferman, S.

(1962) 'Transfinite Recursive Progressions of Theories', *Journal of Symbolic Logic* 27, 259–316.

(1977) 'Categorical Foundations and Foundations of Category Theory', in J. Hintikka and R. Butts (eds.), *Logic, Foundations of Mathematics and Computability Theory*, Reidel.

Feyerabend, P.

(1975) *Against Method*, New Left Books.

(1978) 'In Defense of Aristotle', in G. Radnitsky and G. Anderson (eds.), *Progress and Rationality in Science*, Reidel.

Field, H.

(2003) 'A Revenge-Immune Solution to the Semantic Paradoxes', *Journal of Philosophical Logic* 32, 139–77.

(2005) 'Is the Liar Both True and False?', chapter 2 of Beall and Armour-Garb (2005).

Fitch, F. B.

(1952) *Symbolic Logic*, Donald Press.

(1964) 'Universal Metalanguages for Philosophy,' *Review of Metaphysics* 17, 396–402.

Fitzgerald, P.

(1966) *Salmond on Jurisprudence*, 12th edn, Sweet & Maxwell.

Føllesdal, D. and Hilpinen, R.

(1971) 'Deontic Logic: an introduction', in Hilpinen (1971).

Forrester, M.

(1982) *Moral Language*, University of Wisconsin Press.

van Fraassen, B.

(1968) 'Presupposition, Implication and Self Reference', *Journal of Philosophy* 65, 136–51.

(1970) 'Truth and Paradoxical Consequence', in *The Paradox of the Liar*, ed. R. L. Martin, Yale University Press.

Fraenkel, A., Bar-Hillel, Y. and Levy, A.

(1973) *Foundations of Set Theory*, North-Holland.

Friedman, H. and Meyer, R. K.

(1992) 'Whither Relevant Arithmetic?' *Journal of Symbolic Logic* 57, 824–31.

Fuller, L.

(1969) *The Morality of Law*, Yale University Press.

Gale, R. M. (ed.)

(1967) *Philosophy of Time*, Anchor Books.

Garfield, J. and Priest, G.

(2003) 'Nāgārjuna and the Limits of Thought', *Philosophy East and West* 53, 1–21. Reprinted as chapter 5 of J. Garfield, *Empty Words*, Oxford University Press, 2002, and as chapter 16 of the 2nd edn of Priest (1995).

Gasking, D. A. T.

(1940) 'Mathematics and the World', *Australasian Journal of Philosophy* 18, 97–116. Reprinted as pp. 390–403 of P. Benacerraf and H. Putnam (eds.), *Philosophy of Mathematics: selected readings*, Oxford University Press, 1964.

Goddard, L. and Goldstein, L.

(1980) 'Strengthened Paradoxes', *Australasian Journal of Philosophy* 58, 211–22.

Gold, T.

(1966) 'Cosmic Processes and the Nature of Time', pp. 311–29 of G. Colodny (ed.), *Mind and Cosmos*, University of Pittsburgh Press.

Gödel, K.

(1947) 'What is Cantor's Continuum Problem?' *American Mathematical Monthly* 54, 515–25. Reprinted in P. Benacerraf and H. Putnam (eds.), *Philosophy of Mathematics*, Blackwell, 1964.

Goldstein, L.

(1979) 'Four Alleged Paradoxes of Legal Reasoning', *Cambridge Law Journal* 38, 373–91.

Goodship, L.

(1996) 'On Dialethism', *Australasian Journal of Philosophy* 74, 153–61.

Graham, A. C.

(1978) *Later Mohist Logic, Ethics, and Science*, Chinese University Press.

Grice, H. P.

(1957) 'Meaning', *Philosophical Review* 66, 377–88.

(1968) 'Utterer's Meaning, Sentence Meaning and Word Meaning', *Foundations of Language* 4, 1–18.

Grünbaum, A.

(1967) 'The Anisotropy of Time', chapter 10 of T. Gold (ed.), *The Nature of Time*, Cornell University Press.

(1967*a*) 'The Status of Temporal Becoming', pp. 322–53 of Gale (1967).

Guest, A. (ed.)

(1969) *Anson's Law of Contract*, 23rd edn, Oxford University Press.

Gupta, A.

(1978) 'Modal Logic and Truth', *Journal of Philosophical Logic* 7, 441–72.

(1982) 'Truth and Paradox', *Journal of Philosophical Logic* 11, 1–60.

Gupta, A. and Martin, R. L.

(1984) 'A Fixed Point Theorem for the Weak Kleene Valuation Scheme', *Journal of Philosophic Logic* 13, 131–5.

Haack, R. J. and Haack, S.

(1970) 'Token Sentences, Translation and Truth Value', *Mind* 79, 40–57.

Haack, S.

(1974) *Deviant Logic*, Cambridge University Press.

Hacking, I.

(1975) *Why does Language Matter to Philosophy?*, Cambridge University Press.

Hallett, M.

(1984) *Cantorian Set Theory and Limitation of Size*, Oxford University Press.

Hamblin, C.

(1969) 'Starting and Stopping', *Monist* 54, 410–25.

Hare, R.

(1963) *Freedom and Reason*, Oxford University Press.

Harman, G.

(1972) 'Deep Structure as Logical Form', in Davidson and Harman (1972), 25–47.

Hart, H. L. A.

(1954) 'Definition and Theory in Jurisprudence', *Law Quarterly Review* 70, 37–60.

Hegel, G. W. F.

(1812) *Wissenschaft der Logik*, published in English translation by A. V. Miller as *Hegel's Science of Logic*, Allen & Unwin, 1969.

(1830) *Philosophy of Nature*, English translation by A. V. Miller, Clarendon Press, 1970.

(1840) *Lectures on the History of Philosophy*, English translation by E. S. Haldane, Kegan Paul, 1892.

(1955) *Lectures on the History of Philosophy*, vol. 1, trans. E. S. Haldane and F. H. Simpson, Routledge & Kegan Paul.

Henkin, L.

(1953) 'Some Notes on Nominalism', *Journal of Symbolic Logic* 18, 19–29.

Herzberger, H.

(1970) 'Paradoxes of Grounding in Semantics', *Journal of Philosophy* 67, 145–67.

(1982) 'Notes on Naive Semantics', *Journal of Philosophical Logic* 11, 61–102.

Hilpinen, R. (ed.)

(1971) *Deontic Logic: Introductory and Systematic Readings*, Reidel.

(1981) *New Studies in Deontic Logic*, Reidel.

Hintikka, J.

(1971) 'Some Main Problems in Deontic Logic', in Hilpinen (1971).

Horwich, P.

(1990) *Truth*, Oxford University Press.

Humberstone, L.

(1979) 'Interval Semantics for Tense Logics', *Journal of Philosophical Logic* 8, 171–96.

Ilyenkov, E. V.

(1977) *Dialectical Logic: essays on its history and theory*, Progress Publishers.

Kaye, R.

(1991) *Models of Peano Arithmetic*, Clarendon Press.

Klenk, V.

(1976) *Wittgenstein's Philosophy of Mathematics*, Nijhoff.

Knuuttilla, S. and Lehtinen, A. I.

(1979) 'Continuity and Contradiction: a fourteenth century controversy', *Synthèse* 40, 189–207.

Kretzmann, N.

(1982) 'Continuity, Contrariety, Contradiction and Change', chapter 10 of N. Kretzmann (ed.), *Infinity and Continuity in Ancient and Medieval Thought*, Cornell University Press.

Kripke, S.

(1975) 'Outline of a Theory of Truth', *Journal of Philosophy* 72, 690–716.

(1976) 'Is there a Problem about Substitutional Quantification?' in G. Evans and J. McDowell (eds.) *Truth and Meaning*, Oxford University Press.

Kroon, F.

(2004) 'Realism and Dialetheism', chapter 15 of Priest, Beall, and Armour-Garb (2004).

Kuhn, T.

(1962) *Structure of Scientific Revolutions*, Chicago University Press.

Lakatos, I.

(1962) 'Infinite Regress in the Foundations of Mathematics', *Proceedings of the Aristotelian Society*, supp. vol. 36. Reprinted in Lakatos (1978), Vol. II.

(1968) 'Changes in the Problem of Inductive Logic', in I. Lakatos (ed.), *The Problem of Inductive Logic*, North-Holland. Reprinted in Lakatos (1978), Vol. II.

(1970) 'Falsification and the Methodology of Scientific Research Programmes', in I. Lakatos and A. Musgrave (eds.), *Criticism and the Growth of Knowledge*, Cambridge University Press. Reprinted in Lakatos (1978), Vol I.

(1976) *Proofs and Refutations*, Cambridge University Press.

(1978) *Collected Papers*, Vols. I and II, ed. J. Worrall and G. Currie, Cambridge University Press.

(1978a) 'Cauchy and the Continuum: the significance of non-standard analysis for the history and philosophy of mathematics', in Lakatos (1978), Vol. II.

Lear, J.

(1980) *Aristotle and Logical Theory*, Cambridge University Press.

Leibniz, G. W.

(1687) 'Letter of Mr. Leibniz on a General Principle Useful in Explaining the Laws of Nature through a Consideration of the Divine Wisdom; to Serve as a Reply to the Response of the Rev. Father Malebranche'. Published in English translation in Leibniz' *Philosophical Papers and Letters*, ed. L. E. Loemker, Reidel, 1969, 351–4.

Leisenring, A.
(1969) *Mathematical Logic and Hilbert's ∈-Symbol*, Macdonald.
Lemmon, E.
(1962) 'Moral Dilemmas', *Philosophical Review* 71, 139–58.
Lewis, D.
(1972) 'General Semantics', in Davidson and Harman (1972).
(1973) *Counterfactuals*, Harvard University Press.
(1982) 'Logic for Equivocators', *Noûs* 16, 431–41.
(2000) 'Academic Appointments: why ignore the advantages of being right?' chapter 15 of *Papers in Ethics and Social Theory*, Cambridge University Press.
(2004) 'Letters to Beall and Priest', chapter 10 of Priest, Beall, and Armour-Garb (2004).
Libert, T.
(2003) 'ZF and the Axiom of Choice in Some Paraconsistent Set Theories', *Logic and Logical Philosophy* 11, 91–114.
Littman, G. and Simmons, K.
(2004) 'A Critique of Dialetheism', chapter 20 of Priest, Beall, and Armour-Garb (2004).
Lucas, J. R.
(1961) 'Minds, Machines and Gödel', *Philosophy* 36, 112–27. Reprinted in A. Anderson (ed.), *Minds and Machines*, Prentice Hall, 1964.
Łukasiewicz, J.
(1971) 'On the Principle of Contradiction in Aristotle', *Review of Metaphysics* 24, 485–509.
Mabbott, J. D.
(1951) 'Our Direct Experience of Time', *Mind* 60, 153–67. Reprinted as pp. 304–21 of Gale (1967).
Makinson, D.
(1990) Review of *In Contradiction*, *Mathematical Reviews* 90f:03007, pp. 3247–8.
Mares, E.
(2004) 'Semantic Dialetheism', chapter 16 of Priest, Beall, and Armour-Garb (2004).
Martin, R. L.
(1967) 'Towards a Solution of the Liar Paradox', *Philosophical Review* 76, 279–311.
Maund, J. B.
(1981) 'Colour: a case of conceptual fission', *Australasian Journal of Philosophy* 59, 308–22.
Mayberry, J.
(1977) 'On the Consistency Problem for Set Theory: an essay in the Cantorian foundations of classical mathematics, (I)' *British Journal for the Philosophy of Science* 28, 1–34.
(1980) 'A New Begriffsschrift, (II)', *British Journal for the Philosophy of Science* 31, 329–58.
McConnell, T.
(1978) 'Moral Dilemmas and Consistency in Ethics', *Canadian Journal of Philosophy* 8, 269–87.
McGee, V.
(1990) *Truth, Vagueness and Paradox*, Hacket.
Mellor, D. H.
(1984) *Real Time*, Cambridge University Press.

Meyer, R. K.

(1976) 'Relevant Arithmetic', *Bulletin of the Section of Logic, Polish Academy of Sciences* 5, 133–7.

Meyer, R. K. and Mortensen, C.

(1984) 'Inconsistent Models for Relevant Arithmetics', *Journal of Symbolic Logic* 49, 917–29.

Meyer, R., Routley, R. and Dunn, J. M.

(1979) 'Curry's Paradox', *Analysis* 39, 124–8.

Montague, R.

(1974) *Formal Philosophy*, Yale University Press.

Mortensen, C.

(1985) 'The Limits of Change', *Australasian Journal of Philosophy* 63, 1–10.

(1987) 'Inconsistent Nonstandard Arithmetic', *Journal of Symbolic Logic* 52, 512–18.

(1988) 'Inconsistent Number Systems', *Notre Dame Journal of Formal Logic* 29, 45–60.

(1990) 'Models for Inconsistent and Incomplete Differential Calculus', *Notre Dame Journal of Formal Logic* 31, 274–85.

(1995) *Inconsistent Mathematics*, Kluwer Academic.

(1997) 'The Leibniz Continuity Condition, Inconsistency and Quantum Dynamics', *Journal of Philosophical Logic* 26, 377–89.

(2002) 'Change', in E. Zalta (ed.), *The Stanford Encyclopedia of Philosophy* (December 2002 edn), at http://plato.stanford.edu/entries/change/.

(2004) 'Darmakīrti and Priest on Change', *Philosophy East and West* 54, 20–8.

Mortensen, C. and Priest, G.

(1981) 'The Truth Teller Paradox', *Logique et Analyse* 95–6, 381–8.

Nelson, D.

(1959) 'Negation and Separation of Concepts in Constructive Systems', pp. 208–25 of A. Heyting (ed.), *Constructivity in Mathematics*, North-Holland.

Olin, D.

(2003) *Paradox*, Acumen.

Papineau, D.

(1979) *Theory and Meaning*, Oxford University Press.

Parsons, C.

(1971) 'A Plea for Substitutional Quantification', *Journal of Philosophy* 68, 231–7.

(1974) 'Sets and Classes', *Noûs* 8, 1–12.

Parsons, T.

(1984) 'Assertion, Denial and the Liar Paradox', *Journal of Philosophical Logic* 13, 137–52.

(1990) 'True Contradictions', *Canadian Journal of Philosophy* 20, 335–53.

Peacocke, C.

(1978) 'Necessity and Truth Theories', *Journal of Philosophical Logic* 7, 473–500.

Peano, G.

(1906) '*Addition* E', *Rivista di Mathematica* 8, 143–57.

Popper, K. R.

(1940) 'What is Dialectic?', *Mind* 49, 403–26. Reprinted in Popper (1963).

(1954) 'Self Reference and Meaning in Ordinary Language', *Mind* 63, 162–9. Reprinted in Popper (1963).

(1963) *Conjectures and Refutations*, Routledge & Kegan Paul.

Prawitz, D.
(1967) *Natural Deduction*, Almqvist & Wiksell.

Priest, G.
(1979) 'Indefinite Descriptions', *Logique et analyse* 22, 5–21.
(1979*a*) 'Logic of Paradox', *Journal of Philosophical Logic* 8, 219–41.
(1979*b*) 'Two Dogmas of Quineanism', *Philosophical Quarterly* 29, 289–301.
(1980) 'Sense, Entailment and *Modus Ponens*', *Journal of Philosophical Logic* 9, 415–35.
(1982) 'To Be and Not To Be: dialectical tense logic', *Studia Logica* 41, 249–68.
(1983) 'Logical Paradoxes and the Law of Excluded Middle', *Philosophical Quarterly* 33, 160–5.
(1983*a*) 'An Anti-Realist Account of Mathematical Truth', *Synthèse* 57, 49–65.
(1984) 'Semantic Closure', *Studia Logica* 43, 117–29.
(1984*a*) 'Logic of Paradox Revisited', *Journal of Philosophical Logic* 13, 153–79.
(1985) 'Inconsistencies in Motion', *American Philosophical Quarterly* 22, 339–46.
(1986) 'Contradiction, Belief and Rationality', *Proceedings of Aristotelian Society* 86, 99–116.
(1987) 'Unstable Solutions to the Liar Paradox', in S. J. Bartlett and P. Suber (eds.), *Self Reference: reflections on reflexivity*, Nijhoff.
(1988) 'Consistency by Default', Technical Report TR-ARP-3/88, Automated Reasoning Project, Australian National University.
(1989) '*Reductio ad Absurdum et Modus Tollendo Ponens*', in Priest, Routley, and Norman (1989).
(1989*a*) 'Classical Logic *Aufgehoben*', in Priest, Routley, and Norman (1989).
(1989*b*) 'Denyer's $ Not Backed by Sterling Arguments', *Mind* 98, 265–8.
(1990) 'Dialectic and Dialetheic', *Science and Society* 53, 388–415.
(1991) 'Was Marx a Dialetheist?' *Science and Society* 54, 468–75.
(1991*a*) 'Minimally Inconsistent *LP*', *Studia Logica* 50, 321–31. Reprinted as chapter 16 of this book.
(1992) 'On Time', *Philosophica* 50, 9–18. Reprinted as chapter 15 of this book.
(1993) 'Another Disguise of the Same Fundamental Problems: Barwise and Etchemendy on the Liar', *Australasian Journal of Philosophy* 71, 60–9.
(1993*a*) 'Can Contradictions be True? II', *Proceedings of the Aristotelian Society*, suppl. vol. 67, 35–54.
(1994) 'Is Arithmetic Consistent?' *Mind* 103, 337–49.
(1994*a*) 'What Could the Least Inconsistent Number Be?', *Logique et analyse* 37, 3–12.
(1994*b*) Review of V. McGee, *Truth, Vagueness and Paradox*, *Mind* 103, 387–91.
(1994*c*) 'Gödel's Theorem and the Mind . . . Again', pp. 191–201 of M. Michaelis and J. O'Leary-Hawthorne (eds.), *Philosophy in Mind: the place of philosophy in the study of mind*, Kluwer Academic. Reprinted with a different introduction as 'Gödel's Theorem and Creativity', pp. 107–15 of T. Dartnall (ed.), *Artificial Intelligence and Creativity: an interdisciplinary approach*, Kluwer Academic, 1994.
(1995) *Beyond the Limits of Thought*, Cambridge University Press; 2nd, extended, edn, Oxford University Press, 2002.
(1995*a*) 'Gaps and Gluts: reply to Parsons', *Canadian Journal of Philosophy* 25, 57–66.
(1995*b*) 'Multiple Denotation, Ambiguity, and the Strange Case of the Missing Amoeba', *Logique et Analyse* 38, 361–73.
(1996) 'Everett's Trilogy', *Mind* 105, 631–47.

(1996*a*) 'On Inconsistent Arithmetics: reply to Denyer', *Mind* 105, 649–59.

(1997) 'Inconsistent Models of Arithmetic, I: finite models', *Journal of Philosophical Logic* 26, 223–35.

(1998) 'What's So Bad about Contradictions?' *Journal of Philosophy* 95, 410–26. Reprinted as chapter 1 of Priest, Beall, and Armour-Garb (2004).

(2000) 'Inconsistent Models of Arithmetic, II: the general case', *Journal of Symbolic Logic* 65, 1519–29.

(2001) *Introduction to Non-Classical Logic*, Cambridge University Press.

(2002) 'Paraconsistent Logic', pp. 287–93, vol. 6, of D. Gabbay and F. Guenthner (eds.), *Handbook of Philosophical Logic*, 2nd edn, Kluwer Academic.

(2003) 'Inconsistent Arithmetic: issues technical and philosophical', pp. 273–99 of V. F. Hendricks and J. Malinowski (eds.), *Trends in Logic: 50 years of* Studia Logica (*Studia Logica Library*, vol. 21), Kluwer Academic. Reprinted as chapter 17 of this book.

(2003*a*) 'On Alternative Geometries, Arithmetics and Logics: a tribute to Łukasiewicz', *Studia Logica* 74, 441–68.

(2004) 'Wittgenstein's Remarks on Gödel's Theorem', chapter 8 of M. Kölbel and B. Weiss (eds.), *Wittgenstein's Lasting Significance*, Routledge.

(2005) *Towards Non-Being: the logic and metaphysics of intentionality*, Oxford University Press.

(2005*a*) 'Spiking the Field Artillery', chapter 3 of Beall and Armour-Garb (2005).

(2006) *Doubt Truth to be a Liar*, Oxford: Oxford University Press.

(forthcoming *a*) 'Paraconsistent Set Theory', in A. Irving (ed.), *Essays on Set Theory*, Blackwell; reprinted as chapter 18 of this book.

(forthcoming *b*) 'Conditionals', in I. Ravenscooft (ed.), *Minds, Worlds and Conditionals: themes from the philosophy of Frank Jackson*, Oxford University Press.

(forthcoming *c*) 'The Paradoxes of Denotation', in T. Bolander, V. F. Hendricks, and S. A. Pedersen (eds.), *Self Reference*, CSLI Publications.

(forthcoming *d*) 'Paraconsistency and Dialetheism', ch. 3, vol. 8 of D. Gabbay and J. Woods (eds.), *Handbook of the History of Logic*, Elsevier.

(forthcoming *e*) 'Motion', in D. Borchert (ed.), *Encyclopedia of Philosophy*, 2nd edn, Macmillan.

(forthcoming *f*) 'Beyond the Limits of Knowledge', in J. Salerno (ed.), *New Essays on the Knower Paradox*, Oxford University Press

(forthcoming *g*) 'Reply to Slater', in Carnielli *et al.* (forthcoming).

Priest, G., Beall, JC, and Armour-Garb, B. (eds.)

(2004) *The Law of Non-Contradiction: new philosophical essays*, Oxford University Press.

Priest, G. and Crosthwaite, J.

(1987) 'Relevance, Truth and Meaning', in R. Routley and J. Norman (eds.), *Directions of Relevant Logic*, Nijhoff.

Priest, G. and Routley, R.

(1982) 'Lessons From Pseudo-Scotus', *Philosophical Studies*, 42, 189–99.

(1983) *On Paraconsistency*, Research Report 13, Logic Group, Research School of Social Sciences, Australian National University. Reprinted as chs. 1, 2, 5, 13 and 18 of Priest, Routley, and Norman (1989).

Priest, G., Routley, R., and Norman, J. (eds.)

(1989) *Paraconsistent Logic: essay on the inconsistent*, Philosophia Verlag.

Prior, A.

(1961) 'On a Family of Paradoxes', *Notre Dame Journal of Formal Logic* 2, 16–32.

(1971) *Objects of Thought*, Oxford University Press.

Quine, W.

(1953) *From a Logical Point of View*, Harper & Row.

(1970) *Philosophy of Logic*, Prentice Hall.

(1973) *Roots of Reference*, Open Court.

(1976) 'Whither Physical Objects?', in *Essays in Memory of Imre Lakatos*, Boston Studies in the Philosophy of Science, Vol. 39, Reidel, 497–504.

Reichenbach, H.

(1956) *The Direction of Time*, University of California Press.

Rescher, N.

(1969) *Many-Valued Logic*, McGraw-Hill.

Rescher, N. and Brandom, R.

(1980) *The Logic of Inconsistency*, Blackwell.

Rescher, N. and Urquhart, A.

(1971) *Temporal Logic*, Springer Verlag.

Restall, G.

(1992) 'A Note on Naive Set Theory in *LP*', *Notre Dame Journal of Formal Logic* 33, 422–32.

(2004) 'Assertion, Denial, Accepting, Rejecting, Symmetry, Paradox, and All That', paper given to the annual meeting of the Australasian Association of Philosophy, available at http://consequently.org/writing/assertiondenialparadox.

Routley, R.

(1977) 'Ultralogic as Universal', *Relevant Logic Newsletter* 2, 50–89, 138–75. Reprinted as an appendix in Routley (1980).

(1980) *Exploring Meinong's Jungle and Beyond*, Research School of Social Sciences, Australian National University.

(1984) 'The American Plan Completed: alternative classical style semantics, without stars, for relevant paraconsistent logics', *Studia Logica* 43, 131–58.

Routley, R. and Plumwood, V.

(1989) 'Moral Dilemmas and the Logic of Deontic Notions', in Priest, Routley, and Norman (1989).

Routley, R. and Routley, V.

(1972) 'Semantics of First Degree Entailment', *Noûs* 6, 335–58.

(1975) 'The Role of Inconsistent and Incomplete Theories in the Logic of Belief', *Communication and Cognition* 8, 185–235.

Routley, R., Plumwood, V., Meyer, R., and Brady, R.

(1982) *Relevant Logics and their Rivals*, Vol. I, Ridgeview.

Russell, B.

(1903) *Principles of Mathematics*, Cambridge University Press.

Russell, B. and Whitehead, A.

(1910) *Principia Mathematica*, Cambridge University Press.

Ryle, G.

(1950) 'Heterologicality', *Analysis* 11, 61–9.

Sainsbury, R. M.
(1987) *Paradoxes*, Cambridge University Press; 2nd, rev., edn, 1995.
Schotch, P. and Jennings, R.
(1981) 'Non-Kripkean Deontic Logic', in Hilpinen (1981).
Shapiro, S.
(2002) 'Incompleteness and Inconsistency', *Mind* 111, 817–32.
(2004) 'Simple Truth, Contradiction, and Consistency', chapter 20 of Priest, Beall, and Armour-Garb (2004).
Shoenfield, J.
(1967) *Mathematical Logic*, Addison Wesley.
Slaney, J.
(1989) '*RWX* is not Curry Paraconsistent', chapter 17 of Priest, Routley, and Norman (1989).
Slater, B. H.
(forthcoming) 'Dialetheias are Mental Confusions', forthcoming in Carnielli *at al.* (forthcoming).
Smart, J. C.
(1949) 'The River of Time', *Mind* 58, 483–94; reprinted as chapter 10 of A. Flew (ed.), *Essays in Conceptual Analysis*, Macmillan, 1956.
(1963) 'Quine's Philosophy of Science', in D. Davidson and J. Hintikka (eds.), *Words and Objections*, Reidel.
Smiley, T. J.
(1993) 'Can Contradictions be True? I', *Proceedings of the Aristotelian Society*, suppl. vol. 67, 17–33.
Smith, J.
(1991) Review of *In Contradiction*, *Noûs* 25, 200–3.
Spade, P.
(1982) 'Quasi-Aristotelianism', chapter 11 of N. Kretzmann (ed.), *Infinity and Continuity in Ancient and Medieval Thought*, Cornell University Press.
Stalnaker, R.
(1968) 'A Theory of Conditionals', *Studies in Logical Theory*, American Philosophical Quarterly Monograph Series, no. 2, Blackwell.
Steiner, M.
(1975) *Mathematical Knowledge*, Cornell University Press.
Takeuti, G.
(1975) *Proof Theory*, North-Holland.
Tanahashi, K. (ed.)
(1985) *Moon in a Dewdrop: Writings of Zen Master Dōgen*, Farrar, Straus, & Giroux.
Tarski, A.
(1936) '*Der Wahrheitsbegriff in den formalisierten Sprachen*', *Studia Philosophia* 1, 261–405. Reprinted in English in *Logic, Semantics and Metamathematics*, Oxford University Press, 1956.
Tennant, N.
(2004) 'An Anti-Realist Critique of Dialetheism', chapter 21 of Priest, Armour-Garb, and Beall (2004).
Thomason, R.
(1981) 'Deontic Logic as Founded on Tense Logic', in Hilpinen (1981).

Thompson, J. F.

(1962) 'On Some Paradoxes', in R. J. Butler (ed.), *Analytical Philosophy* (First Series), Blackwell.

Tooley, M.

(1988) 'In Defence of the Existence of States of Motion', *Philosophical Topics* 16, 225–54.

Van Bendegem, J. P.

(1993) 'Strict, yet Rich Finitism', pp. 61–79 of Z. W. Wolkowski (ed.), *First International Symposium on Gödel's Theorems*, World Scientific Press.

(1994) 'Strict Finitism as a Viable Alternative in the Foundations of Mathematics', *Logique et analyse* 37, 23–40.

Wallace, J.

(1972) 'On the Frame of Reference', in Davidson and Harman (1972).

Wang, H.

(1962) *A Survey of Mathematical Logic*, Science Press.

Weir, A.

(2004) 'There are No True Contradictions', chapter 22 of Priest, Beall, and Armour-Garb (2004).

Williams, D. C.

(1951) 'The Myth of Passage', *Journal of Philosophy* 48, 457–72. Reprinted as pp. 98–116 of Gale (1967).

Wittgenstein, L.

(1953) *Philosophical Investigations*, Blackwell.

(1956) *Remarks on the Foundations of Mathematics*, Blackwell.

(1964) *Philosophical Remarks*. Page references to the English translation, Blackwell, 1975.

Woodruff, P.

(1984) 'Paradox, Truth and Logic, Part 1', *Journal of Philosophical Logic* 13, 213–32.

von Wright, G.

(1963) *Norm and Action*, Humanities Press.

(1969) *Time, Change and Contradiction*, Cambridge University Press.

Xu, M.

(1994) 'Doing and Refraining from Doing', *Journal of Philosophical Logic* 23, 621–32.

Yablo, S.

(1982) 'Truth and Grounding in Semantics', *Journal of Philosophical Logic* 11, 117–37.

Index

absorption 83, 86, 248, 249, 251, 253, 269–70
abstraction, set-theoretic 10, 28, 30–2, 141–2,
    144–5, 148, 247, 250, 278
acceptability, rational 72, 100–3, 104–5, 113–15,
    274–5, 276
Ackermann fallacies 91
action: and belief 97–8
    at a distance 167
Aczel, P. 265
adjunction 190, 196
aesthetics, and dialetheism 295
agnosticism, and acceptability and rejection 99,
    103
ambiguity 286–7
    typical 19–20, 35, 37, 38 n.21
analyticity, and set theory 146–8, 153
Anderson, A. and Belnap, N. 84, 90 n.8
anti-realism, mathematical 152–7
antinomies: in Hegel 3–4
    in Kant 3
antisatisfaction conditions 129–30, 138–40
Aquinas, St Thomas 184
Aristotle 205
    and law of non-contradiction 94–5, 273
    and truth value gaps 65
arithmetic: and basic statements 40
    collapsed models 232–4
    Peano 128, 130, 135, 231, 240–1
    recursive functions 39, 41, 46
    and substitutional semantics 144–6, 155, 157
    and theory of syntax 155
    transfinite 21, 150, 209
    see also Goedel, K.
arithmetic, inconsistent 231–46, 266
    v. consistent 234–6
    and naive notion of proof 237–9
    and Shapiro 239–43
    structure 244–6
Armour-Garb, B. 267, 269
Armour-Garb, B. and Priest, G. 285 n.2
Arrow Paradox (Zeno) 173, 174–5, 180, 281,
    297, 298
ascent, semantic 23–5
assertion: and belief 96
    and content 94–5

of contradiction 94, 96
    and denial 292
    mathematical 149–51, 152
    and truth 23, 61, 62–4, 94, 100, 267–8
assertion principle, and absorption 83, 86
Augmentation Constraint (AC) 272–3
Axiom of Choice 142, 248
Axiom of Foundation 250
Axiom of Infinity 250
axiomatic theories 236, 239

Barwise, J. and Etchemendy, J. 263 n.5
Batens, D. 120 nn.10,11, 121 n.12, 222,
    225 n.11
Beall, JC 267–9
Beall, JC and Priest, G. 285 n.2
Beall, JC and Ripley, D. 285 n.2
Bedegem, J. P. van 234 n.4
belief: acceptance and rejection 98–9, 100–3,
    104–6, 262, 274–5
    and contradiction 96–9, 275
    rational 99–103, 199, 262
    rational change 103–4
Bell, J. 35, 202 n.31
Berry's paradox 9, 16, 25–7, 264, 286 n.6
Bobenrieth, A. 302 n.32
Bolzano, B. 208
Boolos, G. and Jeffrey, R. 241 n.18
Bradley, F. H. 181
Brady, R. 25 n.26, 221
Bromand, J. 287 n.9, 290
Burali-Forti's paradox 9, 10, 29
Burge, T. 20 n.19

Cantor, G. 29, 33, 209, 266 n.9
Cantor's Theorem 9, 142, 253
cardinality 228
    and syntax 154–8
cardinals: as Aleph 33
    inaccessible 34–5, 36, 266
    limit 142
Carnap, R. 107
Carroll, L. 260
categories, in Kant 3, 47

category mistakes, and semantic paradoxes 14,
    65, 259, 300
category theory 150
    and cumulative hierarchy 33–5, 37, 48, 157–8,
        203
causation, backward 179
change: cinematic account 162, 168, 173, 176,
        281, 298
    and continuity principle 165–71, 181
    and contradiction 159, 171, 172, 181, 214
    instant of 160–2, 295–8
    metaphysics of 159–71, 281
    and motion 171, 172–81, 214
    see also spread hypothesis
Characterisation Principle 278–80
Chihara, C. 200 n.24
Chomsky, N. 207 n.1
Church, A. 41
closure, semantic 125–40, 143, 155, 276–8
    conditions 11–12, 17–18, 23, 125–30, 132
Collapsing Lemma 227–8, 229–30, 232–4,
        256–7
command, as obligation 194
Compactness Theorem 229
completeness, and consistency 39, 47
comprehension *see* abstraction, set-theoretic
computation theory, inconsistent 240, 241–3
concepts: as incoherent 5
    as inconsistent 3–5, 9, 47–8, 201, 204, 299
conceptualism 153; *see also* intuitionism
conditionals: biconditionals 17–18, 59, 125, 131,
        157, 240, 249, 254, 260–1
    detachable 221–2
    enthymematic 255
    intensional 71, 269–70
    material 59, 83, 88, 221, 249, 254, 256, 259,
        260–1
    non-contraposible 71, 88, 252, 276
    non-material 232
    relevant 231, 251–6, 270–1
    truth conditions 74, 88
confirmation 107–9
connectives: conditional 59, 270–3
    extensional 60, 73–81, 85, 92, 110, 164, 256,
        269–71
    implication 73, 82–3, 84, 86–9
    intensional 59, 71, 76 n.5
    monotonic 227 n.12
    see also entailment
consequence: minimally inconsistent 225,
        275

semantic 36–7, 84–6, 92–3, 163–4, 190, 225,
        285–6
*consequence 119–22, 143, 275
consistency: and belief 96, 100–2, 104
    and completeness 39, 47
    in empirical world 159–71
    and expressibility 16, 24
    and language 5–6, 9, 73
    and mathematics 141
    and metalanguage 24–5, 70
    and recursiveness 42, 46
    and set theory 28–30
    and transconsistency 207–9, 222
    and truth 132
continuity condition (Leibniz) 165–9, 181, 281
    and contradiction 169–71
Contraction *see* absorption
contracts: and discharge by frustration 183, 194
    and inconsistent obligation 182–3
contradiction: as *a priori* improbable 106, 114–17
    and change 159, 171, 172
    crucial 114–15, 116–17
    non-dialetheic 116
    in the world 299–302
    see also dialetheias
contraposition: and conditionals 71, 88, 252, 276
    and entailment 71, 79, 88, 139, 141–2 n.2
    and T-scheme 71, 79, 129, 139, 141–2 n.2,
        161 n.3, 268–9, 276
CP *see* Characterisation Principle
Craig's theorem 44
criticisability, rational 104
criticisms of dialetheism 284–302
    and expressibility 290–5
    and extended Liar Paradox 287–90
    and logic 284–7
    and motion 295–9
cumulative hierarchy: and category theory 33–5,
        37, 48, 157–8, 203
    and logic 36–7
    and mathematics 202
    and set theoretic paradoxes 30–8, 48, 265–6
    and set theory 30–8, 157–8, 256–7, 259
    and type theory 35
    and ZF set theory 31, 38, 256–7
Curry, H. 131
Curry's Paradox 83–4, 248, 269
Cut Theorem 78, 110

Da Costa, N. 248
Davidson, D. 57, 134 n.9, 135

de Morgan algebra 27, 72, 92, 139, 254
Dedekind, R. 33, 142, 208, 280
deduction: and entailment 84
    informal 237
definability paradoxes 10
deflationism 59–61, 267, 268–9
denial 292
denotation paradoxes *see* Berry's paradox
Denyer, N. 284 n.2
detachment, material 59, 71, 110, 250–1, 259;
    see also disjunctive syllogism
Devlin, K. 31
Dharmakīrti 297–8
diagonalisation 48–9, 83, 130, 135, 259
Dialectic, Transcendental: and Hegel 3–4
    and Kant 3
dialetheias: deontic 188–95, 282
    in empirical world 159–71, 172–81, 299–302
    frequency 116
    Goedel's first incompleteness theorem 39–50
    legal 184–8, 201, 302
    logical paradoxes 9–10, 115, 293
    moral 198–9
    resolution 200–2
    semantic paradoxes 10–38
    set theoretic paradoxes 28–38
    in social world 182–204
    as true contradictions 4–5
dialetheism:
    applications:
        and change and motion 159–71
        and change and time 159–71, 181
        and philosophy of law 182–204
        semantic closure 125–40
        set theory 141–58, 277–80
    classical 66, 70
    and Goedel's theorem 44–6
    intuitionist 66, 69
    and logic:
        criticisms 284–7
        and disjunctive syllogism 110–22, 208,
            221, 276
        and entailment 82–93, 247, 269–70
        and extensional connectives 73–81, 221
        and metaphysics of change 159–71
        and pragmatics 94–109
        and truth and falsity 53–72, 270–2
        see also LP
    metaphysical/semantic 299–302
    and pragmatics 94–109
    as self-refuting 104

and truth and falsity 67–9, 266–9
    see also criticisms
disjunctive syllogism (DS) 110–22, 208, 221,
    225, 253–4
    and material conditional 221, 254,
        259
    and Methodological Maxim 116, 118
    and Principle R 113–14, 276
divine command theory of morality 198
DS *see* disjunctive syllogism
Dummett, M. 152, 238
    and assertion 64–5
    and law of excluded middle 149
    and naive proof 42, 43
    and redundancy theory of truth 60–1
    and verificationism 57
Dunn, J. M. 232

Eklund, M. 285 n.2
Engels, F. 97, 159
entailment 4 n.5, 82–93
    bientailment 129, 137, 196
    contraposible 71, 79, 88, 139, 141–2 n.2
    and Curry's Paradox 83–4, 269
    First Degree 16, 233 n.2, 269
    and obligation 191–2, 196
    and relevant logic 89–92, 231
    and strict implication 82–93
    and tense logic 164
    and truth and falsity preservation 5, 84, 89,
        190, 270, 286
Everett, A. 284 n.2, 287 n.9
ex contradictione quodlibet principle 5–6, 42, 103,
    185, 193, 202, 221, 247
    and implication 84, 110
exclusion principle 112, 268–9
    and acceptance and rejection 98
    and set theory 144–6
    and T-scheme 70–2, 126, 130,
        136–8
    and truth and falsity 75, 79, 292–3
    and truth and untruth 70–2
exhaustion principle 268–9
    and acceptance and rejection 98
    and change 161
    and truth and falsity 75, 79, 293
    and truth and untruth 70, 71
Explosion 247, 291
    see also ex contradictione quodlibet
expressibility, and consistency 16,
    23–4

Facts: and extensional connectives 76, 78, 80–1, 85–7, 88, 93
  and metaphysical dialetheism 300–1
  and truth 65–6, 67, 69, 268
falsehood, necessary 91
falsity: and antisatisfaction conditions 129–30
  and dialetheism 67–9, 292–4
  falsity predicate 80
  and negation 64, 88
  preservation 84, 89, 286
  and rationality 99–100
  and truth 53–72, 75, 267, 292–4
  and truth value gaps 64–6
  and untruth 69–72, 267
Feferman, S. 43 n.10, 44 n.13
Feurbach, L. 203 n.35
Field, H. 263 n.5, 285 n.2
finitism 234 n.4
Fitch, F. B. 20 n.18, 285 n.4
Frege, G.: and classical logic 207
  and mathematical realism 151
  and set theory 28, 110 n.1, 158
  and truth conditions 57

Gale, R. M. 181 n.15
Galileo Galilei 208
games: language games 203–4
  and rules 199–200
gap theory *see* truth value gaps
Gentzen's *LK* 78, 110
Gödel, K. 148, 236–9, 266, 283 n.50
  first incompleteness theorem 39–50, 236–7
    and dialetheism 44–6
    and inconsistency 46–8, 266
    and naive theory of proof 40–4
    proof 48–50
  second incompleteness theorem 24, 231, 237
  and undecidable sentences 236–7, 239
Goldstein, L. 123
good Samaritan paradox 191–2
Goodship, L. 251 n.7, 276 n.38
Grelling's paradox 9, 10
Grice, H. P. 57 n.8, 63, 291
Guest, A. 183 n.2
Gupta, A. 18 n.17, 21 n.20
Gupta, A. and Martin, R. L. 16 n.15

Hare, R. 193
Hart, H. L. A. 186
Hegel, G. W. F. 159

  and change 213–14, 215, 216, 220
  and contradiction 3–4, 5, 47, 97, 170, 204, 208, 263
  and motion 175–81, 281, 296–7, 298–9
Heisenberg's uncertainty principle 181
Henkin, L. 147 n.12
Heracleitus 97, 159, 175
Herzberger, H. 21 n.20, 24 n.24
hierarchy of interpretations 20–3
hierarchy of truth predicates 18–20, 43, 44 n.13, 48, 101
Hintikka, J. 192, 196 nn.19,20
Horwich, P. 267

idealism, Hegelian 3–4, 159
identity: in formal semantics 78, 93, 251 n.8
  predicate 273
implication 82
  and assertion principle 84, 86
  falsity conditions 129
  intuitionist 66
  material 74, 76 n.5, 83, 88, 249
  and material detachment 110
  non-contraposible 71, 88–9, 129
  as non-extensional connective 73, 86
  and relevant logic 89–92
implicature, conversational 74, 291–2
impredicativity, of set theory 147
Inclosure Schema 251 n.7, 263
incoherence, and inconsistency 5–6
incompleteness theorems *see* Goedel, K.
inconsistency: improbability 115–17
  and incoherence 5–6
  and the infinite 208–9
  and language 200–2
  and logic 110–12, 118–19
  minimal 222, 224, 275–6
  and motion 175–9
  and naive set theory 142, 201
  and obligation 182–4, 189
  and proof 44–6, 47, 131, 136–40, 277
  and rational belief 100–2, 104
  and time 159–71, 181
induction: informal 136–7
  transfinite 21
induction hypothesis 137–40
inexpressibility thesis 23–4, 133–4
inference: and absorption 83, 249
  classical 225
  and crucial contradiction 114–15, 116–17
  and *LPm* 225, 226

quasi-valid 110–11, 113–15, 116–17, 118, 276
rules 11–12, 110, 203
and truth preservation 12, 18, 36
validity 259–60, 269–70, 277, 286
see also disjunctive syllogism
infinity, and inconsistency 208–9
intention, and assertion 63
intuitionism: and logic 207, 222
and mathematics 40 n.3, 98–9, 103, 141, 150, 152–3, 221
and metatheory 258
and paraconsistent logic 231
and proof 42
and revisionism 221, 248
and truth value gaps 13, 16, 66, 69, 268
intuitions, and categories 3
is/ought distinction 196

Kant, I. 263
and categories 3, 47
and obligation 193
knowledge: of abstract objects 150, 153
of truth 54
Koenig's paradox 9, 154 n.26
Kripke, S. 144 nn.7,8, 154 n.25, 156–7
and groundedness 14, 264
and semantic paradoxes 19, 21 n.20
Kuhn, T. 40 n.3

Lakatos, I. 25 n.25, 31 n.6, 45, 101 n.13, 104, 201 n.27, 202 n.30
language, logical: and abstraction 73–4
and closure conditions 11, 125–30
and consistency 5–6, 9
and cumulative hierarchy 36–7
and extensional connectives 73–81, 221
and truth conditions 133
see also Liar Paradox
language, natural: and closure conditions 11–12, 125, 132
and consistency 4–5, 9, 73, 200–2, 299
as hierarchy of semantically open languages 18–20
language games 203–4
and true contradictions 12, 67, 131, 299–300
and truth value gaps 12–16
universality 134
law 182–204
and dialetheias 184–8, 201
and exceptive clauses 187–8

and inconsistent obligations 182–4, 189
and legal norms 182–97, 201, 282, 302
law of excluded middle 293
and denotation paradoxes 16, 25, 263
and deontic semantics 282
and disjunctive syllogism 120
and first-degree entailment 74–6, 269, 271–2
and impossible worlds 270–2, 282
and intuitionism 98, 99, 103
and realism 149
and set-theoretic paradoxes 29–30
and teleological theory of truth 66, 267–8
and truth value gaps 13, 15–16, 71–2
law of non-contradiction 76, 94–5, 208–9, 267, 273, 298
Leibniz continuity condition 165–9, 181, 281
and contradiction 169–71
Leibniz, G. W. 165–71, 283 n.50
Lemmon, E. 164
Lewis, D. xix, 57, 104 n.16
L'Huilier, S. 166
liar paradox 9, 23, 29, 79, 264–5, 293–4, 304
extended 15–16, 18, 19, 22–3, 71–2, 135–6, 287–90
and Hegel 263
Lin, F. 226
Lin's Lemma 226, 227, 228–9
Littman, G. and Simmons, K. 287 n.9, 288
Löb's Theorem 237
Loewenheim–Skolem theorem 36–7
logic: classical 117–19, 160, 207, 221–2, 258–60, 275–6, 285, 291
and cumulative hierarchy 36–7
depth relevant 251–6
dialectical tense 162–5, 177–9, 281
and dialetheism 53–72, 73–81, 110–11, 275–6
criticism 284–7
and entailment 82–93, 247, 269–70
and extensional connectives 73–81
and metaphysics of change 159–71
and pragmatics 94–109
and truth and falsity 53–72, 270–2
see also LP
and fallibility of theory 207–8
and inconsistency 110–12, 118–19
modal 92
paraconsistent 73, 231, 247–8, *see also* LP
and pragmatics 94–109
relevant 89–92, 142, 231, 270–1, 277
and truth predicate 78–80
see also language, logical; truth

LP (paraconsistent logic) 221–30, 249–51, 261
  and classical reasoning 221–2
  and inconsistent arithmetics 232–4, 235–7
  and minimal inconsistency *see LPm*
  and proof theory 247–8, 285
  semantics 73–81, 223–4, 277, 286–7
  and set theory 247–61
  and truth values 269
LPm 222–30
  and inference 225, 226
  as non-monotonic 224–5, 251
  properties 224–5
  and Reassurance Theorem 226–8
  semantics 224, 228–30
Łukasiewicz, J. 95

M *see* Maxim M (Methodological Maxim)
M (possibility operator) 90, 129
McGee, V. 263 n.5
McTaggart, J. 181
Mares, E. 299–302
Martin, R. L. 14
Marx, K. 151, 203, 263
mathematics: and anti-realism 152–4
  and basic statements 40
  classical 152–4, 157–8, 221, 248
  and consistency 141
  and cumulative hierarchy 202
  and disjunctive syllogism 116, 221
  and intuitionism 40 n.3, 98, 103, 141, 150,
    152–3, 221
  and naive proof 41
  and realism 45 n.17, 141, 143, 148–51,
    154–6, 278–9
  see also arithmetic; philosophy of mathematics;
    semantics
Maxim M (Methodological Maxim) 116, 118
Mayberry, J. 32, 37–8 n.19
meaning: and assertion 63
  proof-theoretic account 285
  and T-scheme 56–8, 60, 132–6
  and truth conditions 57, 60, 132–3, 135, 146,
    267, 285
  and truth value gaps and hierarchy of
    interpretations 21
metalanguage: and consistency 24–5, 70
  set theoretic 10, 37, 38, 156–7
metamathematics, classical 231, 243
metatheory: of arithmetic 235
  intuitionist 258
  and object theory 70

paraconsistent 247, 248–60, 277
Meyer, R. K. 221, 231, 271
Meyer, R. K. and Mortensen, C. 231
Mirimanoff's paradox 9, 29, 257 n.17
model theory: and domain-and-satisfaction
    semantics 148–9, 152
  homophonic 294–5
  and paraconsistent metatheory 258–60
  and paraconsistent set theory 256–8, 259,
    277–8, 294
  and validity 247, 277
modus ponens principle 50
  and conditionals 226, 248, 251, 271
  and material implication 83, 86, 249
  and paraconsistent set theory 248, 249, 251
Montague, R. 57
morality: and moral norms 197–8
  transcendent standards theories 198
  and utilitarianism 198
Mortensen, C. 221, 231–2, 281 n.44, 295, 297–8
motion: cinematic account 173, 176, 281, 298
  as continuous state of contradiction 171,
    172–81, 214
  and continuum 176–7, 281, 297
  crititique of paraconsistent account 295–9
  Hegelian account 175–81, 281, 296–7, 298–9
  orthodox account 172–5, 180, 181, 281, 296–
    7
  and Relativity Theory 298–9
  spread hypothesis 177–9, 180, 281, 298

necessity: and entailment 85
  and mathematical realism 149–50, 152, 153
  and possible worlds semantics 85
negation: and antisatisfaction conditions 139
  Boolean 227 n.12
  and denial 292
  and falsity 64, 88
  paraconsistent 294–5
  and reasonable rejectability 98–9, 102–3,
    114, 275
  truth conditions 66, 67–9, 126, 131, 294–5
  and truth gap theory 264–5, 267–8
Nelson, D. 231
neo-Meinongianism, and realism 148–9
neo-Platonism, and realism 148, 279
Newton, I. 283 n.50
nominalism, and anti-realism 153–4, 157–8,
    277, 278
noneism 279–80
norms 182–204

legal 182–97, 201, 282, 302
  moral 197–9
  of rationality 199, 283
number theory: as set theory 110 n.1, 158
  and syntax 154–5

objects, inconsistent 260
obligations: as commands 194
  conditional 196 n.20
  conjoined 191, 192–3, 194–5
  and deontic semantics 188–95, 282
  inconsistent 182–4, 185, 195, 197–9
  moral 197–9
  "ought" and "can" 193–4
  rational 199, 283
  transmission 191–3, 196
Olin, D. 276 n.39
omniscience of G 86–7
ordinals: and cumulative hierarchy 31, 33
  limit 142
  and rank 19–20, 30
  transfinite 21
  von Neumann 29, 142
ought/can distinction 193–4
ought/is distinction 196

PA *see* Peano arithmetic
paraconsistency: logic *see* LP; LPm
  set theory 247–61, 265–6, 277, 289
    material strategy 249–51
    and metatheory 247, 258–60, 277
    model theoretic strategy 256–8, 259,
      277–8, 294
    relevant strategy 251–6
paradox of the arrow (Zeno) 173, 174–5, 180,
  198, 281, 297
paradox of the preface 100
paradoxes, logical 6, 9–10, 67–8, 101, 131–2,
  200, 263–5, 286 n.6, 294, 299
  and Goedel's theorem 46–8
  and law of non-contradiction 208–9
  and local inconsistency 115
  as rationally acceptable 72, 101, 103, 117
  and truth conditions 147
paradoxes, semantic 10–38, 263–5
  and expressibility 291
  extended 15, 23–5, 135
  and heterological paradox 11
  and hierarchy of truth predicates 18–20, 101
  as inclosure paradoxes 11–12, 263

and non-wellfounded truth conditions 132,
  147–8
and rejection of T-scheme 134
and truth value gaps 12–16, 17–18, 22, 65,
  99 n.10, 135, 264
see also Berry's paradox
paradoxes, set theoretic 10, 28–38, 247
  and cumulative hierarchy 30–8, 48, 265–6
  and category theory 32–5
  lack of rationale 30–2
  as inclosure paradoxes 263
  and non-wellfounded truth conditions 148,
    265
Parsons, C. 38 n.21, 99 n.10, 144 n.7
Parsons, T. 264, 267, 284 n.2
Peacocke, C. 18 n.17
Peano arithmetic 231, 280
  as inconsistent 240–1
Peano, G. 9, 231, 280
Petersen, U. 110 n.1
philosophy of mathematics, and realism and set
  theory 45 n.17, 141, 143, 148–58,
  278–80
place, and motion 175–80
Plato 150, 203, 283 n.50
Popper, K. R. 104 n.16, 117
positivism, and law 186
possibility, and entailment 85
possibility operator (M) 90, 129
possible worlds semantics: and entailment 87,
  88–9, 270–3
  and impossible worlds 89, 270–2, 282
  and necessity 85
  and T-scheme 18 n.17, 57, 60 n.11, 133, 134
postulates: large cardinal 265–6
  classical 117–18
  Groethendieck 34, 38
Pradine *v.* Jane 183
pragmatics 94–109
  and assertion 94–5
  and belief 96–9
  and probability theory 107–9
  and rational belief 99–103
  and rational change of belief 103–7, 262, 274
predicates: falsity 80
  satisfaction 11, 17, 125–30
  see also truth predicates
present: instantaneous 181
  specious/extended 217, 218–19
Priest, G. 25, 144 n.7, 181 n.15, 221, 226, 232,
  234 n.4, 263, 281

Priest, G. and Routley, R. 125 n.1, 141 n.1
Prior, A. 200 n.25
probability, epistemic 115, 116
probability theory 107–9, 274
proof, naive notion 40–4
    and Goedel's theorem 46–8, 286 n.6
    as inconsistent 44–6, 47, 131, 136–40, 277
    and inconsistent arithmetics 237–9
    as recursive 41–4, 46
proof conditions 152
proof theory 78
    and *LP* 247–8, 285
    and naive set theory 141–3
proofs, quasi-valid 113
Pseudo Scotus 91

quantification: in deontic semantics 191
    in formal semantics 28, 76–8, 92–3
    restricted 76 n.5, 254–5
    substitutional 57, 144–6, 153, 154–6, 278
quantifiers: constant-domain 273
    extensional 110, 256, 269
    propositional 226
    referential 155
    truth conditions 154
quasi-validity 53, 110–11, 113–15, 116–17,
    118, 276
Quine, W. 146–8, 158 n.30
    and cumulative hierarchy 31

rationality: and belief 99–103, 199, 262, 273–5
    and change of belief 103–7, 262, 264
    and obligation 199
realism, mathematical 45 n.17, 141, 148–51,
    278–80
    and anti-realism 152–7
    noneist 279–80
    and semantics 143, 154–7
realism, metaphysical 300–2
Reason, as inconsistent 47
reasoning: classical 117–19, 152–3, 221–2, 228
    and consistency 3, 9
    and disjunctive syllogism 116–17, 221, 222,
    225
    inductive 117, 122
    and logic 207
    and paraconsistent logic 221–30
    valid 118, 119
Reassurance Theorem, and *LPm* 226–8
recursiveness: and naive proof 41–4, 46
    and Peano arithmetic 240–1

and truth theory 135, 144, 147
reductio see law of excluded middle
rejectability, rational 102–3, 104–6, 116,
    274–5, 276
    and Principle R 113–15, 276
relativisation 137
Relativity Theory 97, 298–9
Rescher, N. 258 n.22
Restall, G. 251 n.6, 260, 264, 268
revisionism, and intuitionism 221, 248
rights: and deontic semantics 189
    and legal dialetheias 186–7
Ross's paradox 192
Routley, R. 4 n.4, 57, 148, 221, 271
Routley, R. and Routley, V. 90 n.9,
    113 n.5
rules, of games 199–200
Russell, B. 207, 260, 301
    and hierarchy of truth predicates 18
    and motion 172–5, 176, 177–81, 281, 297
    and number theory 110 n.1
    and set theory 158
Russell's paradox 9, 10, 29, 31 n.7, 142, 247
Ryle, G. 14

satisfaction conditions 10, 11–12, 57–8, 125–6,
    130–1, 138–40, 143–5
science: and inconsistent theories 101–2
    and search for certitude 107, 262
self reference 83, 130–2, 238–9, 251 n.7;
    see also paradoxes, logical
semantics: and closure 11–12, 17–18, 125–40,
    143, 155, 276–8
    conditional 88–9, 269–70
    and consistency 70, 202
    constant domain 92–3, 273
    constructive 153
    deontic 188–97, 282
    dialetheic 73–81, 223–4, 269, 286–7,
    299–302
    domain-and-satisfaction 148–9, 153, 154–5,
    157
    and extensional connectives 74–6
    formal *see* language, logical
    and inexpressibility thesis 23–4, 133–4
    mathematical 9, 143, 148–9, 152–3
    and mathematical realism 143, 154–6
    modal 84–6, 92, 164
    naive 28, 125–40
    for paraconsistent logic 73, 223–4,
    228–30, 277

possible world 18 n.17, 57, 60 n.11, 85, 87, 88–9, 133
propositional 191
realisability 231
of relevant logics 251, 270
and set theory 37–8, 153–4, 265, 277
substitutional 143–6, 147, 153, 154–7, 278
of tense 163–4, 169–70, 177–9, 281
truth conditional 54, 57, 131, 133, 188–9, 302
truth-functional 73–81, 85
see also paradoxes, semantic
sentences: closed atomic 144–5
content 94–5
embedded 292
false 64–9
and genuine conditionality 59
grounded 14, 264
and meaning 56–8
stable/unstable 21–3
true 54–61, 147
truth valueless 13–16, 66, 135
undecidable 236–7
sequence principle 130, 140
set theory: abstraction scheme 10, 28, 30–2, 141–2, 144–5, 148, 247, 250, 278
and analyticity 146–8, 153
axioms 145–6, 147
and cardinality and syntax 154–8
and category theory 33–5
*consequences 143
and cumulative hierarchy 30–8, 157–8, 256–7, 259, 265–6
formal and informal 38
and impredicativity 147
inconsistent 142–3, 201
and mathematical anti-realism 152–7
and mathematical realism 148–51, 279–80
and metalanguage 10, 37, 38, 156–7
naive 28–30, 110–11 n.1, 141–58, 277–80
NF 31
and number theory 110 n.1
paraconsistent 247–61, 265–6, 277, 289
material strategy 249–51
and metatheory 247, 258–60, 277
model theoretic strategy 256–8, 277–8, 294
relevant strategy 251–6
paradoxes 10, 28–38, 148
and semantics 37–8, 153–4, 265, 277
and substitutional semantics 143–6, 147, 153, 154–7, 278
and triviality 84, 131, 142–3, 248, 250, 253

and truth conditions 131, 143–5, 146–8, 153, 154–5
ZF *see* ZF set theory
sets: empty 75 n.3, 142, 253–6
fuzzy 220
infinite 33, 142
power set 37–8, 142, 253
Russell 260, 265
universal 142, 251, 254
Shapiro, S. 232, 239–43, 285 n.2, 291 n.20, 292–4
Shoenfield, J. 31 n.7
Slater, B. H. 285 n.2
Smart, J. C. 148 n.15, 288 n.13
Smiley, T. J. 284, 287 n.9, 288 n.11
space, and time 216, 219
spread hypothesis: and motion 177–9, 180, 281, 298
and time 213–14, 215–16, 217, 219–20, 281
Stalnaker, R. 71
statements: as primary truth bearers 54
and proof 40
substitutivity: of bientailments 137
of equivalents 83
of identicals 137–8
syllogism, disjunctive *see* disjunctive syllogism
syntax: and cardinality 154–8
first order theory 155
and number theory 154–5

T-scheme: and abstraction scheme 141–2 n.2, 144
contraposibility 70–1, 79, 129, 139, 141–2 n.2, 161 n.3, 268–9, 276
in formal language 125–30
and Goedel's theorem 46–7
and hierarchy of interpretations 20–3
homophonic/non-homophonic 134–5, 156 n.28
as material biconditional 17–18, 59, 125, 131
and meaning 56–8, 60, 132–6
proofs 136–40
satisfaction conditions 11–12, 125–6, 130–1, 138–40, 143
and semantic paradoxes 15, 134
and truth 55–61, 70–1, 132–6
and truth conditions 57, 131, 132–3, 135
and truth value gaps 17–18, 135
universal validity 55–6
see also truth predicates

Tarski, A. 132–4
  and closure conditions 11–12, 17–18, 23,
    125, 132
  and hierarchy of truth predicates 19–20, 43, 44
    n.13, 101
  and satisfaction conditions 10, 138
  and semantics 28
  and set theory 9–10, 38
  and truth 54, 55, 57–8, 235, 237
  and universality of natural language 134
  see also T-scheme
tautologies: as analytic 146, 153
  as logical truths 85, 95
Tennant, N. 285–6
tense, reality 216–17, 219–20
tense logic 162–5
  and change 169–71, 177–9, 281
  and Leibniz Continuity Condition 165–9
theology, negative 265
Thomason, R. 194 n.18
thought, and dialetheism 47–8
time: and change 159–71, 181, 213–20
  and continuity principle 165–9, 181, 281
  direction and duration 216–17, 218
  flow 215–16, 218
  as inconsistent 159–71, 181
  instants/intervals 161–2, 295–8
  Kantian view 3
  and motion 173–5, 176–80, 295–6
  sorites argument 218–20
  and space 216
  and specious present 217
  and spread hypothesis 213–14, 215–16, 217,
    219–20, 281
Tooley, M. 281, 295–9
transconsistent 207–9, 221–2, 248, 283
Trichotomy 287–8, 290
triviality: and classical logic 291
  and dialetheias 202
  and inconsistent arithmetic 237
  and set theory 84, 131, 142–3, 248, 250, 253
  and T-scheme 131, 132, 276
  and truth conditions 147 n.13
truth: and assertion 23, 61, 62–4, 94, 100, 267
  and consistency 132
  correspondence theory 65, 149, 268, 300, 302
  deflationary accounts 59–61, 267, 268–9
  and dialetheism 67–9, 266–9
  disquotational features 55–6
  and falsity 53–72, 75, 100, 267, 270–2, 292–4
  in interpretation 223, 294

knowledge of 54
necessary 91
redundancy theory 61
stable 21–3
teleological account 61–2, 63–4, 66, 94,
  186, 266–7
and untruth 69–72, 267
see also T-scheme
truth conditions: and conditionals 74, 88
  and deontic semantics 188–9
  homophonic 145, 294–5
  and meaning 56–8, 60, 132–3, 135, 146,
    267, 285
  and negation 66, 67–9, 126, 131, 294–5
  non-wellfoundedness 131–2, 147–8
  recursive 144, 147
  and satisfaction conditions 11–12, 57–8,
    125–6, 130–1, 138–40, 143–5
  and set theory 131, 143–5, 146–8, 153, 154–5
  substitutional 154–7
  and T-scheme 57, 131, 132–3, 135
truth predicates 11, 17–18, 78–80, 112, 135,
  155–7, 269 n.15, 276
  and Goedel's theorem 47
  hierarchy 18–20, 43, 44 n.13, 48, 101
  hierarchy of interpretations 20–2
  of inconsistent arithmetics 235–6
  and set theory 38
truth preservation 113, 140, 163
  and entailment 5, 84, 89, 190, 270, 286
  and inference 12, 18, 36
truth value gaps 64–6, 71
  and semantic paradoxes 12–16, 17–18, 22, 65,
    99 n.10, 264, 267
truth value gluts 15, 265, 295
type theory 20 n.18, 247
  and cumulative hierarchy 35

uncertainty principle (Heisenberg) 181
universality: of classical logic 207
  of natural language 134
untruth 69–72, 267
utilitarianism, and moral norms 198

vagueness, and language 68, 299
validity: and cumulative hierarchy 36
  model-theoretic definition 247, 277, 285
  see also quasi-validity
valuelessness 13–16, 66, 135
verificationism 57, 186
  and dialetheism 69 n.26, 282 n.46, 285

Wallace, J. 18 n.17
Weir, A. 257–8 n.20, 274–5, 286
Wittgenstein, L. 37 n.18, 40 n.3, 45, 150–1, 203–4, 283 n.50
Woodruff, P. 21 n.20
Wright, G. von 162 n.5, 194

Zeno of Elea 159, 162, 165, 173–5, 180, 281, 297, 298
Zermelo, E. F. F. 33
Zermelo-Fraenkel set theory *see* ZF set theory

ZF set theory 101, 247
and *consequence 143
and cumulative hierarchy 31, 38, 256–7
and inconsistent arithmetics 243–4 n.21
and material strategy 250–1
and metatheory 259, 277
and model theoretic strategy 256–8, 277–8
and ordinality 31
and relevant strategy 253
Zorn's Lemma 228

...and as soon as contradiction ceases, life, too, comes to an end, and death steps in.

Engels (1894), p.140

Made in the USA
Lexington, KY
09 April 2013